Marketing Plans for Services

Marketing Plans for Services

A Complete Guide

Third Edition

Malcolm McDonald,
Pennie Frow
and
Adrian Payne

WILEY
A John Wiley & Sons, Ltd, Publication

Library of Congress Cataloging-in-Publication Data
McDonald, Malcolm.
    Marketing plans for service businesses : a complete guide / Malcolm McDonald,
  Pennie Frow and Adrian Payne. — 3rd ed.
      p. cm.
    Includes bibliographical references and index.
    ISBN 978-0-470-97909-9 (pbk. : alk. paper)
      1. Service industries—Marketing.   2. Service industries—Planning.   I. Payne,
    Adrian.   II. Frow, Pennie.   III. Title.
  HD9980.5.M388   2011
  658.8'02—dc23   2011017544

ISBN 978-0-470-97909-9 (paperback), ISBN 978-1-119-95186-5 (ebk),
ISBN 978-0-470-97941-9 (ebk), ISBN 978-0-470-97944-0 (ebk)

A catalogue record for this book is available from the British Library.

Typeset in 10/12pt Palatino Roman by MPS Limited, a Macmillan Company, Chennai, India.
Printed in Great Britain by TJ International Ltd, Padstow, Cornwall, UK

Contents

Preface

This latest edition recognizes the growing importance of the service sector in most economies and of significant differences between product and service marketing.

The world of services marketing has changed dramatically during the past decade. The easy, high-growth markets have been replaced by mature, low-growth demand patterns that have forced suppliers to question their erstwhile successful business models, such as, for example, those that consisted largely of making 'products' and selling them to intermediaries, who magically got rid of them somehow to an unsophisticated general public who were in awe (or ignorance) of complicated products such as pensions.

Today, however, there is in most developed countries a situation of government regulation, oversupply, and more importantly a more sophisticated consumer who has been empowered by the Internet. This has forced service providers to pay greater attention to the needs of the consumers of their services. This means that they have been forced to pay greater attention to marketing.

The three authors work with many of the world's leading service organizations in their role as professors of marketing at three of the world's leading business schools. We have sought to combine the acknowledged leadership of Cranfield University in the domain of marketing planning (Malcolm McDonald) with the experience of two experts in the field of services marketing (Pennie Frow and Adrian Payne) to produce a unique text for those who are faced with the special challenge of producing world-class marketing plans for services where there are no tangible products.

The approaches outlined in this book have been used extensively by us in a large number of services organizations.

We believe you will find, in the pages of this book, the answer to the challenge of creating marketing plans that produce significantly improved bottom-line results.

Malcolm McDonald
Pennie Frow
Adrian Payne
September 2011

The structure of this book and how to use it

This book consists of 13 chapters, some examples of marketing plans and a glossary of terms used in marketing planning.

Chapter 1 provides a broad view of marketing as it relates to services. It describes the marketing concept and some misunderstandings about marketing.

Chapter 2 considers the nature of services and relationship marketing.

Chapter 3 provides an overview of the four key phases of the marketing planning process.

Chapter 4 looks at the barriers that can prevent a service organization being successful in introducing marketing planning.

Chapters 5 to 10 provide a detailed examination of each of the four phases in the marketing planning process and an explanation of the frameworks and techniques which are useful in undertaking these tasks.

Chapter 11 examines some of the key organizational aspects relating to marketing planning. These issues, although not directly part of the marketing planning process itself, have an important and profound impact on its ultimate effectiveness. Here we discuss the role of marketing intelligence systems; market research; to what extent the introduction of marketing planning is appropriate at the different stages of development of an organization; and finally, the issue of how a service organization can develop or improve its marketing orientation.

Chapter 12 examines the growing importance of measuring financially the effectiveness of marketing expenditure.

Chapter 13 provides structures for a three-year strategic marketing plan, a one-year detailed marketing plan and a headquarters consolidated plan of several strategic businesses unit (SBU) strategic marketing plans. These structures will help with implementing the processes and frameworks outlined earlier in this book. Also, in the 'Examples of Marketing Plans' are a number of illustrations of what strategic marketing plans actually look like in different types of service organizations.

Those readers who have read widely on the services sector and are familiar with the services marketing literature can start at Chapter 3.

We suggest that all readers should undertake a close examination of the process aspects in the text, covered in Chapters 5 to 10. We also recommend that Chapter 9 is read thoroughly as, although not directly about the marketing planning process, it addresses many of the issues which are critical to successful implementation of a marketing planning system.

> However, it should be recognized that a little learning is a dangerous thing. While Chapter 13 and the examples of marketing plans provide a clear overview as to how a marketing plan is structured, we advise a thorough examination of the detailed discussion of each of the key steps. For those seriously interested in either initiating marketing planning or in improving the quality of their marketing planning, we strongly recommend them to study the whole book before attempting to use any of the systems and plans provided at the back of the book.

Finally, we have provided references for statements made in the text, but in order to make this book easier to read, we have included these at the end of the book rather than at the end of each chapter.

Best of luck – and happy and profitable marketing planning in your service organization.

List of Figures

1 Marketing and services

The growing importance of the service sector

Since the Second World War, North America and Western Europe have seen a steady and unrelenting decline in their traditional manufacturing industries. Their place has been taken by numerous service-based enterprises that were quick to spot the opportunities created by both organizational needs and by the increased personal affluence and the consequent raised lifestyle expectations of the population.

There has been very substantial growth in services over the last two decades. This growth has been widespread but is now especially pronounced in developing countries where services represent the engine of their economic growth.

> So successful has been this transition from an essentially industrial society that today more than 70 per cent of most Western economies are now in the service sector, whether measured in terms of income or numbers employed.

Figure 1.1 shows estimates of the size of the service sector as a percentage of gross national product (GNP) for different countries These statistics, published by the US Central Intelligence Agency in 2011,[1] show the dramatic transformation of the global service landscape. Hong Kong leads the world with 92% of its economy in the service sector. China's economy a few decades ago was principally an agricultural economy. The service sector in China has grown by 191% over the last 25 years. Today, services represent over 44% of China's GNP.

As Jim Spohrer, the director of IBM Almaden Services Research Centre, has observed, 'This shift to services represents the single largest labour force migration in human history. Global communications, business and technology growth, urbanization, and low labour costs in the developing world, are all in part responsible for this dramatic shift.'

The service-led 'second industrial revolution'

This shift in emphasis has been so pronounced that some observers refer to it as the 'second industrial revolution'. As individuals spend

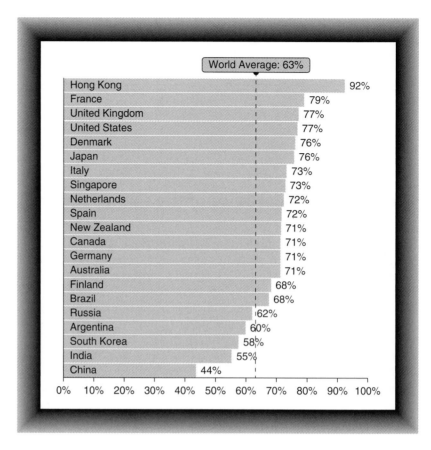

Figure 1.1
Size of the service
sector as % of GNP for
different countries

greater proportions of their income on travel, entertainment and
leisure, postal and communication services, restaurants, personal
health and grooming and the like, so has the service sector responded
by creating businesses and jobs. In addition, the growing complexity
of banking, insurance, investment, accountancy and legal services has
meant that these areas of activity showed a similar inclination to
expand, in terms of their impact on the economy as a whole.

Although there is a realization that it is essential for a country to have
some kind of industrial base, there is little to suggest that this trend
towards the service sector is slowing down. Based on research by
IBM,[2] Figure 1.2 shows the projected growth of employment in
services in the USA to the year 2050 and demonstrates the anticipated
strong growth in services over the next few decades.

Indeed, the manufacturing industry itself is showing a greater
propensity to subcontract out a wide range of service-related
activities which at one time were carried out in-house.

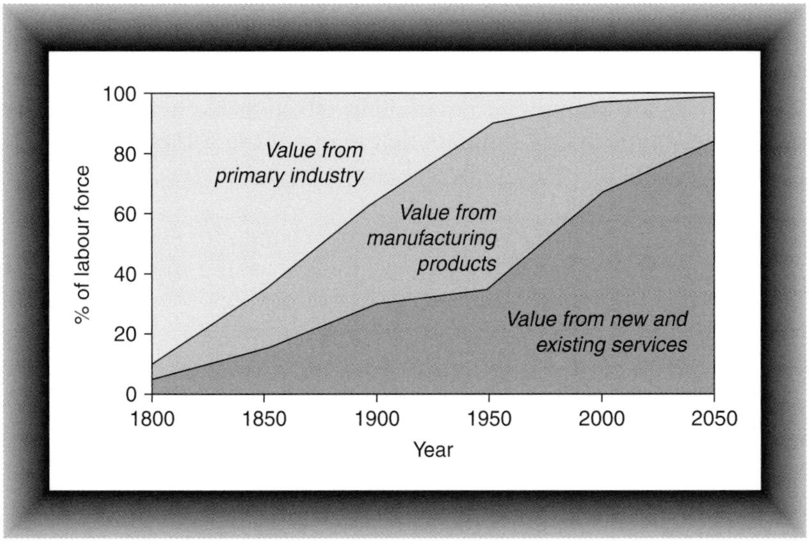

Figure 1.2
Projected growth of
employment in
services in USA to 2050

For example, outsourcing is continuing to increase in areas such as cleaning, catering, recruitment, deliveries, computer services, advertising, training, market research and product design. These are all areas where it has been found that external specialists can provide a cost-effective alternative to a company's own staff. More and more companies are choosing to contract out for specialist services and concentrate attention on their core activities.

Service businesses and marketing effectiveness

For many years business schools and consultancy firms have emphasized how important it is for companies to develop a marketing orientation. At first sight this message would appear to have hit home, because today many companies claim to be market-led and customer-focused. However, from our position of working with senior managers and marketing staff from a wide range of companies, we can see that this so-called 'marketing orientation' has, for most of them, not been accomplished.

Marketing has not yet stormed the citadels of many service organizations

> There is more emphasis on rhetoric than actions. In fact, we estimate that less than one service organization in five has a deep understanding of its customer base and an effective strategic marketing plan based on this understanding.

One of the major UK banks recruited hundreds of consumer goods-trained marketing personnel, yet still has no observable differential advantage in any of its operations. It is clear that such organizations have confused marketing orientation with selling and promotion. The result is that they have merely succeeded in creating a veneer and a vocabulary of marketing.

Research by the authors into marketing effectiveness across a variety of service organizations suggests that many of the companies studied operated well below their potential marketing effectiveness.

One of the authors, in his work conducting courses for executives from service businesses, has demonstrated this by asking many groups of senior managers from different service organizations these two simple questions:

1. To what extent does your chief executive in your service organization declare publicly: 'we are a customer-driven firm'; or 'we are a customer-oriented organization'; or 'we are market-focused and customer-centric as a business'; or some similar statement?

2. What percentage of the service businesses that you deal with, either as a company executive or as an individual consumer, is truly market oriented?

In answering this latter question, these executives were asked to consider all their firm's service suppliers, including: transportation and logistics companies; IT suppliers; accountants; solicitors; banks and financial services organizations; as well as training organizations. They were also asked to consider those services they used as a consumer, including hotels, banks, utilities such as water, electricity and gas, their mobile and fixed line telephone companies, and so on.

We have now put these questions to over 1,500 managers on executive programmes. The answers have been remarkably consistent. For large service organizations, in excess of 90% of chief executives claim their organization is market-oriented or customer-focused. However, when executives were asked about their experience with their service suppliers, they considered only 5–10% of the organizations they dealt with were market-focused. This confirms much work remains to be done in developing a customer-oriented culture in service firms.

> With organizations paying only lip-service to being marketing-oriented, the results suggest a dramatic need for improvement in marketing effectiveness.

Philip Kotler has developed an audit to help provide organizations with a measure of their marketing effectiveness.[3] This audit is generic to all organizations, but can be adapted to a specific service sector or organization. We have modified this audit for use in a range of service sectors including banking, professional service firms, not-for-profit services and schools.

We use an audit developed for professional service firms as an illustration here. The audit identifies five attributes that can be used to audit the marketing effectiveness of the organization. Adapting these to reflect a professional firm environment, they include:

1. *Customer philosophy* – to what extent does the senior partner acknowledge the importance of the market place and client needs and wants in shaping the firm's plan and activities?

2. *Integrated marketing organization* – to what extent is the firm staffed for market analysis, competitive analysis, planning, implementation and control?

3. *Adequate marketing information* – does management receive the kind and quality of information necessary to conduct an effective marketing programme?

4. *Strategic orientation* – does the firm management generate innovative marketing strategies and plans for long-term growth and profitability, and to what extent have these proved successful in the past?

5. *Operational efficiency* – does the firm have marketing plans which are implemented cost effectively, and are the results monitored to ensure rapid action?

The audit rates the firm on each of these five attributes. The five sections of the audit each include three questions with a maximum score of six points being possible for each of the attributes.

Each of the five attributes has several questions. For example, under 'adequate marketing information' the following questions are asked:

- When were the last market research studies of clients, referrals, sources, premises and their location and competitiveness conducted?

- How well does the firm's management know its sales potential and the profitability of different market segments, clients, territories, services and forms of marketing promotion?

- What effort is expended to measure the cost effectiveness of different marketing expenditures?

To find full details of this audit, refer to this chapter's references.[3] (References for all the chapters appear towards the end of the book.) We have used this modified audit with over 25 professional service firms. The results we have obtained suggest that most professional firms are operating well below their potential in terms of marketing effectiveness. The results for a number of different professional service firms are shown in Figure 1.3 which shows each firm's ranking on the five attributes.

We have chosen professional service firms simply as an illustration of the use of the marketing effectiveness audit. Interestingly these firms

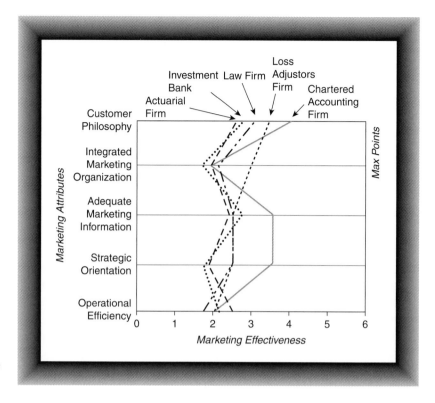

Figure 1.3
Marketing
effectiveness ratings
for professional service
firms

are all larger ones and are considered leaders in their sphere of professional services.

We have used this audit over many years with a large number of service organizations. These have included banks, insurance companies, airlines, retailers, hotel chains, industrial plant hire, motoring clubs, not-for-profit organizations and charities to name a few. While the concepts in this book apply equally to a wide range of service organizations, some modification of them may be necessary, given that service covers such a huge range of organizational types. We explore the nature of different types of services in the next chapter.

> An audit's primary purpose is to find and communicate to senior executives the perceived level of marketing effectiveness within the firm. It provides useful evidence of the need for a programme to improve the firm's marketing orientation. These are its primary functions; it is not intended to replace the rigorous marketing audit that is carried out as part of the marketing planning process and which is discussed in detail in Chapter 7.

From our consulting work with a wide range of service organizations, and surveys of executives in service organizations and from our extensive use of this audit we conclude that the vast majority of enterprises in the service sector have much distance to travel to improve their marketing effectiveness. Somewhat depressingly, this does not appear to have improved much over the past 15 years.

What is clear is that many service companies are misdirecting their energies and resources and thereby are failing to create competitive advantage and capitalize on market opportunities.

The purpose of this book

This book sets out to demonstrate how service businesses and other service organizations can formulate strategic marketing plans which contribute to the creation of competitive advantage. It focuses on *how* world-class strategic marketing plans should be developed, as this process results in an output – a plan – which encapsulates the resulting objectives, strategies and actions.[4]

It examines the marketing planning process in some detail and shows how successful companies tackle its difficult elements. Where necessary, relevant marketing theory, techniques and research results are introduced so that the reader can better understand the implications of taking particular actions at various stages of the process. In addition, it is important to consider the demands a new approach to planning places on the organization.

> For marketing planning to take root, not only must new skills be learned, but often new attitudes have to accompany them. Indeed, many of the barriers that hamper the acceptance of marketing planning can be attributed to outmoded or inappropriate organizational behaviour.

The purpose of this opening chapter is briefly to examine the importance of services in the global economy and the critical notion of the marketing concept. In the next chapter we explore to what extent the marketing of services differs from the marketing of products. We will also look at the diverse range of services in terms of establishing some threads of 'commonality'. In doing this, it makes it possible for the service manager to learn from other companies which may not necessarily be in the same business field. The next chapter will also develop reasons why the service marketer must formulate an enlarged and more sophisticated marketing mix than has traditionally been the case, and why focusing solely on customer markets will not prove to be enough for a guaranteed long-term marketing success.

The marketing concept

Marketing as a source of competitive advantage

The central idea of marketing is to match the organization's capabilities with the needs of customers in order to achieve the objectives of both parties. If this matching process is to be achieved, then the organization has to develop strengths, either from the nature of the services it offers or from the way it exploits these services, in order to provide customer satisfaction.

The matching process is complicated by the ever-changing business environment

Since very few companies can be equally competent at providing a service for all types of customers, an essential part of this matching process is to identify those groups of customers whose needs are most compatible with the organization's strengths and future ambitions. It must be recognized that the limitations imposed by an organization's resources, and the unique make-up of its management skills, make it impossible to take advantage of all market opportunities with equal facility. Companies who fail to grasp this fundamental point, which lies at the heart of marketing, are courting commercial disaster.

This matching process is further complicated in that it takes place in a business environment which is never stable for any length of time. External factors continue to have a major impact on the company's attempts to succeed. For example, new competitors might enter the business, existing ones may develop a better service, government legislation may change and as a result alter the trading conditions, new technology may be developed which weakens their current skills base – the possibilities are almost endless. However, not every external factor will pose a threat. Some environmental developments will undoubtedly provide opportunities.

Figure 1.4 provides a visual summary of the matching process, which is the essence of marketing. As it shows, the environment has an impact not only on the matching process, but also on the 'players'. So,

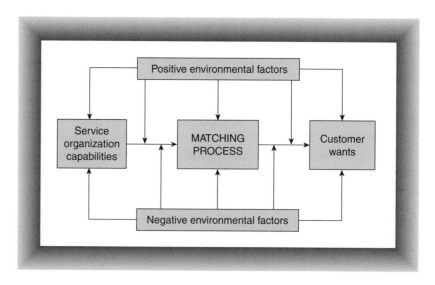

Figure 1.4
Marketing: a matching process

for example, local labour conditions might limit the company in recruiting a workforce with the appropriate skill levels. Equally, changed levels of unemployment can have a drastic impact on customer demand, making it either much greater or much less.

Misunderstandings about marketing

One of the biggest areas of misunderstanding is that concerned with customer wants. Many people, unfortunately some of them in marketing, have a naive concept of customers. They see customers as people, or organizations, who can be manipulated into wanting things that they do not really need.

In the long run, customers always have the final say

However, commercial life is not really that simple. Customers are not prepared to act so unthinkingly at the request of the supplier, as evidenced by a very high proportion of new products and services that fail to make any impact in the market place. All the evidence suggests that it would be foolish to deny that the customer, in the end, always has the final say. Moreover, customers invariably have a choice to make about how they satisfy their particular requirements.

> In the final analysis, they will choose those services that they perceive to offer the benefits they seek, at the price they can afford.

Another area of misunderstanding is the confusion of marketing with sales. Some ill-informed organizations actually believe that marketing is the new word for what was previously called sales. Others perceive marketing to be a mere embellishment of the sales process. That such companies exist is a sad reflection on the standard of management and suggests that marketing education has been less than effective. By failing to recognize that marketing is designed to provide a longer-term strategic, customer-driven orientation rather than a short-term tactical triumph, such an organization is certain to under-achieve. Not surprisingly, the chief executive of one such company was overheard to say: 'There is no place for marketing in this company until sales improve!'

Marketing should not be confused with sales

Marketing should not be confused with advertising

A similar misunderstanding occurs which confuses marketing with advertising. Here, gloss is seen as the magic formula to win business. However, without integrating advertising into an overall strategic marketing plan, hard-earned budgets can be completely wasted. Throwing advertising funds at a problem is no way to resolve an underlying issue which might have its roots in the fact that the service on offer has been superseded by another superior offer.

Marketing should not be confused with having a good service or product

Another misconception is that it is enough to have a high-quality service or product to succeed. Sadly, this has proved not to be the case

Marketing should
not be confused
with customer
service

time and time again. No matter how good the service or product, unless it is appropriately priced and promoted it will not make any lasting impact.

The final area of confusion, and one to which we will return in more detail later, is to think that marketing is synonymous with customer service. With misguided enthusiasm, many organizations subscribing to this belief have rushed into organizing 'customer service' programmes for their staff.

> Had they bothered to find out what their customers really wanted, perhaps they would have responded differently.

Train passengers might have travelled in less dirty and cramped conditions, and might have arrived at their destination on time more frequently. Those customers using banks might have found them open at more convenient times, and with more than one cashier on duty during the busy lunch period (the only time working customers can get there!). Instead, customers have been treated to cosmetic 'smile campaigns', where, regardless of their treatment, they were thanked for doing business with the supplier and encouraged to 'have a nice day'. Most people can recall an incident of this nature.

This is not to say that 'customer care' programmes are not important. What we contend is that unless the core service and the associated intangibles are right such programmes will fail. Such programmes ought to be part of the overall integrated set of marketing activities, not a substitute for them. The warning signs are there for those who care to look for them.

> One US study showed that, while 77% of service industry companies had some form of customer service programme in operation, less than 30% of chief executives in these companies believed that it had any significant impact on profit performance.

A definition of marketing

Before outlining the nature of services marketing, we need to move from what we have described as the marketing concept to a meaningful definition of marketing which will be used as the basis for this book.[5]

Marketing is a specialist function, just like HR, or Logistics, or IT, or Finance, or Manufacturing, and Business Schools and marketing practitioners really must stop the trend towards aggrandizing what is, in effect, a relatively simple if vital role.

The need to define marketing more tightly arose from a Cranfield research club 'Improving Marketing Effectiveness through IT'. Clearly, if managers were to understand what kind of marketing tasks needed to be supported by what kind of IT applications, a tight definition and a map were needed to help managers navigate this domain.

Surprisingly, in spite of literally hundreds of definitions of marketing, most of them hopelessly wrong, we couldn't find such a map anywhere, so we started with our *own* definition of marketing. But, before giving it, let us stress once again that, wherever the function of marketing is located in the organization and no matter what it is called, it will be ineffective unless the whole company is market-driven ('customer-driven', 'customer-needs driven', 'demand-driven', are other expressions for the same thing). This market-driven philosophy has to be led from the board downwards.

On the assumption that this is in place – a mega assumption indeed! – let us turn to our definition of marketing.

Marketing is a process for:

- Defining markets
- Quantifying the needs of the customer groups (segments) within these markets
- Determining the value propositions to meet these needs
- Communicating these value propositions to all those people in the organization responsible for delivering them and getting their buy-in to their role
- Playing an appropriate part in delivering these value propositions to the chosen market segments
- Monitoring the value actually delivered.

But marketing never has been, nor ever will be, responsible for delivering customer value, for this is the responsibility of everyone in the organization, but particularly those who come into contact with customers, which is a central difference between service organizations and manufacturing organizations, as in the former it is often people who make up the actual product – but more about this later.

An overview of the new marketing process

With this in mind, we can now examine a map of this process – see Figure 1.5.

This process is clearly cyclical, in that monitoring the value delivered will update the organization's understanding of the value that is required by its customers. The cycle may be predominantly an annual one, with a marketing plan documenting the output from the

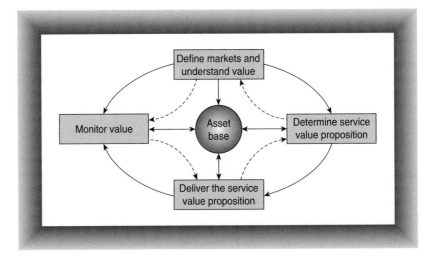

Figure 1.5
Overview of
marketing map

'Understand service value' and 'Develop service value proposition' processes, but equally changes throughout the year may lead to an accelerated iteration around the cycle so the organization can respond to particular opportunities or problems.

We have used the term 'Determine service value proposition' to make plain that we are here referring to the decision-making process of deciding what the offering to the customer is to be – what value the customer will receive, and what value (typically the purchase price and ongoing revenues) the organization will receive in return. The process of delivering this value, such as by making and delivering a physical product or by delivering a service, is covered by 'Deliver service value proposition'.

Thus, it can be seen that the first two boxes (top and right-hand) are concerned with strategic planning processes (in other words, developing market strategies), while the third and fourth boxes (bottom and left-hand) are concerned with the actual delivery in the market of what was planned and then measuring the effect. Throughout, we use the word 'proposition' to indicate the nature of the offer from the organization to the market.

It is well known that not all of the value proposition delivering process will be under the control of the marketing department, whose role varies considerably between organizations. The marketing department is likely to be responsible for the first two processes, 'Understand value' and 'Determine service value proposition', although even these need to involve numerous functions, albeit coordinated by specialist marketing personnel. The 'Deliver service value' process is the role of the whole company, including, for example, product development, operations, purchasing, sales promotion, direct mail, distribution, sales and customer service.

The various choices made during this marketing process are constrained and informed not just by the outside world, but also by the organization's asset base. Whereas an efficient service organization with much spare capacity might underpin a growth strategy in a particular market, an organization running at full capacity would cause more reflection on whether price should be used to control demand, unless the potential demand warranted further capital investment. As well as physical assets, choices may be influenced by financial, human resources, brand and information technology assets, to name just a few.

We are using this framework in order to position this book firmly within the total marketing process of service organizations, albeit most of the book is about only the first two of these boxes.

Define markets and understand value

Inputs to this process will commonly include:

- The corporate mission and objectives, which will determine which markets are of interest
- External data such as market research
- Internal data which flows from ongoing operations.

The process involves four major subprocesses, shown in Figure 1.6.

First, it is necessary to define the markets the organization is in, or wishes to be in, and how these divide into segments of customers with similar needs. The choice of markets will be influenced by the corporate objectives as well as the asset base. Information will be collected

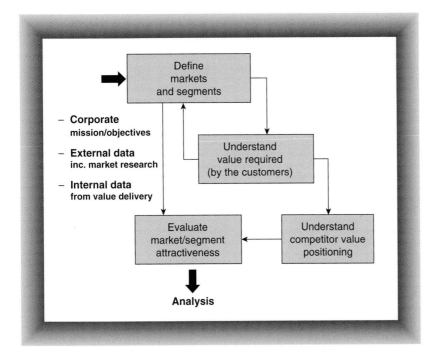

Figure 1.6
Define markets and understand value

about the markets, such as the market's size and growth, with estimates for the future.

Once each market or segment has been defined, it is necessary to understand what value the customers within the segment want or need. This value is most simply thought of as the benefits gained from the offer, but it can also encompass the value to the customer of surrounding services such as maintenance or information. This step also encompasses what the customer is prepared to give in exchange, in terms of price and other criteria, such as lifetime cost or convenience of a purchase. One way of expressing customer value requirements is via a critical success factor analysis which might list such criteria as offers specification, quality or reliability, the quality and range of services, price and the ease of purchase, and which might also include weights to illustrate their relative importance to the customer in the buying decision. This step of 'Understand value required' also includes predicting the value which will be required in the future. We will discuss this more in Chapter 9.

In performing this step, it may emerge that subsets of the customers within a market have very different requirements. In this case, the market may need to be further segmented to represent these subsets. Hence there is an important feedback loop from this step to the 'Define markets' step.

'Understand competitor value positioning' refers to the process of establishing how well the organization and competitors currently deliver the value that the customers seek. To illustrate in terms of critical success factors, this process would correspond to scoring the organization and its competitors on each of the customers' success factors. (We will show an example of this analysis later in the book.) Again, it involves looking into the future to predict how competitors might improve, clearly a factor in planning how the organization is to respond. SWOT (Strengths, Weaknesses, Opportunities, Threats) analysis is one tool used here.

From these three processes, the relative attractiveness of the different markets or segments can be evaluated in order to determine where to prioritize the organization's resources.

Determine Value Proposition

The definition of the value proposition to the customer contains five subprocesses, shown in Figure 1.7 (more commonly referred to by us as strategic marketing planning). Unfortunately, the term value proposition is typically tossed about casually and applied in trivial fashion in companies, rather than in a much more strategic, rigorous and actionable manner.[6] To obtain an overview of the use of the term value propositions in industry, we survey groups of managers attending five executive events on three continents. Some 265 senior and mid-level

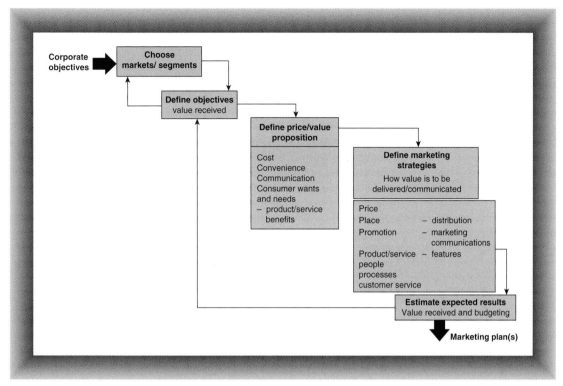

Figure 1.7 Determine value proposition

managers participated in this study. Two questions were addressed: first, 'Is the term "value proposition" one that is in regular use within your organization?'; second, 'If so, is the term just used in a general sense without specific meaning attached to it, or is there a structured underlying process resulting in a clearly articulated written customer value proposition within your organization?' On average, the term was used within 65% of the organizations. However, only 8%, of those who were using the term value propositions, stated they had a formal process for developing them and that written value propositions were developed and communicated within their organization.[7] This survey confirms that the term appears to have little substance in most organizations.

> Creation of a strong value proposition is critical for service organizations.

The key input to this process is the prioritization of target markets, based on an analysis of customer needs and the relative attractiveness of different customer segments, which was produced by the previous process.

The next two subprocesses define the core of the value proposition to the customer. While they can occur in either order, organizations typically start by defining the value they hope to receive from the segment: 'Define objectives'. This involves defining marketing objectives in terms, for example, of market share, volume, value or contribution by segment.

The other half of the equation is defining the value to be delivered to the customer in return. This price/value proposition can be thought of as using the four 'Cs': 'Cost', 'Convenience', 'Communications' and 'Consumer wants and needs'. These translate what the organization does in terms of the marketing mix to what the customer cares about. For example, the customer is concerned with 'convenience' of purchase, which influences how the organization will make the service available. Similarly, instead of 'product' or 'service', we have the 'consumer wants and needs' which are met by the product or service. The customer is interested in the total 'cost' to them, not necessarily just the upfront 'price'. And finally, 'promotion' translates into the two-way 'communications' in which customers declare their requirements and learn about the organization's offerings.

The fourth subprocess may involve iterations with the third one since, in defining the marketing strategies – how the value is to be delivered and communicated – it may be necessary to reconsider what the value can actually be. We have listed the four traditional aspects of this process – the four 'Ps' – as well as three additional marketing mix elements: people; processes; and customer service. These additional elements are discussed in Chapter 2. While separate plans, or plan sections, may be produced for each of these, the decisions are closely intertwined: for example, the choice of 'place' will impact what communications are feasible, what surrounding services can be delivered and what price can be charged.

Once these issues have been resolved, an estimate of the expected results of the marketing strategies can be made, in terms of the costs to the organization and the impact of the price/value proposition on sales. This final step closes the loop from the original setting of objectives, as it may be that iteration is required if it is considered that the strategies that have been defined are not sufficient to meet the financial objectives.

The output from the 'Determine value proposition' process is typically a strategic marketing plan, or plans, covering a period of at least three years. In some cases, specific plans are produced for aspects of the particular 'Ps', such as a pricing plan, a distribution plan, a customer service plan or a promotions plan. However, even when no plans are produced, the organization is implicitly taking decisions on the offer to the customer and how this offer is to be communicated and delivered. The content of these plans has to be communicated to and agreed with all departments or functions responsible for delivering the customer value spelled out in the plans.

Deliver value proposition

The third major process is to deliver the value proposition. This is illustrated in Figure 1.8.

The major input to this process is the strategic marketing plan(s) derived from the previous stage.

It will be seen that the top line is an adaptation of Michael Porter's value chain. However, we suggest that there are a number of marketing activities which shadow these value chain activities, under the general heading of 'Communicating the offer'. In today's one-to-one world, these communications often occur in parallel with all the tasks involved in value delivery. One might, for example, check a service offer with customers at the R&D stage. The offer may be tailored by the customer, resulting in changes and so on.

Communicating the offer is typically managed by designing, implementing and monitoring a number of marketing communications

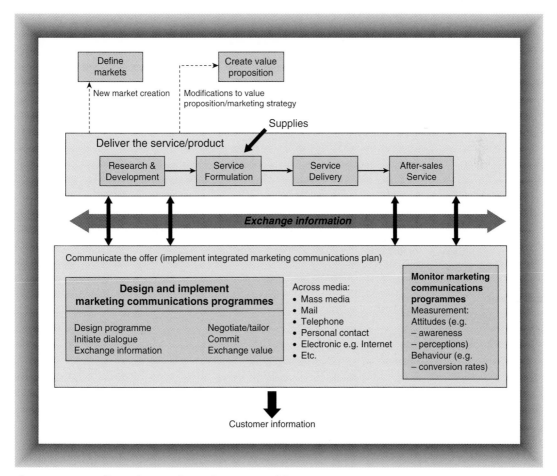

Figure 1.8　Deliver the service value proposition

programmes. A communications programme could be, for example, a direct mail campaign; an advertising campaign; a series of sales seminars; an in-store promotion; and so on. We have also extended the term 'marketing communications programmes' to include management of such media as the sales force, which may be managed in a more continuous way, with annual targets broken down by quarter or month.

Figure 1.9 illustrates traditional views of the sales and purchasing process, with our revised interaction perspective between the two. The tasks may have an unfamiliar look: in order to represent the interactive, one-to-one nature of today's marketing, we have renamed the classic steps in the sales process.

Traditional 'push-based' models of marketing, in which, after the product is made, prospects are found and persuaded to buy the product, are illustrated on the left. The delivery and service that follow are operational functions with little or no relationship to marketing.

Traditional models of buyer behaviour, illustrated on the right of the figure, assume more rationality on the part of buyers, but underplay

Service supplier perspective		Interaction perspective		Service buyer perspective	
Advertising	**Selling**	**Marketing activity**	**Interaction**	**Decision theory**	**Consumer behaviour**
		Define markets/ understand value			
		Create value proposition	Recognize exchange potential	Problem recognition	Category need
Brand awareness					Awareness
	Prospecting	Initiate dialogue			Attitude
Brand attitude • info *re* benefits • brand image • feelings • peer influence	Provide information	Exchange information		Information search	Information gathering and judgement
Trial inducement	Persuade	Negotiate/tailor		Evaluation of alternatives	
	Close sale	Commit		Choice/purchase	Purchase process
	Deliver	Exchange value			
Reduce cognitive dissonance	Service	↓	Monitor	Post-purchase behaviour	Post-purchase experience

Figure 1.9   Rethinking the sales process for service businesses

the importance of what the buyer communicates back to the seller. The seller's offer is assumed to be predetermined, rather than developed in conjunction with the buyer.

The stages of the process of communicating value are therefore rede-scribed as follows:

- 'Recognize exchange potential' replaces 'category need' or 'problem recognition'. Both sides need to recognize the potential for mutual exchange of value.

- 'Initiate dialogue' replaces 'Create awareness' or 'Prospecting'. The dialogue with an individual customer may be begun by either party. One feature of the Web, for example, is that on many occasions new customers will approach the supplier rather than vice versa.

- 'Exchange information' replaces 'Provide information'. If we are to serve the customer effectively, tailor our offerings and build a long-term relationship, we need to learn about the customer as much as the customer needs to learn about our products.

- 'Negotiate/tailor' replaces 'Persuade'. Negotiation is a two-way process which may involve us modifying our offer in order better to meet the customer's needs. Persuading the customer instead that the square peg we happen to have in stock will fit their round hole is not likely to lead to a long and profitable relationship.

- 'Commit' replaces 'Close sale'. Both sides need to commit to the transaction, or to a series of transactions forming the next stage in a relationship, a decision with implications for both sides.

- 'Exchange value' replaces 'Deliver' and 'Post-sales service'. The 'post-sales service' may be an inherent part of the value being delivered, not simply as a cost centre, as it is often still managed.

One-to-one communications and principles of relationship marketing, then, demand a radically different sales process from that traditionally practised in service organizations. This point is far from academic, as an example will illustrate.

The company in question provides business-to-business financial services. Its marketing managers relayed to us their early experience with a website which was enabling them to reach new customers considerably more cost-effectively than their traditional sales force. When the website was first launched, potential customers were finding the company on the Web, deciding the products were appropriate on the basis of the website, and sending an email to ask to buy. So far, so good.

But stuck in the traditional model of the sales process, the company would allocate the 'lead' to a salesperson, who would telephone and make an appointment, perhaps three weeks hence. The customer would by now probably have moved on to another online supplier who could sell the product today, but those that remained were subjected to a sales pitch, complete with glossy materials, which was totally unnecessary, the customer having already decided to buy. Those that were not put off would proceed to be registered as able to buy over the Web, but the company had lost the opportunity to improve its margins by using the sales force more judiciously.

In time, the company realized its mistake, and changed its sales model and reward systems to something close to our 'interaction perspective' model. Unlike those prospects which the company proactively identified and contacted, which might indeed need 'selling' to, many new Web customers were initiating the dialogue themselves, and simply required the company to respond effectively and rapidly. The sales force were increasingly freed up to concentrate on major clients and on relationship building.

The changing nature of the sales process clearly raises questions for the design of marketing communication, such as: Who initiates the dialogue, and how do we measure the effectiveness of our attempts to do so across multiple channels? How do we monitor the effectiveness not just of what we say to customers but what they say back? And how about the role of marketing communications as part of the value that is being delivered and paid for, not just as part of the sales cost?

Monitor value

Monitoring the value delivered to the customer, and received from the customer, is the purpose of 'Monitor value' illustrated in Figure 1.10.

There are four main areas where monitoring can occur, corresponding to the main types of information dealt with in the planning process of 'Understand value' and 'Determine service value proposition'.

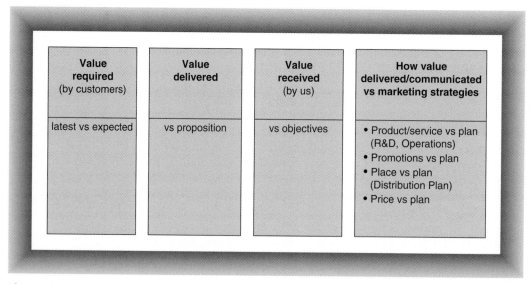

Value required (by customers)	Value delivered	Value received (by us)	How value delivered/communicated vs marketing strategies
latest vs expected	vs proposition	vs objectives	• Product/service vs plan (R&D, Operations) • Promotions vs plan • Place vs plan (Distribution Plan) • Price vs plan

Figure 1.10 Monitor value

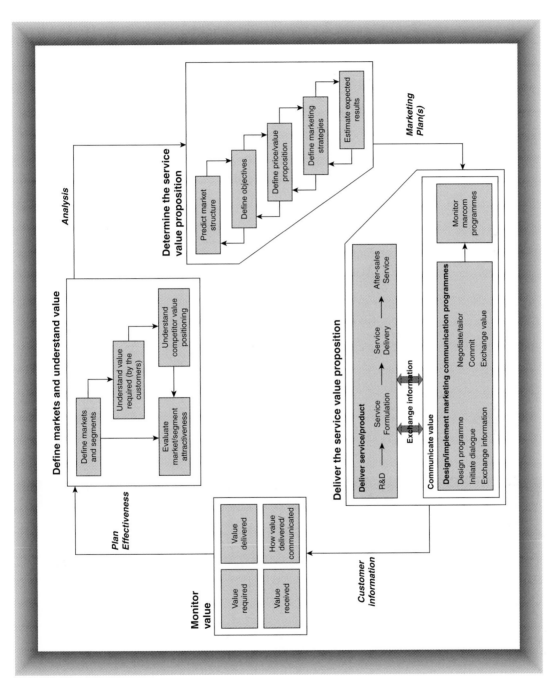

Figure 1.11 Summary of marketing map

First, the organization can monitor whether the value the customers actually require corresponds to the previous analysis of customer requirements carried out as part of 'Understand value'. The information for this may be gathered partly from the information gained in the 'Deliver service value proposition' process, or it may require special activity such as market research.

Second, the value delivered can be monitored against the value proposition which was defined during the 'Determine service value proposition' process. As all aspects of value are as measured by the customer's perception, this will again involve asking the customer by some means.

The organization will also wish to monitor the value it receives against the marketing objectives defined during the 'Develop service value proposition'. This is the area that most organizations are best at, through monthly analysis of sales by product, channel and so on (though analysis by segment or customer is often poorer than analysis by product, with customer profitability or lifetime value generally difficult to obtain). But as the financial results are a result of customer satisfaction, monitoring the value delivered to the customer is equally important, and for many organizations one of the simplest ways of improving performance.

Finally, the overall effectiveness of marketing strategies by which the value was delivered may be evaluated.

Figure 1.11 shows a consolidated summary of the marketing process.

From here, this book deals in the main with Box 2, 'Determine the service value proposition', as it is this above all else that defines the service offer and how the organization intends to create value for all its markets. Box 1, 'Define markets and understand value', is dealt with as part of the marketing planning process in Chapter 9.

Summary

In this chapter, we have taken a broad-ranging review of marketing and services. The spectacular growth in service businesses in the last few decades in all developed economies has been largely due to the favourable business environment which prevailed over this period. Today, the business environment is more competitive and this calls for a more analytical and strategic approach that only thorough and detailed marketing planning can provide.

We then outlined a detailed map of marketing which highlights the point that marketing is a professional function needing high-level skills. This map of marketing addresses four key related activities: define market and deliver value; determine the service value proposition; deliver the service value proposition; and monitor value.

While this book covers most of the marketing domain, we particularly emphasize the development of the service value proposition as it is at the heart of the strategic marketing plan for a service business.

2 The nature of services marketing

So far, much of what has been said could be equally applicable to either a product or a service. So, is there anything special about services marketing?

At one level, the theory of marketing has universal application – the same underlying concerns and principles apply whatever the nature of the business. However, the nature of a particular service business may dictate a need to place much greater emphasis on certain marketing elements, which in turn could lead to different marketing approaches.

It is frequently argued that services have unique characteristics that differentiate them from goods or manufactured products. The four most commonly ascribed to services are:

> Intangibility – services are to a large extent abstract and intangible.
>
> Heterogeneity – services are non-standard and highly variable.
>
> Inseparability – services are typically produced and consumed at the same time, with customer participation in the process.
>
> Perishability – it is not possible to store services in inventory.

From the 1980s these characteristics, known as 'IHIP' (intangibility, heterogeneity, inseparability and perishability) were widely discussed in the academic literature and textbooks in services marketing. However, the huge diversity of types of service businesses suggests that it is difficult to fit services into a neat definition. The universality of these characteristics has been increasingly challenged over recent years.[1–3] As we comment on shortly, not all services possess all of the above characteristics and some even possess high levels of the opposite of these characteristics (tangibility, homogeneity, separability and durability). However, most services do not involve the transfer of ownership in the way that occurs with physical goods.

Services possess other special qualities of importance to marketers. Services offer significant opportunity for resource sharing, such as through line-rental or timeshare agreements, where personalized access to telecommunications or a holiday home is kept at an affordable level by sharing access to goods, physical facilities, systems and expertise. The duration of usage, or time element, extends the perspective for pricing strategy beyond relative quality and value. Thus, while activity-based costing is widely used in manufacturing, time-based pricing may be a desirable option in the provision of services. Further scope for competitive differentiation may exist where price-sensitive customers can take advantage of lower cost time periods and time-sensitive customers are willing to pay extra for speed or last-minute convenience.

Arguably, marketing's traditional emphasis on the provision of goods as the basis for economic exchange is being replaced by an emphasis on the provision of services – elevating the importance of marketing planning for service businesses.

> One of the issues in defining a service is to do with the fact that, whereas a product is seen to be tangible and a service intangible, there are in reality many variations on the degree of tangibility.

Kotler[4] has identified four categories, varying from a 'pure' product to a 'pure' service.

(a) A pure tangible product	A tangible offer, such as sugar, coal, or tea. No services are bought with the product.
(b) A tangible product with accompanying services such as commissioning, training, maintenance	Here, the offer has built-in services to enhance its customer appeal, e.g. computers, machine tools.
(c) A service with accompanying minor goods (or services)	Here, the offer is basically a service but has a product element, e.g. property surveyors, whose expert inspection is encapsulated in a report. Similarly, airlines offer in-flight meals, or entertainment.
(d) A pure service, where one buys expertise	Here, the offer is a stand-alone service such as psychoanalysis.

These categories can be placed on a continuum which embraces all possible degrees of intangibility.

Figure 2.1 identifies the continuum of tangible–intangible possibilities. Point (a) on the left-hand side of this figure illustrates an offer where

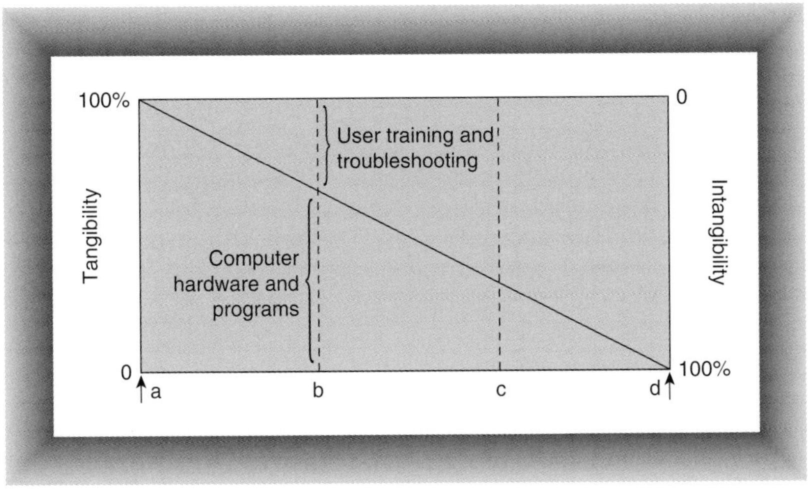

Figure 2.1
Continuum of tangible–intangible possibilities

there is no service element and so the product is highly tangible. At the other end of the continuum, point (d) illustrates a product which is entirely a service and is therefore highly intangible. Points (b) and (c) show varying mixes of tangibility/intangibility. For example, point (b) illustrates the mix of tangibility and intangibility for a computer company. Computer hardware and programs are highly tangible and can be regarded as commodities; however, the service elements of user training and troubleshooting are largely intangible.

Viewed in this way, the difference between a product and a service becomes far less discrete. The distinction between services and manufactured products has become increasingly blurred as many manufacturing companies have seen the opportunity to add services to their portfolios.[5] Many manufacturing organizations now have substantial service businesses. Rolls-Royce and IBM stand out as two exemplar organizations that have embraced services. Both these organizations have achieved huge growth in the services component of their businesses.

Jet engine manufacturer Rolls-Royce introduced their 'power by the hour' initiative which provides airline operators with a service that involves a fixed engine maintenance cost over an extended period of time. Typically Rolls-Royce retains ownership of the engines and airline operators are assured of an accurate cost projection by buying 'power by the hour' with guaranteed performance standards. They also avoid the costs associated with unexpected engine breakdowns.

IBM, once primarily a manufacturer of large computers, has significantly increased the share of its business derived from services. IBM has shifted its focus from commoditized hardware to higher-margin services and software. This is being achieved by both organic growth and purchase of service businesses like the consulting division of PricewaterhouseCoopers. IBM's Global Services organization is the world's largest business and technology services provider. It is the fastest growing part of IBM, with over 190,000 workers serving customers in more than 160 countries.[6]

In addition to organizations operating solely in the service sector and manufacturing companies with a substantial component of service activity in the businesses, there is also a substantial amount of internal services undertaken by companies in all sectors. These internal services include accounting and payroll administration, legal services, recruitment, transport and logistics, cleaning and catering. Increasingly these services are being incorporated to form subsidiaries or outsourced to external service providers, thus adding further to the growth of the 'formal' service sector.

Service marketing does not only apply to service industries services	Theodore Levitt, recognized as one of the world's leading marketing experts, has commented that 'everybody is in service'. He points out that all industries are in services, although some have a greater or less service component than other industries.[7] Services scholar Evert Gummesson makes a similar point when he points out that: 'The former special case of the service sector has now become the universal case.'[8]

> It follows that to define services as being confined only to service industries is not strictly true.

This view has been increasingly recognized since the publication of Stephen Vargo and Robert Lusch's award-winning research on service-dominant (S-D) logic.[9] This research, first summarized in an article in 2004, provides a new perspective on goods and services. Although a detailed review of service-dominant logic and the closely related area of service science[10] work are beyond the scope of this book, some brief comments should be made on this important topic.

Vargo and Lusch contend that services are more prevalent than goods and goods need to be considered as a 'medium' for a firm's service. They consider all firms are in the business of providing services. Companies that produce goods only, such as an automobile manufacturer, are in fact creating a service for their customers – in this case a 'service' that enables customers to go from 'point A' to 'point B'. Many of the issues addressed by Vargo and Lusch have appeared previously within the services and relationship marketing literatures. However, what they present in their work is an integration of many of the somewhat disparate concepts and principles of services marketing.

Central to this work is the recognition of the need for a shift from a firm perspective to a customer perspective. S-D logic emphasizes that companies need to become continuous learning organizations working more closely with their customers and that communication with customers should be characterized by conversation and dialogue. By adopting this perspective the customer shifts from being a passive audience to an active player whether engaged more deeply in joint value creation or 'value co-creation'.[11]

There is an increasing trend towards differentiating what were once considered to be tangible products by exploiting the intangible service elements of the offer. The service elements can be added to provide unique features matching customer needs. For example, in the highly competitive photocopier business, service has become a major factor in the buying decision. Photocopiers are leased or sold with service contracts which tie customers to the supplier.

Nevertheless, it will be difficult to proceed without attempting to define a service in some way. Therefore, while recognizing that any definition might prove to be unduly restrictive, and that somewhere a service may exist which does not conform to what we say, our definition is:

> A service is an activity which typically has some element of intangibility associated with it. It involves some interaction with customers or property in their possession, and does not result in a transfer of ownership. A change of condition may occur and provision of the service may or may not be closely associated with a physical product.

Services encompass a wide range of organizations dealing with both consumers and businesses. Within the for-profit sector they include airlines, banking and finance, insurance, telecommunications, utilities, hotels, restaurants, travel and tourism, transportation and many more. Firms operating in the areas of accounting, architecture, legal services and management consulting and market research are generally referred to as professional services. The services sector also include most organizations operating in the not-for-profit sector including schools, libraries, health care services, public hospitals, the opera and ballet and a wide range of government and municipal services. Government at all levels has grown in size in most countries, creating a huge infrastructure of service departments. Today, non-profit making organizations such as charities, hospitals and government departments are discovering the need for services marketing planning.

As discussed above, the universality of the service characteristics of intangibility, heterogeneity, inseparability and perishability have been increasingly put under scrutiny in recent years. While it is true that these characteristics describe the context of many services, when compared to traditional goods, there are many exceptions. Evert Gummesson provides the following examples of where these characteristics do not apply[12]:

> *Intangibility* – a surgeon operating in the health care sector. The surgeon cuts you open, performs invasive surgery and sutures you back together. This could not possibly be perceived by the provider or the patient as something intangible!

Heterogeneity – a withdrawal from an automatic teller machine. This is an example of a highly standardized mass production service activity which is highly homogeneous, except perhaps when the cash machine runs out of money.

Inseparability – a substantial number of services are separable ones that do not involve the customer's direct participation. Such services include transporting freight, laundry of clothes, lawn mowing services and parcel delivery.

Perishability – while many services are perishable, others are not. For example, live performances such as entertainment, music and religious services can be recorded for subsequent broadcast or can be developed into physical goods in the form of tapes or DVD or electronic media.

While the universality of the service characteristics of intangibility, heterogeneity, inseparability and perishability has been challenged, we conclude that while many services possess the IHIP characteristics, others do not. Further, they may exhibit these characteristics to different degrees. Clearly there is a continuum of tangibility ranging from highly intangible to highly tangible. This concept of a continuum is useful when considering the other characteristics discussed above. Services can only be described as having a tendency towards a higher degree of the intangibility, heterogeneity, inseparability and perishability characteristics. For any given service there is, potentially, a different combination of each of the four factors. This suggests a continuum for each of the four characteristics, as shown in Figure 2.2.

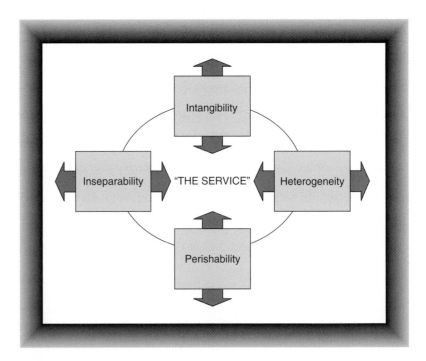

Figure 2.2
A continuum for each of the four service characteristics

The concept of a continuum for each of the four characteristics of services recognizes that emphasis on each of these characteristics can vary for a given service, and can also provide a source of competitive differentiation. Understanding the positions of a particular service on each continuum, along with the position of competitors, is an important means of considering potential sources of competitive advantage. In the same way, manufacturers of products can seek competitive advantage by focusing on 'service' elements. The services marketer should consider the extent to which each of these characteristics might be addressed. For example, the service marketer may wish to make the service more tangible by providing testimonials and elaborate documentation with a customer's pension plan. On the other hand, a marketer could seek to intrigue customers by making an offer less tangible and surrounding it with mystique, such as a surprise luxury holiday destination. Of course, marketers generally will seek to make their offers more tangible.

Classification of services

There have been a number of approaches used to develop a classification scheme for services. The intention behind this work was to provide service managers with a means of identifying other companies who, though operating in different types of industries, shared certain common characteristics.

Some of these early approaches were not always helpful in aiding the development of service marketing strategies. In some cases, the fault lay in the oversimplification of the classification scheme used, which did not offer enough strategic marketing insights to be of much value. In other cases, service managers were not open-minded enough to recognize where similarities with other industries could exist. This led Christopher Lovelock, a distinguished services researcher and former Harvard Business School professor, to develop a more substantial classification framework.

> Much can be learned by looking at other types of service organizations

His framework yields valuable marketing insights in response to five crucial questions[13]:

1. What is the nature of the 'service act'?
2. What style of relationship does this service organization have with its customers?
3. How much room is there for customization and judgement?
4. What is the nature of supply and demand for the service?
5. How is the service delivered?

Lovelock examines each of these questions in a series of two-dimensional matrices. Based on his work, each of the five questions and the matrices associated with them are now examined in more detail. (For a review of other services classification schemes, see the work by Sandy Ng and her colleagues.[14])

1. *What is the nature of the service act?*

The primary considerations here are whether or not the service is largely tangible or intangible and if it is addressed essentially to people or to 'things', be they property, systems or equipment. Not only can these factors be combined in the matrix shown in Figure 2.3, but they also raise further issues for the inquisitive service manager, such as:

- What benefits does the service provide?
- Does the customer need to be present as the service is delivered?
- Is the customer changed as a result of the service?
- Does the customer have to come out to receive the service, or can it be provided at home (or at the office)?

Exploring possible answers to these questions might enable the service manager to gain new insights, thereby repositioning the service by making it more beneficial or convenient to the customer. For example, a hairdressing salon might develop an 'at-home' service for customers who are incapacitated or who find travelling difficult. If this proved to be successful, it could reduce the need for having an expensive high street establishment. Indeed, it might eventually lead to withdrawing from fixed premises entirely.

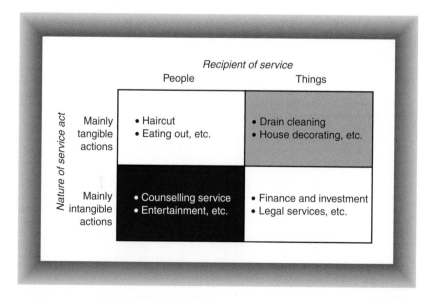

Figure 2.3
Nature of service matrix

2. What style of relationship does the service organization have with its customers?

The prime factors which underpin this question concern whether or not the customer has some type of formal relationship with the provider of the service, and whether the service itself is provided continuously or in discrete transactions. These considerations lend themselves to the matrix in Figure 2.4.

Clearly, there are advantages for the service provider to have customers as 'members', whether this is done in a contractual sense or just by mutual agreement. By knowing personal details about the customers, it becomes easy to contact them via direct marketing and to tailor special offers around their particular needs. Thus, market segmentation becomes relatively straightforward and it is possible to build up customer loyalty by trading on the special relationship that membership brings.

In contrast, when the relationship is informal, next to nothing is known about the customer. Another problem is assessing how to charge for a continuous delivery, informal relationship type of service. In the examples provided in the matrix, they come 'free', but are of course funded by the taxpayer.

The key questions this matrix raises for service managers are:

- Can anything be done to move 'informal' into 'member' relationships (e.g. random cinema visitors become cinema club members; regular tool hirers get a privilege card; etc.)?

- Where can there be trade-offs between pricing and usage rates (e.g. season ticket holders for theatre or sports entertainment; book clubs that give price incentives for membership)?

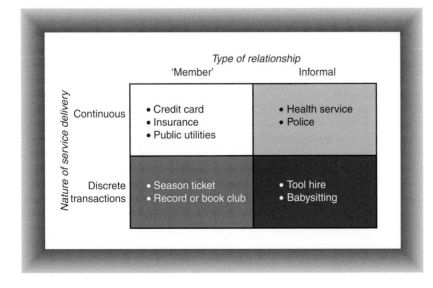

Figure 2.4
Style of relationship matrix

3. How much room is there for customization and judgement?

Here, the issues centre on the degree to which the service can be tailored to meet specific needs, and the degree of judgement required by staff who come into contact with the customer. This is illustrated in Figure 2.5.

The questions this matrix raises for the service manager are, on the whole, bound up with cost and the availability of the right calibre of staff. For example:

> • Is it desirable to limit the degree of customization and thereby benefit from 'standardization' and economies of scale?
>
> • Should customization be increased in order to reach a wider range of customers?
>
> • Should services be simplified so that less judgement is required by contact staff?
>
> • Should the service be updated in order to capitalize on the expertise of staff?

In answer to questions like these, a general management consultancy firm might start to specialize in just one or two specific areas. Similarly, the landscape gardener might focus on paths and patios.

The level of customization will often create friction between the marketing and operations function. Service market managers will often

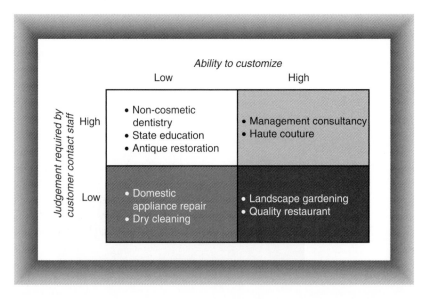

Figure 2.5
Customization and
staff judgement matrix

see the need for a high level of customization which poses greater demand on operational staff. Higher levels of service customization often require employees at the point of service delivery to make decisions based on their own judgement. This means that employees require greater levels of training and a wider skill base. For example, a waiter who prepares food at the customer's table requires a higher level of training than one who delivers food from the kitchen to the table.

4. What is the nature of supply and demand for the service?

In other words, are demand fluctuations large or small, and can peak demands be met relatively easily? The matrix these questions provide is shown as Figure 2.6.

As was stated earlier, a service usually cannot be stored, so if demand exceeds supply it is an invitation for another supplier to step in. This indicates that it is important for the service manager to understand demand patterns over time, knowing why and when peaks occur, and taking steps to work out what alternative strategies might be used for 'smoothing' them. Some examples of how this works in practice would be:

- The DIY store, whose busiest time is weekends, expands 'capacity' by employing temporary staff.

- Railway companies provide reduced price 'off-peak' travel.

- Restaurants provide a reduction for early evening diners during the week, but restore normal pricing at weekends.

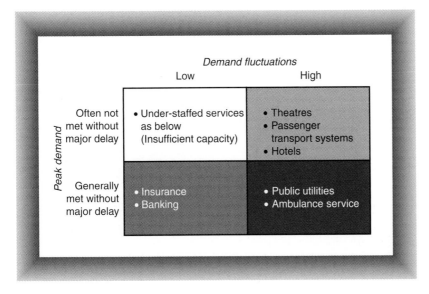

Figure 2.6
Supply and demand matrix

Typical of the questions that supply and demand prompt in the minds of service managers are:

- ● How susceptible to peaks and troughs is the business?
- ● To what extent can peaks be coped with?
- ● Should alternative strategies be adopted for creating capacity?
- ● Should alternative strategies be adopted for introducing differential pricing?
- ● Should a new mix of strategies be experimented with, involving both capacity and pricing?

Coping with demand fluctuation can cause serious problems for service managers. Computer technology helps delivery scheduling for services. For example, on the underground train network in Singapore, the passenger flow is constantly monitored via a computer-linked ticketing system. If passenger flow suggests additional trains are required, the system will immediately trigger action to correct the situation.

5. How is the service delivered?

The method by which the service is delivered to customers can be another area where a change of marketing strategy could pay dividends. The factors to consider are shown in Figure 2.7.

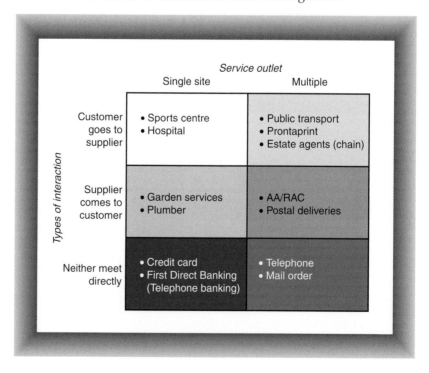

Figure 2.7
Service delivery matrix

This matrix raises another set of questions for the service manager:

- Should the service be delivered at a single site or through multiple outlets?
- What is the most convenient type of transaction for customers?
- If the type of interaction changed, would the service quality improve or deteriorate?
- Can suitable intermediaries be used in order to achieve multiple outlets (e.g. franchises)?

Service delivery is of great importance to the customer's overall perception of service quality. Services that generally require the customer to come to the supplier have a greater opportunity to control the delivery experience. For example, a client visiting a lawyer's office will gain an impression of competence and professionalism from the 'atmosphere' of the waiting area and the friendliness and efficiency of the receptionist. However, increasingly, many services are being delivered without the customer and supplier meeting. For example, telephone banking and the use of email, the Internet, fax machines and EDI (electronic data interchange) have been introduced within many service sectors.

Lovelock's five questions (and the associated matrices) clearly raise a number of important issues for the service provider. The advantage of this particular method of classification is that it can cut across service industry barriers, thus enabling comparisons to be made with, and lessons learned from, service companies in other business fields. They also highlight key issues that need to be addressed in the marketing plans of service organizations.

The strategic value of services in manufacturing

As was shown earlier, the 100% tangible product is a rarity. Apart from a few commodity items or foodstuffs, most products have an element of service attached to them.

Many manufacturers have been quick to realize that, although their basic product might be in the 'me-too' category, they can bring about some differentiation from the way they manage the service element of the product.

The types of services that can feature in an expanded 'product package' are:

- Training
- Consultancy
- Service contracts
- Customization
- Fast-moving troubleshooting
- Help with financing
- Special delivery arrangements
- Stockholding or inventory control for the customer
- No-quibble guarantees

Adding services can become a major source of differential advantage in the manufacturing sector

As manufacturing companies become more sophisticated and as technological advantages become ever more transitory, services begin to represent an area of significant profit potential. This trend has even earned itself a new piece of jargon, 'servitization of business', coined by Sandra Vandermerwe and Juan Rada.[15] Not surprisingly, manufacturing is now looking more and more at the service sector in order to learn from its experience. As a result, what was once a clear divide between two quite different types of businesses is becoming increasingly blurred.

This section on the nature of services was prompted by a seemingly simple question about the difference between marketing a product and a service. As we have seen, not only is it not easy to define where a product finishes and a service begins, but even the difference between manufacturing as an industry and the traditional notion of a service industry is becoming ever less clear.

This discussion was important, because it should help the reader to have a much clearer idea about how a business should be defined in terms of the intangibility of its service and the other characteristics that give it a particular identity. Knowing this makes it easier to recognize how the marketing planning process can be best adapted for particular circumstances.

The marketing mix

Earlier, marketing was described as being a process which matches the supplier's capabilities with the customer's wants. We also saw that this matching process took place in a business environment which could pose threats for the supplier, but which also created opportunities.

The marketing mix is, in effect, the 'flexible coupling' between the supplier and customer which facilitates the matching process. Traditionally it was said to consist of four elements, namely:

- *Product* – The product or service being offered.
- *Price* – The price or fees charged and the terms associated with its sale.
- *Promotion* – The communications programme associated with marketing the product or service.
- *Place* – The distribution and logistics involved in making the product/service available.

From this, the shorthand term for the marketing mix became the 4Ps, for reasons which are obvious. However, it must be remembered that within each 'P' is subsumed a number of subelements pertinent to that heading. So, for example, promotion will include not only face-to-face communications provided by contact staff, but also indirect communications such as advertising, sales promotions, publications and direct mail.

Services and the marketing mix

In recent years, those charged with developing the application of marketing in the service sector have questioned whether the 4Ps approach to the marketing mix was sufficiently comprehensive. As a result, there has been a marked shift of opinion and most service marketers now consider that an expanded marketing mix is appropriate for service businesses – one that ensures that all important elements are not overlooked.

In services marketing, the 4Ps need to be expanded

Added to the original 4Ps are:

- *People* – Since people are an essential element in the production and delivery of services, the quality of the service is largely determined by the quality and behaviour of the company's staff. This is particularly true in respect of those whose jobs involve high levels of customer contact.
- *Processes* – The procedures, routines and policies, which influence how a service is created and delivered to customers, can clearly be instrumental in determining how 'customer friendly' the company is perceived to be.
- *Customer service* – As customers demand higher levels of service, this element becomes a competitive weapon with which a company can differentiate itself. In the longer term it helps to build closer and more enduring relationships with customers.

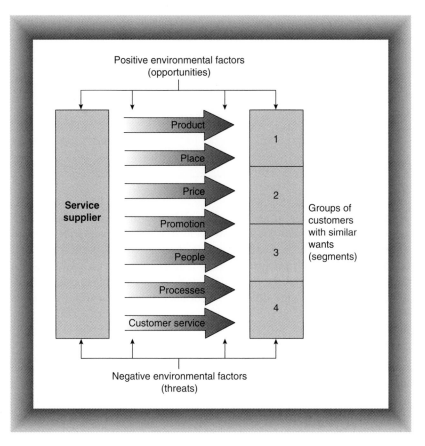

Figure 2.8
The marketing process

This expanded marketing mix is robust enough to cover most service marketing situations. Figure 2.8 provides a more detailed representation of how the marketing process for services works.

It should be noted that some authors argue that physical evidence should form a separate element of the services marketing mix.[16] While its importance is undoubted, so too is that of advertising and personal selling. Just as advertising and personal selling are sub-elements of the promotion element of the marketing mix, we consider physical evidence should be viewed as a sub-element of the product element of the mix. However, it is important that the significance of physical evidence is recognized, and attention directed at it, regardless of whether it is viewed a sub-element of product or a marketing mix element in its own right.

The output of the service provider results from the effort it puts into its services marketing mix.[17] Most service organizations now divide their customers into customer segments and provide a different marketing mix best suited to the needs of each one, as shown in Figure 2.8.

| Success depends on careful market segmentation

Across these segments, perhaps the service product provided is slightly different, perhaps the pricing varies from segment to segment, perhaps the promotion is different with, say, one segment influenced by indirect communications and another by face-to-face methods, perhaps the place element of the mix is different for each segment, or perhaps it is customer service which is differentiated.

There is, in reality, a tremendous range of options open to the marketer who chooses to explore all of the services marketing mix possibilities, but of course the whole marketing process really hinges on how accurately the needs and wants of customers are known, and how astutely they are grouped into segments which meet the following criteria:

- They are adequate in size to provide the company with a good return for its effort.
- Members of each segment have a high degree of similarity, yet are distinct from the rest of the market.
- Criteria for describing the segments are relevant to the purchase situation.
- Segments are capable of being reached through communications.

It goes without saying that a company should not try to work with too many different segments. There is a danger that some will be too small but, more importantly, the company will not be capable of managing its dealings with too many different segments without diluting its efforts.

Like an individual, a company cannot be all things to all people. It must learn to focus on its strengths and on markets where it has the best chance of succeeding.

Market segmentation is discussed in more detail in Chapter 6.

A brief history of marketing in the service industry

It would be fair to say that professional marketing does not have an especially long history in the service sector. An early study in 1970 compared 400 service and manufacturing companies and discovered that the service companies were:

- Less likely to have marketing mix activities carried out in the marketing department.
- Less likely to do comparative analysis of service products.

- Less likely to use outside agencies for their advertising (they showed a preference to do it themselves).

- Less likely to have an overall sales plan.

- Less likely to have sales training programmes.

- Less likely to use market research firms and marketing consultants.

- Less likely to spend as much on marketing as a percentage of gross sales

More service businesses should study best practice from other organizations

In general, the service industry has demonstrated considerable growth over the past four decades. However, with increasing globalization and deregulation, competition has also become far more intense. Today, we find a sector that has grown, but one that in general marketing terms still lags behind best practice in consumer goods and the industrial sector. However, the picture is not all bad, for many service companies have become very sophisticated in their marketing and would compare favourably with examples of best practice anywhere in the world.

It was only in the 1980s that serious attention was given to service marketing. Some of the work developed since then has suggested that service companies alter their 'marketing' focus as they evolve and develop. These different phases are shown in Figure 2.9. However, it should be noted that this is a general pattern that companies follow. Some individual companies might have reached these focus points in a slightly different sequence, or indeed might have jumped some of the steps completely.

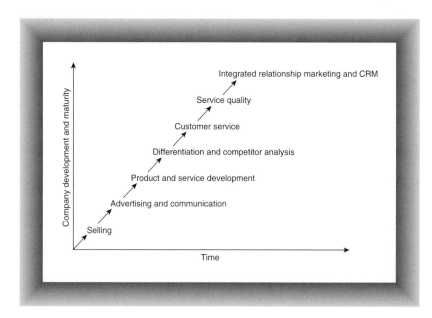

Figure 2.9
General development pattern of marketing approaches

The pattern shown in Figure 2.9 is not surprising, because it conveys a learning process whereby each step is almost a natural extension of moving forward. In fact, it could be argued that this sequence closely follows the various phases of activity which certain kinds of service companies exercised from their activities in the 1970s to the present day. Those wishing to gain a deeper perspective of service marketing should see the 2010 contribution by Ray Fisk and Stephen Grove who survey the evolution of the services field.[18]

Seeking to reach the final stage requires the service company to:

- Integrate all marketing activities
- Develop a realistic and focused approach to marketing planning
- Develop a marketing-oriented culture
- Recognize the importance of quality transactions both inside the company and with customers
- Capitalize on the use of database marketing techniques
- Engage in appropriate digital marketing and social media activities
- Explore greater engagement with customers through co-creation
- Develop a Customer Relationship Management (CRM) strategy that focuses on shareholder value creation rather than on the adoption of IT solutions
- Increase profitability through balancing customer acquisition and customer retention.

This last point is not always fully appreciated by service companies and it merits some further elaboration.

Customer retention and profitability

Acquiring customers can be expensive. Usually it involves certain one-off costs, such as, for example, advertising, promotion, the salesperson's time, and even the cost of entering data into the company's data bank. Thus, every customer represents an investment, the level of which will vary from business to business.

Retaining customers is extremely profitable

If they are treated correctly and remain customers over a long period, there is strong evidence that they will generate more profits for the organization each year they maintain the relationship. Across a wide range of businesses this pattern is the same (Figure 2.10).[19]

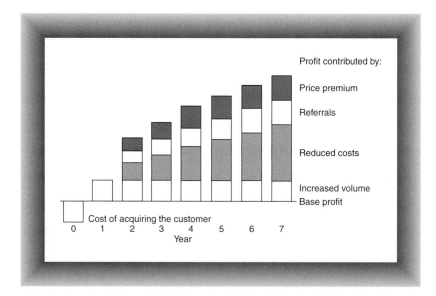

Figure 2.10
Retaining customers
pays off

> For example, an industrial laundry almost doubled its profits per customer over five years. A car servicing business expects fourth-year customers to generate three times the profit of a first-year customer. A distributor of industrial products found that net sales per account continued to rise even into the nineteenth year of the relationship.

This trend holds true for many types of service companies. As the relationship extends, the initial 'contact' costs, such as checking creditworthiness, no longer figure on the balance sheet. In addition, the more that is known about the customer as the relationship develops, the more offers can be tailored effectively to meet their needs. Thus, the customer gets greater value, which in turn encourages more frequent and larger purchases.

> It follows, therefore, that when a company lowers its customer defection rate, average customer relationships last longer and profits climb. Viewed in this way, the costs of providing enhanced customer service could be seen as an investment in customer retention.

Integrated relationship marketing and CRM

For an organization to reach the last level of sophistication shown in Figure 2.9 it needs to reappraise the way it relates, not only to customers, but also to all other areas which have an impact on the business. It involves a recognition that in order to achieve success, the organization is dependent upon the outside world for everything: its skills (through the workforce), its materials, the equipment it uses and, as we saw earlier, the trading conditions under which it operates. Of course relationship marketing is not about having a deep relationship with each and every customer. Rather it is a process that involves determining the *appropriate* relationship with customers and customer segments. This relationship marketing approach for customers applies equally to other 'non-customer' stakeholders.

There are six 'markets domains' or stakeholder groups that need to be considered within this broader vision of relationship marketing,[20] as shown in Figure 2.11. Only the central area is concerned with traditional customer markets and it is on this that the remainder of this book will focus. It is in its customer markets that the company's services, which are the *raison d'être* for the organization's existence, have special currency.

> There are six 'market domains' that need to be managed by the organization

> All of the six markets are interrelated and influence each other, but it is the customer market which is the central focus of the organization's goal.

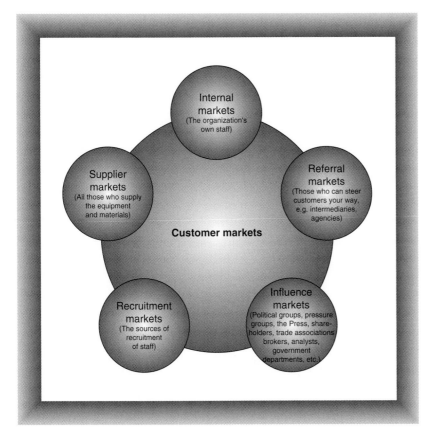

Figure 2.11
Relationship marketing – a broadened view of markets

Relationship
marketing is more
profitable than one-
off transactions

An organization needs to successfully engage with all these stake-holder groups or market domains. However, while it is important to understand this concept, it is equally important to understand that it is not the primary role or function of an organization's marketing department to prepare 'marketing plans' for these other five 'satellite' market domains. (However, the tools and methodologies of market-ing planning outlined in this book can be used to develop market plans for these other satellite markets.) Clearly, managing these other markets is the ultimate responsibility of the board of directors, through both the functional chiefs who manage each area and the management of cross-functional activities within the service organi-zation. For example, the recruitment and internal market domains should be managed by the human resources function, the sharehold-ers and external analysts within the influence market domain by the corporate affairs function and the supplier market domain by the procurement function. All these non-customer market domains need to be managed with a view to achieving success within the customer market, since this is the whole point of what we call 'relationship marketing'.

With customers being the prime focus of the organization's marketing efforts, this new orientation calls for there to be a switch from seeking 'one-off' transactions with any customer who can be inveigled to buy, to building long-term relationships. This change from 'transaction marketing' to 'relationship marketing' has very real implications for the organization. Some of these are listed below.

Transactional marketing focus	*Relationship marketing focus*
● Single sale	● Customer retention
● Service features	● Service benefits
● Short timescale	● Long timescale
● Little emphasis on customer service	● High emphasis on service customer
● Moderate customer contact	● High customer contact
● Limited customer commitment	● High customer commitment
● Quality is the concern of 'production'	● Quality is the concern of all

A similar shift in orientation needs to accompany this change of focus with respect to the other 'markets domains' shown in Figure 2.11. Thus, a more open, long-lasting and committed relationship is called for in the organization's dealings with what we have termed internal markets, referral markets, influence markets, recruitment markets and supplier markets.

> By building longer-term quality relationships in this way, the organization can establish stability in the restless, ever-changing business environment.

Not only is this mutually beneficial to the parties involved in the short term, but it also makes it easier to plan ahead with greater accuracy.

Not all 'satellite' markets are equally important

Clearly, not all of these satellite markets are going to be of equal importance to companies. Therefore, each organization will have to make decisions regarding what levels of attention and resources they devote to each one. The corporate thinking process is likely to follow these steps:

> 1. Which of these areas has the greatest impact on our future success?
>
> 2. Who are the key participants in these markets?
>
> 3. What are the expectations and requirements of these participants?
>
> 4. To what extent is the company currently meeting these expectations and requirements?
>
> 5. What strategy needs to be formulated to bring these relationships to the desired level?
>
> 6. Are any of these strategies sufficiently complex or resource intensive to justify the need for a formal written plan?

As an aid to these deliberations, a relationship marketing network diagram or 'radar chart', as illustrated in Figure 2.12, can be used. This has two axes representing customer markets – existing and new – and five axes representing the 'satellite' markets. Each axis has a scale ranging from 0 to 10 on which it is possible to plot the current and desired levels of emphasis on each market.

In the example shown of the changing emphasis of the management of an international airline, the greatest improvement is required in influence and internal markets, whereas the other markets call for more modest changes in emphasis.

> Of course, the more the measurements on the radar chart diagram are based on research or objective criteria, the more accurate and useful the finished diagram becomes regarding policy-making.

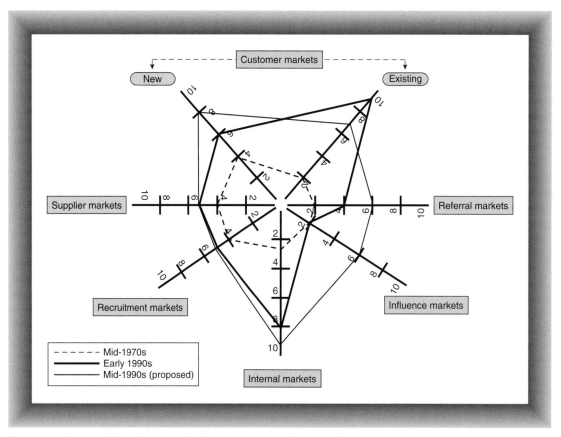

Figure 2.12   Relationship marketing network diagram for a major international airline

While this is not intended to be a book specifically about relationship marketing and strategies for customer retention,[20] it should be obvious that in preparing a strategic marketing plan the only real justification for giving up resources to complete this task is if the final result spells out clearly how the organization is going to get and keep customers.

The services plan, then, will show clearly what it is that your organization is offering to your target customers that makes them want to buy from your organization, rather than from any other that happens to be in the market. This involves true relationship marketing.

Summary

Although products and services are on the surface quite different, closer inspection reveals that a 'pure' service or product rarely exists. Most services contain a tangible product element and most products have an intangible service element. The relative weight of tangibility to intangibility in a company's offer will indicate whether or not the service can be marketed much like a traditional product or if a new approach is required. Indeed, such is the range and diversity of services that service managers can often learn from other industries where services are provided which, although different, have some of the same inherent characteristics as their own.

Marketing was described as a matching process which tries to optimize the company's capabilities in the context of meeting customer needs. The 'flexible coupling' in this matching process is the marketing mix, which consists of the product/service, price, promotion, place, people, processes and customer service. While many organizations claim to subscribe to a marketing approach, there is considerable evidence to show that they do in fact misunderstand some of the basic principles that should be followed. Indeed, such has been the evolution of marketing over recent years that only the more mature and sophisticated organizations have grasped the fact that the more traditional approach, which we called 'transaction marketing', is no longer likely to bring lasting success. Instead, 'relationship marketing' is more in keeping with the times in which we live.

However, in order to adapt to the principles behind relationship marketing, the organization needs to look afresh not only at its customer markets, but also at what we have termed 'market domains' or satellite markets – the internal, influence, referral, recruitment and supplier markets. In fact, what this new approach demands is an entirely new kind of marketing orientation, which in turn often requires that there is a change in the organizational climate and the attitudes of staff throughout the company.

Finally, as we have seen, there is a potential problem of confusing customer markets with satellite markets, thereby causing a blurring of focus of the company's efforts. The satellite markets are aimed at supporting the customer market and the delivery of shareholder value. This problem can be avoided by remembering that, whatever else might be provided, the organization's key output, the service(s) upon which its very existence depends, are directed and tailored to meet the needs of customer markets. In order not to compound any confusion about this, for the remainder of this book we will use the term 'service product' to indicate the main output and to distinguish it from the array of other supporting services the company might provide. Figure 2.13 puts into perspective what constitutes the service product and the product surround.

Having discussed the specific nature of services and the need for services businesses to shift to a relationship orientation, we will now proceed to examine the processes and problems in developing marketing plans for service businesses.

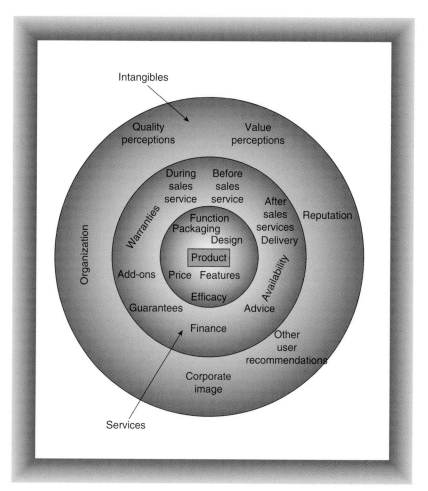

Figure 2.13
The 'service product'
and the product
surround

3 Marketing planning for services: the process

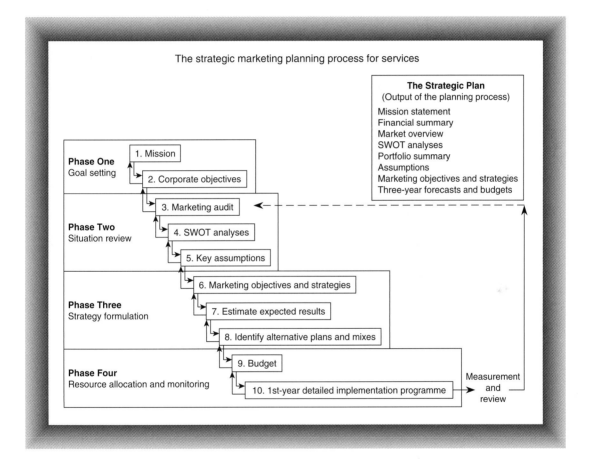

The strategic marketing planning process for services

The Strategic Plan
(Output of the planning process)

Mission statement
Financial summary
Market overview
SWOT analyses
Portfolio summary
Assumptions
Marketing objectives and strategies
Three-year forecasts and budgets

Phase One
Goal setting

1. Mission
2. Corporate objectives

Phase Two
Situation review

3. Marketing audit
4. SWOT analyses
5. Key assumptions

Phase Three
Strategy formulation

6. Marketing objectives and strategies
7. Estimate expected results
8. Identify alternative plans and mixes

Phase Four
Resource allocation and monitoring

9. Budget
10. 1st-year detailed implementation programme

Measurement and review

In this chapter, we will take an overview of the strategic marketing planning process for services, shown above, and also a brief look at some of its component parts. We will also consider some of the reasons why service organizations do not always manage to take advantage of the benefits that strategic marketing planning should bring. The four phases shown above will be examined in detail later in Chapters 5 to 10.

What is marketing planning?

In essence, marketing planning is a series of activities which are tackled in a logical sequence in a way that leads to the setting of marketing objectives and the devising of programmes to meet them. Thus, the marketing plan becomes a framework for identifying where and why marketing resources are going to be allocated, when they are to come into play and how they are to be integrated in order to make maximum impact.

The output of this process is the strategic marketing plan, the contents of which will be spelled out later in this chapter.

Marketing plans are now an essential aspect of business

As we saw in the previous chapter, when business life was less volatile and complex than it is today service companies were able to survive and sometimes prosper without paying very much attention to marketing planning. Indeed, there are no doubt a few fortunate companies who are still in growth sectors, or who happen to be in the right place at the right time and, as such, see little benefit in devoting resources to marketing planning.

> However, for the vast majority, the more uncertain their prospects become, the greater their necessity to have the life-line that a well-formulated marketing plan can offer.

During periods of recession there is often an increased interest in marketing planning and how it can help organizations deal with economic downturn.

Research shows that, not only will a marketing plan bring about a better coordination of activities and individuals whose actions are interrelated over time, but it will also result in a discipline that will:

- Increase the likelihood of identifying external developments
- Prepare the organization to meet change
- Minimize non-rational responses to the unexpected
- Improve communications between executives and departments
- Reduce conflicts that inevitably arise when organizational direction is unclear
- Force management to think ahead systematically
- Balance corporate resources more effectively against market opportunities

- Provide a framework for the continuing review of operations

- Most telling of all, lead to a higher return on investment (as shown in evidence from the PIMS[1] study).

At first sight, with all these benefits on offer, it is surprising that more service organizations have not invested in more detailed and comprehensive marketing planning.

Marketing planning involves organizational change

However, what on the surface appears to be a fairly straightforward planning process, does, in fact, raise a number of deeper issues for the organization.

To introduce marketing planning is more than a cognitive process because inherent in this new approach are implications that can impact on all parts of the business, from the boardroom down. If the planning task is tackled properly, no organizational areas are immune. Marketing planning needs to permeate all parts of the organization, to the extent that even its structure and traditional power patterns have to stand up to scrutiny and change if they are found wanting.

Other approaches to marketing planning

This book is about the scientific, normative type of marketing planning described in many articles and textbooks during the past 30 years. There are, of course, other strategic decision-making models and it would be remiss not to mention what these different approaches are, together with their strengths and weaknesses.[2] There appear to be six accepted models of perspectives of strategic decision-making. These are:

1. *A planning model* – Here, strategic decisions are reached by use of a sequential, planning search for optimum solutions to defined problems. This process is highly rational and is fuelled by concrete data.

2. *An interpretative model* – Here, the organization is regarded as a collection of associations, sharing similar values, beliefs and perceptions. These 'frames of reference' enable the stakeholders to interpret the organization and the environment in which it operates. Information which does not fit with the dominant reference system is actively ignored or downgraded. The same could be said of people. In this way, a particular culture emerges which

encourages individuals to lend themselves to self-fulfilling organizational prophecies, uncontaminated by deviant behaviour or information. Strategy thus becomes the product, not of defined aims and objectives, but of the prevailing values, attitudes and ideas in the organization.

3. *A political model* – Here strategy is not chosen directly, but emerges through compromise, conflict and consensus-seeking among interested stakeholders. Since the strategy is the outcome of negotiation, bargaining and confrontation, those with the most power have the greatest influence.

4. *A logical incremental model* – Here, strategies emerge from 'strategic subsystems', each concerned with a different type of strategic issue. Strategic goals are based on an awareness of needs rather than the highly structured analytical process of the planning model. Often, due to a lack of necessary information, such goals can be vague, general and non-rigid in nature. The commitment to a firm's strategy for reaching the 'image of the future' is delayed as long as possible, as various 'first steps' are evaluated. As events unfold and movement towards the strategic goals proceeds, more information becomes known and strategic action can be adjusted and brought into sharper focus.

5. *An ecological model* – In this perspective, the environment impinges on the organization in such a way that strategies are virtually prescribed and there is little or no free choice. In this model, the organization which adapts most successfully to its environment will survive in a way which mirrors Darwin's natural selection. In reality, restriction of strategic choice is not solely attributable to the external environment. Blinkered perception and the feeling of powerlessness by decision-makers also play their part.

6. *A visionary leadership model* – Here, the strategy emerges as the result of the leader's vision. It is not necessary for the leader to have originated the idea, but his or her commitment to it, their personal credibility, and how they articulate it to others, can provide the necessary organizational momentum. However, to be successful, the vision has to have some resonance with the followers and the surrounding circumstances. In other words, it must be attractive and timely.

It is unlikely that a given service organization will use a pure version of any of these models. In all probability, its strategic decision-making model will be a hybrid of some of them. However, it is possible that one or two of these will predominate and thereby give strategic decision-making a distinctive 'flavour'.

Strengths	Weaknesses
Planning model • Systematic • Unemotional • Clear analysis of problems • Various strategic options are considered before selecting the most appropriate one • It provides a framework which can be communicated and understood through the organization • It provides a discipline of review and evaluation for managers	• Assumptions are made that the environment is predictable over the strategic time-span • It is implied that the organization is not directly affected by the environment over this time • There is separation between those who make decisions and those in possession of the most useful information • It can become bureaucratic and ritualistic, e.g. the annual numbers game • It assumes that people are rational and have the skills to handle information in an unbiased way • It is impossible to assemble all the data required to make a truly rational choice
Interpretative model • There is a conscious effort to establish shared values or beliefs through the organization • Individuals contribute in a way which is congruent with personal values, therefore their commitment is high	• Symbols and mythology assume greater importance than hard data • Strategy is not related to defined aims, but common perceptions held by the organization • Information which does not confirm the model is rejected or downgraded • If change becomes necessary, a radical shake-up and readjustment programme is required, in order to kill off the old paradigm and those who promoted it
Political model • There is a recognition of the realities of power • Only serious issues get put on the agenda, i.e. those with bargaining power • Strategic decisions are acceptable to dominant interest groups	• Strategies, coming as they do from conflict and compromise, are rarely unanimously accepted doctrines • There is an overemphasis on jockeying for position, at the expense of 'keeping an eye on the ball' • Personal success takes precedence over organizational success • The 'out-voted' minorities will often subvert strategies to meet their own ends
Logical incremental model • There is widely shared consensus for action among top management • The organization is open to learning from the environment • Key players are encouraged to view issues dispassionately • Tentative strategic options are tested before being adopted fully • Ongoing assessment of the environment enables strategy to be modified if necessary • Resources are generally allocated to those parts of the organization which promise most • Change is evolutionary not revolutionary	• The formal processes of the organization cannot analyse and plan all possible strategic variables concurrently • Strategic goals are arrived at by a 'muddling' process, rather than analysis • The process does not allow much scope for creative options • Strategies seem to focus on 'no lose' and organizational health, rather than 'winning' • New problems can disrupt the 'up and running' strategy in a disproportionate way
Ecological model • Organizational variations which match the environment produce definite advantages	• Decision-makers mistakenly believe that they are powerless to develop strategy options, whereas they could exercise choice in terms of market segmentation, product differentiation, and so on
Visionary leadership model • It simplifies complex organizational issues • It communicates at a 'gut' level • It can generate high levels of commitment and motivation among 'believers'	• The process is heavily dependent on the visionary's dream • Visions might be inadequate or out of synchronization with the times • The organization can remain too committed to an out-of-date vision

Figure 3.1   Strengths and weaknesses of alternative marketing planning models

It will be of interest for the service organization to be aware of the ways in which its strategy-forming processes are 'biased', because each of the models described above has inherent strengths and weaknesses (Figure 3.1).

The reason this book deals with the planning model, rather than the others, is that the authors' research has shown that this is the most effective way of coping with the turbulence and rate of change which now characterizes most service businesses. Also, it is a model that can easily be adapted to take account of organizational size and complexity.

The marketing planning process

In the last chapter, it was explained how the marketing perspective has to change from being essentially concerned with short-term transactions to longer-term relationships. This being the case, the marketing planning process needs to be considered over a reasonably long time-frame and in a strategic context.

> Indeed, the blame for the failure of so many companies in recent years can be firmly traced to short-term, financially dominated objectives; and to being overconcerned with immediate sales performance and profit ratios which reflect historical and current conditions, rather than long-term growth.

A strategic approach
is essential

A reasonable compromise between short-termism and looking so far ahead as to render it meaningless is to consider a planning period of about three years. Of course, for some types of services, this might still prove to be too long (for example, in computer services) or too short (for example, in energy utilities), but these companies will have to establish a planning window which is appropriate for their particular businesses. Thus, right from the outset, the emphasis is on a three-year (or longer, where necessary) marketing strategy rather than on a one-year tactical plan.

> It has been shown that many of today's organizational problems stem directly from a historical overemphasis on short-termism. Many organizations that were tactically efficient died because they did not have an effective strategy towards their markets. Doing things right (tactics) is not an effective substitute for doing the right things (strategy).

It is crucial to do the
right things as well
as to do things right

'Doing the right things', in the context of strategic marketing, simply means ensuring on a continuous basis that customers have good reasons to want to do business with one's own organization rather than with any other competitor who happens to be around. This, in turn, requires an ongoing dialogue with specific groups of customers, whose needs are understood in depth, and for whom offers are developed that have differential advantages over the offers of competitors.

To do this effectively means predicting the changes that are taking place in the business, economic, legislative, technical market and competitive environment, setting objectives and strategies for a period of around three years and then setting in motion the necessary tactical changes in the first year of the plan (the tactical plan). In the absence of a strategic marketing plan, it is simply impossible to do this by means of only a one-year tactical plan. In its turn, of course, a strategic marketing plan is likely to be more effective if appropriate strategic tools are utilized, such as scenario planning, as well as the methods outlined in this book. The really crucial document, however, will always be the strategic marketing plan.

Because research has shown that it is effective strategic marketing planning that is so difficult and elusive, this book focuses solely on this form of planning – the strategic marketing plan.

The planning process which follows is one that has been tried and tested at the Cranfield School of Management for the past two decades. The framework provided originates from research carried out by one of the authors, Malcolm McDonald.[3] In outline there are four major phases:

> Phase One: Establishing the strategic context
>
> Phase Two: Conducting a situation review
>
> Phase Three: Formulating marketing objectives and strategies
>
> Phase Four: Allocating budgets and developing a detailed first-year implementation plan.

In turn, these four phases can be broken down into a series of steps, as shown in the figure at the start of this chapter. This figure shows how the four phases are divided into ten discrete steps. For the sake of clarity, the ten steps in the marketing planning process are shown as quite distinct activities.

> In practice, many of the steps are interrelated and the whole process is highly interactive.

Thus, instead of starting at Step 1 and pushing on relentlessly to the end, it is likely that there will be quite a lot of interaction and doubling back, as the feedback arrows or 'loops' that connect each step of the marketing planning process indicate. We emphasize that the services marketing planning process is not a linear one, rather it is an iterative and recursive process. This means that activities, information and insights gained in a later step in the process may have an impact on earlier steps in the plan, possibly causing them to be revisited and revised.

Chapters 5 to 10 focus on the four phases in the planning process in some detail. However, at this point we will briefly explain what each of the ten steps involves before expanding on each of them so as to turn them into actionable propositions.

It is important to understand, however, that the process itself is only the means of producing the output, i.e. a strategic marketing plan.

Step 1   Mission

It is important for all companies to have a sense of mission. By encapsulating this into a brief, highly personal and meaningful statement, it gives the various stakeholders in the service organization a clear purpose and sense of direction.

The service mission statement is an important device that can provide an understanding for staff working in different parts of the organization, enabling them to pull together and uphold the corporate values and philosophy. However, it is essential that the mission statement is communicated clearly to all stakeholders and is perceived to be both relevant and realistic. Unless these requirements are met, the mission statement is unlikely to have any real impact on the organization. This is explained in detail in Chapter 5.

Step 2   Corporate objectives

The purpose of corporate objectives is for the stakeholders to measure the success of the mission. Seen in this light, the only true objective of a company is what is stated as being the principal purpose for its existence. In most commercial service companies, this is expressed in terms of profit, since profit is the one universally accepted criterion by which efficiency can be evaluated. It is profit which provides the means of satisfying shareholders and owners alike. It is also profit which provides the wherewithal to reinvest in the business to make it grow. For non-profit-making service organizations, such as government departments or charities, objectives such as economic efficiency, funds raised or projects completed might be more realistic measures of performance.

From this, it follows that stated desires such as to 'expand market share', 'increase sales' or 'improve productivity' are not objectives, but are actually *strategies* at a corporate level, since they are the means by which the company will achieve its profit objectives.

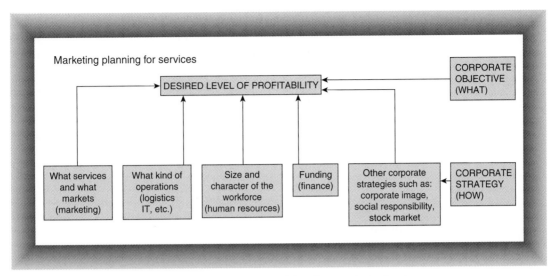

Figure 3.2   Relationship between corporate objective and strategies

Some typical corporate objectives and strategies for a commercial organization are shown in Figure 3.2. From this, it can be seen that, at the next level down in the organization, i.e. at the functional level, 'what services and what markets' become *marketing objectives*. In turn, the *marketing strategies* for meeting these, such as using advertising or personal selling, become *departmental objectives* for those particular parts of the business.

When viewed in this way, it can be seen that within the whole organization is a hierarchical chain of interlinking objectives and strategies.

> With such a protocol in operation, an objective or strategy set at even the lowest reaches of the organization should be capable of being traced upwards in order to discover how it contributes to the overriding corporate objective.

This, then, is how, when taken together, the mission statement and corporate objectives provide the strategic context for what follows in the marketing planning process.

More about this stage of planning is given in Chapters 6, 7 and 8.

Step 3   Marketing audit

> The purpose of the marketing audit is to gather all the relevant data which can determine how well equipped the service organization is to compete in its chosen marketing arena now and in the future.

Much of the data collected comes from external sources, and is concerned with the business and economic environment, together with market and competitor analysis. Not only is the current situation analysed, but also future trends and their significance are considered. Internal sources provide additional information and help to identify the company's strengths and weaknesses.

In its search to understand the business environment, the sensible service organization will be selective in terms of what it strives to uncover, knowing that 20% of relevant data will provide it with 80% of the answers it needs to know. Unless the organization is practical in its approach to the marketing audit, the task can become extremely time-consuming, with huge volumes of data which overwhelm the process of identifying key relevant information.

This is discussed in more detail in Chapter 6.

Step 4   SWOT analyses

The purpose of the SWOT (Strengths, Weaknesses, Opportunities and Threats) analysis is to identify the key components of marketing information from the vast amount of data generated by the audit. By grouping all the salient information under these four headings, it becomes possible for the organization to highlight the external opportunities and threats, and to weigh them against its current internal strengths and weaknesses. Once in possession of this information, the way forward becomes clearer.

Detailed guidelines on how to complete a SWOT analysis for each market segment are given in Chapter 7.

Step 5   Key assumptions

The marketing audit and the subsequent SWOT analysis can only reflect reality if some assumptions are made about the future. These might concern the number of competitors, the political climate, the general economic well-being of certain markets, and so on.

Such assumptions, or educated guesses, should be few in number and be addressed only to key factors that have a bearing on the planning period.

They should also be communicated properly so that everyone involved in the planning process understands how the 'playing field' might be expected to change over time. Key assumptions also identify areas which may need to be addressed through 'contingency plans'.

Assumptions are discussed in more detail in Chapter 7.

Step 6 Marketing objectives and strategies

The SWOT analyses and key assumptions steps provide the marketing planner with the data with which to set marketing objectives and strategies. The marketing objectives will be concerned with which services are provided for which markets. The possible combinations of these are illustrated in a neat way by the matrix developed by **Ansoff**,[4] shown in Figure 3.3.

Clearly, the quadrant representing current business (present services to present markets) reflects the arena about which the company knows most. In that sense, it is the area of least risk, unlike new services to new markets (diversification) which represents the least known, hence most hazardous, way forward.

As Figure 3.3 shows, marketing objectives bring with them a strong sense of what the marketing strategy should be to achieve them. In Chapter 8 we will explore strategy formulation in more detail. For now, it is enough to recognize that the marketing strategy has its roots in an analytical process.

● Definition: Igor Ansoff is an American planning guru who constructed a matrix known as the Ansoff matrix, which has two dimensions and four boxes – existing products, new products, existing markets, new markets

Step 7 Estimate expected results

Because the marketing objectives and strategies have to contribute to the corporate objectives in the way shown earlier, the financial outcome of Step 6 has to be calculated as accurately as possible. If the expected results far exceed the corporate objectives, then it could be that the

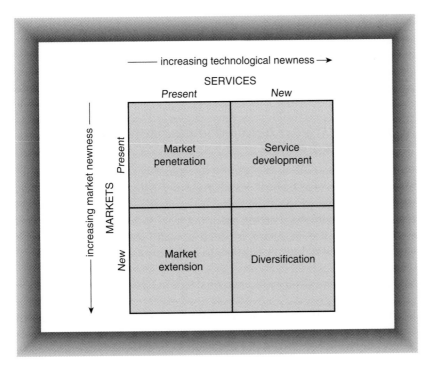

Figure 3.3
Ansoff matrix

corporate objectives need to be set at a higher level. Conversely, if the expected results fall short of the corporate objectives, the next step considers if they can be met by a revised alternative marketing mix.

This is further considered in Chapter 8.

Step 8   Identify alternative mixes

In this step, the SWOT analysis and key assumptions are reappraised in order to identify if there are other, more productive, mixes of marketing objectives and strategies which get closer to achieving (or exceeding) the corporate objectives. If, after considerable creative experimentation, there is still a shortfall, it has to be considered that the original corporate objectives were unrealistic and they should be adjusted accordingly.

Even if the first attempt at marketing objectives and strategies yields the right level of expected results, it is still recommended that some alternative mixes are considered, as the first solution is not always the best one. The step of alternative mixes helps identify the most appropriate and rewarding marketing objectives and strategies.

This is further considered in Chapter 8.

Step 9   Budget

Once the marketing objectives and strategies are agreed, it becomes possible to cost out the various programmes for the contributing marketing activities. The nature of the advertising input, sales staff, distribution and so on can be determined and budgets allocated accordingly.

The output of this total process is a strategic marketing plan covering a period of between three and five years.

Step 10   First-year detailed implementation programme

With the strategic plan as a guide, the detailed implementation programme or one-year tactical plan can be developed. In effect, this one-year tactical plan propels the company towards its strategic goals. Of course, the sensible marketing planning system has a monitoring and control procedure in order to ensure what was planned actually happens – and if it doesn't happen, to know the reason why.

Steps 9 and 10 are dealt with in more detail in Chapter 9.

With the ten-step planning process we have just outlined, it becomes a relatively easy task to monitor progress and to identify the root causes of any 'derailments'. By taking whatever corrective action is shown to be necessary, and by learning from its mistakes, the company does, in fact, develop a stronger and more effective planning process for the future.

We have found relatively few service organizations whose planning 'systems' possess all of these steps linked in this way.

> Those whose marketing planning closely follows this approach do, on the whole, manage to cope with their environment much more successfully than those who rely mainly on a 'sales forecasting and budgetary control' approach.

Moreover, the genuine marketing planners are more prepared and so have less need to 'fire-fight' ongoing events. In short, they suffer fewer operational problems and, as a result, tend to be more effective organizations.

Summary

In this chapter we defined marketing planning and identified the benefits it could bring to an organization. We went on to outline a marketing planning process for service organizations which consists of four phases: establishing the strategic context; conducting a situation review; formulating marketing objectives and strategies; allocating budgets and devising a detailed first-year implementation plan.

These four phases can be further broken down into ten interactive and interrelated process steps. Each of the steps was described briefly as an introduction to what is to follow in Chapters 5 to 9. However, the amount of text devoted to each step in the following chapters will vary considerably, based on their complexity, importance and the amount of detail with which they need to be addressed.

Before examining the finer points of the marketing planning process, it is useful to consider some of the most common barriers to effective marketing planning. These are described in the next chapter.

4 Marketing planning for services: the problems

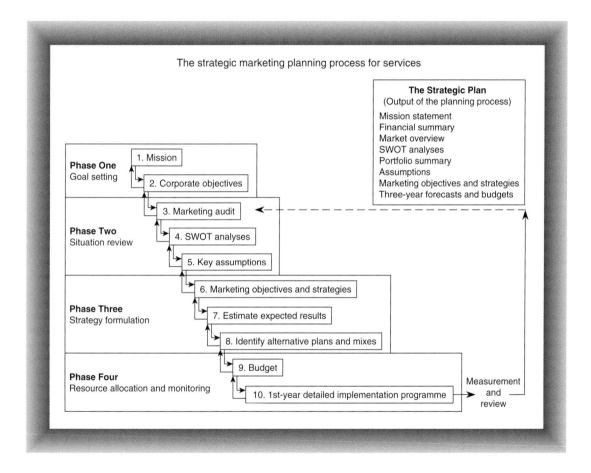

The strategic marketing planning process for services

The Strategic Plan
(Output of the planning process)
Mission statement
Financial summary
Market overview
SWOT analyses
Portfolio summary
Assumptions
Marketing objectives and strategies
Three-year forecasts and budgets

Phase One
Goal setting

1. Mission
2. Corporate objectives

Phase Two
Situation review

3. Marketing audit
4. SWOT analyses
5. Key assumptions

Phase Three
Strategy formulation

6. Marketing objectives and strategies
7. Estimate expected results
8. Identify alternative plans and mixes

Phase Four
Resource allocation and monitoring

9. Budget
10. 1st-year detailed implementation programme

Measurement and review

Marketing planning and services

Having reviewed the ten key steps in the marketing planning process, we next briefly discuss some formal studies on the use of marketing planning by companies and consider the key problems associated with marketing planning. We review these studies chronologically in order to show how the study of marketing planning has evolved.

The need for effective planning in the services sector has been recognized for a considerable time. For example, as long ago as 1975 Chisnall[1] pointed to the growing services sector and emphasized that in planning services, whether it be in the commercial or public sector, greater attention should be given to input/output measurement to ensure that resources used reflect their contribution to the efficiency of the organizational output. He described the relevance of marketing techniques such as marketing research, strategic planning and marketing control to help improve the development of service organizations, but argued that there was an institutionalized reluctance of service industries to develop a more realistic and market-oriented approach to marketing planning.

Marketing planning has been slow to develop in the service sector

By the 1980s, there was little evidence that service organizations had adopted marketing planning on a widespread and successful basis. Hooley[2] and his colleagues found that 43% of their sample of 529 service firms claimed to have both one-year and long-range marketing plans but noted that their mailed surveys were skewed towards more successful companies. No attempt was made to evaluate formally how comprehensive the marketing planning was.

Greenley[3] examined marketing planning practices in 50 UK service companies from a number of industries including: banking and insurance; freight forwarding and transport; management and market research consultancy; technical consultancy; catering; television entertainment; and the gas and electricity sector. He compared the headings of the major sections of marketing plans of these service companies with a typical list of headings suggested in the marketing literature, which included: situation analysis; objectives; strategy statement; action programme; budget; and control. Greenley concluded that marketing planning in service companies was not well developed.

The research on marketing planning in service organizations follows more general research on marketing planning. Despite the obvious and theoretically supported benefits of marketing planning, a review of empirical studies that have been carried out suggests that as few as 10% of companies actually use a comprehensive marketing planning process and even the most optimistic of these studies only offered a figure of 25%.

Studies in the 1990s showed slow adoption of sophisticated marketing planning approaches. A study of 385 medium and large firms in the UK found that just over half attempted to prepare marketing plans. Of these, 73% were described as 'having a go at the entire marketing planning model, whilst doing little of it comprehensively'.[4]

The 1994 study by Greenley and Bayus[5] of marketing planning processes in US and UK companies suggested that only 13% of the companies could be described as sophisticated marketing decision-makers. A further study by the Conference Board, a global research network based in New York, found that much remained to be done in asserting the role of marketing and marketing planning in the boardroom.[6]

A study of marketing planning in the UK, published in 2001, showed that only 50% of companies had long-term marketing plans as well as annual marketing plans.[7] Brian Smith's 2003 Ph.D. thesis, concluded that marketing planning is not widely used, even if it is a good prescription and the literature is a poor description of what happens in practice.[8] A further piece of research published in 2004[9] points to the lack of success in marketing planning and how management processes should be given greater emphasis in the development of strategic marketing plans.

A 2010 study of marketing planning,[10] drawing on a sample of 750 companies, confirmed that there is a positive relationship between higher company performance and undertaking formal marketing planning. Over 65% of the firms studied were within the services sector. This study identified a statistically significant relationship between higher company performance and 14 key strategic marketing practices including: conducting a comprehensive situation analysis; adopting a proactive approach to the future; carrying out self-generated market research; the commissioning of market research; setting longer-term profit objectives; setting more offensive marketing objectives; adopting a strategic focus of market expansion; competing on the basis of superior value-to-the-customer; introducing new ways of doing business; developing and introducing new products; and using a marketing intelligence-gathering system to monitor changes in competitor behaviour, customer behaviour, technology, and business/economic trends.

Another 2010 study of 216 business organisations[11] concluded that marketing planning is positively associated with executives' perception of change in their company's overall financial performance. The results showed a positive association between formal marketing planning and the market share performance. Higher levels of formal marketing planning were associated with higher levels of market share achieved. The study also found a difference between those organizations that formally prepare marketing plans and those that do not. Those organizations that had adopted a formal marketing planning process showed higher performance levels than those that did not.

Of course just having a marketing plan is by no means sufficient. There needs to be strong leadership behind it and company-wide commitment to it. In an article entitled 'Strategic Marketing Planning: A Twenty-First Century Perspective', Keegan, drawing on his much earlier study of the Japanese approach to strategic market planning, concluded: 'An essential element of a Strategic Market Plan is vision and commitment to that vision. This requires strong leadership by dedicated individuals. The successful Japanese companies have had this kind of leadership. At the same time, a successful Strategic Market Plan also requires the commitment of the entire organization to its goal and objectives. One of the functions of strong leadership is to create and support this commitment throughout the organization.'[12] Keegan points out that his earlier conclusions about leadership and commitment line up with contemporary best standards of twenty-first century advanced practice in marketing planning.

There are some signs of an improved approach to marketing planning in the service sector

A review of marketing planning literature published over the past three decades shows a growing recognition of the importance of marketing planning and an increasing body of literature focusing on the preparation of marketing plans. However, our own research suggests many service companies lag behind accepted best practice and there is much opportunity for improvement.

> The question is – does it matter if service organizations don't bother with strategic marketing planning?

There can be little doubt that marketing planning is essential when we consider the increasingly hostile and complex environment in which companies operate and the many services companies who have declined or failed in recent years. Hundreds of external and internal factors interact in a bafflingly complex way to affect our ability to achieve profitable sales. Also, let us consider for a moment the four typical objectives which companies set: maximizing revenue; maximizing profits; maximizing return on investment; and minimizing *costs*. Each one of these has its own special appeal to different managers within the company, depending on the nature of their particular function. In reality, the best that can ever be achieved is a kind of 'optimum compromise', because each of these objectives could be considered to be in conflict in terms of equivalences.

Definition:
Costs are charges incurred in running an enterprise. They can take many forms including overhead, direct, indirect, attributable, avoidable and others.

> Managers of a company have to have some understanding or view about how all these variables interact and must try to be rational about their business decisions, no matter how important intuition, feel and experience are as contributory factors in this process of rationality.

Most managers accept that some kind of formalized procedure for marketing planning helps sharpen this rationality so as to reduce the complexity of business operations and add a dimension of realism to the company's hopes for the future. Because it is so difficult, however, most companies rely on sales forecasting and budgeting systems. It is a well-known fact that any fool can write figures down! All too frequently, however, they bear little relationship to the real opportunities and problems facing a company. It is far more difficult to write down marketing objectives and strategies.

Apart from the need to cope with increasing turbulence, environmental complexity, more intense competitive pressures, and the sheer speed of technological change, a marketing plan is useful:

- For the marketer
- For superiors

- For non-marketing functions
- For subordinates
- To help identify sources of competitive advantage
- To force an organized approach
- To develop specificity
- To ensure consistent relationships
- To inform
- To get resources
- To get support
- To gain commitment
- To set objectives and strategies.

The benefits of a marketing plan are:

1. Better coordination of activities
2. It identifies expected developments
3. It increases organizational preparedness to change
4. It minimizes non-rational responses to the unexpected
5. It reduces conflicts about where the company should be going
6. It improves communications
7. Management is forced to think ahead systematically
8. Available resources can be better matched to opportunities
9. The plan provides a framework for the continuing review of operations
10. A systematic approach to strategy formulation leads to a higher return on investment.

Effective marketing is enhanced greatly by a well-thought-through and developed marketing plan. Such a plan helps bring all the service firm's marketing activities together in an integrated manner and helps create a positive future for the firm. However, a number of problems create barriers to the development and implementation of marketing planning.

What gets in the way of marketing planning?

(For readers who want to go straight to the details of the marketing planning process itself, please move to Chapter 5.)

Service organizations facing difficulties in their markets instinctively recognize the need for an integrated approach to marketing planning.

Indeed, many have attempted to adopt a new planning approach. However, it is clear that any attempt to introduce a formalized marketing planning system, like the one described in this book, carries with it serious organizational and behavioural implications for the company. It is not a quick remedy for a service organization's problems.

> The introduction of this type of approach strikes at the very heart of how the organization is managed and unless it recognizes this and faces up to the new problems which surface, then real improvements will not take place.

Our research and experience suggest there are a number of barriers which get in the way of successful marketing planning. Here are some of the common barriers which prevent genuine change taking place and an effective services marketing plan being developed in service organizations. In addition, there are other barriers which will be described throughout this book.

1. Short-termism

Too many service organizations are so engrossed in what is happening today that they neglect the future of the company. Managers who are evaluated and rewarded on the basis of current operations will naturally enough find it difficult to concern themselves with the corporate future. Decisions are, therefore, based on short-term results.

> It is obviously safer and easier for managers to concentrate on managing current services and customers in order to achieve their current budget rather than concerning themselves with the future.

Similarly, there is a reluctance to invest in tomorrow's services, technologies, and even managers. Of course, there are always cogent arguments why such investment must be delayed, but the truth is that for most managers, tomorrow never comes.

2. Weak support from the chief executive and top management

Senior managers are extremely influential in establishing a corporate climate or culture. While top management might not deliberately set out to do this, subordinates are quick to spot what excites and interests the 'culture carriers'. These areas then become the unwritten agenda for corporate politics, which is all about getting noticed, getting resources and getting on.

> Unless the chief executive understands marketing planning, sees the need for it, and, above all, shows an active interest in it, then it will be virtually impossible for a senior marketing executive to make any real progress in improving marketing planning.

Historically, marketing planning has been taken less seriously in service firms than in the consumer products and industrial products sectors.

Where the chief executive pays only lip-service to marketing planning and starves it of adequate resources, it is not likely to flourish and be a successful value-adding activity for the organization. Moreover, other managers will see the low level of priority given to marketing planning and judge for themselves if it is worth getting associated with an out-of-favour activity. Thus, the notion that marketing planning is not really important becomes a self-fulfilling prophecy.

In contrast to this restrictive scenario, the chief executive who champions marketing planning will ensure that it is regularly on the agenda of management meetings, will be chasing up for progress reports, will be seen frequently talking about marketing planning, will see to it that marketing planning skills figure in criteria for recruiting or promoting managers, and so on. There would be no doubt whatsoever in the minds of the staff in this company that marketing planning is *really* important.

> The active interest of the chief executive and top management is vital if a formalized marketing planning system is to be successful

3. Lack of a plan for planning

It is one thing to establish a marketing planning system on paper, yet another to make it come alive. As with any significant organizational change process, there has to be a plan for introducing the new system in such a way that it becomes part of the service organization's fabric, rather than an élitist, peripheral activity. Several issues need to be addressed:

- There is a need to mobilize top management support (for reasons explained above).

- There is a need to communicate throughout the company why a new approach to planning is required.

- There is a need for training programmes to equip people for the new roles they have to play.

- There is a need to set up the subsystems which are required to provide the data to fuel the planning system.

- There is a need to ensure that adequate resources are available and in place to make the new system work.

- There is a need to make a 'dummy run', or small-scale trials, before plunging headlong into the new approach.

- There is a need to tailor the process so that it fits the specific needs of the organization.

All of these things take time. They cannot just be ignored or glossed over, otherwise marketing planning will be ineffective. By planning the introduction of planning, companies are more likely to get it right first time. In our experience, it can take several years from making a decision to introduce strategic marketing planning to getting it right at an operational level. Taghian[13] points out that marketing planning needs to be practised formally and periodically to be more useful and that it needs to include both a top-down and bottom-up structure to incorporate the participation and involvement of the talents, skills, and support of all key managers and their supporting staff.

Figure 4.1 shows how both top-down and bottom-up perspectives on marketing planning are required. Typically, in the year a proper strategic marketing planning process is started, there is limited clarity when the first cut at strategic marketing planning is made. In the next period, as the strategic marketing plan is cascaded down to the business or segment level, first cut segment and tactical plans are developed. As these latter plans are developed in detail, inevitably as the

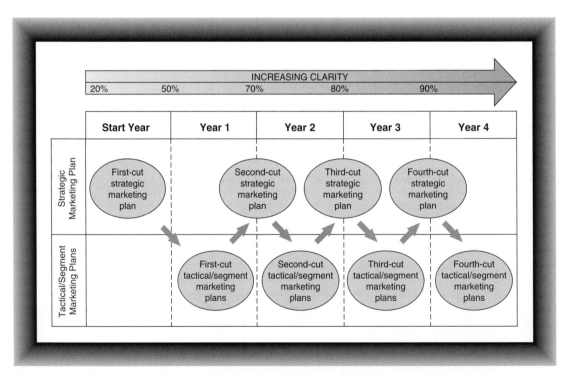

Figure 4.1   Marketing planning requires top-down and bottom-up perspectives

segment and tactical plans are consolidated upwards, further development and changes need to be made as the second cut strategic marketing plan evolves in the next period. Over time, the organization gains increasing clarity and confidence in its marketing plans.

4. Lack of line management support

> Line managers, that is to say those with a responsibility for delivering the service product, are often knowingly or unknowingly the repositories of exceedingly valuable marketing information, be it about particular customers or trends they have spotted. For this reason, they have a significant role to play in terms of contributing to the formulation of the marketing plan.

At the same time, these managers are already likely to be very busy doing their 'real job', as they would probably describe it. Therefore, it is essential for those responsible for coordinating marketing planning to win such staff over to their cause and thereby gain access to the information they possess. How this is achieved will vary from company to company. It might be through training, it might be through getting the line managers involved in designing the way data is collected, or it might be through redesigning their jobs. Whatever the chosen method, one thing is certain, unless there is the committed support from these managers to the marketing planning process, it will be fatally handicapped.

5. Confusion over planning terms

Those charged with setting up a marketing planning system are frequently well qualified in this field. For them, marketing terminology and jargon are convenient verbal shorthand with which to communicate to fellow professionals. However, in order to win over the hearts and minds of others in the organization, the planning terminology used must be understood by all managers. Too much talk to non-marketing managers about missions, matrices, strategic thrusts, positioning, and so on, is inappropriate and may well 'turn off' those who need to be influenced.

Companies with successful planning systems have used terminology which is acceptable to operational managers, and where terms like 'objectives' and 'strategies' are introduced these are clearly defined. To help with this definition a glossary of marketing terminology is provided at the end of this book.

Marketing terminology should be consistent and clearly understood

6. An over-reliance on numbers

Many managers are highly numerate. Quantities, percentages, discounts, success rates, sales revenue, costs and the like are the bread and butter of their everyday lives. It is numbers that make their world turn round. They are evaluated on the basis of numbers and, not surprisingly, in turn judge others in much the same way.

However, when they are asked (as marketing planners often do) to elaborate on causal factors for past performance, to assess expected results, to highlight external opportunities, or to provide a critique of the key issues facing them, they have difficulty doing this.

They appear to be far happier extrapolating numbers and projecting current performance into the future, rather than expressing the logic of how they perceive their current business situation and how that impinges on their objectives and strategies.

A 'numbers-driven' mentality may encourage parochial and short-term thinking, whereas the required approach needs creative analysis. There has to be a new balance between quantitative data and qualitative thinking if there is to be effective services marketing planning.

7. *Too much detail, too far ahead*

Associated with the issue above is an alternative response from managers. If they are short of the analytical skills to isolate the really key marketing issues, they may overreact and identify far more problems and opportunities than the company can ever hope to cope with. When this happens, the really important strategic issues can get buried deep in a deluge of useless information and over-elaborate detail. Not surprisingly, the ensuing plan will lack focus and confuse those for whom it was supposed to provide guidance. There is also a danger that the company could become overextended, heading off in too many directions at once.

Companies and individuals must learn that it is high-quality intelligence they seek, not a high quantity of data. Systems that generate too much information are not only ineffective, they are also demotivating for those who have to struggle to use them.

Organizations that have overcome these types of problems have done so by ensuring that all levels of hierarchy are clear about the nature of the contribution they are expected to make. At each successive level of management, lower-level analyses are synthesized in ways that ensure that only key decision-making information reaches the next level up. Thus, in effect, there is a hierarchy of audits, SWOT analyses, assumptions, objectives, strategies and plans, each pertinent to the level and sphere of influence that go with its position in the total enterprise.

Such a scheme of things ensures that top management of a service organization is charged with addressing mainly macro-issues and lower management concentrates more on key micro-issues. In this way, everyone plays more to their strengths.

Too much misleading and unreliable data can also be generated if the company's time-frame for planning extends too far into the future. Although anticipating the future is vital, if the time-frame is too long then judgement becomes less reliable and realistic and the credibility and usefulness of the marketing plan then come into question.

8. Once-a-year ritual

In companies where marketing planning is not properly understood, rather like the seasons, 'marketing planning time' comes round once a year. Its arrival is signalled by thick sets of pro-forma sheets arriving on managers' desks, accompanied by a memo proclaiming the urgency of returning the same by a given deadline. The weeks that follow are characterized by a flurry of activity as managers investigate and compete for information. Once the forms are returned, organizational life can get back to normal and managers can relax in the comfort of knowing that their peace will not be disturbed for another 12 months.

One bank we have worked with has a planning process which has a close resemblance to what we have described.

> Managers of this bank would make painstaking and diligent inputs to the system, then hear nothing more.

Any plans that did emerge were, apparently, filed away, never to be referred to again. Not surprisingly, in this bank, 'involvement' in the planning process was seen to be a demotivating chore, and marketing is quite rightly interpreted as relatively unimportant.

Companies who tackle marketing planning seriously do not fall into this trap. They have a planning calendar which operates *throughout the year*, as will be explained further in Chapters 11 and 13. When the task is tackled in this way, marketing planning becomes an integral part of the service manager's job, not a temporary 'bolt-on' extra.

9. Confusion between operational and strategic marketing planning

From what has been said so far, it should be obvious that we advocate that a service organization should consider all the strategic implications of its position and set marketing objectives and strategies for about three years hence. Having done this, the company can then devise the one-year operational marketing plan, which in effect represents the first steps towards reaching those objectives.

Many companies do not do this. Instead, they argue that because the future is so uncertain, they can only look ahead for the next year. Accordingly, they prepare a marketing plan and operational plan rolled into one. From this, they will extrapolate forward to arrive at their longer-term 'strategic' objectives. Clearly, this approach fails to grasp the fact that the future is not likely to be the same as today, and it avoids looking at the real strategic issues which face the company.

> Successful service companies understand that their operational marketing plans are derived from their strategic marketing plans, not vice versa.

By operating with this protocol, both the operational and strategic plans will be integrated and mutually supportive.

10. Failure to integrate marketing planning into the corporate planning system

It is clear that the marketing plan should be an integral part of the total corporate planning process. However, it is implicit in this relationship that both are operating over the same timescale and have a similar level of formalization. Indeed, other major functions such as information systems, finance and personnel should also be planned in a similar way over the same period. The linkages and integration between corporate planning, strategic marketing and other functional planning are illustrated in Figure 4.2.

Marketing planning should be an integrated, not an isolated, activity

By having all the planning processes integrated in this way, the fullest advantage can be taken of the company's multi-functional strengths, weaknesses, opportunities and threats, and trade-offs can be made at a functional level between what is needed and what can be afforded.

When marketing planning operates in isolation, it will be found more difficult to gain the participation of other key functions in the company which might be major determinants of success. For example, the marketing plan might call for more manpower and skill levels than personnel can deliver in time. This is why the creation of cross-functional linkages, shown in Figure 4.2, is so important.

11. Delegation of planning to a 'planner'

Most of the literature sees the marketing planner basically as a coordinator, not as an initiator of goals and strategies. In many companies where there is a person with the title of marketing planning manager, the appointment was made to resolve some significant marketing

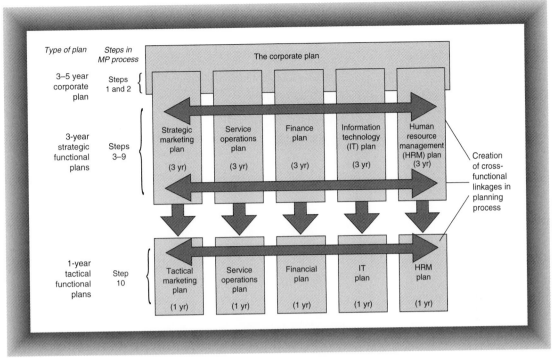

Figure 4.2   Integration of corporate planning, strategic marketing planning and tactical marketing planning

problems and to take the pressure off the marketing director (or CEO). As a result of this, the newcomer, who is often young and highly qualified, is given a (frequently remote) staff position responding directly to the marketing director or CEO.

Such new managers are then told that their task is to design a marketing planning system, coordinate the inputs and formulate overall objectives and strategies for the board.

> This puts the marketing planner in the invidious position of having uncertain status and power, yet being expected to make an impact on organizational behaviour at all levels.

Some individuals have the personality, tenacity and political skills to operate from such an unpromising position and eventually win through. Most, however, never earn the respect or cooperation of line managers and, as a result, try to do more and more of the planning themselves.

Understandable though this situation might be, the resulting plan, deprived of crucial line management input, is usually critically flawed. Not surprisingly, those who resented the planner's attempts to

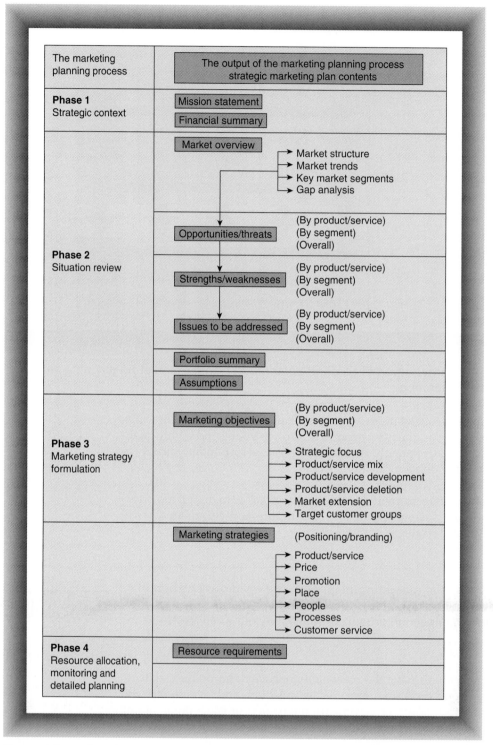

Figure 4.3   What should appear in a services strategic marketing plan

Source: Based on M. McDonald (2002), *Marketing Plans: How to prepare them, how to use them*, 5th edn, Butterworth-Heinemann, Oxford

establish some sort of order in the first place will happily pick holes in the plans produced, and be heard to make comments about the problems of 'not living in the real world'.

The problems for the marketing planner raised above occur directly as a result of the abdication of top management in giving thought to the formulation of overall marketing strategies.

> However, when market pressures call for a more robust or radical response from the company, top management must get involved and be prepared to play its part.

Planners, by themselves, are relatively impotent to make an impact on the organization.

12. Uncertainty about what should appear in the marketing plan

Just as an architect's working sketches and rough calculations would never appear on the final blueprints, even though they played a crucial part in the design, so should a marketing plan be free of unnecessary detail. Like any good report, the finalized marketing plan should be authoritative and easy to understand. Its major function is to determine where the company is, where it wants to go and how it can get there. It lies at the heart of the company's revenue-generating activities, such as the timing of cash flow and the size and nature of the workforce. It is in effect a 'selling document' for the service organization's marketing strategy.

What should appear in a written strategic marketing plan is shown in Figure 4.3. The items mentioned in this figure will be elaborated on in later chapters.

Summary

Although the planning process in services marketing looks straightforward when considered in the abstract, it actually presents a number of problems when considered in an organizational context. This is because the introduction of marketing planning is more than a cognitive process. It strikes at the heart of how a company is managed and structured. Many organizations have suffered serious financial consequences as a result of a lack of focus on their markets.

For this reason, there are a number of barriers which prevent a service organization from taking full advantage of marketing planning or introducing it successfully. We considered some of the more common barriers, which were:

1. Short-termism
2. Weak support from the chief executive and top management
3. Lack of a plan for planning
4. Lack of line management support
5. Confusion over planning terms
6. An over-reliance on numbers
7. Too much detail, too far ahead
8. Once-a-year ritual
9. Confusion between operational and strategic marketing planning
10. Failure to integrate marketing planning into the corporate planning system
11. Delegation of planning to a planner
12. Uncertainty about what should appear in the marketing plan.

All of these issues serve to underline the point that strategic marketing planning in service organizations is not an easy task. Its introduction needs careful consideration and, sometimes, nothing short of a change of corporate culture is required if it is to be successfully implanted.

Having discussed the broad strategy marketing planning process and the barriers that need to be overcome for planning to be effective, subsequent chapters expand on each of the four key planning phases.

5 Marketing planning Phase One: the strategic context

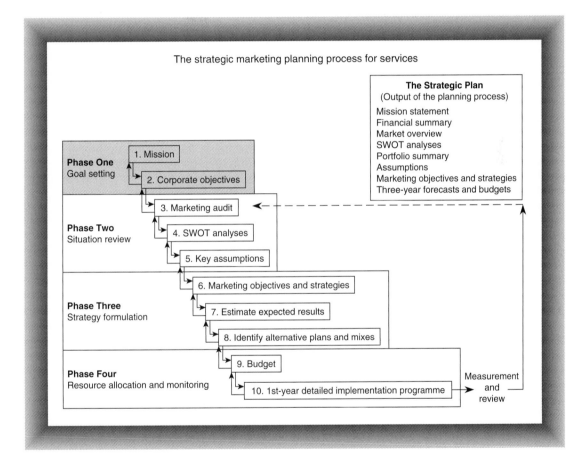

The strategic marketing planning process for services

The Strategic Plan
(Output of the planning process)

Mission statement
Financial summary
Market overview
SWOT analyses
Portfolio summary
Assumptions
Marketing objectives and strategies
Three-year forecasts and budgets

Phase One
Goal setting

1. Mission

2. Corporate objectives

Phase Two
Situation review

3. Marketing audit

4. SWOT analyses

5. Key assumptions

Phase Three
Strategy formulation

6. Marketing objectives and strategies

7. Estimate expected results

8. Identify alternative plans and mixes

Phase Four
Resource allocation and monitoring

9. Budget

10. 1st-year detailed implementation programme

Measurement and review

In each chapter, we will stress the difference between the *process* of marketing planning and the *output* of this process – *the strategic marketing plan*. What should appear in the written output of the strategic marketing planning process was shown in Figure 4.3 in the previous chapter.

We have seen that the first phase of the marketing planning process involves determining (or re-examining) the mission statement and setting corporate objectives. In this chapter, we will look at both of these issues in some detail, using examples from the service industry to illustrate how some companies have set about these tasks. Particular attention will be given to the problematic issue of mission development. These two steps form the strategic context and provide the pivotal link between the corporate plan and the marketing plan, as outlined in Figure 4.2.

Step 1 Mission

A mission for services

Business strategy is a top management responsibility that involves both identifying the future direction of the organization as well as managing the creative interaction of the functional disciplines of operations, marketing, finance and human resource management. It is both a process and a way of thinking which leads to the development of a set of strategies that assist the business in achieving its corporate objectives.

If the organization has no clear notion about its vision and values, it may be in a quandary regarding the way forward

Virtually all companies have a business strategy; however, this may be implicit or explicit. While some companies are successful with only an implicit strategy guiding the chief executive and the management team, it is our experience that companies developing an explicit strategy through a planned approach have a greater chance of long-term success.

The process of business strategy formulation should commence with a review and articulation of the company's mission. As briefly explained in Chapter 2, the mission (or vision) encapsulates the company's identity in terms of what it is, what makes it special, what it stands for, and where it is heading. It should explicitly reflect the basic beliefs, values and aspirations of the organization, providing an enduring statement of purpose that distinguishes the organization from its competitors and an important device for coordinating internal activity.

Mission statements must not be so broad as to make them meaningless

Studies conducted over the past 25 years reveal two important points. First, companies have been slow to develop mission statements that add value. Second, companies that develop well-thought-through mission statements and achieve high levels of employee engagement derive strong benefits. We briefly review these studies below.

Research in the late 1980s showed a relatively low take-up of mission statements by US organizations. One study[1] based on 181 of the top 1,000 corporations in the USA showed that 50% had not developed a formal mission. Another study by Byars and Neil[2] examined 157 mission statements from 208 members of the Planning Forum (the world's largest membership organization on planning and strategic management) and concluded that most of these were so broadly written that they had little meaning.

A 2001 study by three Canadian professors examined the relationship between the mission and organizational performance.[3] Drawing on data from 83 large North American organizations they found that commitment to the mission, and the degree to which an organization aligns its internal structure, policies and procedures with its mission, were both associated with employee behaviour. It was this latter variable which was observed to have the most direct positive relationship with financial performance. This highlights the importance of engaging employees with the mission.

A study published in 2004 assessed the quality of 56 European, Japanese, and US firms' mission statements.[4] A number of quality measures were identified. The study results showed that the mission statements generally fell short of meeting these quality criteria.

A 2009 study by two European professors argued that mission statements can only be considered effective or successful if they stimulate organizational members to (a) process the information within the mission statement and (b) to reach a common understanding about the meaning of the information within the mission statement with respect to the conveyance process.[5] This study's results indicated that mission statements fulfil their expected role. The results also suggested that organizational employees are satisfied with their formal mission statement if the organizational image expressed by the mission statement is seen to be (1) difficult but feasible, (2) reasonably clear and understandable, (3) worthy/worthwhile, legitimate, (4) interesting, exciting, (5) important, influential, and (6) distinctive.

By the latter part of the 2000s, most large organizations had developed mission statements. A 2006 study found that 415 Fortune 500 firms, or 83% of these firms, had posted a mission statement on their website.[6] A later study published in 2010 found that 96% of the top 50 *Fortune* companies had adopted mission statements.[7] This study also compared the changes in the mission statements of the top 50 *Fortune* companies in 2000 and 2008. It found that there was a significant increase over this period in the number of companies that emphasized 'ethical behaviour' and 'global reach' in their mission statements. There was also a real increase in the number of companies that include 'employees' in their mission statements. Most of these companies also underlined the importance of creating excellent goods or services for the customers.

These investigations and our own research suggest that most large service organizations have developed formal mission statements. However, this adoption is much less in medium-sized and smaller firms. We conclude that across the whole service sector many organizations have yet to develop effective mission statements.

> In contrast, service companies that have taken the development of a mission seriously have benefited significantly from the discipline and direction it has provided.

A study of the top 25 management methods and techniques deployed by senior managers around the world, published by US consulting firm Bain & Company in 2009, found that the mission statements were rated as one of the top five management tools. However, while senior managers' satisfaction rates with mission statements had improved in recent years, they lagged behind their satisfaction rates with strategic planning.[8]

It seems that, as with marketing planning itself, there still is some confusion among companies regarding how to define a mission. As a result, instead of a mission that reflects a unique commitment to corporate values and direction, what emerges can be a bland set of generalizations and meaningless statements. Not surprisingly, such missions are greeted at best with scepticism, at worst with derision.

While recognizing that different service organizations might use other terminology such as business definition, credo, statement of business philosophy, belief statement, vision statement, statement of purpose, and so on, we define a mission as follows:

> A mission is an enduring statement of purpose that provides an animated vision of the organization's current and future business activities, in service and market terms, together with its values and beliefs and its points of differentiation from competitors. A mission helps determine the relationships with each of the key markets with which the organization interacts, and provides a sense of direction and purpose which leads to more correct independent decisions being made at all levels of the organization.

As already mentioned, it has to be recognized that some organizations might have a mission which, although strongly embedded in their culture, does not appear in writing. Such might be the case in smaller organizations, or in those with a strong, charismatic leader.

> Thus, while it is not essential for the mission to appear in writing, we would recommend that it should do, in order that it does not run the risk of being misinterpreted or loses its impact at lower levels within the organization.

The nature of corporate missions

An examination of what has been written about missions suggests that a number of key issues are important and need to be taken into consideration. They are:

1. It is dangerous to define the mission too narrowly or too broadly.
2. The audience for the mission should be considered carefully.

> 3. It is crucial to understand the business one is in.
>
> 4. The mission should be unique to the organization preparing it.
>
> 5. The mission should be need-oriented, rather than offer-oriented.
>
> 6. Within any organization, there will need to be a hierarchy of mission statements.

Each of these issues gives rise to a number of interesting questions which need to be addressed.

1. How does one get the balance between too narrow and too wide?

One of the classic examples of a services sector business which defined its mission too narrowly was the railway industry in the USA. In his early seminal paper on the topic, Levitt[9] argued that by defining itself to be in the locomotive business, rather than helping customers solve their transportation needs, the industry as a whole failed to identify and capitalize on opportunities, and thereby hastened its own demise.

Another example would be football clubs in Europe and elsewhere, whose narrow focus on the game itself obscured the fact that their customers' needs for entertainment could be met by other more sociable and comfortable alternatives. They just did not perceive themselves to be in the entertainment business and, with only a few exceptions, attendance figures fell dramatically.

Gestetner, a UK duplication machine manufacturer, defined its business narrowly as the duplication market. In 1995 Gestetner, along with other companies such as Lanier, Savin and Rex-Rotary, was taken over by Ricoh, the Japanese electronics and office equipment manufacturing company. In the 1990s IBM moved away from its long-standing mission and defined its business too narrowly as mainframe computers, with disastrous consequences, subsequently it developed a new mission and a focus on services and it eventually recovered – more about this later. In the last decade many diverse 'product' companies, including IBM with its consulting services, photocopier manufacturers which have developed bureau services, and jet engine manufacturers such as Rolls-Royce with their services-based concept of selling 'power by the hour', have successfully broadened the scope of their mission to embrace services.

> However, just as there are dangers in defining the business too narrowly, to have no bounds can be equally ruinous.

The mission statement has to provide some focus on the activities of an organization

Indeed, this might be the more common of the two faults. For example, the deregulation of the financial services sector in many countries led to banks diversifying away from their core business into stockbroking and investment banking, with disastrous results. Similarly, retailers have undertaken diversification away from what customers perceived to be their traditional realms. Finding they were unprofitable in these areas, they struggled to get back to their core retailing business. The fashion retailer Laura Ashley provides a good example of this.

Sometimes, their identity gets lost in the process. For example, with hindsight the attempts of Woolworths in the UK to diversify might now be seen as a fit of corporate folly, where all its old strengths were thrown away and nothing of substance put in their place. Another example is US energy services company Enron. This company entered into deals and projects which were beyond the scope of its mission. Creative accounting and corporate fraud added to their problems which led to their demise in the early part of the 2000s. Enron clearly did not emphasize 'ethical behaviour' in their mission and behaviour.

> In these cases, if *effective* missions had been formulated, with the requisite strategic focus that this implies, it is questionable if some of them would have diversified into the non-core, non-profit-making, non-integrated business areas that they entered in recent years.

2. Who is the target audience for the mission and what are its expectations?

The reasons for writing a mission statement can vary. Some organizations might do it for public relations purposes; some might do it because they see that other companies have them. As we said earlier, however, it should be for the purpose of strategically focusing the business activities. By being clear about the mission's purpose, it becomes easier to define the target audience and to know the level of sophistication of their requirements.

Figure 5.1 identifies how a bank might consider its key audiences and their expectations, in terms of formulating a mission. This is based on a consideration of all the stakeholders described in the opening chapter. For some types of business, like water services, there might be additional stakeholders to consider such as environmentalists, whose concerns will be about issues like the extraction of water from rivers and the effluent pumped back into rivers or the sea.

It is important that the mission statement is not too long

While this framework can be extremely useful for identifying and mapping the relative importance of each of these groups, clearly a mission which tried to embrace every group and issue equally could end up exceedingly long. Therefore, some decisions have to be made regarding which target audiences the company wants to recognize within the mission. The context for such decisions will be the nature of the service product, the current position of the firm in its industry sector, and who the key players are among the stakeholders.

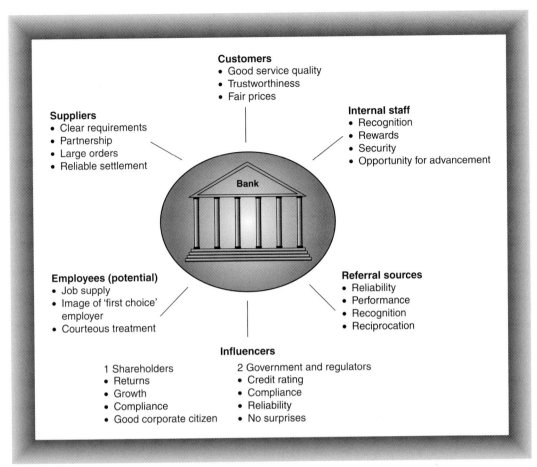

Figure 5.1 Key audiences and their expectations in a bank

There is a view in many service organizations that the key messages in the mission should be concerned primarily with providing a sense of strategic direction and motivation of the *internal staff*.

When necessary, a modified version of this statement can be used for external purposes and reflect the considerations of other stakeholders.

There is, however, an obvious danger that, in producing an internally focused mission statement, the interests of two other principal stakeholders – the shareholders/owners of the business and the customer – are neglected.

Perhaps the approach to recruitment attributed to Bill Marriott of Marriott Hotels puts this in context. When he interviews prospective managers he says, 'There are three important groups we need to satisfy – shareholders, customers and our employees. Which is the most important one to focus on?' To get the job you have to answer 'the employees'. Marriott argues that it is only by focusing on employees that he will have happy customers and only through happy customers will he provide good return to his shareholders.

3. What business are we in?

This question is closely related to the earlier one about defining the business too narrowly or too broadly. While many companies might claim that the answer is obvious, we have found that when asked to write it down without conferring, senior managers from the same service organization rarely come up with the same answer. This then poses another question: 'If *they* are confused, how must those at lower levels feel?'

Failure to recognize distinctive competences can lead to lost opportunities

The trap managers fall into is that they are guided by the nature of their output rather than the company's specific competences. Thus, the claim that their company was in the 'retail business' could, on deeper analysis, be found to be actually in the 'getting latest fashions into the High Street quickest' business. Similarly, the company that claims that it is in 'computer software' is likely to be really in the business of helping other companies to resolve managerial control problems, perhaps of a very specific nature.

Too often, companies fail to recognize their distinctive competences and, as a result, miss valuable opportunities to play to their strengths.

4. How unique is the mission statement?

Service organizations are in different sectors, have different facilities, staffing, levels of morale, geographic locations, track records, management styles, expertise, values, hopes and ambitions. Taking these into account, it is unlikely that all these areas of potential difference should lead to one company having a mission much the same as any other. Yet, in our dealings with many service companies, that is what we find. This is especially true of banks and professional service firms.

> It is as if the mission has been bought off the shelf rather than made to measure.

All service organizations are different and this should be reflected in the mission statement

Not only may a service organization have specific competences, but it should also seek some differential advantages over its competitors. It might be closer to markets, be more efficient, be more aggressive, and so on. Any of these things ought to make the mission somewhat different. (Of course, the corollary of this statement is that, if the company genuinely cannot identify any differential advantages, it should seek to establish some.)

The underlying philosophy in striving for uniqueness is that success lies in obtaining a competitive advantage, in a preferred way, with a selected customer base. The acid test which discloses whether or not this has been achieved is to substitute a competitor's name into your mission. If it still makes sense, then you are implying that both companies are the same – something which is usually untrue.

5. Is the mission market-oriented?

Organizations that focus too closely on their service product rather than market needs can have an inclination to develop new improved services or spin-offs which, brilliant though they might be, may not be required by the market. The message is clear. In order to avoid this, the mission should be market-oriented and focus on customer needs.

Increasingly, organizations such as airlines, hotels and banks are considering customer needs and using this knowledge to make an input into the design of the services they offer.

6. At what level in the service organization is the mission statement being prepared?

Service organizations may have international headquarters, several national headquarters, divisional headquarters and, almost certainly, a number of individual service product, or business, centres. Clearly, then, it is unlikely that one central mission statement will suffice in providing the direction to these several hierarchical levels in the organization. It is suggested, therefore, that all the guidelines provided in this section can be applied equally well to any organizational level. This issue is expanded on later in this chapter.

Here, we can see two levels of mission. One is a *corporate* mission statement; the other is a lower level or *purpose* statement. But there is yet another level, as shown in the following summary:

Type 1 – These are generally found inside the annual reports and are designed to make shareholders feel good. They are invariably full of 'motherhood' statements and organizational puffery. As missions, they have little practical use and should not be confused with Type 2.

Type 2 – The real thing. A meaningful statement, unique to the organization, which impacts on behaviour at all levels of the company.

Type 3 – This is a 'purpose' statement (or lower level mission statement). It is appropriate at the strategic business unit, departmental or service level of the organization.

An example of Type 1 is given in Figure 5.2. This statement could apply equally to almost any organization in the world. They achieve nothing and it is difficult to understand why these pointless statements are so popular. Employees mock them and they rarely say anything likely to

Figure 5.2
The generic mission
statement

> **The generic mission statement**
>
> Our organization's primary mission is to protect and increase the value
> of its owners' investments while efficiently and fairly serving the needs
> of its customer. [... insert organization name] seeks to accomplish this
> in a manner that contributes to the development and growth of its
> employees, and to the goals of countries and communities in
> which it operates.

give direction to the organization. We have entitled this example 'The Generic Mission Statement' and they are to be avoided.

The following should appear in a mission or purpose statement, which should normally run to no more than one page:

1. *Role or contribution* – For example, charity, profit seeker, innovator, opportunity seeker.

2. *Business definition* – This should be done in terms of benefits provided or needs satisfied, rather than the services offered.

3. *Distinctive competences* – These are the essential skills, capabilities or resources that underpin whatever success has been achieved to date. Competence can consist of one particular item or the possession of a number of skills compared with competitors. All should be considered in terms of how they confer differential advantages, i.e. if you could equally well put a competitor's name to these distinctive competences, then they are not distinctive competences.

4. *Indications for the future* – This will briefly refer to what the firm will do, what it might do and what it will never do.

Example of service organization mission statements

In examining actual mission statements for service companies, it is clear that there are vast differences in their length, structure and content. Some are more general statements of philosophy, while others are much more specific. In this section, we will review some examples of different approaches to the development of service organization missions and illustrate the wide range of approaches that are adopted which, in the view of the authors, represent good practice.

Bain & Company mission statement

- Bain & Company's mission is to help our clients create such high levels of economic value that together we set new standards of excellence in our respective industries

- This mission demands:
  - The Bain vision of the most productive client relationship and single-minded dedication to achieving it
  - The Bain community of extraordinary teams
  - The Bain approach to creating value, based on a sharp competitive and customer focus, the most effective analytic techniques, and our process for collaboration with the client

- We believe that accomplishing our mission will redefine the management consulting business and will provide new levels of rewards for our clients and for our organization.

Figure 5.3
Bain & Company
mission statement

The mission statement for Bain & Company, shown in Figure 5.3, emphasizes special competence in creating added value through a commitment to mutually productive relationships between the firm and their clients. This was developed as a result of a five-day intensive workshop retreat by senior management at Bain. We consider this to be an especially useful way of structuring a mission statement – starting with a general statement of strategic intent, followed by specific bullet points on what is required to achieve the mission. In 2011, commenting on Bain & Company's mission statement, a partner of the firm stated that even though this mission statement was developed in 1985 'every time we peer into it, it's just as real, it's just as current, it's just as vibrant as it was years ago'.[10]

The Bain & Company example is a good illustration of the possible longevity of a carefully constructed mission statement. However, for many service firms, mission statements need to evolve over time. The following discussion of mission statements for IBM and British Airways illustrates this process of evolution.

Thomas Watson, IBM's founder, articulated his company's philosophy in the phrase 'IBM means service'. IBM defines itself as a *service* company and the corporate philosophy articulated by Watson was not just to be a *good* service company, but to be the *best* service company in the world. The IBM mission espoused by Watson in the 1960s is shown in Figure 5.4.

Watson argued that the basic philosophy of the organization was more concerned with its customer service performance than with technical

Figure 5.4
Organizational
statement of
philosophy for IBM

> **IBM**
> - Respect for the individual
> - Provide the best customer service of any company in the world
> - Pursue all tasks with the idea that they can be accomplished in a superior fashion.

or economic resources, organizational structure, innovation or timing. Some 20 years later, the then IBM chairman stated: 'We've changed our technology, changed our organization, changed our marketing and manufacturing techniques many times, and we expect to go on changing. But through all this change, Watson's three basic beliefs remain. We steer our course by those stars.'

> The problems suffered by IBM in the 1990s stemmed from a lack of focus on these basic beliefs. A number of books written on IBM's problems provide evidence that during this period they began to focus more on technology than on customer needs. Their subsequent turnaround in the 2000s was based on a renewed emphasis on the customer and transformation to a service-based company.

Missions which are statements of business philosophy, such as this, give overall guidance in terms of values, but do not give much focus to service and product areas on markets. Clearly in the case of IBM during the 1990s this proved to be a weakness. Since then IBM has reinvented itself by focusing on services rather than products.

IBM is now more focused on articulating who they are, what they do, and what they offer as outlined in their new mission statement, the statement of values and business model shown in Figure 5.5. In developing these values all IBM staff around the world and selected other parties were invited to engage in an open 'values jam' on the IBM global intranet. The 'values jam', held over a 90-hour period in October 2008, had some 90,000 log-ins that generated over 32,000 posts. In their responses staff were thoughtful and passionate about the company they want to be a part of and were also brutally honest.[11] Such a Web-based initiative provides an opportunity to canvas a large number of staff and receive their views on the mission and values of the firm within a short time period.

IBM Mission Statement

At IBM, we strive to lead in the invention, development and manufacture of the industry's most advanced information technologies, including computer systems, software, storage systems and microelectronics.

We translate these advanced technologies into value for our customers through our professional solutions, services and consulting businesses worldwide.

IBM Values

- Dedication to every client's success

- Innovation that matters, for our company and for the world

- Trust and personal responsibility in all relationships

IBM Business Model

The company's business model is built to support two principal goals: helping clients succeed in delivering business value by becoming more innovative, efficient and competitive through the use of business insight and information technology (IT) solutions; and, providing long-term value to shareholders. The business model has been developed over time through strategic investments in capabilities and technologies that have the best long-term growth and profitability prospects based on the value they deliver to clients. The company's strategy is to focus on the high-growth, high-value segments of the IT industry.

The company's global capabilities include services, software, hardware, fundamental research and financing. The broad mix of businesses and capabilities are combined to provide business insight and solutions for the company's clients.

The business model is flexible, and allows for periodic change and rebalancing. The company has exited commoditizing businesses like personal computers and hard disk drives, and strengthened its position through strategic investments and acquisitions in emerging higher value segments like service oriented architecture (SOA) and Information on Demand. In addition, the company has transformed itself into a globally integrated enterprise which has improved overall productivity and is driving investment and participation in the world's fastest growing markets. As a result, the company is a higher performing enterprise today than it was several years ago.

The business model, supported by the company's long-term financial model, enables the company to deliver consistently strong earnings, cash flows and returns on invested capital in changing economic environments.

Figure 5.5   IBM mission statement, values and business model

British Airways is a further example of how mission statements need to evolve over time. In the 1990s, the British Airways mission focused on a number of key themes including corporate charisma, creativity, business capability, competitive stance and training philosophy. In 2004 British Airways developed a new set of vision, values and goals. Entitled the 'The BA Way' this new mission represents a statement of British Airways' business strategy, values and goals which was communicated across the company. This initiative involved defining targets and measurements for their non-financial business goals

THE BA WAY OF BUSINESS

British Airways Plc and our subsidiaries strive to be good corporate citizens and to comply with the law in the countries in which we operate. Our activities are underpinned by the BA Way values which will guide our actions as we seek to maximize our opportunities in the marketplace.

The BA Way in the Marketplace

We will do our best to deliver our promises to our customers and our suppliers. We will manage our supply chain consistent with the BA way values.

The BA Way in the Workplace

We aspire to work together as one team, to treat each other fairly, respecting individual and collective rights, and striving for high levels of employee motivation and satisfaction through training, development and honest communications.

The BA Way in the Community

We will work to be a good neighbour.

The BA Way in the Environment

Recognizing the impact of aviation on the environment, we will work to improve our environmental performance.

Figure 5.6   'The BA Way'

including customer advocacy, safety and security, respected company and employee motivation. A key principle underpinning 'The BA Way' is that British Airways relies on the active engagement and support of all stakeholders to deliver business success. This was updated in the latter part of this decade following the appointment of Willie Walsh as Chief Executive of British Airways (see Figure 5.6).

DHL, now part of the logistics group Deutsche Post DHL, has had a number of mission and vision statements over the past two decades. A recent review of DHL websites in different countries identified a number of mission and vision statements including a new much shorter vision for DHL aimed at becoming *'The logistics company for the world.'*[12]

Some companies adopt such short mission statements. For example, the Google mission statement is as follows: *'Google's mission is to organize the world's information and make it universally accessible and useful.'* We view such short statements as 'straplines' rather than proper mission statements. For strategic marketing planning purposes we recommend a more comprehensive mission statement is developed such as the earlier version of the DHL mission shown in Figure 5.7.

DHL will become the acknowledged global leader in the express delivery of documents and packages. Leadership will be achieved by establishing the industry standards of excellence for quality of service and by maintaining the lowest cost position relative to our service commitment in all markets of the world.

Achievement of the mission requires:

o Absolute dedication to understanding and fulfilling our customers' needs with the appropriate mix of service, reliability, products and price for each customer

o An environment that rewards achievement, enthusiasm, and team spirit and which offers each person in DHL superior opportunities for personal development and growth

o A state of the art worldwide information network for customer billing, tracking, tracing and management information/communications

o Allocation of resources consistent with the recognition that we are one worldwide business

o A professional organisation able to maintain local initiative and local decision making while working together within a centrally managed network.

The evolution of our business into new services, markets, or products will be completely driven by our single-minded commitment to anticipating and meeting the changing needs of our customers.

Figure 5.7 DHL World Express – worldwide mission statement

The mission for DHL in Figure 5.7 and the earlier example for Bain & Company in Figure 5.3 both focus on many of the key issues we consider should be addressed in a mission statement for such a firm. It also illustrates the need to develop corporate objectives which are highly integrated with the mission statement. Without a strong linkage, which provides a means of measuring whether the mission can be achieved, much of the potential value of a mission can be dissipated. The relationship between corporate objectives and mission has been well summed up by the chairman and CEO of General Mills:

> We would agree that, unless our mission statement is backed up with specific objectives and strategies, the words become meaningless, but I also believe that our objectives and strategies are far more likely to be acted upon where there exists a prior statement of belief (i.e. a mission) from which specific plans and actions flow.

We return to this issue later in this chapter when, in Figure 5.12, we look at a simple framework for undertaking a consistency check between a mission and the corporate objectives.

Mission statements can be an empty statement on a piece of paper, or can reflect and underpin fundamental values of an organization in pursuit of its strategy.

Levels of mission statement

It is unlikely in most large organizations that one mission statement will suffice

Just as companies have different levels of objectives, ranging from strategic objectives through to tactical objectives and action plans, a service organization should consider to what extent it should develop mission or purpose statements at lower levels of the organization. Cranfield University in the UK has, for example, an overall University Mission Statement, while each of the university's schools (such as Aerospace, Computer Science, Management, etc.) has its own mission statement. Also, within the School of Management, for example, each group, such as the Marketing Group, has its own mission statement, all contributing to this university's outstanding success.

Thus, a bank with diverse financial services operations could have a mission statement for the bank as a whole, as well as individual missions for each business unit: it might develop missions for retail banking, corporate banking, international banking, investment banking, and its insurance and stockbroking activities.

> Many multi-business service organizations are in a similar position of needing to develop missions for their constituent parts.

It may also be appropriate to have missions at individual functional levels. For example, missions could be developed for internal service functions. An example of a mission for a human resource department is shown in Figure 5.8. Some organizations develop a range of missions for internal service activities and departments. A customer service mission statement, for instance, expresses the company's philosophy and commitment to customer service and the need for it follows from the increasing recognition that service quality is an important means of gaining competitive advantage. In some cases, customer service and quality missions are stated separately. In others, they may be combined as part of the statement of a firm's overall mission.

In each case, the 'mission' should focus on the company, business unit, or functional service activity. Where missions are formulated, for example at the departmental level, they should be consistent with higher level missions within the organization.

From mission statements to vision and values

Some companies have expanded their mission statement to include vision and values. The most authoritative work on this topic is that undertaken by consultant Hugh Davidson.[13] His research was prompted by the fact that most of the written materials on missions, visions and values discuss how important they are and provide guidance on how to design statements, but that there is little published

> To develop and promote the highest quality human resource practices and initiatives in an ethical, cost-effective and timely manner to support the current and future business objectives of the organization and to enable line managers to maximize the calibre, effectiveness and development of their human resources.
>
> This will be achieved through working with managers and staff to:
>
> - Develop an integrated human resource policy and implement its consistent use throughout the organization
> - Enhance managers' efficient use of human resources through the provision of responsive and adaptable services
> - Be the preferred source of core strategic HR services
> - Provide high quality tailored HR consultancy
> - Introduce methods to plan for the provision of required calibre and quantity of staff
> - Ensure consistent line accountability throughout all areas within the organization
> - Assist the organization in becoming more customer aware and responsive to changing needs
> - Define and encourage implementation of an improved communications culture throughout the organization
> - Maintain an innovative and affordable profile for HRM.

Figure 5.8   Human resource mission statement

work on how to make them really work in organizations. His research involved interviewing top management (chairpersons and chief executives) in 125 well-run companies and non-profit organizations in the UK and USA. The companies included: BP, FedEx, DuPont, Tesco, Nestlé, Johnson & Johnson, and IBM.

Davidson found that the term 'mission', which has been widely used over the past three decades, has become somewhat less popular in recent years and its use has been subject to criticism because many companies have not developed missions in a thorough and detailed manner. He concluded that it didn't matter which words were used to describe the business vision; what was important were three fundamental questions:

'What are we here for?' – 'Purpose'

'What is our long-term destination?' – 'Vision'

'What beliefs and behaviours will guide us on our journey?' – 'Values'.

A good example of a services company putting this into practice is Goldman Sachs. They are a market leader in their sector and one of the best companies in the investment-banking industry. They define their purpose, vision and values as:

Purpose/Mission: To provide excellent investment and development advice to major companies

Vision: To be the world's premier bank in every sector

Values: – Client first
– Teamwork

But just having a statement of mission, vision and values is not enough. Companies such as Goldman Sachs live these on a day-to-day basis. Goldman Sachs is no longer a partnership but they still maintain a partnership ethos. As Davidson points out, where they differ radically from most other investment banks is on values. They put their client before profit. Everyone at Goldman Sachs understands the importance of always putting the client first. They also place teamwork high on their agenda.

Extending the mission to include the vision and its associated values forms a significant element of an organization's strategy. Put simply, without a clear, concise and well-communicated vision, the organization is unlikely to be highly successful in achieving its goals. Organizations are increasingly realizing that developing a mission, a vision and a set of associated values may be a difficult activity, but it is one that is very worthwhile. Having a strong and appropriate mission, vision and values can enable companies to develop a distinctive culture and a focus for their employees, resulting in a 'people advantage' that is difficult to imitate.

Developing a service mission

Time must be devoted to the mission statement

Many of the examples of missions have the advantage of being short and simple. However, it must be remembered that the few sentences on a piece of paper represent the end result of a 'distillation' process which has extracted the essential few key elements from a mass of raw material.

> To arrive at a meaningful mission statement is, therefore, a time-consuming and sometimes painful experience, not something that can be rushed.

Bearing this in mind, the organization must be genuinely committed to developing its mission (and the vision and values that underpin this) if it is going to get any lasting value out of the investment of time and energy it puts into it. Speed and compromise are not legitimate in the mission formulation process.

Producing the mission statement should be a group process

While the mission can be developed by the chief executive in isolation, or by a management consultant, such approaches miss the vital part of the process – that of creating ownership and gaining organizational acceptance of the outcome. Mission development should therefore be an enterprise-wide consultative process, which involves input from different functional areas and management levels. The example above of IBM using its intranet shows how many staff in different locations can be consulted in a short time.

> The more managers and staff involved in formulating the mission, the more committed to it they will be.

There are a number of ways by which the desired level of involvement can be accomplished. Here are two approaches we have used with success.

Workshops

These can be held in the context of a broader marketing planning exercise, or as stand-alone events. Typically, the participants would be senior executives, but there is no reason why a representative cross-section of other members of the organization could not produce valuable inputs.

How the workshop unfolds will vary from company to company, but it is likely to follow these general steps:

1. *Introduction* – The chief executive explains why it is important for a mission to be formulated. The top-level support the CEO brings leaves participants in no doubt that they are working on a real task.

2. *Orientation* – Time is spent explaining the purpose of missions and what they contain (much as we have done in this chapter). Examples from other companies can be used as visual aids. Participants are encouraged to critique such examples.

3. *Syndicate work* – Small groups of 4–6 people are charged with developing a first draft of the company's mission.

4. *Plenary session* – The individual groups present their missions and all contributions are analysed and discussed regarding their strengths and weaknesses.

5. *Pulling together* – Either by further syndicate work, or through the mechanism of a specially constituted task group, the draft mission takes shape.

6. *Testing* – The draft mission is tested out in other parts of the organization and amended when it is sensible to do so. Thus, the final mission is developed.

Top team approach

This would involve working with the board of directors and so the total group size is only about eight, thereby precluding syndicate work. Here, we adopt a slightly different methodology:

1. *Orientation* – This operates in much the same way as described above.

2. *Individual* – Team members work in isolation to formulate a working mission.

3. *Clarification and review* – Individual contributions are put onto flip charts (without attribution) and posted around the room. Team members then circulate, either:

   a. studying all flip charts unaware of the author; or

   b. each author in turn answers only questions seeking clarification (there is no critique made).

4. *Reformulating the mission* – Working individually, team members, building on the previous phase, reformulate a second draft of the mission.

5. *Clarification and review* – Step 3 is repeated, but this time missions that are essentially the same are grouped together.

6. *Discussion* – The team, through detailed discussions, review the missions, and seek to develop a mission that is both realistic and one to which they are all committed. (In some cases this process extends over several meetings.)

Both of these broad approaches have worked well for us, because we played a catalyst role and were not involved in corporate politics, as well as being unbiased regarding what the outcome should be. We were also able to challenge corporate assumptions which were suspect or just not true, hence establishing a more permissive, and therefore creative, learning environment. As a result of our experiences, we would strongly recommend that a company following the routes we have outlined seeks out an experienced third party, such as a consultant or someone from a business school, to facilitate the event. Furthermore, such a person might also be able to help further develop the final mission and improve its potential as a communications aid. Those wishing to explore mission statements in more detail should refer to the additional references that we provide.[14]

While the mission statement should not be changed often, it should be reviewed regularly

Once established, the mission should not be susceptible to frequent change, because what the company wishes to become should remain more or less the same. The exception to this general rule is if a fundamental change takes place, such as, for example, if new technology develops and renders the company's current technology redundant, or a new strategic direction is determined. Nevertheless, while the mission will not be changed very often, it should be re-examined for its relevance on a fairly regular basis. It should also be introduced to new employees on the first day of their induction programme so they are familiar with the mission and what it represents.

The realizable mission

A mission statement, while seemingly simple in its completed form, may be the result of intensive and critical self-review for the company. The mission should position the services firm clearly in the markets in which it seeks to serve its customers and should provide an animated version with which employees can identify. Describing a mission statement as an 'animated vision' suggests that it should be forward-thinking, inspirational and dramatized. When the mission is communicated it should have the capacity to motivate the workforce towards organizational goals.

Figure 5.9 illustrates that it is necessary to develop a strong overlap between intellectual agreement (the statement of mission) and emotional commitment (the shared values of employees). It is this linkage between mission and values, made by management and other employees, which determines the extent to which the mission is realizable. This was summed up well by Jack Crocker, President of Super Value Stores Inc., who said, 'If a corporation is to succeed and experience continuing, long-term growth, there must exist a meaningful company philosophy [a mission] that justifies the personal commitment and dedication of its people.'

Many missions make the mistake of focusing on shareholders, customers and managers and do not attempt to motivate the non-managerial workforce. Companies should make employee engagement a high

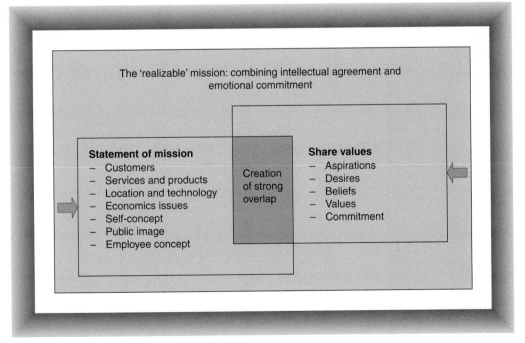

Figure 5.9 The 'realizable' mission

priority in their mission statements, as in a service organization it is often the collective behaviour of employees which brings success or failure.

Step 2 Corporate objectives

Corporate objectives and strategies

Once the mission has been developed, attention needs to switch to the corporate objectives and strategies. By way of recapitulation, how these are related is illustrated by Figure 5.10. From this, we can see that the corporate objectives and strategies need to be consistent with the sense of identity and direction provided by the mission statement. Thus the mission statement and corporate objectives need to be closely integrated. The corporate objectives should enable the organization to determine if its mission is being achieved.

As we saw earlier, the language of the corporate objectives will, in most cases, be in terms of profitability or return on capital invested, for these measures are universal yardsticks of organizational efficiency.

How these objectives will be achieved gives rise to the corporate strategies which impact on the various functional areas of the business. While there can be no absolutes in terms of what corporate

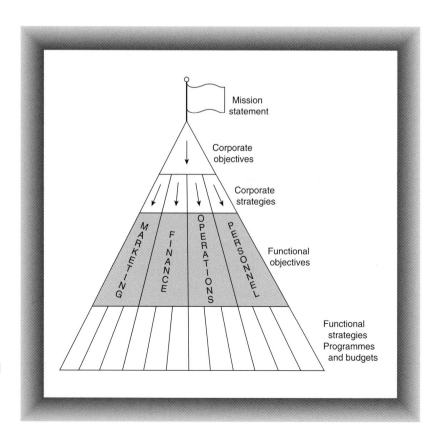

Figure 5.10
Mission statement and the hierarchy of objectives and strategies

strategies should address, it is likely that they will cover much of the following:

1. Market standing, e.g. sales and market share by market segment and the nature of services provided.

2. Innovation, e.g. new avenues of development.

3. Productivity, e.g. productivity of employees; effective use of capital and resources.

4. Financing, e.g. the nature of funding; levels of investment in fixed assets.

5. Staff performance *and development*, e.g. management and worker attitudes; preparedness to change.

6. Social responsibility and sustainability, e.g. to the environment; to the local community; legislative requirements.

From Figure 5.10, it will be seen that what is a *strategy* at a higher level may become an *objective* at the next level down, so giving a hierarchy of objectives and strategies.

Service companies need to consider which specific functional areas will make the largest contribution to achieving the corporate objectives and, in doing this, formulate a mix of strategies which are mutually support-ive. It is unlikely that any functional area can be completely ignored because, clearly, all parts of the organization are interdependent.

Service companies approach the setting of objectives in different ways, as Figure 5.11 shows. Of course, this illustration is fairly general. How-ever, it does show that when a company focuses on its services at the expense of its customers, a certain type of organizational 'culture'

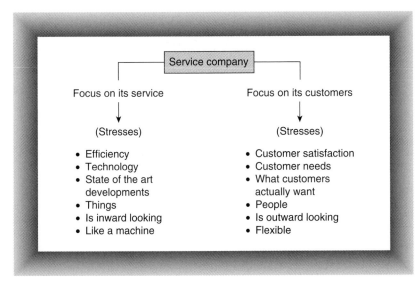

Figure 5.11
Different types of organization focus

almost naturally follows. This is equally true when the company focuses on customers.

That this happens is supported by considering the history of British Airways both before and after its privatization. In its earlier life, it saw itself as being in the business of flying planes. A consequence of this was that it was led by objectives which stressed technical efficiency and customers came a poor second to the pursuit of operational excellence. A major turnaround in profitability was brought about by privatization, which forced the company to modify its objectives and recognize that its future success lay in satisfying passenger requirements. However, as stated earlier, the company lost its pre-eminent position in the late 1990s and it abandoned its focus on customers to a fiscal, cost-cutting orientation. Yet, to switch from one type of culture to another is never easy. In the present competitive environment, it needs to develop a stronger emphasis on both customer service and its cost structure.

As we have said before, only customer-focused objectives and strategies (and organizations) hold the prospect of corporate success in the longer term. Those readers wishing to examine corporate objectives in further detail should consult a strategy text such as Richards.[15]

Quantitative versus qualitative objectives

> While objectives may sometimes be of a qualitative nature for internal company purposes, they must always be capable of being measured.

Objectives should therefore be clear and provide specific targets to be achieved in a given time. If imprecise objectives are allowed, the organization will never have proper yardsticks against which to measure its performance. Thus, if a hotel decided that one of the objectives was to provide the best bedrooms in the area, it would have to spell out the criteria by which it expected to be judged. Then surveys could be conducted to benchmark competitors and to ascertain whether these criteria were being met.

Here is how a financial services company phrased its objectives in quantitative terms:

- *Profit* – Double group earnings over the next five years.
- *Growth* – Treble revenues over the same period.
- *Innovation* – At least one new product or service to be launched every two years, with the intention of its accounting for 10% of total sales revenue within two years of launch.

- *Corporate image* – To improve unprompted recognition (as measured by external research) from 30% to 50% over three years.

- *Services* – Improve advisory and value-added services from 15% to 20% of total revenue over four years.

- *Staff* – Reduce staff turnover by 60% over three years.

Managers working in this organization are left in no doubt about what they are expected to achieve. Everything can be measured.

However, for broad statements of intent that are made public, such as in the annual report, qualitative objectives may be justified.

It is important that the company does not have too many high level corporate objectives. Generally we suggest between six and ten high level corporate objectives are sufficient; however, this may vary from one organization to another. In the case of the financial services company above it had six key quantitative objectives.

A study undertaken by Hackett Benchmarking examined the planning and control practices of world-class companies with non-world-class companies. It found that the mediocre company has 372 line items of objectives and budget detail while the world-class companies have 21. As Chatterjee concludes: 'The process of identifying the few core objectives that drive a top firm's competitive advantage is not easy, but it puts the firm in a much better position to manage the risks of failure than the average company. As a result, the firm does not suffer from information overload, which facilitates better control and communication. Furthermore, focusing resources on the most mission-critical objectives avoids wasted effort and misallocated resources. If something is not performing up to par, it is much easier to spot it from amongst 21 items than 372. However, to cull a large laundry list of objectives down to a handful of critical ones requires the utmost possible clarity as to how your business model is supposed to work.'[16]

To achieve this process, the organization must identify the top six to ten high level corporate objectives and a related set of subsidiary objectives that can be measured and tracked over time. When company's control systems attempt to track everything, they're much less likely to be successful.

As Tim Ambler, a leading researcher into company performance, observes, large companies have far too many measures. Further, often some of the most important measures do not reach board level. He found that measures of important objectives such as customer satisfaction and customer retention only reached board level in 36% and 51% of the companies he surveyed, respectively.[17]

Once a set of appropriate corporate objectives is established, it is important to ensure that these are tightly integrated with the mission. If the mission captures the key strategic essence of what an organization is seeking to accomplish, the corporate objectives should enable the organization to determine if its mission is being accomplished. Unfortunately, we have found few firms that address this issue. How might this be done in practice?

Figure 5.12 provides a structured framework for undertaking this task. It shows the example of how a leading information technology company has ensured its mission and its corporate objectives are closely integrated. It commenced this process by undertaking a content analysis of the key elements within its mission statement. These are shown at the top of this figure and listed with the letters 'a' to 'g'. It then listed the seven key corporate objectives, which it had identified. These are numbered '1' to '7' in this figure. It then considered each element of its mission and determined whether each of the objectives either partially or fully address this element of the mission. These are shown by the small and large text in the figure. It concluded from this process that three new corporate objectives needed to be added to address mission statement elements relating to 'outstanding customer value', 'enhancing the company's role as primary contractors', and 'providing best in-class staff development'. Finally, it identified that the objective of 'new products representing greater than 30% turnover in 5 years' was not addressed as an element within the mission statement. When the top team management considered this, it concluded that this element was so vital to its strategy that it made a further revision to address this issue in its mission statement.

By undertaking this fairly simple process, firms can make sure that the key elements in phase one – goal setting – of the marketing planning process are integrated.

Finally, it must be stressed that for corporate objectives to have any real meaning, they must be based on a deep understanding of customer needs. Consequently, the marketing process has to take place where the customers are, so that a mutual interdependency develops between marketing planning at the operational level and the setting of corporate objectives and strategies.

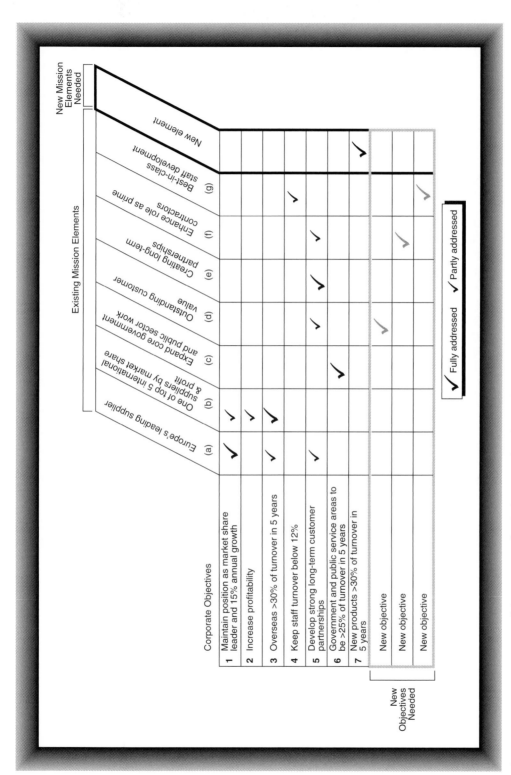

Figure 5.12   Corporate objectives and mission need to be tightly integrated

Summary

In this chapter, we have looked at the first phase of the planning process, which we called the 'strategic context'. It consists of two steps: formulating the corporate mission and setting corporate objectives and strategies. We went on to define the mission statement and to discuss its strategic value. Companies who had trouble in formulating their mission did so partly from ignorance and partly because they fell into some common traps – they made it too broad or too narrow, were unclear about the audience to which it was addressed, were confused about the nature of their business, the mission was not sufficiently unique and representative of the company, it lacked a motivational element, or it focused on the service products rather than on the customers.

Being clear about what the mission means is one thing, formulating it so that it is both realistic and acceptable is something else. We looked at participative methods for arriving at a mission which had organizational value. Methods such as these not only utilized organizational creativity, but also initiated the communication process which is so essential if the mission is to impact on the hearts and minds of managers and staff.

Corporate objectives and strategies are designed to make the mission come alive. We saw that the organization also had to align its objectives and strategies towards meeting customer needs and that, sometimes, this could have profound implications for the corporate culture. Although objectives could be qualitative or quantitative in nature, the latter must be capable of being measured, because they remove ambiguity. However, we did see that there was a role for qualitative objectives in terms of providing a broad backdrop to the organization.

The success of the whole marketing planning process is determined to a large extent by the way these first two steps are tackled. That is why it should be done very thoroughly. No marketing plan can be written properly until these elements of the overall corporate strategy are in place. That they should be in place is the responsibility of top management, not the marketing department.

However, as will be seen, these corporate objectives must inevitably be driven by a deep understanding of customer markets, which entails getting marketing planning done where the customers are. Thus, both top-down corporate objectives and bottom-up, customer-driven marketing plans are mutually interdependent.

6 Marketing planning Phase Two: the situation review (Part 1)

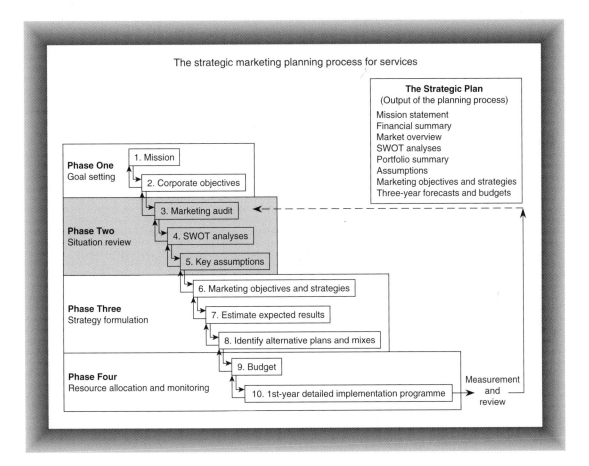

The strategic marketing planning process for services

The Strategic Plan
(Output of the planning process)

Mission statement
Financial summary
Market overview
SWOT analyses
Portfolio summary
Assumptions
Marketing objectives and strategies
Three-year forecasts and budgets

Phase One
Goal setting

1. Mission

2. Corporate objectives

Phase Two
Situation review

3. Marketing audit

4. SWOT analyses

5. Key assumptions

Phase Three
Strategy formulation

6. Marketing objectives and strategies

7. Estimate expected results

8. Identify alternative plans and mixes

Phase Four
Resource allocation and monitoring

9. Budget

10. 1st-year detailed implementation programme

Measurement and review

Once again, we should like to emphasize the difference between the *process* of strategic marketing planning described here and the *output* of this process, the *strategic marketing plan*. What should appear in the written output of the strategic marketing planning process was shown in Figure 4.5 in Chapter 4. In the figure above, we have added a box in the top right-hand corner to emphasize the difference between the process and the output, i.e. the strategic marketing plan.

In this chapter, we will consider in some detail the component steps of Phase Two of the marketing planning process – the situation review. We will look at ways of tackling each of these process steps. In particular, this chapter focuses on market segmentation while Chapter 7 (Part 2) focuses on other tools such as positioning, lifecycle analysis and portfolio management that service companies can use in their situation review.

Once again, we must stress that, for the purposes of clarity, we deal with each of the steps in Phase Two in a linear sequence. In reality, they are highly interactive and far less obvious as 'stand-alone' activities.

Service organizations need to evaluate their future prospects

While the purpose of the previous chapter, the corporate strategic context, was to provide marketing planning with a sense of strategic direction, the situation review is concerned with evaluating the future prospects of the service enterprise. Depending upon the outcome, the company may be well placed to face the future, or, alternatively, it might be found to be lacking in certain areas. Another possibility is that, because of the current circumstances facing the organization, the original corporate objectives of the plan may have to be modified considerably.

The first step of the situation review phase, the marketing audit, provides the information which shapes the subsequent elements of the planning process.

Step 3 The marketing audit

A marketing audit provides the means to enable the service organization to understand how it relates to the environment in which it operates. It also enables internal strengths and weaknesses to be identified in terms of how they match external opportunities and threats. The audit should be a systematic, critical and unbiased review and appraisal of the company's marketing operations. Thus, it provides management with the information to select a position in its particular environment based on known facts. In short, it provides the answer to the question: 'Where is the company now?'

The marketing audit should be kept separate from the marketing plan

It needs to be stressed here that the marketing audit is an essential part of the strategic marketing planning process and that the results of the marketing audit constitute a separate document.

The marketing audit itself is not a marketing plan and only some of the details contained in it should appear in the plan itself. We recommend that a marketing audit be carried out by all commercial managers in their area of responsibility and that this should be a required activity.

By carrying out an audit on a regular basis, e.g. once a year (rather than just at those times when things go wrong), management is more likely to recognize trends and spot underlying problems of a fundamental nature. This means that, instead of responding to symptoms, managers, in fact, address the root causes of organizational and marketing problems.

> Such is the complexity of operating in rapidly changing market conditions that it makes good sense to carry out a thorough situation analysis at least once a year at the beginning of the planning cycle.

Indeed, in many leading organizations, a marketing audit is a *required* activity, which has an equivalent status to a financial audit.

Who should do it?

Sometimes, outside consultants are hired to undertake this task. Experienced though they may be, the cost of using them can be high. Also, it must be asked if they will really have access to all the information which is 'stored' in an informal way by managers within the organization. It is a formidable task for an outsider to win the confidence of all the staff and uncover much of the anecdotal evidence well known to insiders.

Generally speaking, a better solution to the question of who does the audit is to get managers themselves to undertake the analysis within their own areas of responsibility. Where necessary this can be supplemented by the selective use of consultants. This approach has several benefits to commend it:

- The company's own expertise can be tapped and exploited.
- Managers become involved and, therefore, more committed to marketing planning.
- The discipline brought by the analytical process helps to avoid tunnel vision by forcing managers to focus on their total environment on a regular basis.
- Developing a critical appraisal faculty in managers helps them in their personal growth and development.
- Consultants' fees are minimized.

Often, however, the organization's response to the suggestion that their own managers conduct the audit centres on problems of finding the time and not being sufficiently objective. Naturally, time commitment will always be a critical issue.

> Nevertheless, managers ought to find time to stop and analyse the broader issues surrounding their sphere of activity.

Not only does this help the organization, but having this wider vision aids personal performance.

The objection about lack of objectivity can be helped by providing training for the managers, and providing them with easy-to-understand documentation which augments the formal planning approach.

What needs to be covered?

It would be impossible in a book of this length to be able to explain all the possible areas of the marketing audit in specific terms because, undoubtedly, there will be some activities of concern to only a few specialized service companies. However, regardless of their size, or the nature of their business, most companies find that there are certain key determinants to their business. It is on these that we shall focus. (We shall provide some references later in this chapter for those wanting to explore this area in further detail.)

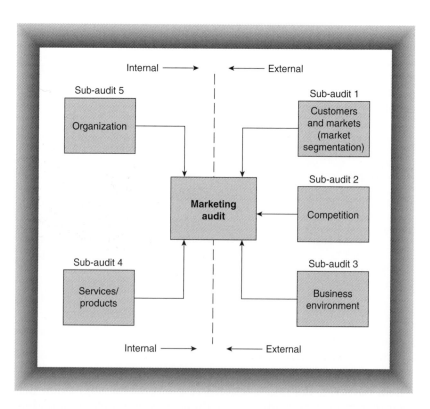

Figure 6.1
The constituent parts
of the marketing audit

In fact, the services marketing audit can be visualized as a set of five interrelating sub-audits, which focus on different aspects of the business, as shown in Figure 6.1. This figure also shows that the marketing audit draws information from outside the company, via the customer, competition and environmental audits, and from inside the company, by auditing the organization and the services it offers.

Let us now consider each of these sub-audit areas in turn.

Sub-audit 1 Customers and markets

Since the whole purpose of marketing planning is to alert and gear the service organization to market opportunities, the customer and market audit is concerned essentially with analysing trends in these areas, both favourable and unfavourable.

> By understanding in depth what is happening to its customers and markets, the company can select those opportunities which offer the best prospects for long-term success.

As the risk of failure is too high to rely on subjective opinion and intuition, the company must be led by accurate, fact-based information.

Market segmentation

In this chapter, a number of diagnostic tools will be introduced. One of the key diagnostic tools of marketing is *market segmentation*; this is a particularly relevant tool to use during the audit process when analysing customers and markets.

The audit process enables the existing methods of segmentation to be reappraised. Sometimes, it can be found that there are more advantageous ways to consider customers when seeking to establish a competitive advantage.

> The segmentation process is concerned with dividing a heterogeneous market into specific homogeneous groups. The **segments** thus identified can then be targeted with specific services and a distinctive marketing mix. The output of this process is a number of segments.

● Definition: A market segment consists of a group of customers within a market who share a similar level of interest in the same, or comparable, set of needs.

The market segmentation process
Introduction (For readers who want a detailed step-by-step process for doing segmentation, see McDonald and Dunbar (2010)[1].)

It has become clear after at least 70 years of formalized marketing that market definition and segmentation are the very core of the discipline. Even the famous PIMS database[2] recognizes that the term 'market share' has to be carefully defined.

How to measure market share has always been at the centre of controversy in discussions of success or failure. Defining a market too broadly or too narrowly can both lead to meaningless statistics.

The remainder of this chapter deals in detail with these problems.

While this is not the place to spell out the academic history of market segmentation, it is so crucial to the success of marketing planning that at least a brief commentary is called for. One of the authors of this chapter did a catholic review of scholarly research into the history of market segmentation (Jenkins and McDonald, 1997)[3] in which 36 references were cited. However, due to scale constraints here is a very brief summary of this research.

The father of market segmentation is widely considered to be Wendell Smith (1956)[4] who prepared market segmentation as an alternative to product differentiation. Yet it wasn't until Wind's (1978)[5] review of the state of market segmentation that the topic went to the top of the agenda of researchers and practitioners. His plea was for new segmentation bases, data analysis techniques and for generally putting market segmentation at the heart of strategic decision-making.

In 2009, a whole issue of the *Journal of Marketing Management* was devoted to market segmentation and for those readers wanting an updated literature review, see Bailey (2009)[6] in that issue. They confirm that most of the work over the intervening years has been primarily around what segmentation bases to use, such as size of purchase, customer characteristics, product attributes, benefits sought, service quality, buying behaviour and, more recently, propensity to switch suppliers, with much of this work being biased towards fast moving consumer goods rather than to business to business and services.

In 2002 Coviello[7] and a host of others, with the advent of relationship marketing and customer relationship management, proposed one-to-one as a successor to market segmentation, although Wilson (2002)[8] found that most CRM projects fail because of poor segmentation. Rigby (2002)[9] summed this up succinctly by saying that trying to implement CRM without segmentation is like 'trying to build a house without engineering measures or an architecture plan'.

Given the amount of academic scholarships and attempts at implementation in the world of practice over the 54 years since Wendell Smith first raised the consciousness of the community to the importance of market segmentation, it is surprising that so little progress has been made. In 2006, Christensen[10], in the *Harvard Business Review* found that of 30,000 new products launched in the USA, 85% failed because of poor market segmentation. Yankelovich's paper[11] in 2006 also reported the widespread failure of segmentation initiatives. This matches the author's own research over a 35-year period. His analysis of 3,000 marketing plans revealed that only 300 contained proper needs-based segmentation – i.e. 90% didn't.

One of the authors of this chapter, having been marketing director of a major fast moving consumer goods company and having worked on practical segmentation with senior teams from leading global multinationals down to SMEs for 35 years, finds much of the academic debate referred to above somewhat arrogant and inward-looking.

The justification for saying this is that anyone who says 'we segment markets by . . .' is totally missing the point. Any market, once correctly defined in terms of needs rather than products, consists of 100% of what is bought, how it is used and why it is bought and used in these ways. The role of any supplier is to understand these behavioural patterns and to discover their rationale, rather than trying to impose some predetermined segmentation methodology onto the market.

Readers who wish to are referred to the *Journal of Marketing Management*, Volume 25, nos 3–4, 2010, which is devoted to bridging the segmentation theory/practice divide.

The purpose here is to spell out proven methodologies for market definition and market segmentation developed over a 20-year period of research at Cranfield School of Management. During this period, a link between shareholder value creation and excellent marketing is shown in the left-hand column of Table 6.1.

Market definition Companies frequently confuse target **markets** with products – pensions or mainframe computers, for example – this, coupled with a lack of knowledge about the sources of differential advantage against each segment, signals trouble. Figure 6.2 shows the first attempt at a market map by a publisher of marketing books. Figure 6.3 shows their second attempt when, instead of defining their market as 'books', they defined their market as the promulgation of marketing knowledge. This led to a whole new corporate strategy.

• Definition: A market is the aggregation of all the products or services which customers regard as being capable of satisfying the same need. (Malcolm McDonald and Ian Dunbar. *Market Segmentation*. Goodfellow Publishing, Oxford, 2010.)

Excellent strategies	Weak strategies
Target needs-based segments	Target product categories
Make a specific offer to each segment	Make similar offers to all segments
Leverage their strengths and minimize their weaknesses	Have little understanding of their strengths and weaknesses
Anticipate the future	Plan using historical data

Table 6.1
The link between excellent and weak strategies

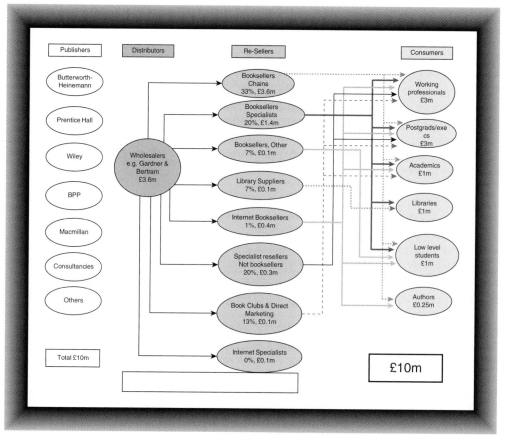

Figure 6.2   Original market map for marketing books market

Table 6.2 is an example from financial services.

Having established changes/developments in products and channels by defining markets in terms of needs, it is still necessary to draw a market map for your major products and services. A method for doing this is now explained.

Many companies pride themselves on their market segmentation even though these so-called 'segments' are in fact *sectors*, which is a common misconception. Everyone with a marketing qualification knows that a segment is a group of customers with the same or similar needs and that there are many different purchase combinations within and across sectors.

But the gravest mistake of all is *a priori* segmentation. Most books incorrectly state that there are several bases for segmentation, such as socio-economics, demographics, geo-demographics and the like. But this misses the point totally. For example, Boy George and the Archbishop of Canterbury are both As, but they don't behave the same! Nor do all 18- to 24-year-old women behave the same (demographics)! Nor does everyone in my street (geo-demographics) behave the same!

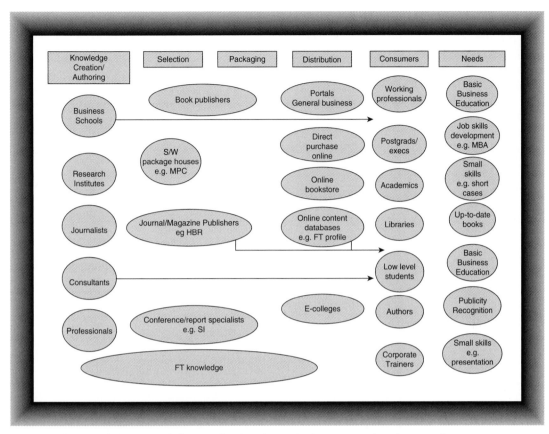

Figure 6.3 Market map of the marketing knowledge promulgation market

All goods and services are made, distributed and used and the purchase combinations that result make up an *actual* market, so the task is to understand market structure, how the market works and what these different purchase combinations (segments) are.

Market mapping A useful way of identifying where decisions are made about competing products and services and, therefore, those who then proceed to the next stages of segmentation is to start by drawing a **'market map'**.

An example of a generic market map is given in Figure 6.4.

It is useful to start your market map by plotting the various stages that occur along the distribution and value added chain between the final users and all the suppliers of products or services competing with each other in the defined market. At the same time, indicate the particular routes to market the products are sourced through, as not all of them will necessarily involve all of these stages.

Note at each junction on your market map, if applicable, all the different types of companies/customers that are found there.

● Definition:
A *market map* defines the distribution and value added chain between final users and suppliers of the products or services included within the scope of your segmentation project. This should take into account the various buying mechanisms found in your market, including the part played by 'influencers'.

Table 6.2
Some market
definitions (personal
market)

Market	Need (online)
Emergency cash ('rainy day')	Cash to cover an undesired and unexpected event (often the loss of or damage to property)
Future event planning	Schemes to protect and grow money for anticipated and unanticipated cash-calling events (e.g. car replacement/repairs, education, weddings, funerals and health care)
Asset purchase	Cash to buy assets they require (e.g. car purchase, house purchase, once-in-a-lifetime holiday)
Welfare contingency	The ability to maintain a desired standard of living for self and/or dependents at times of unplanned cessation of salary
Retirement income	The ability to maintain a desired standard of living for self and/or dependents once the salary cheques have ceased
Wealth care and building	The care and growth of assets with various risk levels and liquidity levels
Day-to-day money management	Ability to store and readily access cash for day-to-day requirements
Personal financial protection for and security from motor vehicle incidents	Currently known as car insurance

A couple of examples are given as Figures 6.4 and 6.5. The airline map is then broken down into more detail in Figure 6.6. The point of this is to understand the leverage (decision) points in the market, for it is here that market segmentation will take place. These leverage points are where most of the major decisions are made about what is bought.

What causes markets to segment?   Here, let us introduce the key concept of market segmentation and why it happens. Clearly, in the early days, markets will tend to be homogeneous. But, as demand grows rapidly with the entry of the early majority, it is common for new entrants to offer variations on the early models, as we have just explained, and consumers now have a choice. In order to explain this more clearly, let us illustrate the approximate shape of markets. If we were to plot the car market in terms of speed and price, we would see very small, inexpensive cars in the bottom left-hand corner (see Figure 6.7). In the top right, we would see very fast, expensive cars. Most cars, however, would cluster in the middle, what we might call: 'The Mr and Mrs average market.'

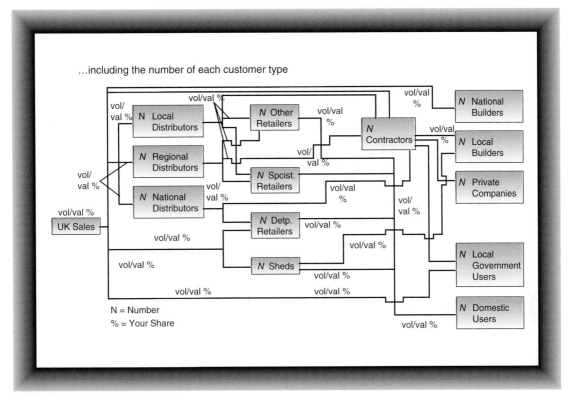

Figure 6.4 Market mapping

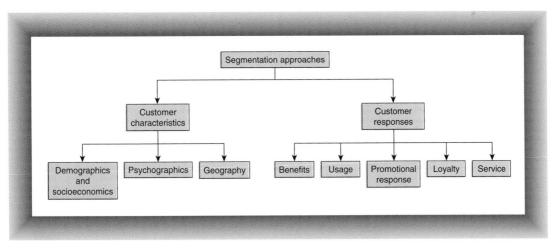

Figure 6.5 Major approaches to services market segmentation

Likewise, the lawn mower market would look very similar (see Figure 6.8). With lawn size on the vertical axis and price on the horizontal axis, at the bottom left would be small, inexpensive, hand-pushed mowers, with expensive sit-on machines for large estates in the right-hand corner. That leaves the mass of the market with average size lawns, and average-sized lawn mowers, which is where the mass market is.

	Mass marketing	Traditional segmentation	Needs-based segmentation	Micro-segmentation	One-to-one marketing
Key focus:	Product	Segment	Segment	Micro-segment	Customer
Market segment:	One segment – homogeneous market	Segments based on demographics, etc.	Segments based on psychographics, lifestyles, etc.	Narrowly defined, high value segments	Segment of one
Product/service offering:	One standard offering	Offerings modified to segment	Integrated offerings to segment needs	Integrated offerings to micro-segment needs	Mass-customization
Communication:	Broadcast marketing	Tailored messages	Tailored messages	Highly tailored messages	Dialogue marketing
Measure of success:	Market share	Segment share	Segment share	Segment share	Share of customer

Vendor ──── **Relationship with customer** ──── Partner

Figure 6.6 Levels of segmentation emphasis

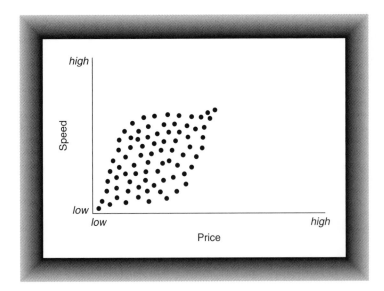

Figure 6.7
Illustration of the shape of the car market

We can now redraw this to represent the shape of any market, particularly at the early growth stage (the shape on the left in Figure 6.9). But when rapid growth begins, new entrants join the market and offer variations on standard products in order to attract sales, and it is at

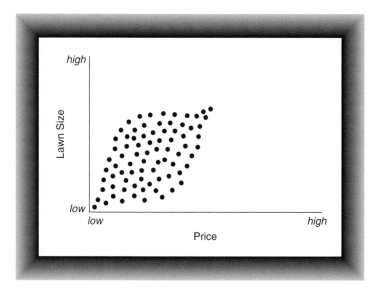

Figure 6.8
Illustration of the shape of the lawn mower market

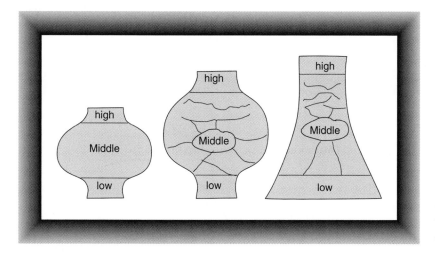

Figure 6.9
The shape of markets from birth to maturity

this stage that markets begin to break into smaller groups, while still growing overall (this is represented by the shape in the middle). Eventually, when markets mature, and there is more supply than demand, any market growth tends to come in the lower price end of the market, while the top end of the market tends to be immune (this is represented by the shape on the right). It is usually the middle market that suffers at this stage, with many competitors vying with each other on price. This, however, is the whole point of market segmentation, for competing only on price is to assume that this is the main requirement of customers, whereas the truth is that this is rarely the case. It is just that a general lack of understanding about market segmentation on the part of suppliers about the real needs of customers in mature markets forces them to trade on price, so encouraging the market to become a commodity market.

It is not widely known that price is rarely the decisive factor in most buying situations. It is certainly the experience of the authors over many years of working on every continent of the world that price accounts for less than 10% of all decisions. The following is a quote from an IPA report (Advertising in a downturn, March 2008, page 5): 'The average proportion of consumers who were motivated by price was around ten per cent and even if this increased during a downturn, the proportion would remain small.'

Let us summarize all of this by showing a product lifecycle representation with some generalizations about how marketing strategies change over time. See Figure 6.10 (product lifecycles are explained in more detail in the next chapter). From this, which we suggest you study carefully, you will see at least four major changes that occur over the lifecycle. At the top of the far right-hand column, you will see the word 'commodity', but the point we want to make is that this is by no means inevitable, and only occurs in markets where the suppliers do not understand the power of market segmentation, as in the case histories provided at the end of this chapter. There are other options, of course, including the option to get out of mature markets. Another is to move the goalposts as it were, somewhat in the manner of First Direct, Direct Line, Michael Dell, Virgin, Amazon.com, and

Key Characteristics	Unique	Product Differentiation	Service Differentiation	'Commodity'
Marketing Message	Explain	Competitive	Brand Values	Corporate
Sales	Pioneering	Relative Benefits Distribution Support	Relationship Based	Availability Based
Distribution	Direct Selling	Exclusive Distribution	Mass Distribution	80 : 20
Price	Very High	High	Medium	Low (Consumer Controlled)
Competitive Intensity	None	Few	Many	Fewer, bigger International
Costs	Very High	Medium	Medium/Low	Very low
Profit	Medium/High	High	Medium/High	Medium/low
Management Style	Visionary	Strategic	Operational	Cost Management

Figure 6.10   The product/market lifecycle and market characteristics

countless others. The strategy we want to concentrate on here, how-ever, is market segmentation, which in our view should be the very first consideration as markets begin to mature.

Market segmentation – how to do it   We can now begin to concen-trate on a methodology for making market segmentation a reality, market segmentation being the means by which any company seeks to gain a differential advantage over its competitors.

Markets usually fall into natural groups, or segments, which contain customers who exhibit a similar level of interest in the same broad requirements.

These segments form separate markets in themselves and can often be of considerable size. Taken to its extreme, each individual consumer is a unique market segment, for all people are different in their require-ments. While CRM systems have made it possible to engage in one-to-one communications, this is not viable in most organizations unless the appropriate organizational economies of scale have been obtained at a higher level of aggregation such as at segment level. Consequently, products are made to appeal to groups of customers who share approx-imately the same needs.

It is not surprising, then, to hear that there are certain universally accepted criteria concerning what constitutes a viable market segment:

- Segments should be of an adequate size to provide the company with the desired return for its effort.

- Members of each segment should have a high degree of similarity in their requirements, yet be distinct from the rest of the market.

- Criteria for describing segments must enable the company to com-municate effectively with them.

While many of these criteria are obvious when we consider them, in practice market segmentation is one of the most difficult of marketing concepts to turn into a reality. Yet we must succeed, otherwise we become just another company selling what are called 'me-too' prod-ucts. In other words, what we offer the potential customer is very much the same as what any other company offers and, in such circum-stances, it is likely to be the lowest priced article that is bought. This can be ruinous to our profits, unless we happen to have lower costs, hence higher margins, than our competitors.

There are basically three stages to market segmentation, all of which have to be completed (see Figure 6.11).

We have already explained about market definition and market map-ping (Step 1).

This first stage should have established the scope of the project by spec-ifying the geographic area to be covered and defining the 'market'

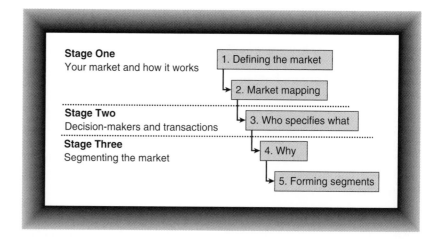

Figure 6.11
The three stages of market segmentation

which is to be segmented, followed by taking a detailed look at the way this market operates and identifying where decisions are made about the competing products or services. Successful segmentation is based on a detailed understanding of decision-makers and their requirements.

The second stage is essentially a manifestation of the way customers actually behave in the market place and consists of answering the question: 'Who is specifying what?'

The third stage looks at the reasons behind the behaviour of customers in the market place and answers the question 'Why?' and then searches for market segments based on this analysis of needs.

The following sections provide an overview of the steps required to complete stages 2 and 3. We can now turn to the process again, and move to steps 3, 4 and 5, although it must be pointed out that segmentation can and should be carried out at all major junctions on the market map, not just at the final user junction.

Essentially, these time-consuming steps involve listing all purchase combinations that take place in the market, including different applications for the product or service. See Figure 6.12, principal forms such as size, colour, branded, unbranded, etc., the principal channels used, when – such as once a year, weekly, etc. – how – such as cash or credit. Next it is important to describe who behaves in each particular way using relevant descriptors such as demographics. For business-to-business purchases this might be standard industrial classifications, size of firm, etc., whereas for consumer purchases this might be socio-economic groups such as A, B, C1, C2, D and E or stage in the lifecycle, or age, sex, geography, lifestyles or psychographics. Finally, and most difficult of all, each purchase combination has to have a brief explanation of the reason for this particular type of behaviour. In other words, we need to list the benefits sought, and it is often at this stage that an organization needs to pause and either commission market research or

Micro-segment	1	2	3	4	5	6	7	8	9	10
Application (if applicable)										
What is bought										
Where,										
When,										
and How										
Who										
Why (benefits sought)										

Figure 6.12
Micro-segments

refer to its extant database of previous market research studies. Although in the figure shown there are only 10 micro-segments, it is normal in most markets for companies to identify between 30 and 50 micro-segments. Remember, these micro-segments are actual purchase combinations that take place in a market.

To summarize, it is clear that no market is totally homogeneous (see Figure 6.13).

The reality is that actual markets consist of a large number of different purchase combinations (see Figure 6.14).

However, as it is impracticable to deal with more than between 7 and 10 market segments, a process has to be found to bring together or cluster all those micro-segments that share similar or approximately similar needs (see Figure 6.15).

Once the basic work has been done, in describing micro-segments, that is steps 2, 3, 4 and 5, any good statistical computer program can carry out cluster analysis to arrive at a smaller number of segments.

The final step consists of checking whether the resulting segments are big enough to justify separate treatment, are indeed sufficiently different from other segments, and whether they have been described sufficiently well to enable the customers in them to be reached by means of the organization's communication methods. In addition, the company has to be prepared to make the necessary changes to meet the needs of the identified segments.

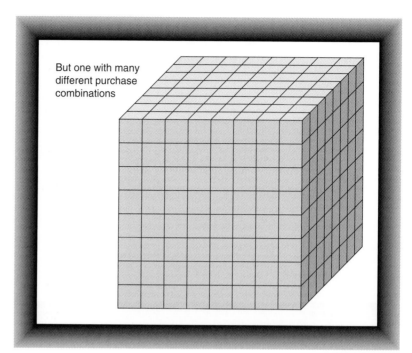

Figure 6.13
An undifferentiated market

Figure 6.14
Different needs in a market

Table 6.3 is a summary of what we have discussed so far. It is obvious that there will be very few markets in the world where all customers have the same needs. Also, once market segmentation has been carried out, positioning products and services to meet the different needs of the different segments is comparatively easy. The difficult bit is

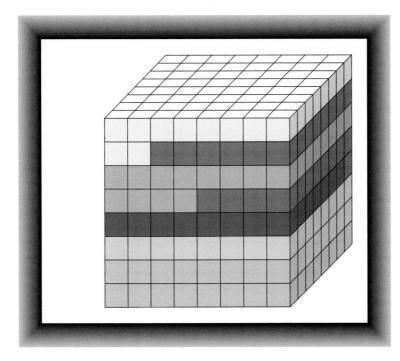

Figure 6.15
Segments in a market

● Not all customers in a broadly-defined market have the same needs
● Positioning is easy. Market segmentation is difficult. Positioning problems stem from poor segmentation.
● Select a segment and serve it. Do not straddle segments and sit between them.
1. Define the market to be segmented and size it (market scope)
2. Determine how the market works and identify who makes the decisions (market mapping)
3. Develop a representative sample of decision-makers based on differences they see as key (including what, where, when and how), note who they are (demographics) and size them
4. Understand their real needs (why they buy, the benefits sought)
5. Search for groups with similar needs

Table 6.3
Understand market segmentation

segmenting markets. The third point is that it is vital to focus on serving the needs of the identified segments, while it is dangerous to straddle different segments with the same offer. This point is made clear in the case histories at the end of this chapter.

The process of market segmentation itself consists of five steps: One, understand how your market works. This involves defining the market and drawing a market map. Two, list what is bought, including where, when, how, and the different applications of the product or service. Three, list who buys using descriptors such as demographics and psychographics. Four, list why they buy, especially the benefits sought. Five, finally, search for groups with similar needs. These will be the final market segments.

Market structure and market segmentation are the heart and soul of marketing. (See Figure 6.16.) Unless an organization spends time on it, driven from the board downwards, it is virtually impossible for it to be market driven, and in any organization that isn't market driven, the marketing function will be ineffective, or at best will spend its time trying to promote and sell product or services that are inappropriate for the market. We will leave you with this figure for you to study. It describes in more detail each of the important steps in the market segmentation process.

There follows a quick segmentation exercise (thanks to Dr Brian Smith[12] of Pragmedic and a Visiting Fellow at the Open University Business School). This will quickly produce a very rough segmentation of your market, but it is no substitute for the proper, more detailed and accurate process described above, as the results will only ever be approximate.

Quick market segmentation solution
- Write down *the main* benefits sought by customers.

- Hygiene factors are benefits that any product or service must have to be acceptable in the market. Try to ignore these.

- Motivators are those benefits that contribute towards the customer's decision about which product to buy.

- Take the 'motivators' and choose the two main ones.

- Draw two straight horizontal lines and make an estimate of the percentage of customers at each end. So, for example, if service level is a key motivator of what is bought. See below.

40% _____ 60%

Low service   High service

Likewise, if the breadth of the product range is a key motivator of what is bought, see below:

40% _____ 60%

low product range   high product range

Take the left hand point of the first horizontal line and drag it over the second horizontal line to make cross as shown.

- Starting at the top, and moving in a clockwise direction, multiply 60% by 60% to give 36% (see first circle).

- Then multiply 60% by 40% to give 24% (see second circle).

- Then multiply 40% (the bottom of the vertical axis) by 40% to give 16% (see third circle).

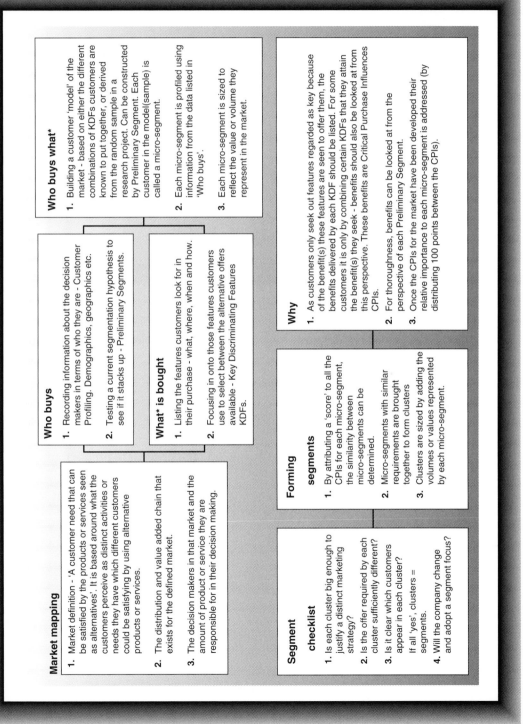

Market mapping

1. Market definition - 'A customer need that can be satisfied by the products or services seen as alternatives'. It is based around what the customers perceive as distinct activities or needs they have which different customers could be satisfying by using alternative products or services.

2. The distribution and value added chain that exists for the defined market.

3. The decision makers in that market and the amount of product or service they are responsible for in their decision making.

Who buys

1. Recording information about the decision makers in terms of who they are - Customer Profiling. Demographics, geographics etc.

2. Testing a current segmentation hypothesis to see if it stacks up - Preliminary Segments.

What* is bought

1. Listing the features customers look for in their purchase - what, where, when and how.

2. Focusing in onto those features customers use to select between the alternative offers available - Key Discriminating Features KDFs.

Who buys what*

1. Building a customer 'model' of the market - based on either the different combinations of KDFs customers are known to put together, or derived from the random sample in a research project. Can be constructed by Preliminary Segment. Each customer in the model(sample) is called a micro-segment.

2. Each micro-segment is profiled using information from the data listed in 'Who buys'.

3. Each micro-segment is sized to reflect the value or volume they represent in the market.

Forming segments

1. By attributing a 'score' to all the CPIs for each micro-segment, the similarity between micro-segments can be determined.

2. Micro-segments with similar requirements are brought together to form clusters.

3. Clusters are sized by adding the volumes or values represented by each micro-segment.

Why

1. As customers only seek out features regarded as key because of the benefit(s) these features are seen to offer them, the benefits delivered by each KDF should be listed. For some customers it is only by combining certain KDFs that they attain the benefit(s) they seek - benefits should also be looked at from this perspective. These benefits are Critical Purchase Influences CPIs.

2. For thoroughness, benefits can be looked at from the perspective of each Preliminary Segment.

3. Once the CPIs for the market have been developed their relative importance to each micro-segment is addressed (by distributing 100 points between the CPIs).

Segment checklist

1. Is each cluster big enough to justify a distinct marketing strategy?

2. Is the offer required by each cluster sufficiently different?

3. Is it clear which customers appear in each cluster?
   If all 'yes', clusters = segments.

4. Will the company change and adopt a segment focus?

Figure 6.16   The market segmentation process – summary

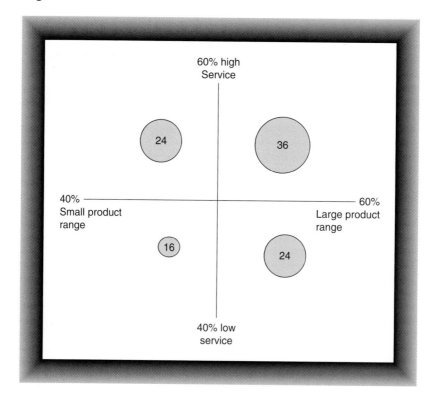

- Lastly, multiply 40% by 40% to give 16% (see fourth circle).

- The circles represent segments in the market.

Interpretation
- The first segment (36%), the biggest segment, requires both high service and a large product range.

- The second segment (24%) prefers a large product range and is less interested in service.

- The third segment (16%) doesn't care much about either a large product range or service.

- The fourth segment (24%) prefers good service and is less interested in a large product range.

- Although not essential, you might consider giving each segment a name.

Action   Ensure your 'offer' including the product, price, service and promotion reflects the differing needs of each segment.

Example   An example of segmentation of the A4 copier paper market follows. Please note that, if as in the case of the A4 paper market, there is one very large segment I (in this case 56%), the exercise can be repeated for just this large segment, resulting in seven segments in total.

- *Service deliver* – Fast, paper always 'there' – point of delivery availability of products; service levels.

- *Product fit for purpose* – High-quality print finish for colour copiers; consistency of quality; paper that doesn't screw up in the machine; print definition, no waste.

- *Environmental factors* – Recyclable.

- *Level of support* – Delivered in small lots; consignment stock; easy ordering (online); delivered to difficult locations.

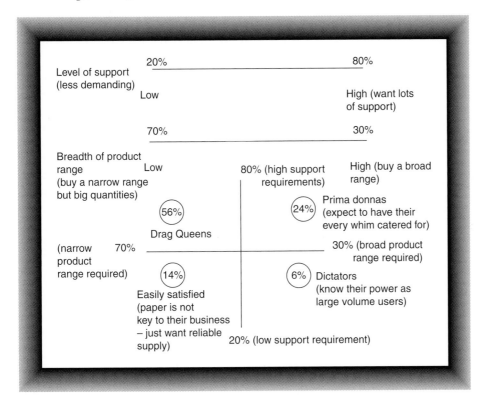

Looking to the future   One final, but crucial, step remains in this part of the marketing audit.

The essence of this stage is to revisit the market map, and consider in what ways it might be affected by e-commerce. Reconfiguring the market map involves examining the current market map, and redrawing it to take account of various anticipated effects of e-commerce. The resulting vision of how the industry could change as a result of e-commerce presents the organization with choices as to how to position itself in the future industry structure and how to manage the transition period. Here is a list of options based on our research of how the market map might be reconfigured.

1. *Disintermediation* – As with other IT-enabled channels such as call centres, e-commerce can enable a link to be removed from the market map, by removing intermediaries whose primary function of

information transfer can be more effectively performed using the internet. An example is the direct sales of greetings cards to the public being trialled by a card publisher, thereby bypassing the retailer.

2. *Partial channel substitution* – This forms a halfway house towards disintermediation, in which an intermediary's role is reduced but not eliminated, through some of its value being provided remotely by the supplier to the intermediary's customer. This is the model adopted by a card manufacturer in its relationship with retailers, where its website is supplementing its agent network rather than replacing it. Similarly, a drinks manufacturer is using data gleaned from its information exchange with distributors to promote directly to retailers, providing 'pull-through' demand which the distributors perceive as of mutual benefit.

3. *Reintermediation* – In some cases, a previous intermediary is replaced by a new online intermediary, rather than bypassed, or an intermediary appears between two types of organization which previously dealt with each other directly. At the time of writing, a groceries' manufacturer is having to define its strategy with respect to the various business-to- business exchanges, or e-hubs, which are appearing in its industry to link retailers to manufacturers. Similarly, the health portals such as Healtheon are forming influential intermediaries between manufacturers of drinks products with a health claim and the consumer.

Why market segmentation is vital in marketing planning In today's highly competitive world, few companies can afford to compete only on price, for the product has not yet been sold that someone, somewhere, cannot sell cheaper – apart from which, in many markets it is rarely the cheapest product that succeeds anyway. What this means is that we have to find some way of differentiating ourselves from the competition, and the answer lies in market segmentation.

The truth is that very few companies can afford to be 'all things to all people'. The main aim of market segmentation as part of the planning process is to enable a firm to target its effort on the most promising opportunities. But what is an opportunity for firm A is not necessarily an opportunity for firm B, depending on its strengths and weaknesses. The whole point of segmentation is that a company must either:

Define its markets broadly enough to ensure that its costs for key activities are competitive; or define its markets in such a way that it can develop specialized skills in serving them to overcome a relative cost disadvantage.

Both have to be related to a firm's *distinctive competence* and to that of its competitors.

All of this should come to the fore as a result of the marketing audit referred to previously and should be summarized in SWOT analyses. In particular, the differential benefits of a firm's product or service should be beyond doubt to all key members of the company.

Even more important than this, however, is the issue of marketing planning and all that follows in this book.

Case examples of market segmentation in the services sector

Two cases are provided. One is an excellent case history of a service organization. It demonstrates clearly how a company losing market share through lack of focus recovered to high levels of profitability, principally through excellent market segmentation. We have included a considerable amount of detail in this case so that the process of segmentation may be fully understood. The second is an example of an insurance company's segmentation for annuity products.

Case study – GlobalTech[†]

This case study describes the use of market segmentation to assist in the development of a service product. Customer requirements were captured via qualitative research and the segmentation was completed through the use of quantitative research. The result was a set of segments that enabled the development of a new approach to delivering service while improving customer satisfaction.

GlobalTech is the fictitious name of a real company marketing hi-tech and service products globally. Customers are counted in hundreds of thousands. The markets are mainly business to business with a very few large customers buying thousands of items. Service is a major revenue stream measured in billions of dollars. The lessons learnt from this case study could be of interest to any organization having to care for large numbers of customers.

Background

A failed segmentation

An internal GlobalTech team tried to complete a marketing audit in 2000. This included market definition, market segmentation and quantification. Each product division conducted their audit separately. They used mainly brainstorming techniques to define their markets and to produce the data required.

Company insight 1

Markets transcend your internally-defined product divisions. Therefore, it is best to understand the markets and monitor your overall performance in those markets. To reshape market information to meet the needs of internal reporting will lead to misinformation.

On completion, the results were compared across the divisions. It rapidly became apparent that each division addressed almost all the markets. However, the market definitions they

[†] Taken from *Market Segmentation: How to do it, how to profit from it*, by M. McDonald and I. Dunbar, Goodfellow Publishers, Oxford, 2010.

produced were different with significant bias to just the products they offered. Similarly, the segments each division identified were in conflict with the outputs from the other divisions.

On reflection it was agreed that the results were unreliable. They could not be used to help shape future strategies or marketing investments.

GlobalTech was now in the uncomfortable situation of being in a market information vacuum. Any confidence they had in their understanding of the market had been destroyed. Consequently, the decision was taken that all future market analysis and understanding tasks would be supported by appropriate investments in market research.

Company insight 2

Do not rely on internally gathered opinions of your sales and marketing staffs to define markets and identify customer requirements and attitudes. Do invest in the necessary market research to provide a reliable segmentation and support for strategy and product development.

First market segmentation

The following year the segmentation was redone, supported by extensive qualitative and quantitative market research. The objective was to understand and group into segments the product buyers in the overall market.

The qualitative study produced a very clear picture and definition of the markets addressed by GlobalTech. It also provided the customers' view of the benefits they sought from the products and the differences in their attitudes towards their suppliers. The questionnaire for the quantitative study was based on the results of the qualitative study. The result was seven clearly defined segments.

This enhanced understanding of the market, assisted the marketing of hardware and software products but did not address service products or customer satisfaction and loyalty issues.

The internal need

At the dawn of the twenty-first century the market cycle had matured. All but the more sophisticated products were perceived as 'commodities'. Consequently, the opportunities for effective product differentiation had diminished. GlobalTech, in common with its competitors, was finding that customers were becoming increasingly disloyal.

For many years, product churns and upgrades from existing customers had accounted for some 70% of GlobalTech's product revenues. Service and exhaust revenues[‡] almost equalled total product revenues. Service was perceived to be a key influencer of loyalty. But the costs of delivering service were becoming unacceptable to customers. Concurrently, service pricing was coming under increasing competitive pressures.

[‡] Exhaust revenues are those revenues that follow on, almost automatically, from an initial product sale. These would normally include service plus training, consultancy, consumables, supplies, add-ons and so on.

The challenge was to increase loyalty while achieving a step function improvement in margins. Thus, it was decided to invest in a better understanding of the service market as an enabler to delivering cost-effective differentiation and loyalty.

This case history covers the project from inception to implementation.

The segmentation project

Buy-in

The GlobalTech main board director responsible for customer service sponsored the project. This was a critical prerequisite, as the outcome would have a significant impact on the organization, its processes and behaviours.

Similarly, the project team included key members of service, marketing and finance to ensure buy-in. However, at that time it was deemed inappropriate to include representatives from all but two of the countries due to travel implications, costs and resource impacts. In retrospect this was not a good decision.

Company insight 3

Try to anticipate the scale of organizational change that may result from a major segmentation project. Then ensure the buy-in planned from the start of the project embraces all those who will eventually have a say in the final implementation.

Business objectives

The project team agreed the overall business objectives as:

1. To develop strategies for profitable increase in market share and sustainable competitive advantage in the service markets for GlobalTech's products.

2. To identify opportunities for new service products and for improving customer satisfaction within the context of a robust customer needs segmentation, which can be readily applied in the market place.

3. To identify the key drivers of loyalty so that GlobalTech may take actions to increase customer loyalty significantly.

4. To provide the information required to help develop a new and innovative set of service products designed and tailored to meet differing customer requirements while significantly reducing internal business process costs.

Results from the qualitative study

The output from the qualitative study was a thorough report documenting the results, in line with the desired research objectives. Some of the more surprising aspects were supported by verbatims. A key output was the polarization of very different attitudes towards service requirements that some buyers had in comparison with others. For example:

- Some wanted a response within a few hours, whereas many others would be equally happy with next day.

- Some wanted their staff thoroughly trained to take remedial actions supported by a specialist on the telephone. Others did not want to know and would just wait for the service provider to fix the problem.

- Some wanted regular proactive communications and being kept up to date. Others wanted to be left alone.

- Some would willingly pay for a premium service, under a regular contract, while others would prefer to take the risk.

- The attitudes of professional buyers, procuring on behalf of user departments, were consistently different from those of the user departments.

Results from the quantitative study

The output from the quantitative study was extensive. Much of the output was detailed demographic data, opportunities information and competitive positioning comparisons. However, the focus was on a fairly extensive executive summary for internal communications within GlobalTech. What follows are summarized extracts from those outputs.

The segments

Six market segments were identified as a result of iterative computer clustering. Initially, the clustering routines had identified more segments but by careful analysis these were reduced to what was decided to be the most manageable level. Some previously very small segments were merged with very similar larger segments. A summary of the six concluding segments appears in Figure 6.10.

Polarizations in attitude

The computer clustering generated the segments by grouping customers with similar attitudes and requirements. This resulted in some marked differences in attitude between segments. As illustrated in Figure 6.11, the Koalas really did not want to know about being trained and having a go, but the Teddies, Polars and Yogis had an almost opposite attitude.

Satisfaction and loyalty

GlobalTech was measuring customer satisfaction for use both locally, as a business process diagnostic tool, and globally, as a management performance metric. These satisfaction metrics were averaged across all customers, both by geographic business unit and by product division to meet internal management reporting requirements.

However, the outputs from the quantitative study clearly showed that these traditionally well-accepted metrics were, in fact, almost meaningless. What delighted customers in one market segment would annoy customers in another, and vice versa. To make the metrics meaningful, they had to be split by key criteria and the market segments.

Loyalty was obviously highest where GlobalTech's 'one-size-fits-all' service deliverable coincidentally best matched a segment's requirements, as illustrated in Figure 6.12.

Correlation between loyalty and customer satisfaction

The lifecycle for many of GlobalTech's products in the market was moving into the 'commodity' phase. Therefore, not surprisingly, customers were becoming less loyal.

Each percentage point increase in loyalty translated into almost the same increase in market share. Each percentage point in market share added many millions of dollars of gross revenues. The cost of reselling to a loyal customer was about one-sixth the cost of winning a new customer. Consequently, each percentage point increase in loyalty had a significant impact on the bottom line.

Because of this, the quantitative study included correlating the key drivers of satisfaction and loyalty within each market segment. The qualitative study identified some 28 key customer requirements of their service provider. The quantitative study prioritized these to provide a shorter list of 17 common requirements. The correlation exercise reduced this to only two requirements that drew a significant correlation between satisfaction and loyalty:

- Providing service levels that meet your needs.

- Providing consistent performance over time.

Although GlobalTech was achieving the second, it was really only delivering the first in two of the market segments.

Segment attractiveness

As an aid to deciding where best to invest, a chart of segment attractiveness was produced using attractiveness factors determined by GlobalTech. Demographic data from the quantitative study was combined with internal GlobalTech financial data. Each factor was weighed to reflect the relative importance to GlobalTech. This highlighted quite a few issues and some opportunities. For instance, the highest margins were coming from some of the least loyal segments. The resulting attractiveness chart appears in Figure 6.13.

Competitive positioning

Fortunately for GlobalTech, its competitors did not appear to have an appreciation of the market segments or the different requirements of their customers. They were also mainly delivering a 'one-size-fits-all' service offering. However, there were some noticeable differences in the offerings. These resulted in each major competitor being significantly stronger in just one or two segments where their deliverables best matched the segment's needs.

The quantitative study provided detailed rankings of the decisive buying criteria (DBCs) and the constituent critical success factors (CSFs) for each market segment. These were to prove invaluable during the phase of designing the service products and developing the strategy to achieve competitive advantage.

Reachability

Key to GlobalTech successfully implementing any strategies or communications that were to be segment-based would be the ability to identify each customer by segment. As part of the quantitative study, two statistical reachability tasks were conducted. The results were as follows:

1. A sampling of internal GlobalTech databases showed that there was sufficient relevant data to achieve better than 70% accuracy, using computer imputation methods, to code each customer with its market segment. This was considered to be good enough to enhance marketing communications measurably, but might not be sufficiently accurate to ensure that the most appropriate offer was always made.

2. Statistical analysis identified four 'golden questions' that would provide acceptable accuracy in segment identification. These questions could then be used during both inbound and outbound call centre conversations until all customers had been coded.

The recommendation was to use both methods in parallel so that accuracy would improve over time. The coding of larger customers, however, should be given priority.

Company insight 4

Understanding the different market segments helps in designing the required offers. But do not get hung up on reachability. It is not essential to code every customer to the right segment from day one. Where you are not really sure, let them see different offers and so position themselves. Similarly, be willing to accept that within a large organization some buyers may fall into different market segments, though the difference will only be on one or perhaps two buying criteria rather than across all the buying criteria.

Strategy development and implementation

Market understanding and strategy development

The challenge now was for the project team to absorb and understand all the findings from the two research studies. The team then had to turn that understanding into realizable strategies. To achieve this, a workshop process covering opportunities, threats and issues (OTIs) was used.

Briefly, the process involved an extensive, but controlled, brainstorming session followed by a series of innovative strategy development workshops.

- A facilitator took the team systematically through every piece of relevant information available.

- Using brainstorming, the team tried to identify every conceivable opportunity, threat or internal issue associated with each item of information.

- The information was also then tested against a predetermined list of business behaviours and processes in an endeavour to entice additional and creative ideas out of the brainstorming.

- Using the DBCs and CSFs from the market model, strengths and weaknesses were added, thus turning the process into a SWOT.

- Similar ideas were merged and de-duplicated.

- Each idea was given two scores in the range of 1 to 9. The first ranked the probable financial impact, the second ranked the probability of success.

- The ideas were then grouped by the similarity of activity and where they had the same or an overlapping financial impact. This ensured that double-counting was eliminated and that opportunities and threats were offset as appropriate. Any one group of ideas would take on the highest single financial impact score and a reassessed probability of success score.

- If the resolution of an internal issue was a prerequisite for capturing an opportunity or overcoming a threat, then the issue plus associated costs and resources was included in the same group as the opportunity or threat. The norm was for a single issue to be attached to many groups.

- The groups were named and then ranked by both financial impact and probability of success. This provided a prioritized shortlist of imperatives that should deliver the maximum realizable benefits to both GlobalTech and its customers.

- Iterative discussions developed into an overall strategy with a number of prioritized sub-strategies.

- Each sub-strategy was supported by a documented description of the opportunity. At this stage encouragement was given to creating innovative yet simple implementation options that would maximize the chances of success. Each implementation option was supported by market, revenue and organizational impact data, associated issues, resources, costs and required control metrics.

- Board members were involved in an option selections and investment approvals process.

- Finally, the implementation programmes and project plans were created.

The strategy

The overall recommendation was to create a set of service deliverables tailored to the individual needs of each segment. These would be complemented by a set of premium add-ons that could be offered to the appropriate segments. By focusing on business process simplification during the design of the offering for each segment, redundancy was eliminated.

The objective of each offering was to increase customer satisfaction significantly with an emphasis on those items that would most positively impact loyalty. Some offerings were quite different from others, both in terms of the deliverable and internal processes that made it possible. This differentiation was also intended to create a measurable competitive advantage in a number of the market segments.

A key to the implementation of the project was a recommended change to the customer satisfaction metrics, so that they became an effective diagnostic tool for tuning the ongoing deliverables for each market segment.

Implementation

Throughout the project, the same core team had been intimately involved with each stage of the project. They guided the work and took on board the results. They delved deeply into the analysis and did their best to understand the markets, their customer requirements and likely competitive impacts. Finally, they worked hard at developing the proposed strategies. They thought buy-in had been achieved by being sponsored by a main board director.

The implementation roll-out across country boundaries became difficult. Each country wanted their say. They had different views of their customer needs and how things should be done in their country. They did not easily understand or even accept the findings of the research and the meaning of the outputs.

The majority of these internal barriers were eventually overcome. Inevitably there were compromises. These led the project team into believing that not all the market segments would be fully satisfied with the new offerings in all countries.

Case study – An insurance company's segments for annuity products

The market for annuities is dominated by individuals at the moment of retirement, who have built up a pensions pot and wish to convert some or all of it to an annuity which pays a guaranteed amount each year until they die. Consumers vary in their attitudes towards such financial decisions, though, on two key dimensions shown in the figure: their need for advice, from highly independent decision-takers to those who prefer to outsource their financial decisions; and their attitude to risk, from those who are very comfortable with risky investments such as shares to those who are risk-averse.

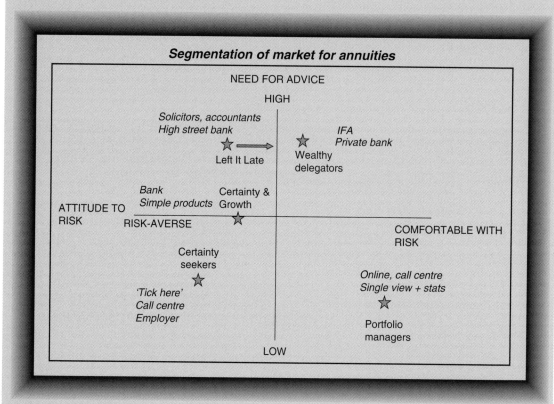

Segmentation of market for annuities

The largest segment is of 'certainty seekers', who wish to convert their pension pot to a guaranteed income with the least possible trouble. This segment typically takes out an annuity with their pension provider. A slightly less risk-averse segment is that seeking 'certainty and growth', representing people who are prepared to take some risk in order to achieve a greater return, for example by investing part of their pension pot in a stock market-based product. 'Wealthy delegators' have a sufficiently large fund that they feel able to take more risk with its investment, and prefer to delegate the fine decisions to an adviser. 'Portfolio managers' may have similar funds but vary in their attitudes from wealthy delegators, preferring to manage their own fund portfolio. Finally, the 'left it late' segment have little or no pension provision.

Clearly the segments vary not just in what product propositions they want but also in what channel to market will best suit them. Certainty seekers can be efficiently served through a simple 'tick here' form, perhaps backed up by a call centre to answer any questions, so as to keep the process as simple and reassuring as possible. Wealthy delegators need to be reached primarily via advice-providing intermediaries such as independent financial advisers. The 'left it late' segment are likely to turn to their bank, and perhaps also their accountant or solicitor. 'Portfolio managers', by contrast, want hard information rather than personal reassurance, and so the Internet backed up by skilled telephone-based advisers may combine a low cost of service with immediacy and a sense of control for the customer.

In this case the most actionable insight for the insurer, though, concerned the growing 'certainty and growth' segment. The company decided that while these customers were unlikely to use an independent financial adviser, they needed some face-to-face contact in order to select the right product and provide reassurance. So distribution via a bank seemed the best option. This led the company to develop a special product variant which was suitable for this channel, and working with a high street bank to distribute it.

Summary

Professional market segmentation is hard work and time-consuming.

It is worth repeating why market segmentation is so important. Correct market definition is crucial for:

1. share measurement

2. growth measurement

3. the specification of target customers

4. the recognition of relevant competitors

5. the formulation of marketing objectives and strategies.

The objectives of market segmentation are:

1. to help determine marketing direction through the analysis and understanding of trends and buyer behaviour

2. to help determine realistic and obtainable marketing and sales objectives

3. to help improve decision-making by forcing managers to consider in depth the options ahead.

7 Marketing planning Phase Two: the situation review (Part 2)

This is the second part of the situation review, in which we introduce some important tools such as life-cycle analysis and portfolio management to help service companies to understand better the factors they have to deal with in their strategies.

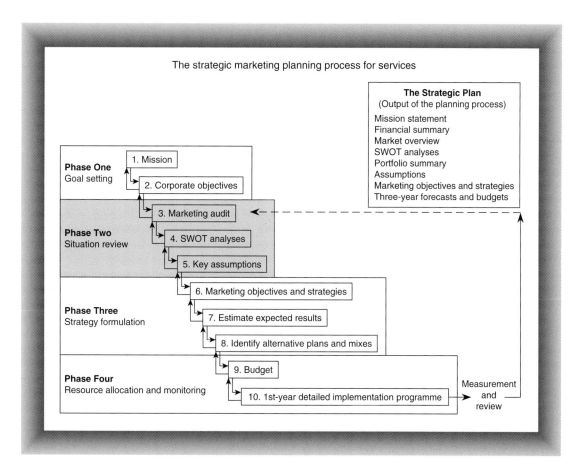

The strategic marketing planning process for services

The Strategic Plan
(Output of the planning process)
Mission statement
Financial summary
Market overview
SWOT analyses
Portfolio summary
Assumptions
Marketing objectives and strategies
Three-year forecasts and budgets

Phase One
Goal setting

1. Mission
2. Corporate objectives

Phase Two
Situation review

3. Marketing audit
4. SWOT analyses
5. Key assumptions

Phase Three
Strategy formulation

6. Marketing objectives and strategies
7. Estimate expected results
8. Identify alternative plans and mixes

Phase Four
Resource allocation and monitoring

9. Budget
10. 1st-year detailed implementation programme

Measurement and review

Sub-audit 2 Competitive position

> In any market segment, there are likely to be one or two critical factors which are the key to success, when looked at from the customer's viewpoint.

There is empirical evidence that 20% of any given population can account for 80% of a result (Pareto's law). In the same way, just as 20% of customers can realize 80% of the sales revenue, or 20% of the possible causes can be responsible for 80% of the total rejects, then just 20% of the possible factors can account for 80% of customer satisfaction.

For example, in the fast-food restaurant business, although customers might seek a wide range of things, their overall satisfaction level can be attributed to just a few. These are called the critical success factors. Let us suppose that research showed these to be:

1. Served quickly (30%)

2. Always a seat (30%)

3. Clean surroundings (25%)

4. Reasonable choice (15%)

Market research should be used to establish customer preferences

It would also be possible to establish by research the relative importance of these factors, as shown by the figures in the brackets above. This means that these customers pay high regard to being served quickly and being able to find a seat. Cleanliness is not quite as important, and having a choice is lower still in their scale of priorities. With this information available, it becomes possible to make a comparison with the main competitors and establish the restaurant's relative strengths and weaknesses, as shown in Figure 7.1.

The first column of figures in Figure 7.1 represents raw scores out of 100, which reflect the extent to which the various fast-food restaurants comply with the listed critical success factors. This shows that, when it

	Weight	Our company	Competitor A	Competitor B
Served quickly	(.30) ×	80 = 24	70 = 21	60 = 18
Always a seat	(.30) ×	50 = 15	80 = 24	90 = 27
Cleanliness	(.25) ×	90 = 22.5	70 = 17.5	80 = 20
Reasonable choice	(.15) ×	90 = 13.5	60 = 9	60 = 9
TOTALS	1.00	75.0	71.5	74.0

Figure 7.1
Example of competitive advantage calculation

comes to speed of service, our company scores 80, which is better than the scores of 70 and 60 of the competitors. However, in terms of seating, our company scores the lowest.

The raw scores are multiplied by the weighting factors established earlier. By adding the adjusted scores, it is possible to arrive at a total which reflects the overall competitiveness. In the example, it shows that our company leads the field, with company B second. However, as all scores are a long way from the perfect 100, there is clearly room for improvement and if our company makes some improvements, it could easily lead the field by a considerable margin.

This type of analysis also discloses other useful information about how this might be achieved, as follows:

> - The seating arrangements must be improved in our company.
> - The speed of service can also be further improved.
> - Too much choice is being offered (hence slowing service and perhaps increasing costs).

This example has obviously been made simple to illustrate the point, yet the principles behind it can be translated into any type of business.

> As companies find themselves in increasingly fierce trading conditions, it becomes ever more important to be clear about competitive strengths and weaknesses,, which may, of course, vary by segment served.

We should stress here that this process, which effectively constitutes part of the strengths and weaknesses (SW) analysis of the SWOT (discussed later in this chapter), is fundamental to the setting of marketing objectives and strategies, so great attention should be paid to this process.

Great attention should be paid to completing SWOT analyses

Competitors will have already featured in analyses of the service's competitive advantage and possible positioning. In fact, like marketing planning itself, all the components considered at the audit stage are interrelated. For example, it is very difficult to consider the service product without connecting it to organizational strengths and weaknesses, competitor activity and the state of the environment at large. Nonetheless it is worthwhile, at least initially, considering the various sub-audits separately in order to bring discipline to the overall marketing audit.

The information which is most valuable in terms of the competitor audit is that which concerns the company's major rivals. To attempt to find out about every competitor would clearly be too costly and time-consuming. What is of particular interest will be knowledge about their:

- Goals and objectives
- Market place behaviour
- Market share
- Growth
- Service quality
- Positioning
- Operations and resources
- Marketing mix strategies.

Without being unethical in any way, much of this information can be gathered from competitors' publicity materials and annual reports, from analysing their communications strategy, from talking to their customers, studying their exhibition stands, carrying out specific market research studies, and so on. Indeed, much of the analysis described earlier in the section on the service audit could not be accomplished without access to pertinent information regarding competitor activity.

Each competitor's service offer and organization has to be put under close scrutiny in much the same way, and with equal rigour, as the company examines its own services, strategies and capabilities. To know about one's competitors is to be prepared.

The area of competition analysis, as a formal area of study, has developed greatly in the past decade.[1]

By carrying out the competitor audit thoroughly, the company can be proactive about the future, rather than being reactive and running the risk of finding itself beaten by the opposition.

Let us now look at the third aspect of the marketing audit.

Sub-audit 3 The environmental audit

While customers rightly occupy much of the attention of the external audit, there are other external factors which can also impact on the service company and, therefore, need to be taken into account. This is the purpose of the environmental audit.

At first sight, scanning the outside world is a daunting task for the marketer, as there is so much to consider that can have a potential

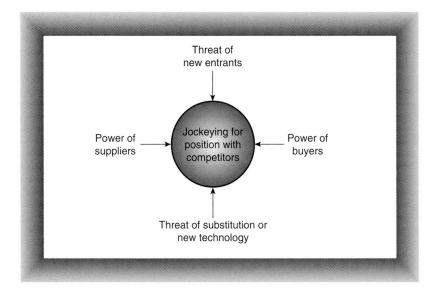

Figure 7.2
Strategic forces impacting on service organizations

influence on the organization's future success. However, it is essential to approach this audit in a fairly pragmatic way and look at only the most critical factors which can affect the business. There are two frameworks which can help with the task of focusing on these critical factors which we will now examine.

Some of the areas for consideration are highlighted by the work of Porter[2] who has identified five areas which will have significant impact on the company's profitability (see Figure 7.2). These are:

1. The success with which the company is *jockeying for position among current rivals*. This means that not only must the service company be aware of its own position, it must also understand its rivals' ambitions and strategies.

2. The environment must also be viewed from the perspective of *identifying new players*, perhaps foreign companies who are looking to expand, or cash-rich firms who are seeking to diversify into our field.

3. *New technology or substitute services* might also pose a threat or an opportunity to the company and should be reviewed on a regular basis.

4. *The power of buyers* might be increasing or decreasing and it is important for the company to understand what forces are at play for this to be happening.

5. Equally, the *power of suppliers* might be shifting in a way that is increasingly helpful or unhelpful to the company's ambitions. Again, the underlying environmental factors that cause this to be happening must be understood.

A detailed audit of these five forces will help to understand the prospect for future profitability of the service organization.

Another model which provides guidance is one that is discussed in Chapter 1, which described six market domains. These were:

- Customer markets (discussed above in Sub-audit 1)
- Referral markets
- Influence markets
- Recruitment markets
- Supplier markets
- Internal markets (this will be addressed in the organizational audit).

It clearly makes sense for the service company to appraise its position within these markets, to be aware of trends within them, and to decide whether or not it could benefit from changing the way it relates with them.

Finally, the environmental audit should address some of the political/ social/legal/economic factors that will have a significant influence on the business. For example, will government fiscal policy have an undue detrimental effect on the business? Are there legal changes or tax incentives which will make it more attractive for customers to buy? Will currency exchange rates work for or against the company? There are clearly a number of questions of this nature which have to be asked – and answered.

> We recommend that the environmental issues that need to be addressed should be specified in sufficient detail by each area to ensure that only relevant data and information are collected.

There is sometimes a blinkered approach adopted by service organizations with respect to the environmental audit. There is a naïve belief that external factors will affect all competitors equally and that, somehow, the status quo will be maintained. This is patently not true and companies that adopt such a posture may find themselves overtaken by their smarter and wiser contemporaries.

Environmental audits will be increasingly important in the future. Hamel and Prahalad[3] have argued that future opportunities are to be found in the intersection of changes in technology, logistics, regulation, demographics and geopolitics. They point to the opportunity that television channel CNN found for global 24-hour television. This grew out of changes in lifestyle (longer and less predictable working hours), changes in technology (Handicam video cameras and highly portable

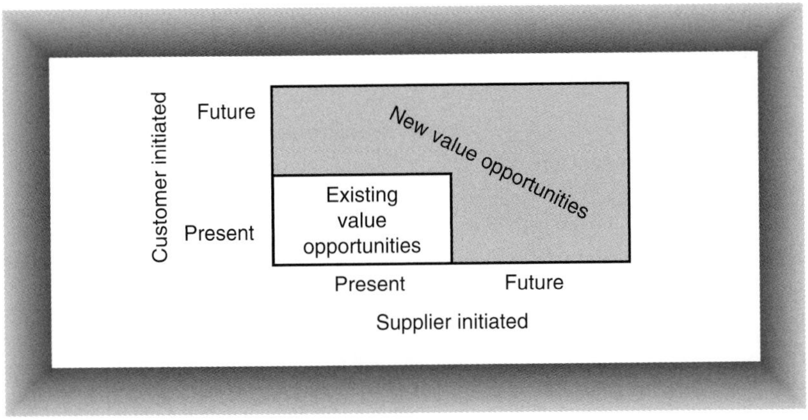

Figure 7.3
The danger of 'current focus'

satellite linkages), and changes in the regulatory environment (licensing and subsequent dramatic growth of cable television companies).

Successful companies such as 3M and Sony rely as heavily on their own creativity and intuition with respect to new market developments as they do on market research. Customers often cannot clearly articulate their future needs, and companies which do not think outside their traditional mindset may find their customers turning to those that do. Figure 7.3 emphasizes the danger of being overly concerned with 'current focus' at the expense of emerging or potential opportunities.

A good example of such creativity is the initiative launched by Starbucks when they introduced their mobile internet service in the early 2000s, enabling customers to have wireless internet connection in Starbucks' retail coffee outlets. This initiative, summarized in Figure 7.4, resulted in a significantly enhanced revenue stream through an initial subscription service as well as increased revenue in its core business. Furthermore, many of the customers using this service did so outside peak times. The revenue model changed over time. As wireless networks became more prevalent Starbucks reduced pricing and had a set fee for two hours of internet use. From 2010, the service in the US became free. Customers who have a registered Starbucks loyalty card can now get two hours of free wireless internet access. Wireless networks have now been replicated by other companies such as McDonald's, but Starbuck's have a 'first mover advantage' and customers have formed a 'Starbucks' habit'.

Sub-audit 4 Auditing the services and products

The services and products currently on offer are generally the things the company knows a lot about. However, sometimes it is possible to be too close to be truly objective about them. Nevertheless, the company must learn to be equally critical about them as it would for all other parts of the marketing audit. In this section we discuss auditing the organization's services and products and look at some tools, including positioning and lifecycle analysis, that are useful in undertaking this sub-audit.

Starbucks' wireless internet initiative

- Starbucks' 'T-Mobile Hot Spot service' offered wireless Internet connectivity in about 2,000 initial locations in the US and Europe in early 2000s.

- Used technology to enhance its core offer – the Starbucks experience.

- $5 for a cup of coffee and initially $49.99 per month for a wireless connection. Later they charged for two hour blocks of usage. From mid 2010 the service became free.

- The average network customer is in the store 45 minutes, which exceeds average, 90% outside peak times; they buy more products and create revenue from the wireless network subscriptions

- Starbucks aims at becoming the 'other place' in people's lives where they can be connected to the Internet.

- Wireless access replicated by others, but customers had formed a 'Starbucks' habit'.

Figure 7.4   Starbucks' 'T-Mobile Hot Spot Service'

Most organizations offer more than one service. Sometimes, these are variations on a theme, as when a restaurant offers a takeaway service, outside catering, and special functions, in addition to its normal provision. Equally, the company might offer distinctly different services, as with a leisure group which is involved in hotels, cinemas, golf complexes and airlines. Each service might come under attack from the same competitors, or there might be a range of different competitors who challenge each service. It is increasingly rare for a service organization to be in the position of a monopoly supplier, because services are relatively easy to duplicate, and they cannot be specified and patented in the same way as a product. Many former service monopolies are now subject to competition from new entrants.

How differentiated is the service product?

It has long been recognized that, when selling a service, the notion of a 'unique selling proposition' can give the salesperson a compelling advantage over competitors.

> However, the USP (as it is called in its abbreviated form) can only exist if the service's unique features can translate into unique benefits.

Therefore, one of the main purposes of the service product audit is to analyse the relative strengths and weaknesses of the company's range of services in comparison with those offered by competitors and help identify points of differential advantage.

Features, advantages and benefits

Sometimes there is confusion about the difference between features, advantages and benefits, even among sales staff. In order to clarify this, it should be remembered that features are the physical character-istics of the service. For example, in the case of a hotel, these might be:

- High-quality accommodation
- French cuisine
- Tennis and golf available
- Trained staff to look after children
- Friendly and informal atmosphere
- Above-average prices.

An advantage is what the service does. For example, high-quality accommodation provides luxuries similar to those in your own home.

A benefit is what the feature provides for the customer *that he or she seeks*. Thus, features and advantages can exist without customers, benefits never can. How a feature translates into an advantage can be illustrated thus:

Feature (what it is)	*Advantages* (what it does)
Tennis and golf available	You can unwind
	You can keep fit
	You can improve your game

However, even in this example, there are the seeds of a problem. Sup-pose some guests arrived at a hotel with the express notion of leaving the children and improving their golf, only to find that the course was filled with amateurs, with little experience, whose objective was to unwind. The former, quite naturally, would be very disappointed. This illustrates that, without knowing a lot about the *benefits* required by customers (from the customer audit), it can be difficult to make a sensible appraisal of the service product.

From what we have said, it is clear that a service organization needs to be able to identify the degree of differentiation of its services when

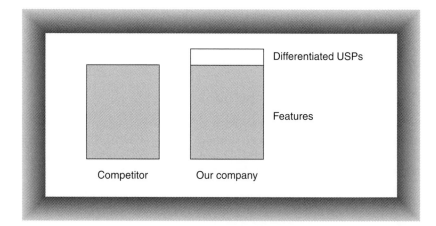

Figure 7.5
Comparison of service features

compared with those of its competitors. It is also essential to understand whether these differences match the benefits required by the target segments.

In Figure 7.5 a competitor's service product is shown to be matched by ours in every respect (the shaded areas). Yet, our company offers some added features which differentiate the service and provide unique selling propositions. These, however, are not necessarily benefits unless they appeal specifically to certain groups of customers.

Of course, with such a comparison, one could equally be disadvantaged when a competing service possesses features that ours does not have. In these circumstances, it would make good sense to try to make the lesser service more competitive by developing these added features, or something even better.

While it is a useful starting point to identify the differential features and advantages, we need to adopt a more systematic approach to benchmarking our products and those of our competitors, as shown in Figure 7.6.

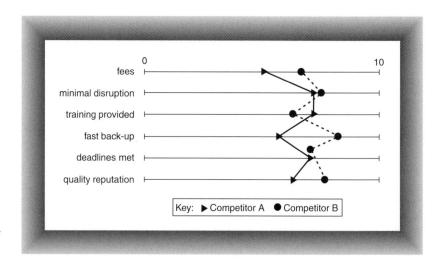

Figure 7.6
Example of comparative analysis – a software company

Figure 7.6 shows a comparison for a computer software company between their services and those of a competitor scored over a number of features, on a 0–10 scale. We can see that in terms of fees, Competitor B charges more. Both of them provide relatively little disruption to existing work practices, but A provides better training than Competitor B. By contrast, they underperform when it comes to back-up services and reputation for quality.

From an analysis like this, it becomes possible to see where a service product performs better or lags behind those against which it is competing. This should be considered not only on aggregate, but also the feature's relative importance within different market segments should be reviewed.

> It is a relatively small step from this type of diagnosis to setting 'benchmarks', or standards, which represent the best practice in each area, thereby measuring the service product against the highest possible relevant standards, not just those of the nearest competitor.

Many service companies are now adopting this type of approach in order to become more competitive.

Service product positioning

> Irrespective of what the company puts into its service product, it is the customer's perception which determines whether or not it is successful.

After all, with 'blind tests' on products, customers often cannot tell the difference between brand X and brand Y. Restore the original brand names, however, and it is another story. Such is the power of branding and the image and expectations it conveys. Because services are intangible, perceptions become ever more important.

It is possible to develop and communicate a differential advantage that makes the organization's service superior and distinctive in the perception of target customers. This is known as positioning. This differentiation can be based on objective criteria (which are fact-based) or subjective criteria (which are more concerned with image and communications).

Positioning can be based on objective or subjective criteria

Every service has the potential for being perceived as different by the customer, because buyers have different needs and are therefore attracted to different offers. The service organization should be keen to discover what differences it can offer which meet the following criteria[4]:

- *Importance* – The difference is highly valued by a sufficiently large or attractive market.

- *Distinctiveness* – The difference is distinctly superior to other services which are available.

- *Communicable* – It is possible to communicate the difference in a simple and strong way.

- *Superiority* – The difference cannot be easily copied by competitors.

- *Affordability* – Target customers will be willing to pay for this difference, i.e. it represents value to them.

- *Profitability* – The service company will achieve additional profits as a result of introducing the difference.

A service company wishing to reappraise its positioning (which already exists in the customers' minds, *even if* it is not the company's intention) should determine which attributes and differences to promote to its target customers. Some marketers advocate promoting a single benefit and striving to gain recognition as leader for that particular attribute. Others recommend that promoting more than one benefit will help to carve out a special niche which can be less easily contested by competitors. Whatever the choice, a successful positioning strategy must take into account existing customers' perceptions of competing market offerings. From this starting point, the company determines the attributes which customers value, but which are not being met by other services. It can then develop and promote these particular aspects of the services it offers. By adopting this approach, it follows that the service organization may have a different positioning strategy for each service and market segment.

While the main emphasis of this chapter is on the positioning of the *goods and services* delivered by the service organization, it must be remembered that positioning can be considered at several levels:

- *Industry positioning*, which seeks to improve customer perception of a service industry as a whole.

- *Organizational positioning*, which seeks to position the organization as a whole.

- *Product sector positioning*, which seeks to position a range of related products and services being offered by the service company.

- *Individual product or service positioning*, which addresses the positioning of specific services.

There should obviously be integration between these levels where companies are positioning at more than one level. Companies need not necessarily be concerned with all of these levels of positioning, just those which hold the prospect of giving it some commercial advantage. It is also advantageous to monitor what major competitors are doing, because shifts in their positioning strategy might require some level of response.

Figure 7.7 illustrates the levels of positioning which might be considered by a bank. In many ways the services and the service sector levels of one bank are very much like those of another, making it important to try to establish superior and differentiated positioning. For this reason, in recent years there have been considerable efforts made at the organizational positioning level, leading to a considerable proportion of total advertising spend being channelled into corporate advertising.

In spite of this, however, in the banking and insurance sectors, very few brands have managed to create a complete set of perceptions in people's minds. A question such as 'What does Barclays offer which is different from Lloyds TSB?' would probably lead to a puzzled silence. The large majority of consumers cannot differentiate significantly between the brands of major banks and insurance companies, in spite of the billions of pounds spent each year on advertising. Exceptions such as First Direct are rare, whereas in the airline industry, there is a clear differentiation between Virgin, Lufthansa and Singapore Airlines. The infamous British Airways advert 'We take more care of you' failed precisely because they forgot to tell their staff!

The challenges marketers face when establishing service brands is illustrated by the history of the UK insurance sector during the last 25 years. Characterized by complex products, pushy salespeople and little understanding of the role of marketing, this translated into a low

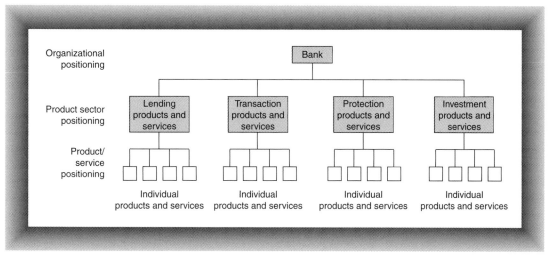

Figure 7.7   Examples of levels of positioning for a bank

degree of brand differentiation. Most companies appointed advertising agencies with a fast-moving consumer goods (FMCG) background, which led to name awareness adverts rather than communicating the benefits of the different insurance brands.

The result was that consumers regarded the products as commodities and intermediaries could therefore easily eliminate a brand from their product portfolio because no one really cared. Just imagine what would happen if Tesco tried to eliminate Heinz, Kellogg's, Mars and Persil from their portfolio!

The deregulation of the UK financial services market in 1986 increased the degree of competition in the insurance sector, allowing other players such as banks to enter the market. This decreased the importance of insurance brokers and responsibility for choosing insurance products moved inexorably towards the consumer. Insurance companies, however, failed to adapt their communication strategies, their point-of-sale material, or their follow-up literature in response to this new consumer power, which positioned the product's generic features in largely technical language at the expense of any competitive brand positioning.

With consumers' ever-increasing demand for better quality, enhanced service and greater convenience, banks and other financial services providers need to learn from companies like Tesco how to transform a commodity into a strong brand. This raises the question about what constitutes a powerful brand and why the financial services sector needs to move away from the traditional FMCG model.

First, a brand is a name, symbol or design on a product, service, person or place. A successful brand, however, creates sustainable competitive advantage for its owner through superior market performance because users perceive unique, relevant added values which match their needs most closely. As Tim Mason, the former Tesco UK marketing director, said: 'Pseudo brands are not brands. They are manufacturers' labels. They are "me too" and have poor positioning, quality and support.' IBM, Cadbury and Tesco are excellent examples of successful corporate brand names, while Persil, Nescafé, Dulux, Castrol GTX and Intel are excellent examples of product brand names.

Second, financial service companies need to realize that the brand is more important than the products they sell. Like the grocery market, banks lack a physical product. A service brand, therefore, is based entirely on the way the company does things and on its values and culture. This is because a customer's perception of the brand depends on individual interactions with the staff of the company.

So brand building needs to be undertaken from the bottom up and involves a profound analysis of every aspect of the interaction between the customer and the company.

Aviva, formerly Norwich Union, subtly and gradually changed its logo to replace lots of regional brands. But it also undertook top to bottom development training at Cranfield to underpin its rebranding with company-wide customer orientation.

The current lack of differentiated powerful brands in the financial services sector clearly illustrates the overall challenges associated with services branding and the need for a new mindset. A successful service brand has to be based on a clear competitive position, requiring the involvement of the entire company. The brand's positioning and benefits should then be communicated to target market segments, taking account of the differing preferences of the members of these segments. This is precisely what differentiates Tesco from ASDA and which accounts for their phenomenal success.

The process of positioning

Service positioning involves five action steps:

1. Determining levels of positioning
2. Identifying the key attributes which impact on selected segments
3. Locating these attributes on a positioning map
4. Evaluating other positioning options
5. Implementing the new positioning strategy.

It will be useful to look at each of these steps in more detail.

1. Determining levels of positioning

Often, the level (or levels) of positioning required is fairly self-evident, because it needs to be consistent with the organization's strategy for succeeding in a given market segment. If the service itself has a strong image or brand, it makes good sense to promote this continually. Conversely, the service might be more of a 'me-too' offer. In this latter case, organizational positioning can be a key strategy for success.

Positioning at a product sector level is now used widely among hotel chains with different types of hotel types. For example, Marriott Hotels have the following hotel 'products', each of which has different positioning:

Marriott Hotels & Resorts

JW Marriott Hotels & Resorts

Renaissance Hotels & Resorts

Courtyard

Residence Inn

Fairfield Inn

Marriott Conference Centers

TownePlace Suites

SpringHill Suites

Marriott Vacation Club International

The Ritz-Carlton

Ramada International Hotels & Resorts Marriott ExecuStay

Marriott Executive Apartments

Among these hotel offers, JW Marriott Hotels & Resorts are positioned as high-quality hotels with exquisite architectural detail and fine dining. Courtyard are hotels designed for business travellers: they provide all the essential services and amenities for business travellers to stay productive while on the road. For extended stays away from home, Residence Inn helps guests maintain a balance between work and life. Spacious suites with full kitchens combine home-like comforts with functionality. The Ritz-Carlton flagship hotels provide the ultimate in luxury and service with among the finest personal service and facilities in the world.

2. Identifying the key attributes

In order to identify the key attributes, it is important to focus on specific market segments and, in particular, on how the purchasing decisions are made. A consideration of the decision-making unit can also help identify key attributes.

Usually, research is carried out to identify the salient attributes and specific benefits required by a target market segment. What must be remembered is that customers make their purchase decision on the basis of *perceived* differences between competing offers. In themselves, what customers look for might not be the most important attributes as perceived by the service company. So, for example, customers' perceptions of a restaurant might rely more on how they are treated by the waiters than on the quality of the meal they are served. Similarly, the decision to invest in a private pension might owe more to the behaviour of the salesperson than to the investment record of the pension fund.

A range of techniques is available to the researcher charged with identifying key attributes. Most of these are computer-based and include perceptual mapping, factor analysis, discriminant function analysis, multiple correlation and regression analysis, and trade-off and conjoint analysis. However, these rather specialized techniques are in the province of the researcher rather than the marketing manager. For that reason, it is not our intention to elaborate on them here.[5]

3. Locating attributes on a positioning map

Usually, two dimensions are used on positioning maps and these are chosen to reflect key customer preferences. Thus, for example, if for a given service these attributes were price and quality it would be

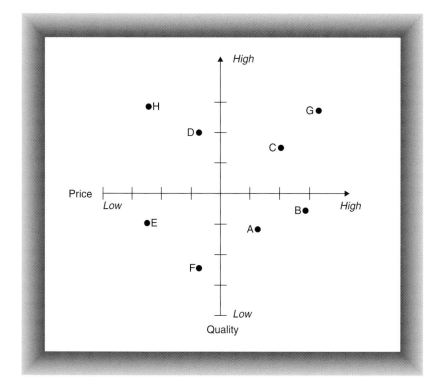

Figure 7.8
Example of a
positioning map

possible to construct a map as shown in Figure 7.8. On such a positioning map, it then becomes possible to plot the various competing services. Of course, in order to plot them accurately, it means that the two
axes are graduated in suitable scales. With such data available in this
form, it can be seen at a glance how the various services compare. For
example, companies E and H offer a service at a similar price, but the
latter provides a much higher level of quality. Similarly, companies H
and G provide almost identical quality, but G is far more expensive.

Positioning maps can be based on either objective or subjective attributes, or on some combination of the two. For example, a pensions company developed a map which had an objective axis ('proportion of
investments used to cover administration'), and a subjective axis
('friendly and courteous service').

In addition to allowing comparisons to be made, such maps can also
indicate the area of core demand, which in Figure 7.8 would be the top
left-hand quadrant, i.e. high quality/low price – the most attractive
combination for customers. Knowing the core demand area enables
the company to devise how it can best reposition any of its services
which fall outside it. The repositioning task might require a significant
communications and advertising campaign being used to alert customers to the changes which are taking place.

Sometimes the area of core demand is not quite as obvious as in the
example above. An example of this might be where there are different

segments with different preferences. In these circumstances, further analysis is required and a technique which was mentioned earlier, i.e. cluster analysis, can be used to identify groups with similar interests. From this, it becomes possible to identify the positioning dimensions which are significant to different market segments.

In highly mature markets, brands are likely to be positioned close to one another, thus indicating that the basic functional or physical characteristics are less likely to be the sole basis on which a product or service is selected.

This brings us to the final component, brand personality. Stephen King said that a product is something that is made in a factory; a brand is something that is bought by a consumer. A product can be copied, but a successful brand is unique and, particularly in mature markets, is a key discriminator in the marketplace.

Brand personality is a useful descriptor for the total impression that consumers have of brands, and in many ways brands are like people, with their own physical, emotional and personality characteristics. Brands are very similar, in that they are a complex blend of physical, emotional and personality characteristics. Thus two brands can be very similar in terms of their functions, but have very different personalities.

For example, just as small Fords, Peugeots, VWs and Fiats all perform about the same along the functional dimensions of size, speed and price, each one has a totally different personality, which is the result of a blend of three sorts of appeal: sensual, rational and emotional. In the same way, any Virgin product or service is seen in a very different light from, say, a British Airways product or service.

Sensual appeal, that is, how the product or service looks, feels, sounds and so on, can have an important influence on buying behaviour. It is easy to imagine how this appeal can differ in the case of, say, cigarettes, or cars.

Rational appeal, that is, how the product or service performs, what they contain and so on, can also have an important influence on buying behaviour.

Emotional appeal, however, is perhaps the most important and has a lot to do with the psychological rewards the products or services offer, the moods they conjure up, the associations they evoke and so on. It is easy to imagine the overt appeal of certain products as being particularly masculine, or feminine, or chic, or workmanlike, or flashy. The point is that, for any brand to be successful, all these elements have to be consistent, as they will all affect the brand's personality and it is this personality, above all else, that represents the brand's totality and makes one brand more desirable, or appealing, than another.

Put at its simplest, it is a brand's personality that converts a commodity into something unique and enables a higher price to be charged for it.

4. Evaluating positioning options

There are three broad options:

(**a.**) *Strengthening current position against competitors*

Ideally, this is done in a way which avoids a head-on attack. A classic example of this was the campaign of Avis car rental, who created a positive benefit from being number two behind market leaders Hertz. 'Avis is only No. 2, so why go with us? We try harder!' they proclaimed. Not only was this seen as truthful, it also appealed to people's natural sympathy for the underdog.

(**b.**) *Identifying an unoccupied position on the map*

This option seeks to find a gap in the market. Using this approach, Virgin Airlines established a foothold in the business passenger market with its 'upper class' in a UK market dominated by British Airways. By striving to provide a better all-round service to customers in this segment, this small airline has developed an intensively loyal and growing group of 'advocates'.

(**c.**) *Repositioning the competition*

In the 1992 General Election in the UK, the Conservative Party was under considerable pressure because it was being seen as the party responsible for creating unemployment and dismantling the National Health Service. For its part, the Labour Party claimed that it would invest in manufacturing, the infrastructure and save the Health Service, all policies with high voter appeal. However, the Conservatives managed to reposition the Labour Party from being investors to being money raisers, i.e. the 'party which stands for high taxation'. This message was repeated with regularity and in no small way helped to reverse what was, according to opinion polls, a potential lost cause. In later elections, however, the Labour Party was able to position itself as the anti-sleaze party, to great effect, only to fall into the same trap as the Conservatives once in office. Their positioning, based on the claim that the economy was in safe hands, was totally destroyed by the 2008 recession.

Regardless of which positioning option is chosen, in order to enhance or sustain a position the following guidelines[6] should be observed:

> ● The positioning should be meaningful for the target market segment.
>
> ● The positioning must be believable. Outrageous claims to be the biggest, or the best, which are clearly untrue will prove to be counter-productive.
>
> ● The positioning must be unique. Companies must find a positioning where they can consistently perform better than their competitors in a given market.

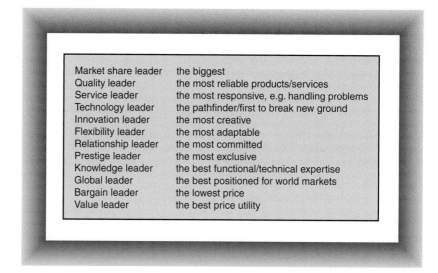

Market share leader	the biggest
Quality leader	the most reliable products/services
Service leader	the most responsive, e.g. handling problems
Technology leader	the pathfinder/first to break new ground
Innovation leader	the most creative
Flexibility leader	the most adaptable
Relationship leader	the most committed
Prestige leader	the most exclusive
Knowledge leader	the best functional/technical expertise
Global leader	the best positioned for world markets
Bargain leader	the lowest price
Value leader	the best price utility

Figure 7.9
Examples of
positioning strategies

Figure 7.9 illustrates ways in which uniqueness might be converted into positioning.

5. Implementing positioning

The new or reinforced positioning strategy needs to be communicated in all implicit and explicit interactions with target customers. This involves the service company, its staff, its policies and image all conveying a consistent message which reflects the desired positioning. This has to carry through in all of the tactical marketing and sales activities.

So, for example, for British Airways truly to be 'the world's favourite airline', its entire staff had to refocus on how they viewed the passengers. Staff had to actually care about the customer and, in turn, the airline itself had to demonstrate a caring attitude towards its employees. Its much publicized 'Putting the Customer First' campaign was an integral part of a coordinated internal and external marketing strategy. Today, however, British Airways has a massive credibility mountain to climb as a result of the long-running strikes by cabin staff and it remains to be seen whether their positioning strategy will survive.

> It must never be forgotten that, like the service itself, a positioning strategy may have a limited lifespan. This means that it should be examined from time to time to ensure that it has not become outdated and that it is still relevant to its target markets.

Because it permits market opportunities to be identified by considering positions which are not met by competitors' services, positioning helps to influence the improvement and redesign of existing offers

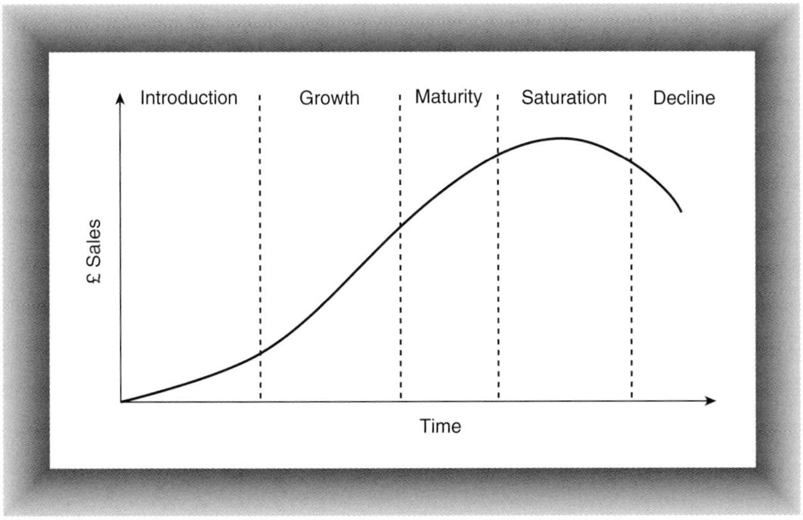

Figure 7.10
The lifecycle curve

and the development of new services. It also allows consideration of competitors' possible moves and responses, thereby providing a further input to strategy formulation.

> Above all, positioning involves giving the target market segment the reason for buying your services, which is clearly the whole purpose of marketing.

The concept of lifecycles

Another key marketing diagnostic tool, which is extremely useful for the purpose of determining appropriate marketing objectives and strategies for the services of an organization, is lifecycle analysis. Historians of technology have observed that many technical functions grow exponentially until they come up against some natural limiting factor, which causes growth to slow down and eventually decline, as one technology is replaced by another. There is empirical evidence which shows that this same phenomenon also applies to products and services.

By plotting the sales of a service over time, the lifecycle curve, shown in Figure 7.10, can be established.

This curve is characterized by five different phases:

1. *Introduction* – Here, there is a slow growth in sales as the new service struggles to get known and accepted.

2. *Growth* – If the service is successful, its sales take off as repeat purchases are made and customers become aware

> of it. Not all new services survive long enough to reach this phase. Moreover, the growth potential attracts other companies into this field and so competition also increases.
>
> 3. *Maturity* – Since all markets are finite, the rapid growth rate of the earlier phase begins to slow down.
>
> 4. *Saturation* – The rate of sales growth eventually levels out. Generally, there are too many firms competing for too little business at this stage. As a result, price wars may break out and there are casualties, or tactical withdrawals, among the competitive companies.
>
> 5. *Decline* – Finally, the market itself falls into decline.

These phases in the lifecycle concept suggest that if a product or service is introduced to the market successfully, then the momentum of buying will increase over time. Consumers will try the product or service and will then often repeat their purchase decision. They will also pass on information about the product to others who, in turn, will test the product. However, the market will eventually reach its peak. As the market matures, there are many firms in the market place and price wars are common as competition develops for market share. Eventually, some firms will be forced out of the market, with the most competitive ones surviving. The market will gradually decline as alternative products are offered and fashions change. The market may be sustained for a small volume, with few producers, though this will often be difficult as economies of scale can be lost.

| Lifecycle analysis can be a useful diagnostic tool

It is possible to extend the lifecycle by taking tactical actions to combat falling sales such as reducing prices, promoting harder, etc., and also by strategic actions which fundamentally reposition the usage of the service. The 'no frills' airline services in the USA, which have become a viable alternative to motor car travel, are a good example of this.

The lifecycle has been much written about in marketing literature during the last three decades and, from the management viewpoint, can focus attention on likely future sales patterns if no corrective actions are taken. More importantly, the various life phases carry with them implications for changes in the way the service is promoted and priced. Indeed, all aspects of the marketing mix need to be adapted over the life of a service. We shall examine, in Chapter 8, how the marketing strategy for a service should be largely determined by its position in its lifecycle.

An understanding of lifecycles of *services businesses* (as well as their services) is also important. The study of lifecycles in services, in this regard, has been relatively limited to date. However, one study of multisite service firms' lifecycles identified five stages, as follows[7]:

1. *Entrepreneurial stage:* where an innovator offers a service at a limited (often one) number of locations.

2. *Multisite rationalization:* where successful service entrepreneurs add a limited number of locations.

3. *Growth:* where a period of rapid expansion occurs, often through the purchase of competitors or franchising or licensing arrangements.

4. *Maturity:* where the rate of growth is reduced through factors such as changing demographics, increased competition, or changing customer tastes.

5. *Decline/regeneration:* where either successful extension of the service concept occurs, or the service firm enters a stage of decline and degeneration.

The concept of lifecycles is useful, but it should be remembered that products or services do not always follow this idealized pattern. The lifecycle concept is helpful as a descriptive model in trying to understand the dynamics of markets. However, it has less value as a predictive model.

In considering lifecycles, we also need to differentiate between the service category, the service subcategory and the service brand. For example, if we take the overnight accommodation market (a service category) it may have a considerably different life from that of business hotels, or motels (a service subcategory). Individual brands, e.g. Stakis Country Club Hotels (a service brand), within a category may also exhibit their own individual lifecycle behaviour.

The stage where the service firm is in its lifecycle needs to be considered carefully and the firm should be aware of different issues and problems it may encounter during the different lifecycle stages. This process can focus attention on future sales patterns and will have a bearing on the key elements to be emphasized within the marketing mix.

Difficulties with drawing a lifecycle are normally connected to the complex question of market share measurement. **_Market share_** is the proportion of volume or value of an actual market rather than with a potential market.

● Definition: Market share is the proportion of volume or value of an actual, not a potential, market

One of the most frequent mistakes made by companies that do not understand what market share really means is to assume that their company has only a small share of some market. However, if the company is commercially successful, it probably has a much larger share of a smaller market segment.

The point to remember is that the lifecycle concept is not an academic figment of the imagination, but a hard reality that is ignored at great risk. Many commercial failures can be traced back to a naïve assumption on the part of managements that what was successful as a policy at one time will continue to be successful in the future.

Diffusion of innovation

An interesting and useful extension of the product or service lifecycle is what is known as the 'diffusion of innovation'. Diffusion is:

1. The adoption

2. of new products or services

3. over time

4. by consumers

5. within social systems

6. as encouraged by marketing.

Diffusion refers to the cumulative percentage of potential adopters of a new product or service product over time. Everett Rogers examined some of the social forces that explain the product/service lifecycle. The body of knowledge often referred to as 'reference theory' (which incorporates work on group norms, group pressures, etc.) helps explain the snowball effect of diffusion. Rogers found that the actual rate of diffusion is a function of a product's or service's:

1. Relative advantage (over existing products/services)

2. Compatibility (with lifestyles, values, etc.)

3. Communicability (is it easy to communicate?)

4. Complexity (is it complicated?)

5. Divisibility (can it be tried out on a small scale before commitment?).

Diffusion is also a function of the newness of a product or service itself, which can be classified broadly under three headings:

- Continuous innovation, e.g. the new miracle ingredient.

- Dynamically continuous innovation, e.g. a 'do-it-yourself' property conveyancing kit.

- Discontinuous, e.g. space tourism.

However, Rogers found that not everyone adopts new products or service products at the same time, and that a universal pattern emerges, as shown in Figure 7.11.

From the real lifecycle analysis shown in Figure 7.12 it can be seen that this retailer was never particularly innovative in buying in new

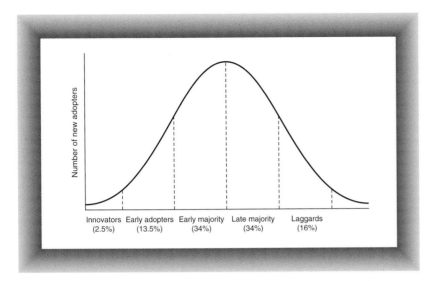

Figure 7.11
Non-cumulative diffusion pattern of innovation curve

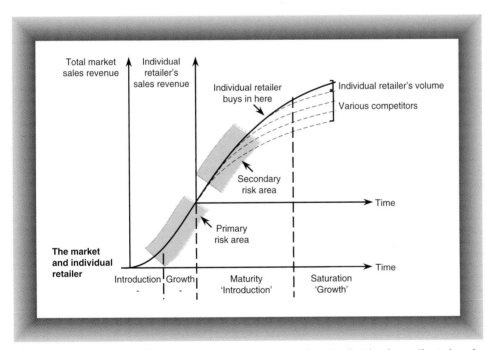

Figure 7.12   Product lifecycle at total market and an individual retailer's level

products. In fact, it shows that he tended to buy in the product at the maturity stage, so giving the market another 'kick'. His policy was then to stock it in depth, price it low, and put a lot of promotional advertising effort behind it. A quick glance at Figure 7.13, however, reveals that, *by mistake*, this retailer occasionally bought into a range of merchandise somewhat earlier in its lifecycle. The trouble was that he still stocked in depth, priced low and promoted heavily, thus giving away margin unnecessarily.

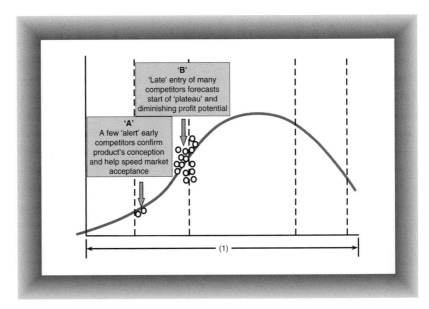

Figure 7.13
Lifecycle illustrating
the potential
advantage of entering
a market early

In general the innovators think for themselves and try new things (where relevant); the early adopters, who have status in society, are opinion leaders and they adopt successful products, including service products, making them acceptable and respectable; the early majority, who are more conservative and who have slightly above average status, are more deliberate and only adopt products that have social approbation; the late majority, who are below average status and sceptical, adopt products much later; and the laggards, with low status, income, etc., view life through the rear mirror and are the last to adopt products.

This particular piece of research can be very useful, particularly for advertising and personal selling. For example, if we develop a typology for innovative customers, we can target our early advertising and sales effort specifically at them. Once the first 3% of innovators have adopted our product or service, there is a good chance that the early adopters will try it, and once the 10–12% point is reached, the champagne can be opened, because there is a good chance that the rest will adopt the product.

We know, for example, that the general characteristics of opinion leaders show that they are venturesome, socially integrated, cosmopolitan, socially mobile, and privileged. So we need to ask ourselves what the specific characteristics of these customers are in our particular market. We can then tailor our advertising and selling message specifically for them.

It can, however, also be both a practical diagnostic and forecasting tool. There follows a worked example of how forecasts, and eventually strategic marketing plans, were developed from the intelligent use of the diffusion of innovation curve in respect of computerized business systems for the construction industry in the UK.

1st estimate of market size	
1. Number of contracting firms (Department of Environment, Housing and Construction)	160,596
2. Number of firms employing 4–79 direct employees	43,400
3. Exclude painters, plasterers, etc.	6,100
4. Conservative estimate of main target area	37,300 (1) or 23% of total
2nd estimate of market size	
5. Using the Pareto (80/20 rule) likelihood that 20% will be main target area, i.e. 160,596 20%	32,000 (2)
3rd estimate of market size	
6. Total number of firms in construction industry (Business Statistics Office)	217,785
7. Number of firms classified by turnover from £100,000 to £1,000,000 (£K) 100–249 (£K) 250–499 (£K) 500–999 (£K)	 26,698 10,651 5,872 43,221 (3)
8. Company's best estimate of size of target market	37,300
9. Company's estimate of the number of micro installations in this segment	3,500 (9.4%)

Plotting this on the diffusion of innovation curve shows:

- Penetration of innovators and early adopters has taken four years. Adoption rate will now accelerate. It will probably be complete within one year.

● *One-year* balance of early adopters $= 6.6\% = 2{,}462$ firms $=$ installed base of 5,968. Sales objective $= 360$ installations plus present base of $400 = 760 = 12.7\%$ market share.

It will be seen from this that three independent estimates were made of the market size in order to establish the current position on the diffusion of innovation curve.

In contrast, a Dutch computer supplier attempted to launch hardware and software into the motor trade using an undifferentiated product at a high sales price. An elementary study would have indicated that this market is already well into the late majority phase, when price and product features become more important. Not surprisingly, the product launch failed.

Retailers need to understand this phenomenon because it relates specifically to the types of customer that frequent their businesses and to the category of products or services in question and where they are on the diffusion of innovation curve. A business not frequented by innovators and early adopters is hardly likely to do particularly well with products or services that are relatively new to the market.

Portfolio of services

While it is quite feasible for a company to operate with a single service (in fact, most new firms start in this way), the lifecycle concept suggests that in the long term innovation is necessary for services which are in decline. Again, the lifecycle curve can provide useful guidance about the best times to introduce (and remove) services from the company's 'portfolio'. If this is done astutely, then the company can meet its objectives by balancing sales growth, cash flow and risk across its range of services (Figure 7.14).

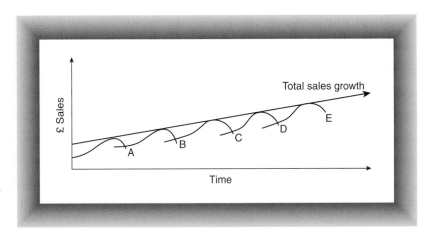

Figure 7.14
How successive services can add to sales growth

> It is, therefore, essential that the portfolio of services is reviewed 'regularly' and that the strategic implications of adding, deleting or promoting existing services are considered in their totality.

How this is done will be covered in detail in the next chapter, since it is central to the setting of marketing objectives and formulating the best strategies to meet them.

Sub-audit 5 The organizational audit

Most organizations are not equally strong in all parts of their business. The sales force might be second to none in some areas, yet the company may fall down in others. The company might be great at coming up with new ideas for services, yet be slow to exploit them.

> The organizational audit sets out to take stock of the company's strengths and weaknesses in terms of how they influence current operations and how they might help or hinder future growth.

The purpose of an organizational audit is to focus on those aspects of organizational performance that have a positive or a negative effect on business performance. There are several areas that should be considered:

Skills

- What skills does the company have?
- How do these compare with competitors?
- What do they best equip the company for?
- What essential skills are lacking or underrepresented?
- What will happen if this skill shortage is not made good?
- If the company heads in a new direction, to what extent will the current skill base be a limiting factor?
- At what organizational level are essential skills in short supply – e.g. strategic, managerial, operational?

There are many questions of this nature which can be asked. In turn, they might focus attention upon the company's recruitment policy and its manpower, training and development.

Resources

In addition to people, how adequate are the resources of the service organization? A number of questions might be asked which, in turn, reflect on past, present and future investment policy. Indeed, resources such as the working conditions could have a direct bearing on the company's capacity to recruit the right kind of people. Equally, the availability of the right data processing systems and equipment can greatly facilitate the availability of data and information into the planning processing.

Systems and procedures

In preparing for marketing planning, the adequacy of the company's management and marketing information systems needs to be evaluated. In addition, there are a number of other procedural issues which could have an impact on business success. For example:

- How are sales leads generated?
- How are they followed up?
- How is the service delivered?
- How are queries and complaints handled?
- How is advertising evaluated?
- How is customer service managed?
- How are new services developed?
- How is lost business analysed and evaluated?

Again, this list will be very much longer for some service organizations. The overriding concern should be to evaluate all such relevant systems and procedures and to identify ways of making them more effective in the context of the company's overall performance.

Roles and relationships

Often organizational problems occur, not because of any of the things listed above, but because people are unclear about the role they are expected to play and how they relate to others. For example, customer contact staff might be unaware of company policy regarding how they should treat customers. Alternatively, interdepartmental rivalry inside the company might get in the way of delivering the best possible service.

> Equally, an overreliance on written rules and job descriptions can lead to the organization getting bogged down in bureaucratic 'red tape' and a lack of people empowered to solve customer problems.

The marketing audit – conclusions

These, then, are some of the issues which have to be addressed in the marketing audit. To find answers to the external factors might result in the company using external market researchers. In some cases, the professionalism and unbiased viewpoint they bring ensures that the information they provide is superior to what might be gathered by the company's own staff.

When a marketing audit is undertaken by internal staff it is useful to have some guidelines, by way of example, to guide the audit process. As an example, a fairly comprehensive marketing audit checklist is shown in Figure 7.15.

Different service organizations from different service sectors will need to develop different guidelines and checklists appropriate to their own businesses. A list of key audit questions developed by an accounting firm is provided in Figure 7.16, as a contrast to the more general list in Figure 7.15.

Those wishing to review more detailed checklists are referred to Wilson.[8] Those interested in reading further on the marketing audit process should see McDonald and Leppard, and Parmerlee.[9]

When the marketing audit is completed, it is possible to move on to the next stage of the planning process.

Step 4 SWOT analyses

If the previous stage could be likened to providing all the pieces of a jigsaw puzzle, the SWOT analysis takes these and tries to make a picture which makes sense to all those within the company.

> The SWOT analysis is one of the most critical stages in marketing planning

It must be stressed here that it is *only* the SWOT analyses that actually appear in the strategic marketing plan itself. This section is, therefore, extremely important and should be read in conjunction with Figure 4.5 in Chapter 4.

These analyses should highlight internal differential strengths and weaknesses *vis-à-vis* competitors, together with key external

EXTERNAL (opportunities and threats)

Business and economic environment

Economic	Inflation, unemployment, energy, price, volatility, materials availability, etc.	as they affect your business
Political/fiscal/legal	Nationalization, union legislation, taxation, duty increases, regulatory constraints (e.g. trade practices, advertising, pricing).	as they affect your business
Social/cultural	Education, immigration, emigration, religion, environment, population distribution and dynamics (e.g. age distribution, regional distribution), changes in consumer lifestyles, etc.	as they affect your business
Technological	Application of technology which could profoundly affect the economics of the industry (e.g. methods and systems, availability of substitutes).	as they affect your business
Intracompany	Capital investment, closures, strikes, etc.	as they affect your business

The market

Total market	Size, growth, and trends (value, volume).
Market characteristics	Developments and trends. *Services*: principal services bought; service characteristics. *Prices*: price levels and range; terms and conditions of sale; normal trade practices; official regulations, etc. *Distribution*: principal method of distribution. *Channels*: principal channels; purchasing patterns (e.g. types of services bought, prices paid); purchasing ability; geographical location; profits; needs; tastes; attitudes; decision-makers; bases of purchasing decision; etc. *Communication*: principal methods of communication, e.g. sales force, advertising, direct response, exhibitions, public relations. *Industry practices*: e.g. trade associations, government bodies, historical attitudes, interfirm comparisons.
Competition	*Industry structure*: make-up of companies in the industry, major market standing/reputation; extent of excess capacity; distribution capability; marketing methods; competitive arrangements; extent of diversification into other areas of major companies in the industry; new entrants; mergers; acquisitions; bankruptcies; significant aspects; international links; key strengths and weaknesses. *Industry profitability*: financial and non-financial barriers to entry; industry profitability and the relative performance of individual companies; structure of operating costs; investment; effect on return on investment of changes in price; volume; cost of investment; source of industry profits; etc.

Figure 7.15 Marketing audit checklist for services (expanded)

INTERNAL (strengths and weaknesses)

Own company
Sales (total, by geographical location, by industrial type, by customer, by product/service)
Market shares
Profit margins
Marketing procedures
Marketing organization
Sales/marketing control data
Marketing mix variables as follows:

Market research	Exhibitions
Service development	Selling
Service range	Sales aids
Service quality	Point of sale
Unit of sale	Advertising
Stock levels	Sales promotion
Distribution	Public relations
Dealer support	After-sales service
Pricing, discounts, credit	Customer service
People	Training
Processes	

Operations and resources
Marketing objectives
Are the marketing objectives clearly stated and consistent with marketing and corporate objectives?
Marketing strategy
What is the strategy for achieving the stated objectives? Are sufficient resources available to achieve these objectives?
Are the available resources sufficient and optimally allocated across elements of the marketing mix?
Structure
Are the marketing responsibilities and authorities clearly structured along functional, product, end-user, and territorial lines?
Information system
Is the marketing intelligence system producing accurate, sufficient and timely information about developments in the marketplace?
Is information gathered being used effectively in making marketing decisions?
Planning system
Is the marketing planning system well conceived and effective?
Control system
Do control mechanisms and procedures exist within the group to ensure planned objectives are achieved, e.g. meeting overall objectives?
Functional efficiency
Are internal communications within the group effective?
Interfunctional efficiency
Are there any problems between marketing and other corporate functions?
Is the question of centralized versus decentralized marketing an issue in the service company?
Profitability analysis
Is the profitability performance monitored by service, served markets, etc., to assess where the best profits and biggest costs of the operation are located?
Cost-effectiveness analysis
Do any current marketing activities seem to have excess costs?
Are these valid or could they be reduced?

Figure 7.16   Marketing audit checklist for an accounting firm

opportunities and threats. A summary of reasons for good and bad performance should be included. It should be interesting to read, be concise, and include only relevant and important information. The analysis should be highly creative, since a fresh and less obvious approach holds a greater prospect of distancing the company from its competitors.

> A well-reasoned SWOT analysis provides the basis for setting objectives and strategies.

Figure 7.17 shows the layout that is recommended for SWOT analyses, which should, of course, be carried out initially on each segment identified in the marketing audit. This is important, because if managers try to do an audit on the overall company, they will only succeed in listing generalities and will fail to get to grips with the real factors that are driving the business. (Guidelines on completing the objectives and strategies part of this form will be given in the next chapter.)

It should be stressed that when inserting CSFs in Figure 7.17 (heading 2), under no circumstances should vague terms such as

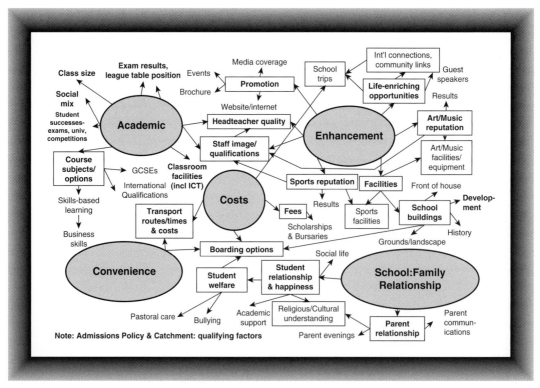

Figure 7.17   Five key buying factors for UK independent schools

- Personality and vision of head
- Exam results
- Class size
- League table position (compared to regional competitors)
- Student academic successes (Oxbridge, major universities, competitions)
- Academic planning: A level, IB, pre-U; IGCSE? New subjects?
- Flexibility of subject choice
- Academic history (results over a number of years)
- Quality/knowledge/experience of staff
- Facilities for teaching and learning
- Learning opportunities outside mainstream subjects (could be vocational skills)
- Reporting procedures
- Innovations in teaching and learning

Figure 7.18
Academic factors

'customer service' be entered, as this could mean virtually anything from on-time-in-full delivery to answering the phones in five seconds. It is in order to enter such terms only if the meaning is spelt out clearly elsewhere.

For example, in the independent schools sector in the UK, while Figure 7.18 shows five major headings, Figures 7.19 and 7.20 list in great detail what the components of each are – and of course the relative emphasis on each component will vary by segment.

Figure 7.21 provides a few guidelines on the criteria for the acronym SWOT.

When these have been completed, a summary of the SWOT analysis can be laid out in the traditional manner shown in Figure 7.22. However, it is our view that SWOT analyses performed in this manner, *ab initio*, and only for the organization as a whole, are of relatively limited use. To improve the value of SWOT analysis we make several suggestions.

First, the SWOT analysis can be made more productive by extending it as shown in Figure 7.23. This extended form can be developed like a decision tree where each individual element may have several implications ('which means') and each implication may have several recommended actions. It is important to add some explanatory notes, where appropriate, to enable the reader to understand the full portent of the analysis.

- Facilities
  - **Buildings and grounds**
  - **Specialist facilities** (floodlit astroturf, ICT centre, theatre)
  - **Development planning**: plans for new/better facilities
- People
  - **Quality of staff** (teaching and specialist – i.e. sports/music coaching)
  - Quality of staff recruitment
  - Front of house/customer focus
  - **Understanding/delivery of mission** by all staff
  - Strong **alumni association**
  - Active **parents' association**
- 'Preparation for Life'
  - Active **careers department**
  - Expertise in **university entrance support**
  - **Work experience, Young Enterprise**, Duke of Edinburgh's Award, Sports Leader's Award, etc.
- Community
  - **Links** through activities (charity fundraising, visits to elderly, working with handicapped, etc.)
  - **Hire of facilities** (pool, theatre, sports, hall for weddings and parties)
  - Compliant with **Charities Act**
  - **Local reputation**
- International links and opportunities
  - Language visits
  - Trips and expeditions
  - Other learning opportunities
- Technology
  - Up-to-date, campus-wide access
  - Resources online to enhance study
- Environmental
  - Clear **policy** and aims
  - Strong **student involvement in campaigns and issues**
  - Clear **priority status** within School – put into action

Figure 7.19 Enhancement/attractiveness factors

Second, the SWOT should be undertaken at several levels:

- For the organization as a whole
- For each major market segment
- For each major service or product
- For the competition.

- **Strengths**
  - It can create value for the organization and customers
  - It is unique
  - It is inimitable
  - It is lasting
- **Opportunities**
  - It is large
  - It is accessible
  - It is lasting

- **Weaknesses**
  - It is meaningful to the customer
  - It is unique
  - It is difficult to fix
- **Threats**
  - It is significant
  - It is lasting

Figure 7.20
SWOT

Finally, the value of SWOT analysis can be improved by quantification.

One way of calculating which opportunities and threats should appear in the SWOT analysis is to consider them from the point of view of their impact and their likelihood of occurring. Using these criteria, opportunities and threats can be appraised using a 'risk' matrix as illustrated in Figure 7.24.

Even though there may be an element of subjectivity in positioning either threats or opportunities on this matrix, it is clear that those which appear in the top right-hand boxes (or closely adjacent to them) are emphasized in the SWOT analysis.

Step 5 Key assumptions

The previous discussion has stressed the need for fact-finding and data gathering to be the foundations upon which the marketing plan is built. However, it is impossible to start with the facts without also starting out with some assumptions. Assumptions establish the basis for objective and strategy setting. Facts and assumptions can become blurred at times, to the extent that one can be mistaken for the other, and it is important to distinguish between them.

To avoid unstated assumptions being ignored, it is important to state them explicitly. By making them explicit, it becomes possible to check and monitor assumptions to be certain that they are, and remain, valid, and if not, to develop contingency plans to deal with them.

It is important to make assumptions explicit

The purpose of the key assumptions step is to identify explicitly those factors which will be critical to the success or failure of the strategic marketing plan. Key assumptions need to be considered in terms of how they impact on the organization as a whole and

Strategic planning exercise (SWOT analysis)

(Note: This form should be completed for each product/market segment under consideration)

1 SBU description
Here, describe the market for which the SWOT is being done

2 Critical success factors
What are the few key things, from the customer's point of view, that any competitor has to do right to succeed?

1
2
3
4
5

3 Weighting
How important is each of these CSFs? Score out of 100

Total 100

4 Strengths/weaknesses analysis
Score yourself and each of your main competitors out of 10 on each of the CSFs. Then multiply the score by the weight

Comp / CSF	You	Competitor A	Competitor B	Competitor C	Competitor D
1					
2					
3					
4					
5					
Total (score weight)					

5 Opportunities/threats
What are the few key things outside your direct control that have had, and will continue to have, an impact on your business?

Opportunities

Threats

6 Key issues that need to be addressed

7 Key assumptions for the planning period

1
2
3
4
5
6
7

8 Key objectives

9 Key strategies

Financial consequences

Figure 7.21 Strategic planning exercise (SWOT analysis)

Figure 7.22
Example of the traditional layout for a SWOT analysis

Strengths	Weaknesses
•	•
•	•
•	•
•	•
Opportunities	**Threats**
•	•
•	•
•	•
•	•

SWOT element	Which means	So actions needed are
Strengths		
• Highly qualified personnel	– Better competence, efficiency and professionalism	1 Promote capability to customers 2 Staff retention programme 3 Incentive package for high achievers
• Larger deposit base	– Better cost base – Higher average deposit	1 Leverage our cost base 2 Automate faster to reduce costs further 3 Emphasize upper and middle tier in bank positioning
Weaknesses		
• Low branch management discretion	– Constant time wasting in referring back to head office	1 Develop improved credit scoring at branches 2 Better training and communications equipment 3 Wider delegation to branch managers 4 Approval 'hot line' at head office
• No overseas representation	– Lost business in key areas	1 Urgent feasibility study for Toronto, New York, Los Angeles and Sydney
Opportunities		
• New Industrial development	– Increased bank lending in commercial area	1 Recruit new industrial team 2 Initiate industrial development seminar for branch managers 3 Representation on government and industrial bodies
• Exploit customers' financial needs	– More income from investment and taxation advisory services – Attraction of new customers to bank	1 Initiate study of new business opportunities 2 Survey of banks in four designated countries 3 Market research to confirm initial service concepts 4 Introduce new service
Threats		
• Increased competition	– Loss of market share	1 Strengthen marketing department 2 Develop a marketing plan 3 Improve customer service 4 Emphasize 'no hidden charges' 5 More aggressive advertising
• Key staff loss	– Need to counter aggressive poaching by private sector firms	1 Improve pay/conditions 2 Introduce staff satisfaction survey 3 Lobby to move outside civil service pay structure 4 Internal marketing initiative

Figure 7.23 Summary of a partial SWOT analysis for a bank

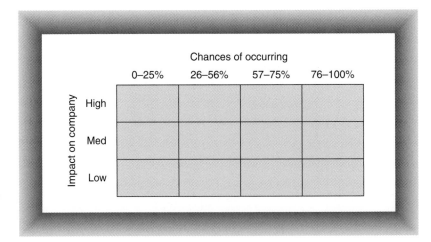

Figure 7.24
Risk analysis matrix for opportunities and threats

on each market segment. Since they are an estimate of the future operating conditions of the marketing plan, they may influence not only its formulation, but also its implementation. Key assumptions might include:

- Inflation rates
- Growth of the economy
- Changes in political/legislative framework
- Interest rates
- Demographic predictions.

In order to be systematic, it can be useful to list key assumptions under a number of general headings such as:

- The general economy
- The service 'industry' sector under consideration
- The company's markets
- Competitors
- Internal organizational factors
- Technological and other developments.

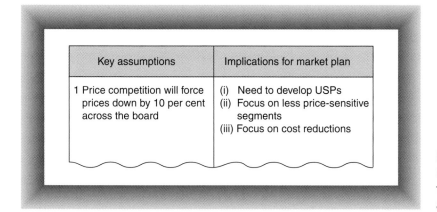

Key assumptions	Implications for market plan
1 Price competition will force prices down by 10 per cent across the board	(i) Need to develop USPs (ii) Focus on less price-sensitive segments (iii) Focus on cost reductions

Figure 7.25
Example of approach for analysing key assumptions

Key assumptions should be relatively few in number. The acid test is that if the achievement of the marketing plan is possible, irrespective of a particular assumption, then that assumption is unnecessary.

When they are identified, it is important to consider their implications for the marketing plan.

A two-column approach can be a useful way of presenting this analysis (Figure 7.25). By using this approach not only are the key assumptions brought into the open, but their impact on the marketing plan is also made explicit. This can remove potential sources of disagreement between managers involved in the planning process and can also indicate where contingency plans might need to be developed, should an assumption prove not to be true. Their usefulness is shown when measuring if a marketing plan is achieving its objectives, and if not why not. The assumptions can then be considered and if they are found to be untrue or inaccurate they can be modified, which in turn will lead to further modification within the plan.

Summary

We saw that Phase Two of the planning process consists of three steps: the marketing audit; the SWOT analysis; and key assumptions. Together, they provide an up-to-date situation review. Of these, the marketing audit is the most far-reaching task and, consequently, most of the chapter was devoted to explaining who should do it and what it involved.

Although outside consultants could tackle the audit, we recommended that the company's own managers should be involved in the auditing process, thereby gaining their interest and commitment. The process itself involves five sub-audits and consists of examining the customers, the services, the business environment, the organization and the competitors in order to identify differential advantages and significant trends. Some tools and frameworks useful in the marketing audit process were also explained.

The mass of auditing information is brought sharply into focus by the SWOT analysis, which identifies all the key factors which will affect the planning period.

Finally, we saw that any plan could only be made in the context of some key assumptions. These need to be put in writing, so that there is no misunderstanding among those who have to contribute to, interpret or implement the plan. They should be few in number and have a direct bearing on the conditions under which the plan is elaborated.

8 Marketing planning Phase Three: marketing strategy formulation

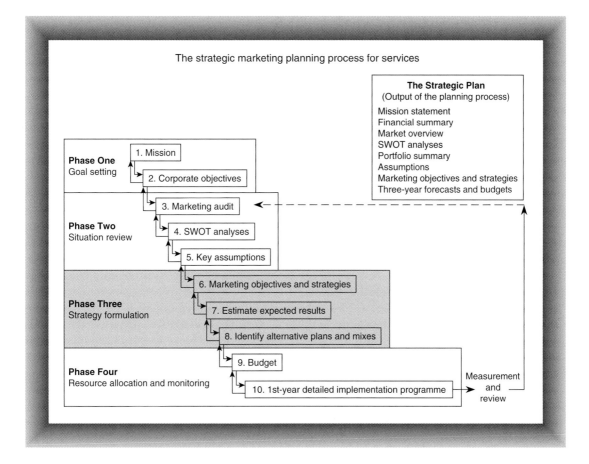

The strategic marketing planning process for services

The Strategic Plan
(Output of the planning process)
Mission statement
Financial summary
Market overview
SWOT analyses
Portfolio summary
Assumptions
Marketing objectives and strategies
Three-year forecasts and budgets

Phase One
Goal setting

1. Mission

2. Corporate objectives

Phase Two
Situation review

3. Marketing audit

4. SWOT analyses

5. Key assumptions

Phase Three
Strategy formulation

6. Marketing objectives and strategies

7. Estimate expected results

8. Identify alternative plans and mixes

Phase Four
Resource allocation and monitoring

9. Budget

10. 1st-year detailed implementation programme

Measurement and review

The situation review should have brought to light most of the key data which enables the marketing strategy formulation phase of the planning process to be undertaken. Even so, it is likely that this next phase will uncover further gaps in the information required if the services organization is to move forward with certainty.

This underlines the point we raised earlier, that the planning process is not as relentlessly linear as the diagram suggests, but is an interactive process, shown by the arrows between the boxes, involving going back to earlier stages from time to time.

The marketing objective and strategy formulation phase of the planning process is, perhaps, the most important of all. Unless this step is carried out well, everything that follows will lack focus and cohesion. Not only does it outline the company's marketing strategy, but it also specifies how it will be accomplished.

In this chapter, we will look at each of the three planning steps in Phase Three in more detail, paying particular attention to the area of developing competitive marketing strategies.

Step 6 Marketing objectives and strategies

It is important to be clear from the outset about the difference between marketing objectives and marketing strategies. Although these terms are frequently used fairly loosely within companies, we consider that they should be defined more precisely for the purposes of marketing planning.

- *A marketing objective* is a precise statement which outlines what is to be accomplished by the service company's marketing activities.

- *A marketing strategy* is the means by which a marketing objective is achieved.

The purpose of setting marketing objectives is to target the profit, revenue and market share we wish to achieve to satisfy the mission. In turn, this provides the guidance for marketing strategies to bring together a marketing mix to achieve the objectives for each segment.

Marketing objectives

With the earlier steps of the planning process behind us, it could appear that the setting of marketing objectives ought to be comparatively straightforward. Unfortunately, this is often not the case, because companies do not always approach the task in a logical way. A logical sequence is:

Level 1   *Set broad marketing objectives*
These would be concerned with long-term profitability and be related to the corporate objectives. By setting broad objectives, communication will be enhanced and a set of expectations will be engendered among staff.

Level 2   *Set objectives for key result areas*
Here, the objectives are defined more precisely, especially for those functions with key roles to play.

Level 3   *Set sub-objectives to support the broad objectives*
The objectives would be based on sales volume, geographic expansion and service offering extension.

A marketing objective should meet several criteria. It must be:

- *Relevant* – in relation to the corporate mission and objectives.
- *Specific* – it should focus on a clear and specific goal.
- *Measurable* – it should be in quantifiable terms.
- *Time bound* – it should have an achievement date.
- *Challenging* – it should be realizable, but at the same time stretching for individuals and the organization as a whole.
- *Focused* – it should be concerned only with markets and services which the company plans to address.

This last point is particularly important, for we support the view that it is only by selling a service to someone (a market) that firms remain in business.

It is wrong to confuse marketing objectives with elements such as pricing, advertising, sales promotion, and so on, which are clearly marketing strategies which help to achieve the objective.

How to set marketing objectives

It is now apparent that when it comes to setting marketing objectives in the way defined above, there are only four possible courses of action:

- Selling existing services to existing markets
- Extending existing services into new markets

> • Developing new services for existing markets
> • Developing new services for new markets.

The Ansoff matrix is a critical structure for setting marketing objectives

For convenience, we reproduce the Ansoff matrix, which was shown earlier in Chapter 3. The matrix captures these options in organized form (Figure 8.1).

An individual service company's ability to cope with technological newness or developing new markets will clearly be a determining factor regarding which quadrants of this matrix become the most significant.

Another point to consider is what constitutes 'new' on the Ansoff matrix. When it comes to markets, the answer would concern how long it took for a company's distinctive competence to become known in a specific market. Anything less than this time could be seen as a new market. In a similar way, new services will be those at the early stages of their lifecycles, where the company is still 'learning' how to deliver them. For example, it might not yet have solved all the technical problems, or managed to get the quality to the same standard as it has for established services.

Since the marketing audit and SWOT analysis should have provided information about why customers buy the services, what factors are affecting their prospects, which market segments offer the greatest

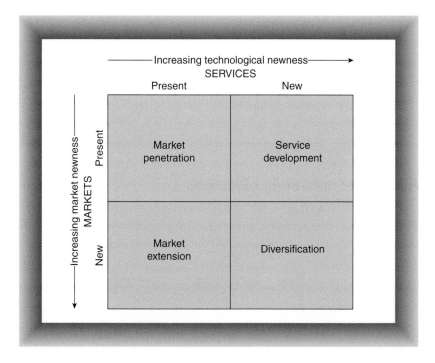

Figure 8.1
Ansoff matrix

rewards, the anticipated activities of competitors, and so on, creative interpretation of this information should make it possible to set objectives for all service/market combinations. Taken together, these should provide the total sales revenue to enable the corporate objectives to be met. A particularly useful tool known as 'gap analysis' can also be used in this process of setting marketing objectives.

Gap analysis

This analytical approach is best understood by reference to Figure 8.2. The figure shows that the initial forecast, or trend, of sales revenue only reaches point A, which falls short of the corporate target, point E. The obvious first thing to do in such circumstances will be to consider actions, such as increasing productivity, that could close the gap without departing too far from current practices.

Actions to penetrate the current markets further could be:

- Improve the mix of services and markets.

- Generate higher sales via a more effective and better managed sales force.

- Improve customer satisfaction with better service.

- Exploit differential advantages with increased pricing.

- Reduce costs and expenses.

- Change the promotional mix, e.g. level of advertising, service levels.

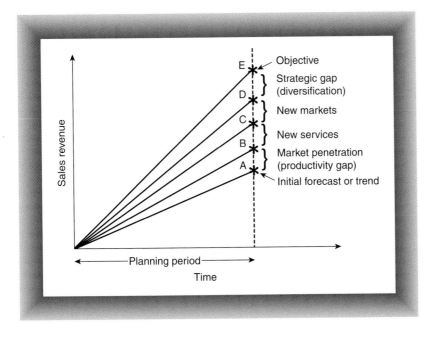

Figure 8.2
Gap analysis

In the example in Figure 8.2, all of these actions have the net effect of pushing the forecast to an improved position, point B. The shortfall between this and the target figure can now only be bridged by having a more radical rethink about the strategies used.

Actions which could be taken to bridge the strategic gap might include:

- Developing new services (taking us to point C).
- Developing new markets (taking us to point D).
- Diversifying (the strategic gap). This can be achieved organically or by acquisition, joint ventures and the like. Hopefully this or the previous actions take the service organization to point E.

Each of these possible actions needs to be investigated to determine its potential impact on reducing the identified gap. If the gap still remains even after a creative and rigorous attempt to close it, then top management might need to be informed that the original corporate objectives are not achievable and are unrealistic. However, this should only be done when all other avenues have been explored.

Before moving on this, however, it is important to understand that gap analysis is only a precursor to producing the strategic marketing plan. It is usual to select a period of about three years into the future (the planning period in Figure 8.2). Completing the gap analysis in the way suggested provides an excellent overview of the likely content of the strategic marketing plan, but in itself it is not a strategic plan.

A summary of the options for filling any identified gaps is given in Figure 8.3. Also, some templates are provided in Chapter 13 for entering new data.

By using the Ansoff matrix and gap analysis, the marketer can begin to focus on marketing objectives and calculate if they will achieve the corporate objectives.

There is, however, another issue to take into consideration and that is whether or not the service portfolio (mentioned in the previous chapter) will be managed effectively. If the company wants to avoid overconcentration of its resources, it will need to invest in those services and markets which will sustain long-term success.

Portfolio Management
This issue was first addressed by the Boston Consulting Group in the USA, who identified that the parameters of relative market share and market growth had a critical bearing on the fortunes of any

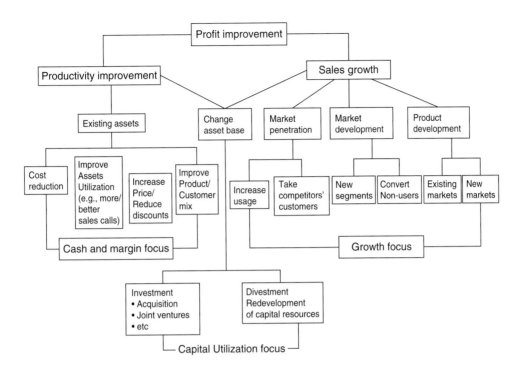

Figure 8.3 Profit improvement

service or product. However, while this consulting firm was extremely successful in applying its concept to a diverse range of businesses, individual organizations (and other consultancies) had problems. They often found it difficult to measure market share with accuracy, or to be confident about market growth rates.

As a development from the so-called 'Boston matrix', General Electric, McKinsey & Co. and, eventually, Shell evolved a multiple factor portfolio matrix[1] (known as the portfolio matrix or directional policy matrix), shown in Figure 8.4. These portfolio management techniques are important for managing existing and new products.

> The directional policy matrix is a more useful development of the Boston matrix

Here, the two axes of the matrix are 'market attractiveness' and 'business strengths'. These are more sophisticated proxies for the Boston parameters of 'market growth' and 'market share'. Indeed, the underlying interpretation of information from both the Boston matrix and the portfolio matrix is very similar. While both approaches have their proponents, we believe the latter is the more realistic and practical approach, as it involves the use of criteria that are more specific to the service organization using it. It is for this reason that we focus on this technique.

Note that, while many texts will show nine boxes, the method described here is a simple and more useful version developed by one of the authors.

The underlying concept of the portfolio matrix is easy to grasp. It is closely related to the lifecycle concept. The rationale behind it is this:

1. There is little point in introducing a new service unless there is an attractive market for it. (What attractiveness means can vary from company to company, as we shall see.) At the same time, the newness of the service means that the company is at the beginning of a learning curve and, sometimes, does not play to as many strengths as it would for a more established service.
   Therefore, in portfolio matrix terms, new services often appear in the top right-hand quadrant.

2. Assuming the service is well received, the company builds up strengths in terms of the service getting known and being able to establish differential advantages, while becoming more efficient. The service, therefore, moves into the top left-hand quadrant and becomes better established.

3. Eventually, the demand for the service falls, because existing customer needs have been met, a new set of services has greater appeal or the market has matured. Thus, the previously attractive and growing market becomes relatively less attractive than other higher growth markets. The service is now more accurately positioned in the bottom left-hand quadrant.

4. Eventually, the less attractive market sometimes encourages the company to switch resources to more promising areas, and the service is denuded of the resources that once led it to success. It now moves into the bottom right-hand quadrant.

All of the service company's offerings should be capable of being positioned on this matrix. There are three very good reasons why this should be done:

1. There are implications for the revenue, costs and profit-generating abilities of the overall service portfolio.

2. The matrix can be helpful in developing strategic insights regarding how each service should be managed.

3. The matrix can provide a forecasting mechanism for revenue generation and can assist strategic thinking.

Revenue generation

Consideration of the four quadrants of the matrix in Figure 8.4 will suggest that, in financial terms, they behave as follows:

- *Upper right-hand box*
  A new service, or one in which the organization has few strengths, will need to be heavily promoted if it is to succeed. At the same time, its sales may be relatively low. It is, therefore, a net user of funds. As such, it is more appropriate to use sales and market share goals as a measure of effectiveness than net present value calculations.

  It is also important to have a service champion that has the necessary entrepreneurial skills to lead this type of business.

- *Upper left-hand box*
  Because of the operation's strong competitive position, the service will be achieving high levels of sales, but its success in this attractive market will attract competition. The result of this is that promotional costs may still be high, which might result in modest margins at best, but which on the whole are neutral in terms of generating funds. Here, it is probably appropriate to use net present value as a measure of effectiveness, probably using a relatively high percentage discount rate, as an organization needs to be sure that it will eventually recover its investment.

  The type of person who should head up this kind of service needs to be experienced, with a higher risk profile than is necessary for some stable markets.

- *Lower left-hand box*
  With the market becoming less attractive, some competitors withdraw and the company may be able to reduce its promotional

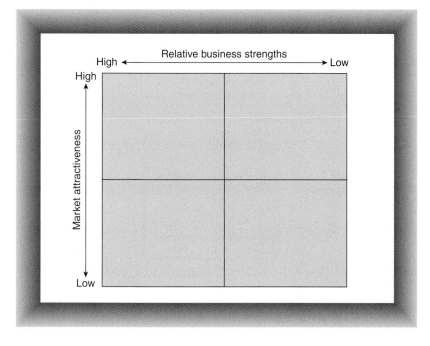

Figure 8.4
The directional policy matrix

efforts and take advantage of its earlier investment in the service. Services in this quadrant are invariably net generators of funds. Here, it is probably appropriate to use return on investment (ROI) or net free cash flow as a measure of effectiveness.

In management terms, it is probably better to have someone in charge of this type of business who is prudent.

- *Lower right-hand box*
  Clearly, sales are at a low level and the company may begin to neglect the service. It might still generate some small amounts of revenue, but questions have to be asked to ascertain whether the resources put into this service would be better invested elsewhere. Unless, as is sometimes the case, these services are necessary to support other more desirable ones, it is often sensible to manage these services for cash. Thus, net free cash flow becomes an appropriate measure of effectiveness.

Figure 8.5 summarizes these rules of thumb.

From the above, it is clear that much of the current revenue and profits come from the services in the bottom left-hand box. It is essential therefore, in terms of managing the portfolio of services, that these exist in sufficient quantities, and that, as they diminish in importance, there are successors to take their place. This means that the development of the portfolio cannot be left to chance. Ideally, there should always be one or two developing services in the top right-hand box that have the potential to become tomorrow's winners (top left-hand box). Similarly, the cash generators of the future commonly come from today's winners. As a general guideline, there should only be a minimal number of services in the bottom right-hand box.

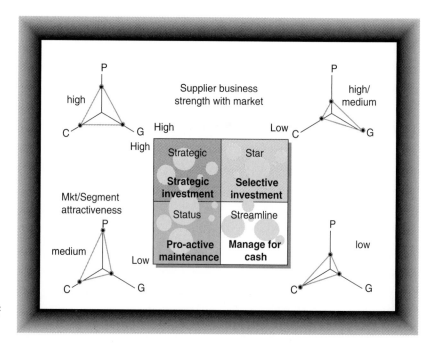

Figure 8.5
Setting expectations of performance

In our consulting work, we often find that a company's portfolio is badly out of balance and, because the full implications of this are not understood, the 'corrective action' they planned to take would, in most cases, have only exacerbated the situation.

Constructing the portfolio matrix

From the outset, a given service organization must be very rigorous with respect to how it defines the components of the axes for the matrix.

First, however, it is essential to decide what constitutes 'markets' for the purpose of completing the vertical axis. Ideally, in a marketing planning context, 'markets' should be genuine segments (i.e. groups of customers/clients with the same or similar needs), but equally, large groups of customers could be used, such as:

- markets, e.g. banks, building societies, universities, etc.

- countries or regions

- key customers/clients.

Figure 8.6 shows a completed matrix for a financial services organization for its major accounts. (For the purpose of this book, the names have been disguised for confidentiality reasons.) For the purpose of this section, we will assume that 'market' means a broader group of customers than segments.

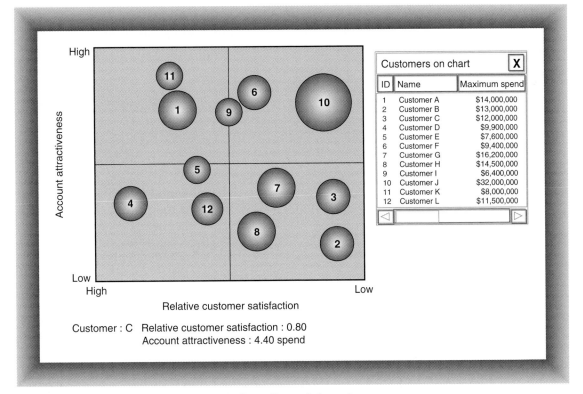

Figure 8.6   Directional policy matrix for a financial services company

In this particular real world example, the biggest and most attractive customer, with a wallet size of $32 million, was positioned in the top right box of the DPM. When seen in the context of the other major customers, it was clear that this insurance company was pursuing the wrong policy for customer J. It was endeavouring to maximize profits, but in doing so was not providing a competitive level of service, so was becoming increasingly less competitive, so that before long the most important customer would no longer deal with them. This resulted in a complete change of objectives and strategies for this customer. This illustrates the power of using the DPM at this stage of the planning process. Not only is it used for evaluating current strategies, but also for deciding future strategies.

The next task is to list these markets.

What constitutes *market attractiveness* will obviously vary from company to company. Here are some of the factors which might come into consideration:

> ● Overall market size; annual growth rate; profit margins; low level of competition; technical requirements; favourable socioeconomic/political background; environmental conditions; quality requirements.

In terms of *business strengths/competitiveness*, factors like the following determine our competitive positioning:

> ● Reputation, e.g. technological; brand/company image; service quality; differential advantages of service; reliability; availability; ability to offer a competitive price.

Since some of these factors will be more important than others, it is usual to weight them, as shown in the example in Figure 8.7.

An example of the Market Attractiveness Factors for an insurance company (disguised for purposes of confidentiality) are shown in Figure 8.8.

While the criteria for market attractiveness may remain constant, the criteria for the competitive position will be different for each market evaluated. Each market should be evaluated according to its attractiveness and according to the organization's strengths in each market.

It is recommended that, in practice, fewer than the seven attractiveness factors are used. Typically, five or fewer are used.

	Weight	Rating (1–5)	Value
Market attractiveness			
Overall market size	0.20	4.00	0.80
Annual market growth rate	0.20	5.00	1.00
Available profit margin	0.15	4.00	0.60
Competitive intensity	0.20	2.00	0.60
Technological requirements	0.15	4.00	0.60
Inflationary vulnerability	0.05	3.00	0.15
Environmental	0.05	3.00	0.15
	1.00		3.90
Competitive position			
Service quality	0.30	4.00	1.20
Brand reputation	0.20	5.00	1.00
Technological reputation	0.15	4.00	0.60
Reliability	0.15	4.00	0.60
Availability	0.10	3.00	0.30
Cost-effectiveness	0.10	3.00	0.30
	1.00		4.00

Figure 8.7
Ranking market attractiveness and competitive position

MFAs	Description	Weight	Score
Profit Pool (a) market economic profit (b) Market size and growth	• Market-wide economic profit pools • Factor in future profit trends from 2007 to 2110	70%	10 = high 1 = low
Competitive Intensity	• Effort required to improve 'share of voice' and hence growth in market share • Ease with which new entrants can enter the market • Different for IFA, and Network	15%	10 = low 1 = high

Regulatory Risk (not included in economic profit assessment)	• Risk assessment of the following items:
	  o Regulatory: risk, price caps, etc.
	  o Market change – pensions replaced by ISAs, life bonds replaced by mutual funds, etc.
		15%	10 = high
			1 = low

		100%	

Figure 8.8 A financial services company's MAFs

If each service is represented on the matrix by a circle whose area is proportional to its sales revenue, then the current balance of the portfolio can be seen at a glance.

It is important to note that the term 'Market Attractiveness' for most service companies will mean 'the potential for growth in our future profits' (usually three years), so at least REVENUE, % GROWTH and % MARGIN will be in the list of market attractiveness factors, as revenue, multiplied by % growth multiplied by % margin equals profit. Also, the actual calculation of each market's position on the vertical axis represents its attractiveness in three years' time, so the circles cannot move vertically in the matrix when setting objectives unless two separate calculations are done – one for attractiveness today and one for attractiveness in three years' time. But this is pointless in reality, so only the one calculation needs to be made.

The portfolio matrix and the future

Additional value can be gained from the portfolio matrix by projecting the position and sales revenue of each service at the end of the planning period and also plotting these. The end result will look like Figure 8.9, which was produced for a business school.

From this example, it can be seen that the pressing need of the business school is to improve the competitive position of some of its services in the top right-hand box. Of the four in contention, which would be the best candidate? On balance, perhaps Distance Education

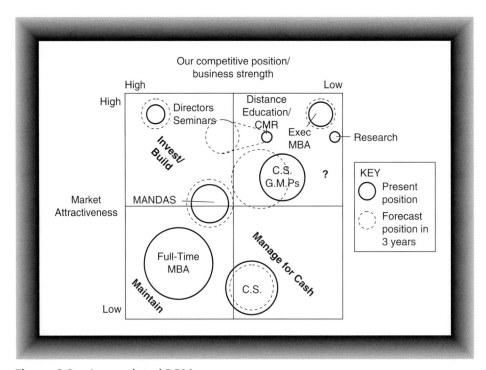

Figure 8.9   A completed DPM

and GMPs would be the ones on which to concentrate if investment funds were limited. However, steps should also be taken to ensure the accuracy of the data collected and to investigate whether it would be possible to expand sales to a higher level than forecast.

It will also be clear, by now, that the directional policy matrix (DPM) is a subtle way of assessing the company's present cash-generating capabilities and the implications for future strategy (see Figure 8.10). Clearly all have different implications, as spelled out in Figure 8.11.

A step-by-step guide to completing a DPM for a service company is provided at the end of this chapter in Figures 8.20 to 8.27.

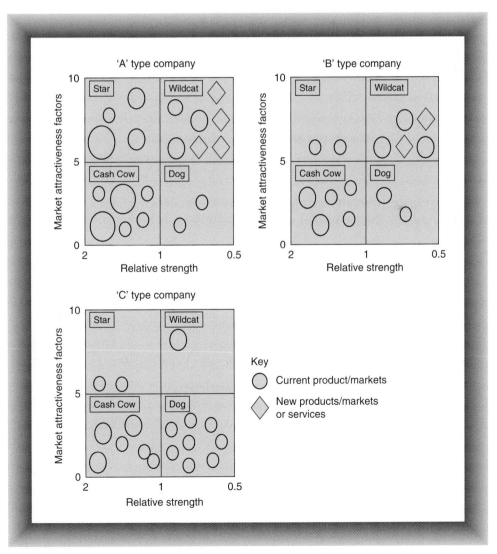

Figure 8.10   Directional policy matrices for three types of company

Type company	Cash-generation
A	Excellent low risk positive cash flow from 'Cash Cows' to invest in 'Stars' and selectively in new products/markets ('Wildcats'). Few 'Dogs'.
B	Excellent low risk positive cash flow from 'Cash cows'. Unfortunately, much of this will be needed to invest in 'Wildcats', so the next few years will entail either: – low profits while building a balanced portfolio, as in 'A' above – paying shareholders the required dividend, a short-term solution which is unlikely to fool investors.
C	Cash rich, from 'Cash Cows', but too many 'Dogs', which may become a cash drain or eventually disappear. There is no future for this company, as there is little or no investment in future products/markets.

Figure 8.11
Cash-generating capabilities of three types of company

The matrix and strategy formulation

From the foregoing discussion of the rationale behind the matrix and its cash-generating implications, it is possible to extract some general 'rules' about marketing strategy. These are illustrated in Figure 8.12. Here, the matrix is shown as a 3 × 3 format so that a finer tuning of strategy can be achieved, depending on where the circles are located.

It is not suggested that the guidelines provided in Figure 8.12 should be followed slavishly. All they do is to provide a general context for the company's marketing deliberations. Similarly, other more specific functional guidelines can be extracted from the matrix, as shown in Figure 8.13. Here, for the sake of simplicity, we have reverted to a four column matrix format.

Developing competitive strategies

We can consider marketing strategies at two levels. First, we consider marketing strategies at the competitive strategy level. There are two factors which have a crucial effect on the development of competitive strategies for any business:

● How successfully it manages its cost base

● The uniqueness of its service.

Porter[2] has combined these factors in the matrix that is shown in Figure 8.14.

		Strong	Medium	Weak
Market attractiveness	High	**Protect position** • invest to grow at maximum rate • concentrate effort on maintaining strength	**Invest to build** • challenge for leadership • build selectively on strengths • reinforce vulnerable areas	**Build selectively** • specialize around limited strengths • seek ways to overcome weaknesses • withdraw if indications of sustainable growth are lacking
	Medium	**Protect position** • invest heavily in most attractive segments • build up ability to counter competition • emphasize profitability by raising productivity	**Selectivity/manage for earnings** • protect existing programme • concentrate investments on segments where profitability is good and risk is relatively low	**Limited expansion or harvest** • look for ways to expand without high risk; otherwise, minimize investment and rationalize operations
	Low	**Protect and refocus** • manage for current earnings • concentrate on attractive segments • defend strengths	**Manage for earnings** • protect position in most profitable segments • upgrade services • minimize investment	**Divest** • sell at time that will maximize cash value • cut fixed costs and avoid investment meanwhile

Business strength

Figure 8.12   Multiple factors matrix – generic strategies

The company with a highly differentiated service (for which it can charge a premium) and a low-cost structure is clearly going to be very successful. The company with a run-of-the-mill, 'me-too' service can only remain competitive if it can keep its costs relatively lower than its rivals (or find a way to achieve differentiation). The company with no means of achieving differentiation and a high cost structure is clearly heading for ruin in the long run. The final case, the highly differentiated offer from a high cost base, does have a prospect of success if it can be focused into niche markets which value the differentiation and are prepared to pay for it.

> Costs and service differentiation are key determinants of commercial success

However, some companies, because of the nature of their business, find their options severely limited. They might, for example, be very labour intensive and, as a result, have inherently high costs which they can do little about. This might suggest that, for them, it will be critical to work at establishing differentiation and to seek niche markets if they are to survive. Of course, they might argue that working on developing a 'special' service would add further to their costs. This does not necessarily have to be the case, as Figure 8.15 illustrates.

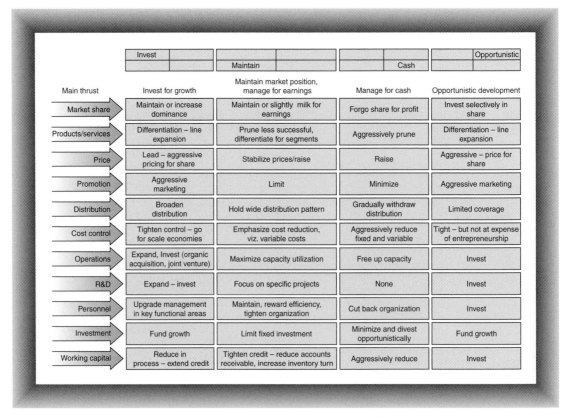

Main thrust	Invest for growth	Maintain market position, manage for earnings	Manage for cash	Opportunistic development
Market share	Maintain or increase dominance	Maintain or slightly milk for earnings	Forgo share for profit	Invest selectively in share
Products/services	Differentiation – line expansion	Prune less successful, differentiate for segments	Aggressively prune	Differentiation – line expansion
Price	Lead – aggressive pricing for share	Stabilize prices/raise	Raise	Aggressive – price for share
Promotion	Aggressive marketing	Limit	Minimize	Aggressive marketing
Distribution	Broaden distribution	Hold wide distribution pattern	Gradually withdraw distribution	Limited coverage
Cost control	Tighten control – go for scale economies	Emphasize cost reduction, viz. variable costs	Aggressively reduce fixed and variable	Tight – but not at expense of entrepreneurship
Operations	Expand, Invest (organic acquisition, joint venture)	Maximize capacity utilization	Free up capacity	Invest
R&D	Expand – invest	Focus on specific projects	None	Invest
Personnel	Upgrade management in key functional areas	Maintain, reward efficiency, tighten organization	Cut back organization	Invest
Investment	Fund growth	Limit fixed investment	Minimize and divest opportunistically	Fund growth
Working capital	Reduce in process – extend credit	Tighten credit – reduce accounts receivable, increase inventory turn	Aggressively reduce	Invest

Figure 8.13 Other functional guidelines suggested by portfolio matrix analysis

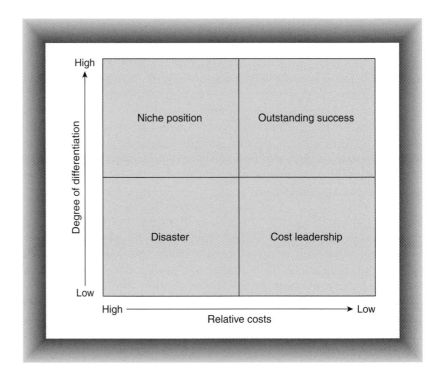

Figure 8.14
The Porter matrix

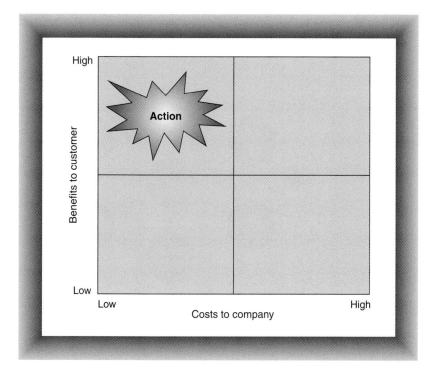

Figure 8.15
Cost-effective service development

By considering those benefits the customer seeks and values highly, which can be provided relatively cheaply, the company may be able to 'customize' its services at little cost.

Marketing strategies

As outlined earlier, what a company wants to accomplish, in terms of such things as market share and volume, are marketing objectives. How the company intends to go about achieving its objectives are marketing strategies. Marketing strategy is the overall route to the achievement of specific objectives and should describe the means by which marketing objectives are to be reached, the time programme and the allocation of resources. It does not delineate the individual courses the resulting activities will follow.

The linkages between marketing objectives and marketing strategies for a service business are shown in Figure 8.16.

There is a clear distinction between strategy and detailed implementation or tactics. Marketing strategy reflects the company's best opinion as to how it can most profitably apply its skills and resources to the market place. It is inevitably broad in scope. The first-year implementation plan which stems from it (discussed in the next chapter) will spell out specific action and timings and will contain the detailed contribution expected from each department.

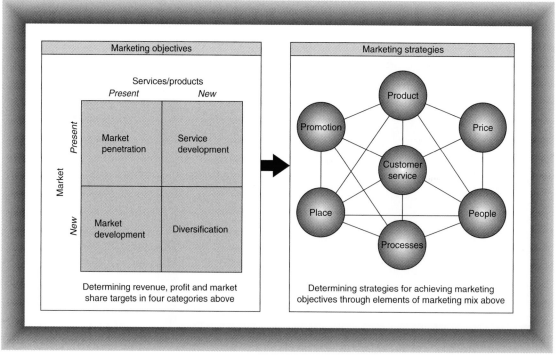

Figure 8.16   Marketing objectives and marketing strategies for a service business

Marketing strategies, within Step 6 of the marketing plan, indicate the *general* content of the marketing strategies. They typically include elements such as:

1. Policies and procedures relating to the services to be offered, such as number, quality, design, branding

2. Pricing levels to be adopted, margins and discounts

3. Advertising and sales promotion – the creative approach, type of media, amount of spend, etc.

4. What emphasis will be put on the sales approach, sales training, etc.

5. What intermediaries might be used, i.e. distribution channels

6. What customer service levels will be required

7. Specification of processes used to deliver services

8. Strategic issues relating to staff.

Thus, marketing strategies are the means by which marketing objectives will be achieved and are generally concerned with the seven major elements of the services marketing mix, as follows:

Product/service – The general policies for product and service deletions, modifications, additions, design, packaging, etc.

Price – The general pricing policies to be followed for product/ service groups in market segments.

Place – The general policies for channels and intermediaries.

Promotion – The general policies for communicating with customers under the relevant headings, such as: advertising, sales force, sales promotion, public relations, exhibitions, direct mail.

People – The general policies for people management as part of the service delivery process.

Processes – The general policies for processes by which a service is created and delivered to customers.

Customer service – The general policies for customer service management, including service level, which help build long-term customer relationships.

Note that these are *general* policies which lead to much greater amplification later in the first-year implementation programme (Step 10 of the marketing plan).

Figure 8.17 provides a list of the marketing strategies (in summary form), which covers the majority of options. The marketing strategies will be made up of three elements: the means; the timetable; and the resources necessary to ensure successful achievement of the objectives. Marketing strategies outline the broad plan of action to achieve marketing objectives through the marketing mix elements.

Marketing strategies are concerned with an overview of the three-year marketing mix strategies which will satisfy customers' needs. The thrust of the marketing mix specification, at this point in the marketing plan, involves creating the differential advantage which makes the service firm's offer different (in a way preferred by the segments that are targeted) from its competitors' offers.

Step 10 in the next chapter, the first-year implementation plan, is devoted to a much more detailed consideration of the marketing mix for services. This next chapter describes what should appear in advertising, sales, price, distribution, processes, people and customer service plans and is intended for those whose principal concern is the preparation of a detailed one-year operational or tactical plan.

From what we have said about setting marketing objectives and strategies, it should now be clear that the services marketer is faced with a wide range of options, which call for creative and, at times, inspirational analysis to address them. This phase of the planning process is closely related to the next two steps.

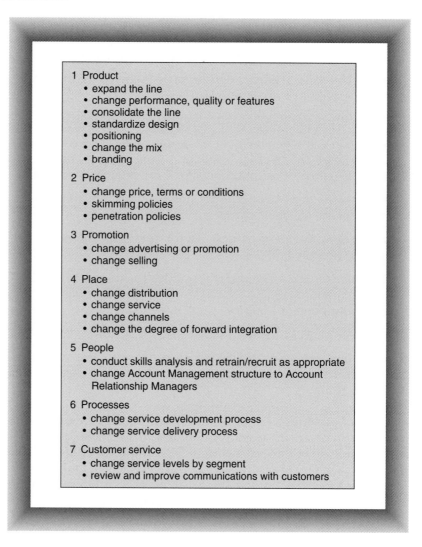

Figure 8.17
Summary of typical
marketing strategies
for a service business

Step 7   Estimate expected results

The purpose of this step is to determine whether the marketing strategies will actually deliver the desired results.

Once the marketing objectives and strategies have been decided for the various service/segment combinations, the financial implications of introducing them need to be evaluated. This will require a detailed review of:

- Projected sales revenues
- The costs of sales
- The costs of marketing

- Operating expenses
- Overhead expenses.

Such an analysis should show that the chosen approach will indeed deliver the anticipated financial contribution to achieve the required targets. If it does not, then the marketing strategies will need to be examined in more depth in order to discover how they might be redeveloped to achieve the expected results.

In times of economic uncertainty, it can be useful to calculate three sets of analyses. These would reflect the estimated results based upon the most pessimistic interpretation of all the salient factors, the most likely result, and that based on the most optimistic levels of demands. In this way, it becomes possible to identify the possible spread of expected results and, in that sense, have a feel for the potential 'margin of error' surrounding the most likely result.

It is necessary to estimate a number of possible outcomes

Forecasting projected sales levels is never easy, particularly as the service cannot be kept in inventory. Several variables need to be considered at this point. These include the capacity of the service company, costs in extending capacity, moving to multisite locations, changing demand patterns through differential pricing, and so on. Although demand and capacity planning is complicated in manufacturing businesses, the characteristics of services make it much more difficult in the services sector. Therefore, techniques such as extrapolation, regression analysis, delphi forecasting, test marketing and consumer surveys can all make a contribution to identifying demand patterns more accurately.

However, because many of the factors under consideration are inter-related, the task is frequently not simple. Thus, although techniques can help to uncover quantitative data, often this must be augmented with qualitative analysis and market research to promise a better understanding of the service market under consideration.

Step 8   Identifying alternative mixes

Even if the original objectives and strategies do produce the expected results, it is still important to discover if a more effective marketing approach can lead to even better results. Therefore, using techniques such as computer modelling, a number of alternative mixes can be evaluated before deciding on the final marketing mix around which the plan will be based.

It is at this stage that plans should be formulated to cover anticipated lower or higher levels of demand. It is often found that the response curves of different marketing mixes can vary considerably. Figure 8.18 shows a representation of predicted revenue against predicted

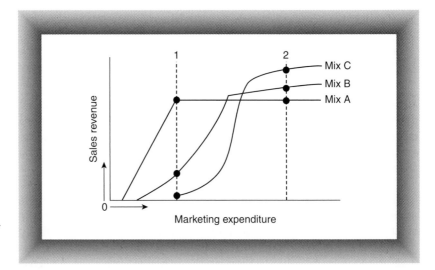

Figure 8.18
Response functions for different marketing mixes

marketing costs for three alternative marketing mixes. The marketing mix chosen will depend on the budget for marketing effort and its impact on revenues and profit. Marketing mix A will produce better results for low levels of expenditure (Point 1) while marketing mix C will provide better results at a higher level of expenditure (Point 2).

Contingency plans[3] should also be considered at this stage of the marketing planning process, in response to the impact of different sets of assumptions which were made earlier. Of course, it will not be possible to develop plans for every eventuality, but it is advisable to have at least:

- A defensive contingency plan, which takes into account the possibility that the assumptions surrounding the marketing audit were unduly optimistic and thus responds to threats that might materialize; and

- An offensive contingency plan, which is really the converse of the one above and seeks to take advantage of opportunities, should they occur.

In an ideal world, possible contingencies can be identified well in advance. Unfortunately, in spite of all good intentions, the dynamics of modern markets can trigger unexpected crises. For example, few predicted the rapid demise of communism and the repercussions it would have in the Eastern Bloc countries. Similarly, events such as the Gulf War or natural disasters can suddenly distort existing supply and demand patterns, making it imperative to modify existing marketing plans, through having contingency planning.

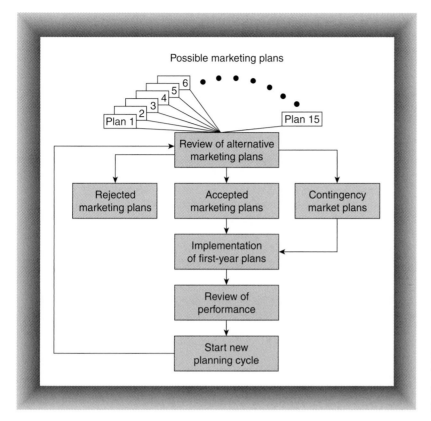

Figure 8.19
The alternative mixes process for a large services company

In these circumstances, it is particularly important to understand if the event in question is a temporary aberration, or something which will have a fundamental and long-lasting effect on the company's markets.

Figure 8.19 shows the phases of alternative mixes for a large services company operating in consumer markets. It shows the rigorous evaluation of 15 possible marketing plans, and the resulting process, as these are selected as marketing plans, contingency plans, or are rejected. The figure also shows the linkages with the formulation of the first-year implementation and the performance review process.

Paradoxically, it is generally not at times of crisis that danger exists, but when things are going well. It is at times like these that companies become complacent and get lulled into a false sense of security. The idea of developing contingency plans fades from the corporate consciousness and, when something does go wrong, the companies are caught completely unprepared. These contingency plans are an important part of the marketing planning process.

A Step-by-step guide to completing a DPM for a service company

Figures 8.20 to 8.27 contain instructions for completing this crucial step in the service organization planning process.

Make an objective assessment of each segment's
attractiveness to your company based on criteria
relevant to what the organization is trying to achieve

1. list the factors you would consider when comparing the
   attractiveness of segments
2. for each of the factors, weight their relative importance to
   each other by distributing 100 points between them
3. define high, medium and low parameters for each factor,
   where very high scores 10 and very low scores 0
4. work out the attractiveness score for each segment using
   the above to arrive at a total between 0 and 10

Factor	Parameters			Weighting	Segment 1	
	10-7	6-4	3-0		Score	Total
1. Segment profitability	>15%	10-15%	<10%	60	6	3.6
2. Cyclicality	Low	Medium	High	40	8	3.2
				Total	100		6.8

Figure 8.20
Market/segment
attractiveness 1

Make an objective assessment of each segment's attractiveness to your company based
on criteria relevant to what the organization is trying to achieve

Factor	Parameters			Weighting	Segment 1	
	10-7	6-4	3-0		Score	Total
1. Segment size (millions)	>£250	£50-250	<£50	15	5	0.75
2. Segment growth	>10%	5-9%	<5%	25	10	2.5
3. Competitive intensity	Low	Medium	High	10	6	0.6
4. Segment profitability	>15%	10-15%	<10%	25	8	2.0
5. Vulnerability	Low	Medium	High	15	6	0.9
6. Cyclicality	Low	Medium	High	10	2.5	0.25
			Total	100		7.0

A score of 7.0 would generally position a segment as 'highly attractive'.

Figure 8.21 Market/segment attractiveness 2

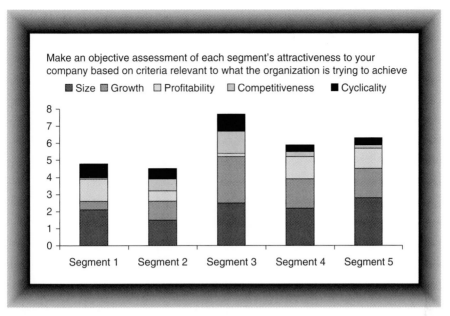

Figure 8.22   Market/segment attractiveness 3

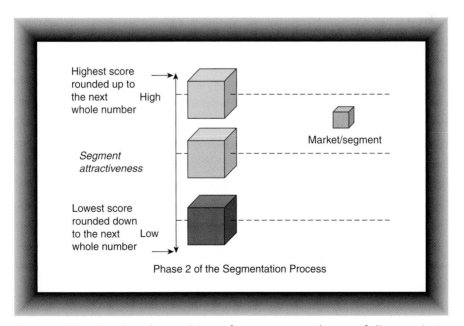

Figure 8.23   Plotting the position of segments on the portfolio matrix 1

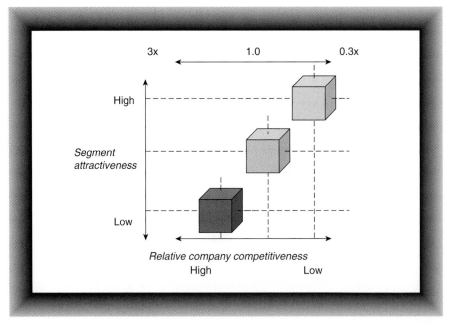

Figure 8.24   Plotting the position of segments on the portfolio matrix 2

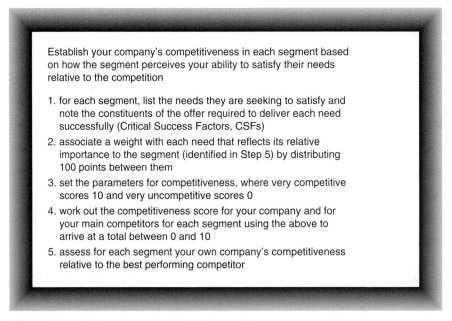

Figure 8.25   Company competitiveness 1

Establish your company's competitiveness in each segment based on how the segment perceives your ability to satisfy their needs relative to the competition

Segment 1: Needs and their associated Critical Success Factors	Weighting	Your company Score	Your company Total	Competitor A Score	Competitor A Total	Competitor B Score	Competitor B Total
1. Product	50	6	3.0	9	4.5	4	2.0
2. Image	25	8	2.0	6	1.5	10	2.5
3. Service	15	8	1.2	8	1.2	6	0.9
4. Price	10	5	0.5	6	0.6	3	0.3
Total	100		6.7		7.8		5.7

Your company's relative competitive strength is your company's Total divided by the highest Total of the competitors expressed as a ratio: 6.7:7.8 = 0.86:1.0

Figure 8.26   Company competitiveness 2

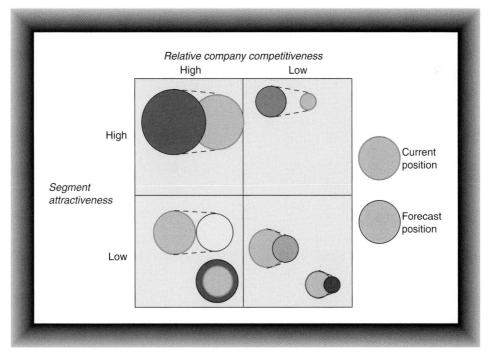

Figure 8.27   Directional policy matrix (DPM)

Summary

In this chapter about the marketing strategy formulation phase of the marketing planning process, we first looked at the differences between objectives and strategies, and at how to set marketing objectives. We saw that, although the marketing audit and SWOT analysis should have provided much of the information required to set marketing objectives, gap analysis might indicate that more needed to be done. Steps might have to be taken to improve productivity and develop new strategies in order to arrive at marketing objectives which met the corporate expectations.

Another consideration was that of managing the service portfolio effectively, bearing in mind that different services have different capacities for either absorbing funds or generating them. By considering the company's output as a 'portfolio', rather than a set of individual services, it was found that underlying strategic issues could influence the way each service was developed and promoted. Indeed, the portfolio matrix provides useful guidelines regarding functional marketing activities.

We saw that developing a competitive marketing strategy is probably the most important phase of the process. Because the planning process is interactive, the steps of setting objectives and strategies, estimating results and considering alternative mixes might have to be reviewed several times before the best formulation emerges.

9 Marketing planning Phase Four: resource allocation, monitoring and detailed planning (Part 1: the budget, the service product plan and the communications plan)

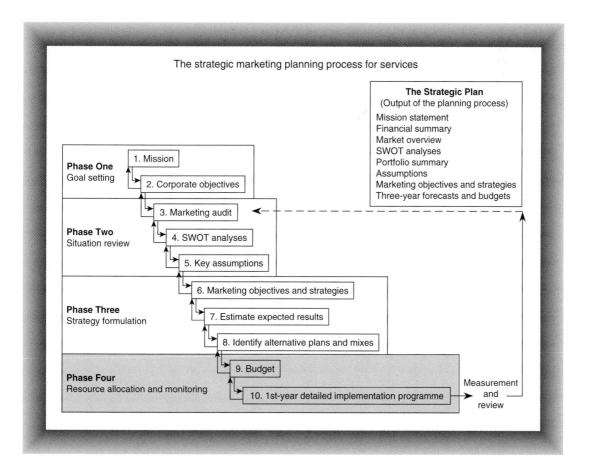

The strategic marketing planning process for services

The Strategic Plan
(Output of the planning process)
Mission statement
Financial summary
Market overview
SWOT analyses
Portfolio summary
Assumptions
Marketing objectives and strategies
Three-year forecasts and budgets

Phase One
Goal setting

1. Mission
2. Corporate objectives

Phase Two
Situation review

3. Marketing audit
4. SWOT analyses
5. Key assumptions

Phase Three
Strategy formulation

6. Marketing objectives and strategies
7. Estimate expected results
8. Identify alternative plans and mixes

Phase Four
Resource allocation and monitoring

9. Budget
10. 1st-year detailed implementation programme

Measurement and review

Chapter 8, on marketing strategy formulation, showed how the marketing audit information could be distilled and used to determine marketing objectives and strategies. Having these available to guide the thinking process, it was then possible to arrive at the services marketing mix, *at a broad strategic level*, which offered the best prospects for achieving the desired results. This chapter, which examines the final phase of the marketing planning process for services, will look first at the marketing budget and then at how the strategic marketing plan can be made operative through the allocation of resources and the formulation of a detailed first-year tactical marketing plan involving considerations of the services marketing mix *at a detailed operational level*. This chapter focuses on the service product plan and on the communications plan. Part 2, in Chapter 10, focuses on pricing, customer service, and monitoring and control.

Step 9   The marketing budget

In arriving at the best strategic marketing mix, all of the options under consideration had to be costed out. In that sense the broad strategic marketing budget is known already. However, it should now be developed in a more detailed and careful manner, as it is going to provide the formal expression of the service organization's commitment to its chosen marketing strategy for the coming three years (or whatever the planning period happens to be).

| Successful budgeting involves cross-functional cooperation

The responsibility for looking ahead in this way is not solely the prerogative of top management, for many executives will have a part to play in translating forecasts, and what is required to achieve them, into monetary values.

> Successful budgeting depends upon the thoroughness with which every aspect of future marketing has been considered and how it impacts on other parts of the business.

The involvement of a wide group of managers in the budgeting process ensures that no important issues are neglected or overlooked. This frequently involves cross-functional cooperation in the planning process, which was discussed in Chapter 4 and illustrated in Figure 4.2. It also serves to remind them that they do have a part to play in working towards a common goal – the future success of the company.

The budget itself can be broken down into a number of component parts.

The revenue budget

As all revenue is ultimately generated by sales, accurate sales forecasts are the critical link in the budgetary process. Not only should they be determined as scientifically as possible, they must also be consistent with the views of field sales staff and others who have an intimate knowledge about customers and the markets for the services under consideration.

- The sales spread, or 'mix', over the principal service lines.

- The volatility of demand for the service(s) both at home and in foreign markets.

- The relationship between sales and the capacity to provide the service(s). For example, capacity might be limited by skill shortages, lack of investment in new technology, and so on, some of which may not be capable of swift expansion.

- Patterns of seasonal demand.

- Special characteristics of the particular service product market.

The 'marketing capacity' budget

This is, in essence, designed to cover marketing staff responsible for providing the services and products over the planning period. It involves a detailed study of what goes into each service, and understanding that labour, material, supplies and equipment need to be available as and when required. Again, no worthwhile conclusions can be reached about the levels of these cost factors without discussion and cooperation between the cross-functional managers involved. From the point of view of maintaining a consistent output as economically as possible, this budget will take into account:

- A consideration of the appropriate levels of service quality to be offered to each major customer segment.

- A detailed study of direct labour involved, expressed in man-hours, taking into account different staff grades that might be required.

- A study of incentives which may influence sales, hence throughput rates.

- The provision of plant, tools and supplies, together with utilities and maintenance facilities.

- A study of the most effective material purchasing procedures.

- Efficiencies achieved through services re-engineering and redesign.

- Other expenses associated with maintaining the marketing output, e.g. use of advertising agency.

The capital expense and finance budget

It will be necessary to draft a long-term capital expense budget for the strategic planning period under consideration. This will address any fixed capital assets which might be required to back up the marketing plans, such as, for example, new service sites, or office expansion.

A cash or finance budget might take into account:

> - Cash flows, i.e. how revenue will match up with operating expenses and payments to suppliers.
> - Short-term loans.
> - Temporary investment for surplus funds.
> - A study of money market conditions and interest rates.
> - The provision for contingent liabilities.

It will be obvious from all of this that the setting of budgets is also more likely to be realistic and related to what the *whole* company wants to achieve when it has this cross-functional emphasis, rather than just having one functional department involved. The problems of designing a dynamic system for budget setting, rather than having poorly-thought-through procedures, are a major challenge to marketing and financial directors of all companies.

Annual zero-based budgeting is an excellent discipline

> Many managers advocate a zero-based approach to budgeting. With this approach the marketing director justifies all marketing expenditure from a base of zero each year, against the tasks which need to be accomplished.

If this is done, then the marketing plan, which in effect links a hierarchy of objectives cascading from the corporate objectives, ties every item of expenditure to the corporate objectives. For example, if customer service demanded a higher proportion of the budget, the rationale for this should be directly attributable to a major objective formulated in the marketing planning process.

> By proceeding in this way, every item of expenditure is fully accounted for as part of a rational, objective and task approach.

It also ensures that when changes have to be made during the period under consideration, they can be made in such a way that least damage is caused to the organization's financial strengths and long-term objectives.

In manufacturing, it is easy to see that incremental marketing expenses are all costs incurred after the product leaves the factory, other than costs involved in physical distribution. In a service company, the dividing line is far less obvious, because a 'factory' does not always exist. Those who 'make' the service product might do so partly in the company's offices and partly on the customer's premises. (The types of interaction in service delivery were discussed in Chapter 2 and illustrated in Figure 2.7.)

Incremental marketing expenses are more difficult to identify in a service organization

> Furthermore, in some services, such as a small management consultancy, the contact person is in effect the service product, the service surround, the salesperson and the company, all at the same time.

Just as with the difficult question of whether packaging should be a marketing or production expense, there are some issues where there are no simple answers. Exactly how a service company defines its marketing expenses will need to relate to its circumstances. Common sense will reveal the most useful and workable solutions. The important point is that careful analysis should be made about what is required to take the company towards its goals, and that items of expenditure should be gathered under appropriate headings. A zero-based budgeting approach lends itself to achieving this result. Those wishing to consider further the relationship between marketing planning and budgeting are referred to Russell Abratt and his colleagues.[1]

There is scant information available on how much money service companies spend on marketing activities relative to their turnover. Some degree of benchmarking of marketing spend may be desirable among friendly companies within the same service sector, or in firms in other service sectors that are comparable to yours.

There is a huge variation in how much service companies spend on marketing activities. For example, in professional services, the average range is between 1% and 2% of fees or turnover. However, while professional service firms include direct marketing expenses and staff within marketing and business development departments, they typically do not include partners' time. Some partners in specialist law firms, accounting firms and management consulting firms may bill their time at a rate in excess of $10,000 a day. Given partners can spend a very substantial amount of time on marketing activities, this can represent a large amount especially if their time is valued at their billing rate.

There is also substantial variation *within* a particular service industry. For example, the IDC 'Marketing Investment Planner 2011 Benchmark

Study' examined marketing expenditure by information technology companies and found companies with a turnover of less than $500 million spend on average 4% of their revenue on marketing, while companies with over $10 billion in revenue spend around 1.8% of their revenue on marketing.[2]

In some sectors of the financial services and professional services market benchmark studies and interfirm comparisons are often available which give indications of what may be appropriate levels of marketing expenditure. However, while benchmarking is very useful we do favour a zero-based approach to the marketing budget, based on the objectives the service organization is seeking to accomplish.

Step 10   First-year implementation programme

Once agreement has been reached regarding budgets, those responsible for the development of the first-year implementation programme of the marketing plan can then proceed to develop details of tasks to be completed, together with responsibilities and timings.

> Such programmes (which in marketing literature are also sometimes called one-year tactical marketing plans, or schedules) constitute detailed guides which ensure that the first-year activities direct the service organization on a journey which will achieve its longer-term strategic marketing objectives.

The customer judges the organization solely on its output

Before starting to formulate the various marketing programmes, it is important to be clear about the activities upon which they are intended to impact. Guidance for this comes from taking a 'customer's-eye view' of the company. As Figure 9.1 shows, the customer views the service organization through the window of its output. This, as we saw earlier, is what is termed the marketing mix, which consists of seven key elements – the traditional four Ps (the service product, promotion, price and place) and three additional elements appropriate to services marketing (people, processes and customer service).

> By managing the components of the marketing mix effectively, the marketer provides a 'window' which enables the customer to view the service organization offer in an integrated manner.

We can now see that marketing programmes involve developing plans for managing all seven components of the marketing mix. However, not all marketing plans will have separate plans for all seven elements

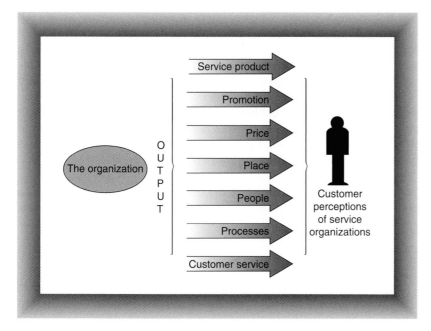

Figure 9.1
The organizational output

of the marketing mix. In some cases elements such as the people and processes may be incorporated into the other elements of the plan. Whether or not these are detailed separately or integrated elsewhere in the marketing plan, it is essential that the implications of all the mix elements are considered as part of the planning process.

Thus, we have no wish to be overly dogmatic on the subject of how many elements of the services marketing mix should have detailed plans developed for them. For a review of alternative approaches to marketing mix development see Constantinides' work.[3] Readers who choose to stay with the 4Ps concept and find that it works for them, may wish not to abandon it. There is also a danger that extended discussion about what constitutes the marketing mix will reach a sterile level of debate. The pragmatic marketer should make up his or her own mind regarding what constitutes the service company's output. The main point is not to overlook anything.

The marketing mix will now be considered in more detail in terms of what goes into the planning for each of its elements.

Mix element 1: The service product plan

Most of the key elements relating to this element of the marketing mix have already been discussed in Chapter 7 (Sub-audit 4: Auditing the services and products) and in Chapter 8 (Marketing objectives) so will not be repeated here. This earlier discussion covered topics relating to the product plan including the product options (in terms of the Ansoff matrix), differentiation, positioning, lifecycles and portfolio analysis.

The formulation of marketing objectives in Step 6 of the marketing plan will have clarified and set targets regarding the quantity and quality of which services go to which markets. What now needs to be done is to schedule the various activities so that they do not compete for scarce resources at the same time, and that they are delivered in sufficient quantity throughout the planning period that the revenue from the total portfolio provides sufficient funds at any one time. The service product plan will also indicate what activities need to go into the development of new services, and over what period of time. It will also show when and how existing services will be withdrawn from the market.

Three further topics, which were not discussed previously, need to be considered within the product plan. These include: branding, physical evidence and new service development strategies.

Branding[4]

The growing importance of the services sector has made firms aware that the creation and development of service brands represents a source of sustainable competitive advantage. Despite similarities between the principles of branding for goods and services, the specific nature of services requires tailored approaches.

One of the most problematic aspects associated with service brands is that consumers have to deal with intangible offerings. In an attempt to overcome this problem, marketers put a lot of emphasis on the company as a brand, especially in sectors such as financial services, as one way of making the service more tangible. However, studies have shown that consumers know little about specific financial products and services, and are often content to assume that the best-known companies have the best financial products. Thus marketers are left with limited scope for achieving product/service differentiation and service brands run the risk of being perceived as commodities.

To overcome this problem, service brands need to be made tangible to provide consumers with well-defined reference points. One means of increasing the tangibility of service brands is to project the brand's values through as many physical elements (symbols, representations, etc.) as possible, such as staff uniforms, office décor and the use of corporate colours. Virgin Airlines, for example, has successfully used its vibrant red livery to reflect the dynamic and challenging position it has adopted. IKEA's yellow and blue stripes not only allude to the company's Scandinavian origins but also guide consumers through the different sections of the store. The first points of contact with a service organization, including the quality of the car parking facilities and the appearance of the reception area, all interact to give consumers clues about what to expect from the service brand.

A successful brand identifies a service as having sustainable competitive advantage

The tangible elements of a service brand encourage and discourage particular types of consumer behaviour. For instance, a 7-Eleven store played classical symphonies as background music in an effort to retain 'wealthier' customers and drive away teenagers who tended to browse without purchasing.

Staff play a critical role in delivering services and shaping brand perceptions. Much of the success of the Disney brand results from the firm's insistence that employees recognize they are always 'on stage' when working, actively contributing to the performance and to the enjoyment of visitors. Staff morale also impacts on consumers. The development of a genuine service culture, which values staff as well as customers, is central to a strong service brand. The development of a service culture at SAS airlines, for example, helped turn the loss-making business into a successful brand under the stewardship of Jan Carlzon.

The way consumers evaluate a service brand depends largely on the extent to which they participate in the delivery of the service. Where service performance requires a high degree of consumer involvement, such as in Weight Watchers' programmes, it is vital that consumers understand their role and demonstrate firm commitment. In service sectors such as airlines where the level of consumer involvement is low (as all that is required is the consumers' physical presence), the onus of responsibility for service performance falls to the company and its employees.

> Brand perception is influenced by the level of consumer involvement in the service delivery

Effective consumer participation may require that consumers go through a process similar to a new company employee – a process of recruitment, education and reward. Brands such as US retailer Nordstoms and UK bank First Direct have been successful because they have effectively communicated the benefits consumers can gain from their participation. Service brands can be strengthened through an effective management of the mix of consumers who simultaneously experience the service. All major airlines, for example, are aware of the need to identify different segments.

A key decision in service branding is whether to build the brand on a specific service or on the corporate identity. Many large service companies, such as banks and insurance companies, consider that they can offer all their products and services through brands that are built on their corporate image. Financial institutions are wise to follow this strategy for well-established products/services and for new market segments which fit into their existing customer base, avoiding the risk of confusing their customers, who would otherwise see the same staff and the same physical evidence for differently named offerings.

This line of thought, however, can inhibit a company from successfully expanding into new market segments or products. Holiday Inn, for example, successfully offers several tailored brands to different target markets: for instance, Crowne Plaza for upscale business travellers.

While a brand can gain from being linked with a company name, the specific values of each brand still need to be conveyed. There are very good reasons why, in certain circumstances, it is advisable to follow the individual brand name route. For one, this allows the marketer to develop formulations and positionings to appeal to different segments in different markets. Another advantage is that if the new line should fail, the firm would experience less damage to its image than if the new brand had been closely tied to the company.

So, branding, formerly the domain of fast-moving consumer goods, is now recognized as being of great importance to services. Branding has an important role in value creation and can help support the positioning strategy that has been determined for the service organization. Of particular importance is the role of employees in building service brands.[5] Establishing a distinctive brand has become a key issue in almost every service sector.

Berry and Parasuraman[6] have outlined the key questions that need to be addressed by service marketers when considering their brand:

1. Are we proactive in presenting a strong company brand to our customers (and other stakeholders)?

2. How does our company name rate on the tests of distinctiveness, relevance, memorability and flexibility?

3. Do we use to full advantage branding elements other than the company name?

4. Is our presented brand cohesive?

5. Do we apply our brand consistently across all media?

6. Do we use all possible media to present our brand?

7. Do we recognize the influence of the service offering on brand meaning?

8. Do we base our branding decisions on research?

9. Are we respectful of what exists when we change our brand or add new brands?

10. Do we internalize our branding?

These questions provide useful guidelines to developing service brands.

Physical evidence

Elements of physical evidence are a means by which, over time, the brand values can be re-informed. Physical evidence is part of the service organization's environment where the services encounter takes place. Physical evidence is a means of providing tangible physical clues for a service which is largely intangible. Physical evidence also helps support the positioning and image of the service firm.

While it has been argued by some writers that physical evidence[7] is of sufficient importance and that it should form a separate element of the marketing mix, our view is that it is a sub-element of the product element of the marketing mix (in the same way that advertising and personal selling are sub-elements of the promotion element of the mix). However, the important issue is that attention is directed at it, regardless of where it is structurally placed in the marketing programme.

Physical evidence can help with the positioning of a service firm and can give tangible support to the outcome of the service experience. For example, banks have traditionally built highly elaborate and decorative façades and banking chambers to give the impression of wealth, substance and solidarity. Currently many service organizations spend large amounts of money to create branding, architecture, layout, furnishings, décor and uniforms that provide physical evidence that reinforces their desired image.

For services which are performed at the location of the service organization, physical evidence has an essential role to play. Familiarity is often a factor used by service franchise operators to provide reassurance. This is achieved by providing systematic physical evidence of what the customer can expect. For example, customers of Ritz-Carlton hotels and Oddbins wine shops have a clear idea of what they can expect when they visit a new outlet.

New product and service development

The option of new product and service development, as part of the product service plan, was mentioned briefly in the earlier discussion of the Ansoff Matrix. This is an area of increasing interest to service researchers. Christopher Lovelock and his colleagues[8] outline six categories of service development:

1. *Major service innovations* – These innovations represent major new markets. Examples include Dyno-rod (drain/sewer unblocking services); Federal Express and DHL (overnight distribution); cellular telephones; and relatively recent web-based TV services. The risk and reward profiles of such major innovations are typically large.

2. *Major process innovations* – These innovations involve utilizing new processes to deliver existing services better, cheaper or with improved benefits. For example, some universities such as Singapore Management University and the University of Phoenix offer courses with radically new non-traditional service.

3. *Product line extensions* – These offer customers greater variety of choices within existing service lines. This is typical of a business in maturity, which already has a core market which the service provider seeks to maintain. For example, major law firms servicing corporate clients have developed increased business from clients by offering advice on environmental law. This supplements the commercial legal services already provided to their clients, but is in response to both new legislation and companies' desire to be perceived as being environmentally conscious.

4. *Process line extensions* – These are less extensive and less innovative than major process innovations. They typically represent new ways of delivering existing products by offering customers more convenience or a different experience. One of the most common forms of process line extension is adding a low-cost distribution channel such as the Internet to an existing high contact channel.

5. *Supplementary service innovations* – This form of innovation involves adding additional service elements to an existing course service. For example, the traditional camera store has transformed its service offerings by adding a range of customized printing facilities for customers using digital cameras.

6. *Service redesign* – This is a common form of innovation. It involves modest changes and improvements to the core product or the surrounding supplementary services offered to the customer. There are a number of different forms of service redesign which include offering customers self-service, moving the point of service delivery to the customer's location (e.g. mobile dog grooming at the customer's home) and redesigning tangible elements of the service experience (e.g. five-star hotels offering a 'pillow menu' from which hotel guests can select from a range of pillow types available for their room).

Managing the service product plan

Grönroos[9] has suggested four key steps that the services marketer needs to manage in providing a service offer:

● *Developing the service concept* – the basic concept or intentions of the service provider.

● *Developing a basic service package* – the core service, facilitating services and goods, and supporting services and goods.

● *Developing an augmented service offering* – the service process and interactions between the service provider and customers, including the service delivery process. It includes a consideration of the accessibility of the service, interaction between the service provider and the customer, and the degree of customer participation.

● *Managing image and communication* – so that they support and enhance the augmented service offer. This is the interface between the promotion and product marketing mix elements.

A consideration of these steps, together with the elements of the product plan addressed in earlier chapters, makes clear some of the linkages with other elements of the marketing mix. When the basic service offer has been decided, attention can then be directed at development of promotion, and the other ingredients of the marketing mix.

This particular plan or programme provides the backbone for many of the other organizational activities. For example, recruitment programmes will be based on it. It will also loom large in cash-flow projections.

Mix element 2: The promotion and communications plan

Before providing some of the more traditional and abidingly essential guidelines on the day-to-day management of communications, it is clear to everyone in business today that technology changes have empowered the customer and the consumer to find out more about suppliers than suppliers know about them. Also, technology change has given customers enormous choice about how they wish to be communicated to. This makes the market mapping process outlined in Chapter 6 even more important.

The changing nature of promotion and distribution

Promotion and distribution are changing in a number of respects. Channels such as the Internet and social media are emphasizing an already growing trend from mass media such as advertising to more interactive media. Integrating these channels within a coherent strategy is not an easy task. Writers in the field of 'Integrated Marketing Communications' (IMC)[10] emphasize that before engaging on detailed planning – writing sales plans or promotions plans, for example – it is necessary to choose which medium to use for which customer interactions. This is illustrated in Figure 9.2.

The choice of channel/medium is generally a complex one, involving different media for different communications with the same customer. The organization will also frequently wish to leave some options in the hands of the customer. For example, a Dell customer may find out about Dell from colleagues or from press advertising; investigate which product to buy, what the price is and what configuration is required using the Web; print out order details and pass them to the purchasing department to place the order via fax; check on the delivery time via telephone; take delivery via a delivery service; and obtain customer service using email. Customers are no longer content to have the medium dictated by the supplier.

The choice of medium is clearly closely intertwined with the distribution strategy. Distribution channels often have a mix of purposes, providing both a means of conveying a service to the customer and a medium for information exchange. A fashion retailer provides a location where the customer's experience of trying on a suit or dress and determining how it 'feels' is difficult to replicate. So the focus on information exchange is closely linked to the often physical issues of

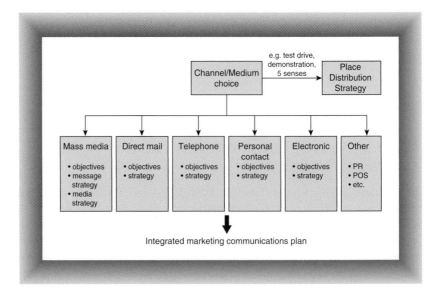

Figure 9.2
Defining a promotion
and distribution
strategy

distribution. However, considering the two separately can result in solutions, such as Internet banking or Internet shopping for CDs (which can be sampled online, but won't need to be 'felt' physically). Choosing the right medium for the right purpose, then, is not a trivial task. There is increasing recognition that this issue needs to be considered afresh, rather than simply following the traditional practice in a given industry. But although writings on IMC explain the problem, there is little practical help for organizations on how to solve it.

A related problem is the changing nature of the sales process, which we will turn to now.

Marketing Operations and the New Sales Process

Once an overall marketing plan has been drawn up, including a plan for promotions, the plan must be implemented. This is the role of marketing operations – the delivery of value to the customer which was specified in the planning process. However, during the course of a year, plenty of finer-grained communications decisions need to be taken. To illustrate, we will look again, in Figure 9.3, at the map of the marketing operations process that we introduced in Chapter 1. In terms of marketing operations, we are physically concerned with the 'deliver value' component within this figure. In Figure 9.4 we provide a detailed map of marketing operations for the 'deliver value' process.

In Chapter 1 we gave a very full and detailed explanation of the 'deliver value' process in the marketing map. It involved a new way of describing the communications process and a definite move away from the now out-of-date theories which assume that the consumer is a passive being, to be analysed and communicated with. What is described here is most definitely a totally two-way, interactive, dyadic process, which has major implications for all organizations, not just service providers.

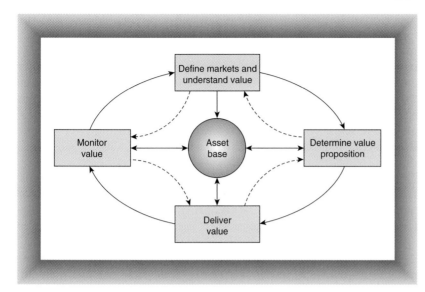

Figure 9.3
Map of the marketing domain

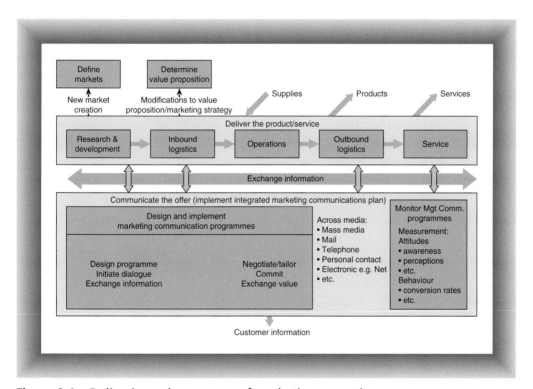

Figure 9.4   Delivering value – a map of marketing operations

The need for CRM systems to underpin tailored communications

The market for integrated CRM systems has largely arisen out of the frustration of many companies with their multiple customer databases developed for different tasks – as many as 40 in one recent case.[11] Most major organizations are working towards a unified view of the customer, so that all aspects of the customer interface can be coordinated. In order to achieve this, systems need to manage customer data independently of the task being performed. For example, if a customer enters their name and address on a website, they do not wish to be asked the same information on the telephone. This requires all tasks to call on a single module which manages this customer data if a spaghetti-like set of system interconnections is not to result. We term this the principle of *task independent data management*.

This point can clearly be seen in Figure 9.5. The 'task management' layer needs to be separate from the 'data management' layer, rather than systems for each task endeavouring to manage parts of the customer data, as is still often the case.

Another point which is clearly illustrated by Figure 9.5 is the importance of *channel independent task management*. The 'channel management' layer of managing different channels or media is often bundled in with particular tasks. A 'direct mail system' will be *the* way in which the organization generates leads; an 'order processing system' will assume that orders come in to an order processing clerk (rather than, say, being made by a website), and so on. Such an architecture is inherently inflexible. An ideal architecture separates the issue of managing

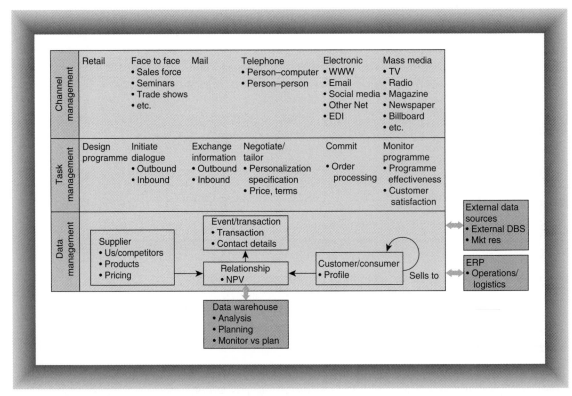

Figure 9.5 Towards a viable CRM structure

the medium from that of managing the task. That way, an order processing system could handle orders that originate over the Web, in-store and from field sales in exactly the same way, without requiring three separate order processing systems.

Two examples follow of an attempt by a major global travel company to understand the information seeking and purchasing processes of different segments. These are given as Figures 9.6 and 9.7

The left-hand row in these figures identifies the various steps of customer interaction, including 'recognize exchange potential', 'initiate dialogue', 'exchange information', etc. The various channels that could be used by customers such as Internet, mobile telephone, interactive digital TV, etc., are shown across the top column of the figures. The different shading shows the relative importance of these channels for each of the stages with the darkest shading representing the most important channel and the lightest shading representing the least important channel.

From an examination of the two segments in Figures 9.6 and 9.7 (there were seven different segments in total for this travel company), it can be seen that the behaviour of each is totally different. Without such segmentation knowledge, an integrated communications plan would be impossible.

As we have seen, 'promotions' in marketing mix terminology mean all the activities by which communications are aimed at customers with a

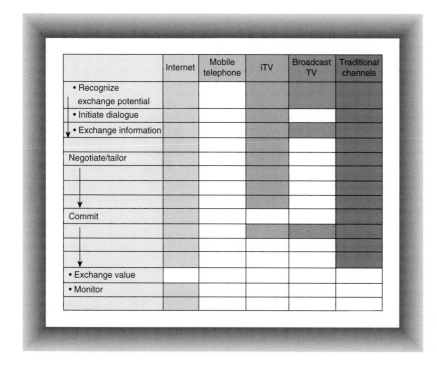

Figure 9.6
The 'Sunlovers'
customer segment

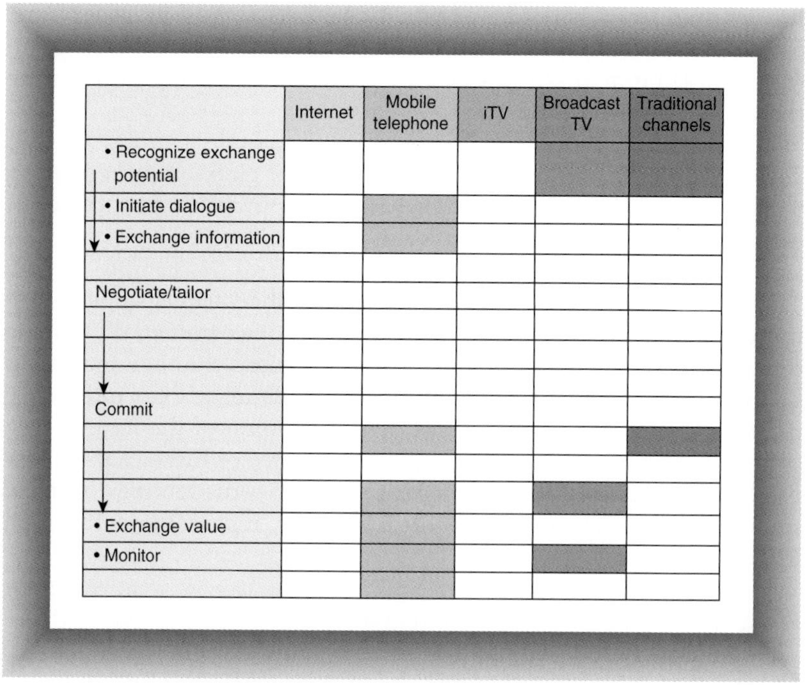
Internet
Mobile telephone
iTV
Broadcast TV
Traditional channels
• Recognize exchange potential
• Initiate dialogue
• Exchange information
Negotiate/tailor
Commit
• Exchange value
• Monitor

Figure 9.7
The 'John and Mary Lively' customer segment

view to influencing the buying decision. For planning purposes, it is often convenient to break these communications into two separate groups:

- Impersonal communications
- Face-to-face communications.

Between them, these methods of communication provide the service marketer with a number of options from which to choose, for they can be used either singly or in combination.

> A key decision is the split between the personal and impersonal communications mix

There is nothing intrinsically better about one means of communication rather than another, for both provide benefits and drawbacks. In essence, personal or face-to-face communications provide a mechanism for a two-way dialogue. However, being 'labour intensive' means that this process is costly to provide. The alternative impersonal methods, such as advertising and promotions, are, in comparison, less expensive (in terms of reaching individuals), yet are limited by the one-way nature of their communication pattern.

Thus, the choice facing the marketer should hinge upon considerations such as:

- Who is the target audience?
- What is it they need to know?

- What is the most cost-effective way of providing this information?
- Can we afford to do it?

Whenever a wide range of options is counterbalanced by a limited budget, it is inevitable that an element of compromise comes into the solution. Having said this, service marketers should do their utmost to provide the optimum communications mix, because intelligent planning can ensure that the two different approaches combine in a way which is mutually beneficial and synergistic.

At the heart of any successful promotion programme is a clear understanding of the communication process, seen from the customer's viewpoint. In general terms, this follows the model shown in Figure 9.8. When it comes to winning customers, the first task of communications is to make unaware customers aware of the service on offer. Having brought customers to that stage, it is important that they fully understand what it is the service will do for them. Next, they need to be convinced that what is said is true and that the service will satisfactorily meet their needs. Finally, the customers need to be energized sufficiently to buy or sign the order.

The communications process must follow a logical sequence

It can be seen that this overall process can be accomplished in a number of different ways. For example, the door-to-door salesperson cold-calling will endeavour to cover the whole process in one short visit. Alternatively, somebody opening a new hair salon might resort to using advertisements in the local newspaper, or a leaflet drop, followed by invitations for prospective clients to have an introductory, free, or reduced price appointment. In providing large-scale business-to-business services, the process may be developed over a long period.

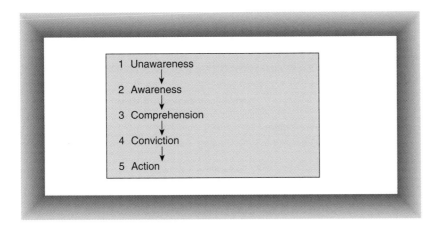

Figure 9.8
Stages of communications

Number of employees	Av. no. of buying influences	Av. no. of salesperson contacts
0–200	3.42	1.72
201–400	4.85	1.75
401–1000	5.81	1.90
1000+	6.50	1.65

Figure 9.9
Buying influences and customer size
Source: McGraw-Hill

The communications process is further complicated in that, in some businesses, it can extend over a long period (e.g. negotiating to supply a service to a government department) or an increasing number of people can become involved at the customer end. For example, in the supply of international telecommunications to the worldwide operations of a major bank, the communications process might be extended over a period of several years.

As Figure 9.9 indicates, if the customer company consisted of 0–200 people, then, on average, three or four people might be involved in the buying decision. As the company size increases, not surprisingly so does the number influencing the buying decision.

> The full significance of this information is contained in the third column, which shows that, on average, a salesperson only makes contact with about one or two of these people.

The issue of company size can also have a bearing on the likelihood of its staff receiving information, as Figure 9.10 shows. In larger companies most information is obtained from the trade and technical press, whereas in smaller companies it is from personal contact.

	% small companies	% large companies
Trade and technical press	28	60
Salesperson calls	47	19
Exhibitions	8	12
Direct mail	19	9

Figure 9.10
Sources of information
Source: MacLean Hunter

Even from this brief discussion about the communications mix, it is evident that its make-up has to be given careful consideration because:

- More than one person can influence what is bought.

- Salespeople do not see all the influencers.

- Customers get their information from different sources.

Digital communications and social media

What's different about digital communications and social media? After all, they have long left their silo in an innovation corner of the marketing function, and become in many ways simply an additional set of communications tools to use in integrated campaigns. Nonetheless, the online revolution has forced marketers to think rather differently about marketing in a digital world. Our '6 Is' framework (Figure 9.11) encapsulates some of these differences. The framework considers six capabilities provided by digital channels which, *when these enhance performance against the customers' buying criteria*, can be beneficial in creation of value for the customer and the firm. We now review each of the elements in this framework.

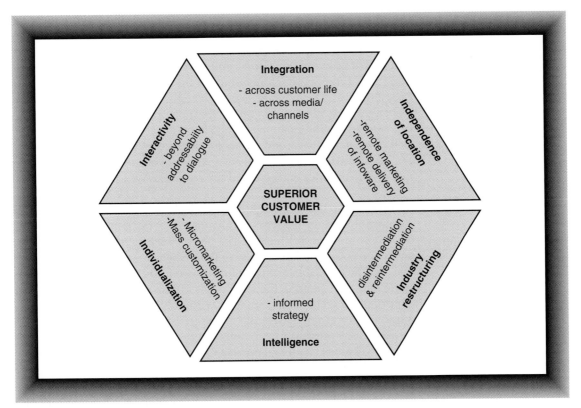

Figure 9.11   The 6 Is of e-marketing

Integration: joining up the customer experience   In the early days of the Internet, the talk was of pureplay business models: businesses entirely dealing with their customers online. But while some highly successful examples of this single-channel strategy clearly flourish, for the great majority of firms, the Internet is part of a multichannel mix. And this is not just in the sense that different customers use different channels: rather, many individual transactions involve a multichannel customer journey from awareness through to information collection, purchase and delivery. A hotel chain found that only 8% of its customers did not touch the Internet at all in their purchase process. An airline found an even lower figure – around 2% – despite many of the final purchases still being made by telephone or with travel agents.

So multichannel integration is as important with the Internet as with any other communication medium, a fact often lost on companies who delegate the website to enthusiasts in an isolated corner of the organization, or outsource its development and operations with minimal provision for information transfer – hence repeating the mistakes often made in the early days of the call centre. Instead, Dell points customers to its website through 'e-value codes' in magazines and brochures, which direct the customer to the exact page they want. This has the crucial benefit of enabling Dell to track the effectiveness of the offline communications. And once on the website, telephone numbers are prominently displayed so the customer does not give up if they need further help.

In similar vein, the dotcom director of a major retailer told us how he had been challenged by a new chief executive as to why he should keep his job. He was able to respond with proof not only that he was making a small but growing profit from online sales, but also that he was generating four times as much revenue for the high-street stores as he was taking online. If a customer searches on his website for, say, a bed, the webpage offers information on the location of the nearest store with the bed in stock, so the customer can go in and try bouncing on it! And like Dell, the retailer is careful to ensure that these cross-channel journeys can be tracked, by such means as giving the customer a code to quote in the store in order to be entered for a prize draw.

A good way to think through how channels fit together in the customer journey is to draw what we call a channel chain diagram – see Figure 9.12 for an example for this retailer. The predominantly online channel chain on the left is the one followed by default when companies first go online. The middle model, starting online and ending offline, had the great advantage of exploiting the company's offline presence – providing an important differentiation compared with pureplay competitors. Furthermore, for some purchases, the customer would start in the store and complete the purchase later online – the right-hand model. We will return to channel chain diagrams in Chapter 10.

The need for management of customer relationships implies the need for systems which manage data on the whole of the customer interaction, throughout the customer lifecycle, from initial contact, through

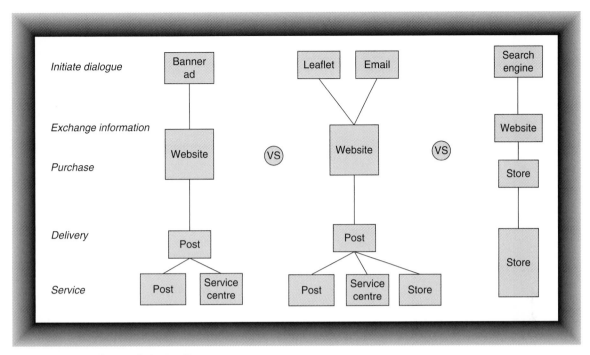

Figure 9.12 Channel chain diagram

configuration and sales, to delivery and post-sales service. The multiple channels by which the consumer demands to be able to reach the supplier implies that this data must also be integrated across communication mechanisms, so a telephone salesperson knows about a service request that was sent yesterday by email, and a sales representative in the field can call on information about previous purchases and customer profitability to assist judgements about discount levels.

Interactivity: beyond addressability to dialogue Knowing your customers means closing the loop between the messages sent to them and the messages they send back. It has been said that this is the age of addressability, as organizations have endeavoured to communicate with individual customers through carefully targeted direct mail, email, paid search and so on. Interactivity goes one step further, listening to the customer and responding appropriately, as one would in a face-to-face conversation. With so many interactive channels now available – websites, social media, call centres, mobile phone apps and so on – marketers need to think differently about the sales process, as customers rightly expect them to use interactivity to hold a true dialogue. In Figure 9.13 we contrast the traditional concept of communication as a one-way bombardment of the customer – apparent from the language of 'campaigns', 'targets', 'persuasion' and so on – with our proposed recrafting of the purchase process as an interaction between equal parties.

Traditional 'push-based' models of marketing, in which after the product is made prospects are found and persuaded to buy the product, are illustrated on the left. The delivery and service that follow are

Supplier perspective		Interaction perspective	Buyer perspective	
Advertising	Selling	Interaction	Decision theory	Consumer behaviour
Brand awareness		*Recognize exchange potential*	Problem recognition	Category need
			Information search	Awareness
Brand attitude	**Prospecting**	*Initiate dialogue*		Attitude
- info re benefits				
- brand image	**Provide**	*Exchange*		Information
- feelings	**information**	*information*	Evaluation of	gathering &
- peer influence			alternatives	judgement
	Persuade	*Negotiate/tailor*	Choices / purchase	Purchase process
Trial inducement	**Close sale**	*Commit*		
Reduce cognitive dissonance	**Deliver**	*Exchange value*	Post-purchase behaviour	Post-purchase experience
	Service	*Monitor*		

Figure 9.13   The purchase process as an interaction between supplier and buyer

operational functions with little relationship to marketing. Traditional models of buyer behaviour, illustrated on the right of the figure, assume more rationality on the part of buyers, but underplay the importance of what the buyer says back to the seller. The seller's offer is assumed to be predetermined, rather than developed in conjunction with the buyer.

The interaction perspective, shown in the centre of Figure 9.13, replaces this one-way process as follows:

- 'Recognize exchange potential' replaces 'Category need' or 'Problem recognition'. Both sides need to recognize the potential for a mutual exchange of value.

- 'Initiate dialogue' replaces 'Create awareness' or 'Prospecting'. The dialogue with an individual customer may be started by either party. One feature of the web, for example, is that on many occasions, new customers will approach the supplier rather than vice versa. All too often, marketers are so busy organizing their next outbound campaign that these ad-hoc queries are not followed up.

- 'Exchange information' replaces 'Provide information'. If we are to serve the customer effectively, tailor our offerings and build a long-term relationship, we need to learn about the customer as much as the customer needs to learn about our products.

- 'Negotiate/tailor' replaces 'Persuade'. Negotiation is a two-way process which may involve us modifying our offer in order to better meet the customer's needs. Persuading the customer instead that the square peg we happen to have in stock will fit their round hole is not likely to lead to a long and profitable relationship.

- 'Commit' replaces 'Close sale'. Both sides need to commit to the transaction, or to a series of transactions forming the next stage in a relationship – a decision with implications for both sides.

- 'Exchange value' replaces 'Deliver' and 'Post-sales service'. The 'Post-sales service' may be an inherent part of the value being delivered, not simply a cost centre, as it is often still managed.

One-to-one communications and principles of relationship marketing, then, demand a radically different sales process from that traditionally practised. This point is far from academic, as an example will illustrate.

The company in question provides business-to-business financial services. Its marketing managers relayed to us their early experience with a website which was enabling them to reach new customers considerably more cost-effectively than their traditional sales force. When the website was first launched, potential customers were finding the company on the web, deciding the products were appropriate on the basis of the website, and sending an email to ask to buy. So far, so good.

However, stuck in a traditional model of the sales process, the company would allocate the 'lead' to a salesperson, who would phone up and make an appointment, perhaps three weeks' hence. The customer would by now probably have moved on to another online supplier who could sell the product today, but those that remained were subjected to a sales pitch, complete with glossy materials, which was totally unnecessary, the customer having already decided to buy. Those that were not put off would proceed to be registered as able to buy over the web, but the company had lost the opportunity to improve its margins by using the sales force more judiciously.

In time, the company realized its mistake, and changed its sales model and reward systems to something close to our 'interaction perspective' model. Unlike those prospects which the company proactively identified and contacted, which might indeed need 'selling' to, many new web customers were initiating the dialogue themselves, and simply required the company to respond effectively and rapidly, which was done with a small desk-based team, who only called on the sales force for

> complex sales where their involvement was needed and justi-
> fied. The sales force was increasingly freed up to concentrate
> on major clients and on relationship building.

Individualization: information-enabled tailoring   Integrated information about the customer provides the basis for individualizing the
product or associated services. Online newspapers from the US's *Wall
Street Journal* to the UK's *Times* can be tailored to provide the topics
you want, and to prompt you when material you are interested in is
available. Dell Premier provides major accounts with a customized
site, which allows easy ordering at individually negotiated prices,
easy tracking, and easy control by the firm's central procurement of
what its staff can see and order. Goods from M&M chocolates to cars
can be customized online, but services can also be customized online.

Inhabitants of virtual world Second Life don't just spend money on
virtual versions of real-world goods from apples to zoos; the traffic
also flows the other way, with services such as Fabjectory 'printing'
the user's online creations such as their avatar as a real-world object.
In a web 2.0 take on individualization, players of EA's Sims 2 game
competed to design an H&M outfit which would be made available in
1,000 H&M stores.

The point is not that we *always* need to individualize just because the
Internet makes it possible; the 6 Is provide e-marketing mix levers, in
the same way that the 7 Ps delineate the overall levers available to any
marketer, to be pulled where necessary in order to achieve marketing
objectives. Individualization is closely linked to independence of location – our next topic.

Independence of location: the death of distance   What is the difference between shoes made to measure by the village cobbler and customized trainers made to order by NIKEiD? Both achieve individualization,
but Nike combines it with post-industrial revolution economies of scale.
It is able to do this because its website can serve a widely spread geographical population, using the data transport provided by the Internet
and the physical transport of our 21st-century infrastructure, plus a
database-driven manufacturing facility. Independence of location
allows individualization to be achieved economically. Niche products
can serve their target markets even if spread globally.

Freeing up the company from the cost of physical facilities *can* lower
overall costs in sectors such as banking, travel and Internet retailing: a
US study calculated costs of 1 cent for a transaction conducted over the
Internet, as opposed to $1.07 for a branch transaction and 27 cents for
an ATM. There are exceptions, however, such as the high rates of stock
returns by clothes retailers – the 26% returns for retailer ASOS being
towards the best that can be hoped for. Another exception is the high

picking and delivery costs for grocery retailers: UK retailer Ocado, loved by its customers for the high reliability that derives from its dedicated high-technology picking centre, has struggled to reach the 6% gross margins which would deliver long-term profits. It announced its first quarterly profit ever early in 2011, ten years after its launch.

The public sector has been slower to exploit independence of location in most countries, but transformations such as the UK's Driver & Vehicle Licensing Agency's (DVLA) switch to Internet ordering of tax discs, which provide evidence that 'road tax' has been paid, show what is possible. Instead of asking car-owners to go with a paper form to their local post office – a high-cost indirect channel partner from DVLA's point of view – the car-owner is now encouraged to visit a website or phone an interactive voice response (IVR) service. Importantly, rather than giving away margin by lowering the price online, the DVLA instead created additional convenience benefits for the customer: the website automatically checks whether the customer has valid insurance and whether the car has an 'MOT' certificate of roadworthiness, saving much searching in drawers at home! This careful focus on the customer's buying criteria, along with a communications campaign, shifted the majority of car-owners to remote channels within two years of launch.

For B2B firms, too, the cost advantages of the Internet can be significant – though mostly as part of a multichannel mix. BT's Business division found that by switching simpler purchases to telephone and the web, it could reduce total sales and marketing costs from 25% of revenue to 18% – putting 7% of revenue straight on the bottom line. Its sales force remained crucial, though, for selling more complex services to high-value customers.

For consumers, too, high-involvement products may require a face-to-face component of the mix. At the high end of the luxury goods retail market, Fabergé's sophisticated website cannot even be viewed without a phone conversation to a service agent based in Fabergé's head office in Switzerland. Its beautiful graphics are backed up by a chat facility with the same service centre, which may lead to the agent offering to fly over to visit the customer to show a five-figure item . . . an offer which one of the authors sadly decided to decline when trialling the service!

If the Internet enables the firm to be independent of its location, the same can be true for the customer. Serving customers wherever *they* are can be enhanced by location-based services on mobile devices which detect their location and advise them accordingly. Location-based social network Foursquare allows users to broadcast their location to others, enabling them to meet old and new friends wherever they are in the world. Gowalla is a game variant on this theme, in which players drop off and pick up items at specified locations. In 2010, the success of such specialists led the major social networking sites such as Facebook and Twitter to launch their own location-based services.

Intelligence: informed strategy Interactivity does not just enable individual customers to get what they want. It also provides a rich source of insight for the firm in order to inform marketing strategy. Financial services provider Egg collects information on service levels through a continuously available online questionnaire, and then displays a summary of the main concerns of customers and how it is responding on the website. Dell collates online buyer behaviour to position its customers into segments such as 'All about price', 'Design is important', 'All about high-end products' and 'Tailored for my country', so it can ensure it has the right offer for each segment without needlessly sacrificing margin by cutting prices across the board.

In a Web 2.0 world, complaints and problems are best looked at as a source of insight rather than as a PR problem to be managed through press releases, as the famous case of Kryptonite locks showed. An online video of these bicycle locks being readily opened with a paperclip led to a defensive response from the company that sounded all too much like advertising copy: 'The world just got tougher, and so did our locks.' The response from bloggers was immediate and devastating: 'We've spent over $100 on these types of locks for our bicycles, and hearing "the world just got tougher and so did our locks" kinda got us a little miffed. The world didn't get tougher, it got Bic pens and blogs and your locks got opened.' The company never recovered.

The Internet, then, provides numerous ways of gaining intelligence, ranging from traditional questionnaires to behavioural analysis. Some of the behavioural techniques available are summarized in Table 9.1.

Industry restructuring: redrawing the market map As with all technological innovations, the effect of digital marketing is sometimes incremental but often radical, with customer needs being met in new ways by new players. Examples that would have seemed unthinkable 20 years ago are all around us. Newspapers face a torrid time as the young gain their entertainment and news from digital sources, and advertising revenues follow audiences online. High-street travel agents are 'disintermediated' by direct online sales by airlines and hotels, and 'reintermediated' by online specialists such as Expedia. Book publishers and business schools who package and disseminate knowledge face the threat of disintermediation from their customers conducting their own research online, or collaboratively creating content such as Wikipedia. Record companies were disintermediated by peer-to-peer file sharing sites and reintermediated by iTunes, allowing many musicians to self-publish with help from YouTube and other social networks.

Each of these innovations can be thought of as a redrawing of the market map which we discussed in Chapter 6. While all predictions have

Table 9.1
Gaining Intelligence
Online: Some of the
Available Tools

Purpose of intelligence	Example measures	Notes
Customer needs and satisfaction	Channel satisfaction (e.g. website) Customer needs Usability	e.g. American Customer Satisfaction Index (www.foreseeresults.com) Online questionnaires, focus groups Testing, online mystery shopping
Promotion effectiveness	Ad impressions Ad clicks Click-through rate Cost per click Cost per acquisition Unique visitors	Number of advertisements seen Clicks on advertisements by users Ad clicks/ad impressions Clicks on ad (or search engine entry)/cost Cost (from ad or intermediary)/ acquired customer Number of different people visiting site
Website effectiveness	Bounce rate Stickiness Attrition rate Conversion rate	Proportion of single page visits Page views/visitor sessions ('PPV') How many visitors are lost at each stage, e.g. from placing items in basket to checking out ('Basket abandonment rate') Purchases/visitors
Performance outcomes	Channel contribution Multichannel contribution	Channel revenue – channel costs Total revenue of multiple channels – sum of channel costs

to be reconsidered constantly in the light of experience, these innovations are not random or fundamentally unpredictable: rather, they succeed or fail according to whether they improve the value proposition for the end customer. So a good way to do at least an initial sense-check of the plausibility of a proposed redrawing of the market map is to evaluate what its impact would be on the end customer's critical success factors, using the quantified approach shown in the section on SWOT analysis in Chapter 13.

The 6 Is, then, are a way of thinking about what is different about digital communications. It is worth reflecting on a company's current position on these 6 Is: which aspects of digital media are currently being exploited well and which are not? There are numerous specific tools which can be used in support of these broad principles; while we cannot cover them in detail here, we summarize some of the main digital communications tools next.

The digital communications mix

We can divide the main tools available for online communications into four categories: see Figure 9.14.

Search engine marketing   As a high proportion of customer journeys online begin with a search engine, search marketing is a crucial part of the communications mix, particularly for customer acquisition. By 2011, over 25% of online ad spend was on 'paid search' – the listings on the search results pages which are reserved for paid-for entries.

Of considerable importance in the online area is search engine optimization (SEO): ensuring that the website naturally occurs high in the listing. And clearly, if paid search costs, say, an average of $3 per click or $8 per 1,000 page impressions ('cost per mille' or 'CPM') it can be cost-effective, too. (Note that this varies considerably. At the time of writing, the cost per click for 'Auto Insurance Quote' was $22.)

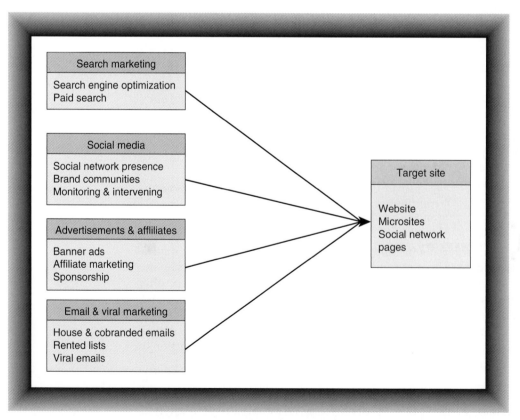

Figure 9.14   Main tools available for online communications

A plethora of advice is available on how Google and other search engines prioritize web pages and optimize web sites to ensure they are ranked high in the list is a specialist skillset, but the basic principles are common sense. Attractive, regularly updated content which many people appreciate, revisit and provide their own links to will find its way up the rankings. Even if these basics are in place, though, it is so important to appear on the first page that it is worth going the extra mile and finding some help from a web designer with SEO skills. A study by icrossing.com found that 95% of all search traffic comes from search results on page one. A luxury hotel chain found that on many commonly used search strings entered by its target customers, such as 'boutique hotel London' in Figure 9.15, it was coming on page 2 or lower. A simple analysis of its better-performing competitors showed why they were ranked higher: they included common search terms within the page title; they repeated these search words several times on the home page; and they had customer review facilities to engage repeat customers with the site, encourage traffic and provide advocacy. Some straightforward amendments brought the site onto the first page of some key search terms.

Social media Social networks such as Facebook, MySpace and LinkedIn – along with online gaming, which is an increasingly social activity – accounted for a third of the online time of Americans by 2010, as against 12% for email and chat. At first glance, it therefore seems odd that advertising spend on social networks is slow to catch up, with only

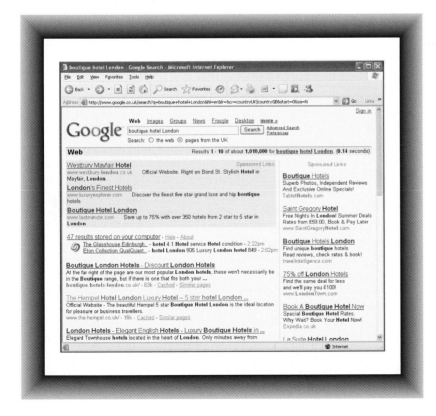

Figure 9.15
Search engine optimization and paid search: a hotel example

around 4% of online spend at that time. In part, this is because the sheer pace of social network expansion has provided a surfeit of advertising space which advertisers struggle to make sense of. While this 4% figure has been increasing fast, though, the truth is that it is nevertheless a vast underestimate of the amount of marketing effort already going into social media. The great majority of the true cost of social media marketing is not advertising on the sidelines, but joining in the conversation: blogging, hosting brand communities and so on. Broadly there are four purposes of social media for the marketer:

1. *Customer insight* – Social media provide a vast repository of free qualitative data about how customers think about the firm's product category and its offerings. UK remote bank First Direct (www .firstdirect.com) is unusual in displaying some of this information straight back to its customers on its home page – what its customers are talking about, how much of it is positive and how much negative, what they want improved and so on. For First Direct, this is a way of endeavouring to turn its highly enthusiastic customer base into powerful advocacy that is visible to non-customers in the notoriously sticky banking market – we are said to change our marriage partners more often than our banks!

   Some companies focus this free market insight by developing communities of innovative, enthusiastic customers – 'lead users' – who develop and evaluate new product ideas. This is the sole source of R&D in the case of clothes retailer Threadless (www .threadless.com), where the most popular ideas submitted by customers are made by the company and sold online. Other interesting examples are Nokia's Design By Community – an exercise to design a phone entirely through user community interaction (www .conversations.nokia.com/design-by-community) – and Volvo's Concept lab (www.conceptlabvolvo.com).

2. *Brand exposure* – The rise of social networking has been accompanied by a stream of statistics on the importance of social networks on purchase decisions, such as Gartner's claim that 74% of consumers are strongly influenced by them. The default reaction of many marketers is to add community facilities to their own website, in the hope of making this the destination of choice for customers in their product category, be it soft drinks, washing powder, accounting software or electrical equipment. This can work well with high-involvement categories such as telecoms or charities. UK Telco BT asked on Facebook how a storyline, running through TV advertisements about two characters Adam and Jane, should end: it received 1.6 million responses. On a smaller scale, Amnesty International asked its supporters for funding for a press ad against Shell's activities in Nigeria: it collected some $65,000. But there are two dangers with this thinking. The first is that not all products have 'social currency': do today's housewives, house-husbands or home workers really want to talk about washing powder? The second danger is that even if there is a relevant conversation to be had – about parenting, say, in the case of P&G – do we want to have it on a brand-owned website?

Practice is developing fast in this area, but some principles are emerging. First, not every brand can host a true destination site, any more than they can hope to host their own television channel. P&G has recognized this in its launch of supersavvyme.com, which aggregates many brands into a lifestyle site for women. At the time of writing the jury is still out on its success: with 200,000 monthly visitors it is gaining some traffic, but also attracting less than ringing endorsements such as this blog post: 'It is full of useful bits and bobs about mothering, and along the way it has competitions featuring Procter and Gamble products, as it is P&G running the whole thing. But is this what mothers really want?'

Which raises the second principle: marketers of all but the strongest brands need to go to where the customers are. There are existing flourishing networks for many areas of professional practice (e.g. JustPlainFolks for musicians), interests (such as e-democracy. org for politics) and affinity groups (BlackPlanet for African Americans, iVillage for women and so on), and the general networks all host these communities of interest too. Cranfield School of Management links with practitioners not just through its face-to-face courses and website but also through a presence on YouTube, Twitter (twitter.com/cranfieldki) and iTunes (e.g. www.youtube .com/user/CranfieldSoM). By 2011, entertainment company Disney's Facebook site had reached 16 million 'fans' and the iTunes' Facebook site had reached 10 million 'fans'.

3. *Relationship building* – Where brand building ends and the sales process begins in earnest is a moot point, but social networks can play a role for customers actively involved in a current purchase. Whether online or offline, word-of-mouth often proves the most powerful communication tool of all, and it has the benefit of being free. Retailer onlineshoes.com found that customers viewing at least one product review were over twice as likely to go on and buy the product than those who don't. And products with more reviews on the retailer's site sold better, irrespective of whether the reviews were positive, negative or mixed! So the retailer positively incentivized reviews, until its customers had developed the habit of posting them regularly.

For business-to-business marketers, social networks can also be important for building personal relationships which so often act as the initial spur to a supplier being shortlisted. IBM were one of the earlier users of virtual world Second Life to build relationships that spill over into the offline world, inviting customers to a Second Life version of Wimbledon where they could watch the tennis, chat to other fans and meet their IBM hosts. A minimum for executives with a front-line role is a strong online presence on networks such as LinkedIn, so they can be found easily when prospective customers are searching for experts on a particular topic.

4. *Customer service* – The final use of social media is perhaps more mundane but no less important: the provision of customer service. Not only is online advice cheaper to provide than telephone support, as

less expert time is typically needed, but also answers to common questions are available to all, providing an economy of scale.

Even better, customers can serve each other, experienced users of a product or service advising less experienced people. This runs counter to the traditional instincts of many marketers to control the customer experience, but loss of control cannot be fought; rather, it is an inevitable part of the increasing customer empowerment which Web 2.0 exemplifies. Apple is active in supporting its user community wherever they are talking to each other: see, for example, becomingatechnician.com and 'The top 100 Apple/Mac blogs'. Zappos is a $1bn online retailer which is well worth looking at as a company built on customer service which uses social media creatively. The extensive customer reviews lower return rates and greatly support search engine optimization. A 'voice of customer' facility builds community and empathy. Word of mouth is facilitated by a facility to 'share' products with other customers. The site has a page aggregating all mentions of Zappos on Twitter without editing: as with First Direct, a move which would seem foolish if its satisfaction levels were lower.

Social media, then, are perfect for customer service. Take-up is only being delayed by the tendency of many firms to delegate social media to a corner of the marketing department – typically the young, digitally literate graduate. A recent *Harvard Business Review* article argues that companies need a new media 'ringmaster' to undertake this role.[12]

Email and viral marketing   Like the banner ad, the email campaign no longer has the excitement of youth in the innovation-obsessed world of digital marketing, but it is nonetheless still an important part of the online communications mix. While response rates (measured by clicking on a link in the email) average out at around 2.8%, this masks much poor mass marketing with undifferentiated content being sent to poorly maintained lists, which can achieve considerably less than 1%. Conversely, well-crafted email campaigns to specific segments using a clean database will often achieve 10–15% click rates. Of course, we are referring here not to unsolicited spam – which now forms three-quarters of email traffic – but to customer-centric information and offers to registered customers and prospects. So, for most firms email forms part of the firm's customer relationship management (CRM) strategy to grow the value of existing customers.

There are exceptions, though, where email can form part of an acquisition strategy:

- Cold emails, using a consumer email list provider such as Experian or a business email list such as Corpdata, are technically opt-in as the recipient may have agreed to receive offers by email, but care is needed as they can feel like spam to the recipient, and response rates are often microscopic.

- Co-branded emails are somewhat better. A department store, for example, teamed up with a grocery retailer to sell products which the grocer did not sell. Advertised to the grocer's email list as part of a regular customer update, the emails generated a healthy 8% response rate and a good return to both parties. Clearly the brands need to be consistent with each other, and the product lines complementary, for this to make sense.

- Finally, the customer may opt into email using another medium. A campaign which has been influential within the car industry was conducted by General Motors around the launch of a new model of the Vectra. In a change from the traditional mass marketing model of this sector, this 'Dialogue' programme provided a response number and website on its advertisements. The 100,000 respondents were asked some simple questions: what car they drove, what kind of car they were interested in, when they were likely to replace their car, and whether they wished to be contacted by email or post. This led to simply tailored quarterly brochures, delivered by mail or email, reflecting the customer's position in the purchase cycle: soft, branding messages to begin with; harder information on model variations and pricing nearer to the customer's estimated replacement date. The end result was 7,000 more cars sold than in a control group who were not contacted – a very healthy return on some simple emails and mailings. The tailoring may have been simple, but it led consumers to feel that they were indeed in a relevant dialogue.

The ease of forwarding emails makes it an ideal vehicle for viral marketing: a promotional message which is passed from peer to peer. Most 'virals' are based on humour. However, successful virals can also be shocking, clever, or compulsively informative.

Finally, we should not forget the importance of *inbound* emails, which may be service queries, but equally may form sales leads. Many companies are so geared up to recruit customers from their outbound campaigns that no-one has time to answer emails from prospects! These are often managed along with chat by a multi-media service centre which is also handling telephone traffic; but however they are handled, it is important in marketing plans to ensure that resources are available to react to customers when they contact us.

Impersonal communications

Generally, the major components of impersonal communications are advertising (in its many different forms), special promotions, public relations (PR) and direct marketing. We will look at these topics in terms of planning them in a way that maximizes their strategic significance. We will also look briefly at direct marketing, an approach which is gaining much prominence in some types of service businesses.

Advertising

Figure 9.16 shows the role of advertising in overcoming the barriers between each step in the communications process.

Thus, for example, for a new service, the role of advertising would be more concerned about establishing a greater level of awareness. In contrast, for a service which is more mature and well understood, its role could be geared to encouraging ownership and motivating potential customers to take action. It would follow that, since the role is different according to the stage of the communication process, so are the objectives and the measures which would be used to monitor their attainment.

Advertising is not the only determinant of sales	There is a popular misconception that advertising success can only be measured in terms of sales increases.

In most circumstances, advertising is only one of a number of important determinants of sales levels (such as price, quality, customer service levels and so on). Not only this, but there will be times when the role of advertising is to create the basis of future success by getting the service known. In this situation, expecting a relationship between the stimulus of advertising and any immediate response in terms of sales is inappropriate.

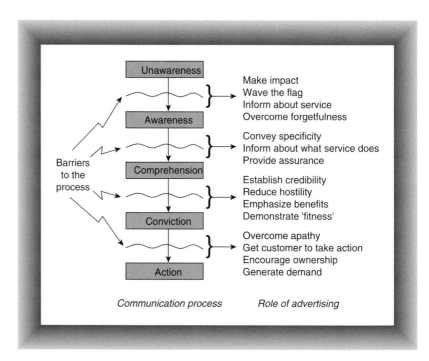

Figure 9.16
Different roles of advertising

Advertising objectives   However, while it is often inappropriate to set sales increases as the sole objective for advertising, it is important to set relevant objectives, which will be explicit and measurable. As Figure 9.17 shows, without identifying advertising objectives, any attempt at measuring the performance of a communications programme will be impossible.

In order to address any of the peripheral activities shown in Figure 9.17, the central advertising objectives must be in place. Setting reasonable, achievable objectives is, therefore, the first and most important step in the advertising plan. All the other steps then flow naturally from this and are summarized in Figure 9.18.

The usual assumption is that advertising is deployed in an aggressive role and that all that changes over time is the creative content. But the role of advertising usually changes during the lifecycle of a product.

> The role of advertising changes over the lifecycle of the service

For example, the process of persuasion itself cannot usually start until there is some level of awareness about a product or service in the market place. Creating awareness is, therefore, usually one of the most

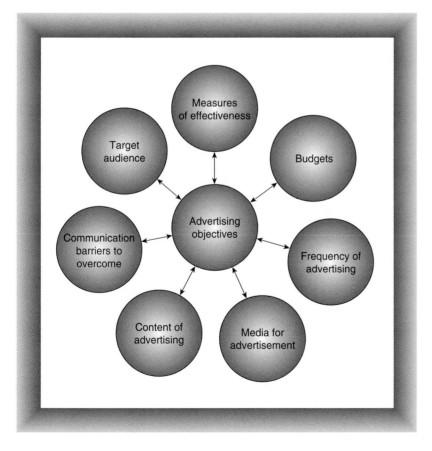

Figure 9.17
The need for advertising objectives

Target market	Type of promotion					
	Money		*Goods*		*Services*	
	Direct	*Indirect*	*Direct*	*Indirect*	*Direct*	*Indirect*
Consumer	Price reduction	Coupons Vouchers Money equivalent Competitions	Free goods Premium offers (e.g. 13 for 12) Free gifts Trade-in offers	Stamps Coupons Vouchers Money equivalent Competitions	Guarantees Group participation events Special exhibitions and displays	Cooperative advertising Stamps Coupons Vouchers for services Events admission Competitions
Trade	Dealer loaders Loyalty schemes Incentives Full-range buying	Extended credit Delayed invoicing Sale or return Coupons Vouchers Money equivalent	Free gifts Trial offers Trade-in offers	Coupons Vouchers Money equivalent Competitions	Guarantees Group participation events Free services Risk reduction schemes Training Special exhibitions Displays Demon- strations Reciprocal trading schemes	Stamps Coupons Vouchers for services Competitions
Sales force	Bonus Commission	Coupons Vouchers Points systems Money equivalent Competitions	Free gifts	Coupons Vouchers Points systems Money equivalent	Free services Group participation events	Coupons Vouchers Points systems for services Event admission Competitions

Figure 9.18 Key steps in determining advertising activity

important objectives early on in the lifecycle. If awareness has been created, interest in learning more will usually follow.

Attitude development now begins in earnest. This might also involve reinforcing an existing attitude or even changing previously held attitudes in order to clear the way for the promotion of a new service. This role obviously tends to become more important later in the product lifecycle, when competitive services are each trying to establish their own 'niche' in the market.

The diffusion of innovation process Also relevant to advertising strategy is an understanding of the 'diffusion of innovation' curve, which refers to the percentage of potential adopters of a new service over time (Figure 9.19). Rogers,[13] the originator of this work, found that, for all new products and services, the cumulative demand pattern conformed to a bell-shaped statistical distribution curve. From this, he was able to distinguish certain typological groups as shown in this figure.

In general, the innovators think for themselves and are active in trying those new services which appeal to them. This 2.5% of the customer population are the fashion leaders, the first to be attracted to the new service offer. The early adopters (13.5%) often have status in society and, because they are not seduced merely by novelty, tend to be opinion leaders.

Winning over the opinion leaders is critical in getting a new service accepted in the market

> They confer on it acceptability and respectability and are, as such, extremely influential in establishing the success of a new service.

The early majority (34%) are more conservative, more deliberate, and usually only adopt services that have been given social approbation by the opinion leaders. When the early majority enter the market, service providers usually enjoy a period of rapid growth in sales. The late majority (34%) are clearly more sceptical. They need to be sure that the service is tried and tested before they risk committing themselves. They also tend to have less money and, often, price becomes more important at this stage. The laggards are often of lower income and status and are the last to adopt the service.

When all potential users of a service become users, the market can be said to be mature and service providers cannot expect the previous high levels of growth.

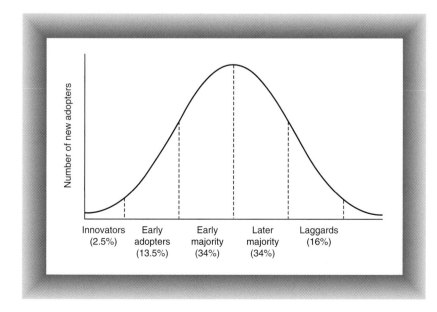

Figure 9.19
Diffusion of innovation curve
Source: Based on a list produced by Professor David Corkindale when at the Cranfield School of Management; used with his permission

> If, from the outset, the company can identify and target its innovators and opinion leaders, it increases the chances of creating interest among the early majority and, thereby, initiates the chain reaction which typifies the diffusion process.

'Other' markets for communication Finally, it should be remembered that advertising and promotion are not directed only at customer markets. In Chapter 2, we described six key market domains that need to be addressed by marketing. Therefore, supplier markets, shareholders, employees – indeed, anyone who can have an important influence on the firm's commercial success – can be legitimate targets for advertising and promotional activity.

Sales promotion

Sales promotion should not be confused with advertising

There is often an element of confusion regarding what constitutes sales promotion. Part of this stems from the fact that, in US textbooks, the term is used to describe all forms of communication, including advertising and personal selling. This all-embracing definition is carried over into the marketing mix, where, as we have seen, 'promotion' covers a wide range of activities.

> It is thus necessary to distinguish between sales promotion as a general expression and 'a sales promotion', which is a specific activity designed to make a featured offer to defined customers within a limited time-span.

In other words, in a sales promotion, someone must be offered something which is different from the usual terms and conditions surrounding the transaction. Such a special offer must include tangible benefits not inherent in the standard 'customer' package. The word 'customer' is put in inverted commas because customers are not always the target of a sales promotion.

The reason for having a sales promotion will be to provide a short-term solution to a problem, hence the reason for it operating over a limited period. Typical objectives for sales promotions are: to increase sales; to counteract competitor activity; to encourage repeat purchase; to encourage speedy payment of bills; to induce a trial purchase; to smooth out peaks and troughs in demand patterns; and so on.

From these examples, it can be seen that, as with advertising, sales promotion is not necessarily concerned with just sales increases. Moreover, since the objective of the sales promotion is to stimulate the recipient's behaviour and bring it more into line with the service organization's economic interests, the promotion can be directed at

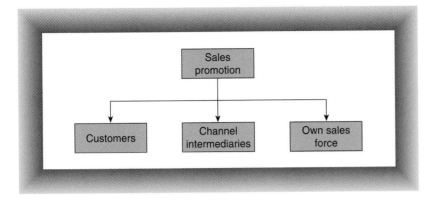

Figure 9.20
Targets of sales promotions

different groups of people (Figure 9.20). Thus, for instance, intermediaries might be induced to increase their sales effort. Similarly, the
company's own sales force might be motivated to sell less popular
services, or open up new geographical territories, if motivated by the
prospect of something over and above their normal remuneration.

Types of sales promotion

The many and varied types of sales promotion are listed in Figure 9.21.
Each one of these is likely to be more appropriate in some situations
than others, because all have advantages and disadvantages. For
example, cash reductions can often lead to pressure for a permanent
price reduction. Then again, coupons, vouchers and gifts might not
necessarily motivate their targets sufficiently, yet could involve high
administrative costs. Therefore, great care is required in selecting a
scheme appropriate to the objective sought.

> It is essential that, even though sales promotions are short-
> term tactical weapons, they should still fulfil their role in the
> overall communications strategy of the company.

Just as advertising has to be utilized to this end, so do sales promotions. There is little point in management subscribing to what is nothing less than a series of unrelated promotional activities with no
overall pattern or coherence. Promotions and advertising need to be
properly planned and integrated.

Preparing the sales promotion plan

> There is widespread acknowledgement that sales promotion
> is one of the most mismanaged of all marketing functions.

Target market	Type of promotion					
	Money		*Goods*		*Services*	
	Direct	*Indirect*	*Direct*	*Indirect*	*Direct*	*Indirect*
Consumer	Price reduction	Coupons Vouchers Money equivalent Competitions	Free goods Premium offers (e.g. 13 for 12) Free gifts Trade-in offers	Stamps Coupons Vouchers Money equivalent Competitions	Guarantees Group participation events Special exhibitions and displays	Cooperative advertising Stamps Coupons Vouchers for services Events admission Competitions
Trade	Dealer loaders Loyalty schemes Incentives Full-range buying	Extended credit Delayed invoicing Sale or return Coupons Vouchers Money equivalent	Free gifts Trial offers Trade-in offers	Coupons Vouchers Money equivalent Competitions	Guarantees Group participation events Free services Risk reduction schemes Training Special exhibitions Displays Demon-strations Reciprocal trading schemes	Stamps Coupons Vouchers for services Competitions
Sales force	Bonus Commission	Coupons Vouchers Points systems Money equivalent Competitions	Free gifts	Coupons Vouchers Points systems Money equivalent	Free services Group participation events	Coupons Vouchers Points systems for services Event admission Competitions

Figure 9.21   Types of sales promotions

This is partly because of the confusion about what sales promotion is, which often results in expenditures not being properly recorded. Some companies include it with advertising, others as part of sales force expenditure, others as a general marketing expense, others as an operating expense, while the loss of revenue from special price reductions is often not recorded at all.

| Sales promotion is an integral part of marketing strategy

Such failures can be extremely damaging because sales promotion can be such an important part of marketing strategy. Also, with increasing global competition, troubled economic conditions, and growing pressures from channels, sales promotion is becoming more widespread and more acceptable. This means that companies can no longer afford not to set objectives, or to evaluate results after the event, or to fail to have some company guidelines. For example, an airline offering $200 allowance on an international airfare with a contribution rate of $600 has to increase sales by 50% just to maintain the same level of contribution. Failure at least to realize this, or to set alternative objectives for the promotion, can easily result in loss of control and a consequent reduction in profits.

In order to manage a service organization's sales promotion expenditure more effectively, careful planning of the process is essential.

> First, an objective for sales promotion must be established in the same way that an objective is developed for advertising, pricing, or distribution.

The objectives for each promotion should be clearly stated, such as trial, repeat purchase, distribution, a shift in buying peaks, combating competition, and so on. Thereafter, the following process should apply:

- Select the appropriate technique
- Pre-test
- Mount the promotion
- Evaluate in depth.

Spending must be analysed and categorized by type of activity (special demonstrations, special point-of-sale material, loss of revenue through price reductions, and so on).

As for the sales promotional plan itself, the objectives, strategy and brief details of timing and costs should be included. It is important that too much detail should *not* appear in the sales promotional plan. Detailed promotional instructions will follow as the sales promotional plan unwinds. For example, the checklist shown in Figure 9.22 outlines the kind of detail that should eventually be circulated. However, only an outline of this should appear in the marketing plan itself.

Public relations (PR)

This is the planned and sustained effort to establish and maintain goodwill between a service organization and its publics. These 'publics' include the 'six markets' referred to in Chapter 2. These can, however, also be other individuals or bodies that might only have an indirect impact on the business, yet merit attention. For example, the main publics of a university are shown in Figure 9.23.

	Headings in sales promotion plan	Content
1	*Introduction*	Briefly summarize content – what? where? when?
2	*Objectives*	Marketing and promotional objectives for new service launch.
3	*Background*	Market data. Justification for technique. Other relevant matters.
4	*Promotional offer*	Detail the offer: special pricing structure; describe premium; etc. Be brief, precise and unambiguous.
5	*Eligibility*	Who? Where?
6	*Timing*	When is the offer available? Call, delivery or invoice dates?
7	*Date plan*	Assign dates and responsibilities for all aspects of plan prior to start date.
8	*Support*	Special advertising, point of sale, presenters, leaflets, etc.; public relations, samples, etc.
9	*Administration*	Invoicing activity. Free invoice lines. Premium (re)ordering procedure. Cash drawing procedures.
10	*Sales plan*	Targets. Incentives. Effect on routeing. Briefing meetings. Telephone sales.
11	*Sales presentation*	Points to be covered in call.
12	*Sales reporting*	Procedure for collection of required data not otherwise available.
13	*Assessment*	How will the promotion be evaluated?

Appendices to plan
Usually designed to be carried by salespeople as an aid to selling the promotion:

- Summary of presentation points
- Price structures/profit margins
- Summary of offer
- Schedules of qualifying orders
- Order forms
- Copies of leaflets.

Also required by the sales force may be:

- Leaflets explaining the service
- Demonstration specimen of premium item
- Special report forms
- Returns of cash/premiums, etc. issued.

Note: It is assumed that the broad principles of the promotion have already been agreed by the Sales Manager.

Figure 9.22 Key elements of a sales promotion plan

The tasks most commonly addressed by PR are:

- Building or maintaining an image
- Supporting other communication activities
- Handling specific problems or issues, e.g. a health scare

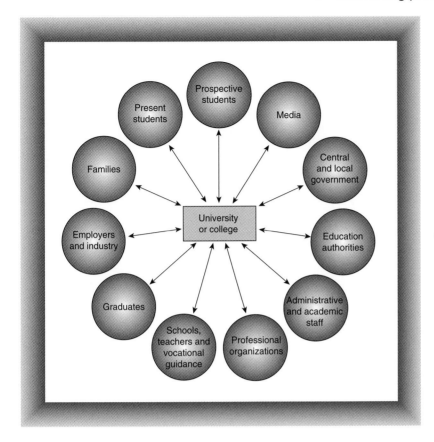

Figure 9.23
Main publics for a university

- Reinforcing positioning
- Assisting in the launch of new services
- Influencing specific publics.

Building a corporate image is of increased importance today.

The reason for this is that customers have become more sophisticated and want to know more about the company with whom they will be entering a relationship.

For their part, companies have used the concept of image development in an attempt to differentiate themselves from competitors. So, for example, we have 'The listening bank', 'The bank that likes to say yes!', and so on.

As soon as the concept of corporate image is introduced, one is immediately drawn into the concept of customer perceptions, rather than reality. In fact, the whole issue of image is complex, because it is so multifaceted. For example, images can exist at several different levels:

- How a market/public actually sees the company
- How the company sees itself
- How the company would like to see itself
- How the company ought to be seen in order for it to achieve its objectives.

If a company is to tackle this area conscientiously, then it is the first and last of the images listed above that need to be researched and understood. It is these which provide the dimensions of the image gap which can be addressed by public relations activity.

Another issue in the process of image building is to ensure that the perceptions are drawn from appropriate customer groups and segments. For instance, just looking at one market could reveal a different set of images depending upon the type of relationship with the customer:

- Regular customers
- Intermittent customers
- One-off customers
- Potential customers
  - with whom the company has been in contact
  - to whom the company is largely unknown.

The major PR objectives will be to assess where important image gaps exist and then take actions to close them. A gap can be closed by:

- Changing the company so that it conforms more with the expected image of the market/public.
- Changing the market/public's perception so that it moves closer to the company reality.
- Some combination of these two broad approaches.

There is no single specific activity that can alter a service organization's image. Everything it does, and every point of contact with a customer, contributes in some way to the end result. The service itself, the quality of dealings with the staff, the nature of its advertising and even the style of the letter headings, all have a part to play. However, it is in no-one's interest to strive for an image which cannot be sustained.

PR 'tools' A wide range of approaches can be used in the design of a PR programme. These could include:

- Publications, e.g. press releases, annual reports, brochures, posters, articles, videos, and employee reports
- Events, e.g. press conferences, seminars, conferences
- Stories which create media interest, e.g. new contracts, design breakthroughs
- Exhibitions and displays
- Sponsorship, e.g. charitable causes, sports events, theatre and the arts, community projects.

As with the other elements of the communications mix, a PR programme should follow an overall process which consists of specifying the objectives, determining the best PR mix of activities, integrating these over the planning period and evaluating the results.

Direct marketing
Direct marketing is often assumed to be another name for direct mail. This is not correct, because it encompasses a number of media, of which direct mail is just one. There are six main approaches to direct marketing:

- Direct mail
- Mail order
- Direct response advertising
- Telemarketing
- Direct selling
- Digital marketing and social media.

In any direct marketing campaign, these can be used either singly or in combination. The objective is to establish a two-way, personalized relationship between the company and its customers.

> When tackled well, that is to say, when well-chosen customers are targeted with personalized communications that are relevant to them, direct marketing is not only very acceptable, but can also deliver spectacular results.

Direct marketing can be very powerful when properly managed

When managed in a poor manner, direct marketing can be seen as an invasion of privacy, a waste of resources (paper, time and money), and a patronizing and inefficient method of communicating.

The initial approach to customers is driven by an identification of prospects which are often obtained through lists which are rented by the company, or built up from its own data banks. Current technology makes it possible for all initial contact with these people to be personalized, not only by use of their name, but also in terms of knowing key aspects about their lifestyle or purchasing intentions. The message will aim to get the recipient to take action of some sort, such as, for example, to attend a demonstration, to call for a free consultation, or to apply for a promotional video or brochure. The purpose is to initiate contact and stimulate the communication process. The service organization can then respond in whatever way is appropriate and move the relationship towards an eventual sale.

As markets become more fragmented, direct sales forces get more expensive to run.

> The advances in technology make it easier to personalize communications and so direct marketing becomes a feasible and more attractive proposition.

One of the major reasons for its success is that its cost-effectiveness can be measured, since the results generated by a programme can be compared with its cost. Direct marketing can account for up to 14% of media expenditure in those companies where its value has been recognized. Companies such as American Express, British Telecom and most airlines and banks are already using direct marketing extensively to build profitable business.

Since special skills and resources are needed to run direct marketing campaigns, a company may wish to use an outside specialist agency rather than rely on its own staff, in the same way that advertising and sales promotions are typically contracted out. Experimentation with providing incentives for customers to stay in 'dialogue' is helping to improve the success rate of direct marketing still further.

As with all the other aspects of planning, it is essential that the programme for direct marketing starts on the basis of having clear

Function	Responsibilities	Examples
Selling	To persuade potential customers to purchase services and/or to increase the use of services by existing customers	Insurance agent; stockbroker; bank calling officer; real estate salesperson
Service	To inform, assist and advise customers	Airline flight attendant; insurance claims adjuster; ticket agent; bank branch manager
Monitoring	To learn about customers' needs and concerns and report them to management	Customer service representative; repair person

Figure 9.24
Personal contact
functions in services

objectives. Once these are in place, it becomes relatively straightforward to schedule the component activities into a coherent plan.

Personal communications

The three main types of customer contact through personal communications are: selling, servicing and monitoring. Figure 9.24 provides a framework for considering the personal contact function in services together with responsibilities and some typical examples.[14] This suggests that while selling is a pervasive activity in many service organizations, other forms of personal contact including service and monitoring are also important.

The most potent element of face-to-face communications is that provided by the sales force. However, the strategic role of sales has to be assessed in the context of the service organization's overall communications strategy. In order to get things into perspective, top management must be able to answer the following kinds of question:

- How important is personal selling in our business?
- What role does it have in the marketing mix?
- How many salespeople do we need?
- What do we want them to do?
- How should they be managed?

The answers to these questions go a long way towards defining the scope of the sales plan.

The role of personal selling

Personal selling is widely used in many service industries. Financial services, for example, use a high level of media advertising, but still rely heavily on personal selling. Here, contact with sales staff is important because with the potential ambiguities surrounding a service, customers need to be able to discuss their needs and the salesperson is needed to explain the choices available.

> Recent surveys have shown that more money is spent by companies on their sales force than on advertising and sales promotion combined. Selling is, therefore, not only a vital element of the marketing mix, but also an expensive one.

Personal selling has a number of advantages over other elements of the marketing mix:

> 1. It provides two-way communication.
> 2. The sales message can be more flexible (than with advertising) and can be more closely tailored to the needs of individual customers.
> 3. The salesperson can use in-depth knowledge of the service to the advantage of the customer, and overcome objections as they arise.
> 4. Most importantly, the salesperson can ask for an order, and, possibly, also negotiate on price and special requirements.

While in front of a customer, the salesperson is, to all intents and purposes, not a representative of the company, but the company itself. This means that any personal credibility the salesperson establishes should reflect well on the organization as a whole. Unfortunately, the converse of this is equally true.

What Does the company want salespeople to do? The immediate response to such a question is simple: 'Go out and sell'. However, there are obviously more specific issues to be addressed, including:

> - How much should be sold? (Value of unit sales volume)
> - What should be sold? (Over the range of services)
> - To whom should it be sold? (Which market segments)

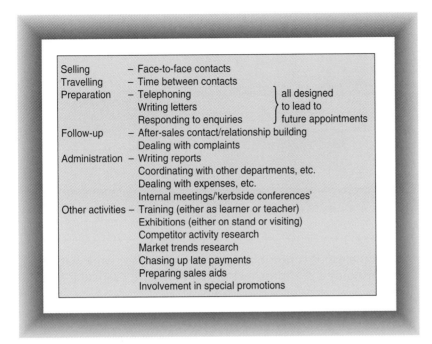

Selling	– Face-to-face contacts
Travelling	– Time between contacts
Preparation	– Telephoning ⎫ all designed Writing letters ⎬ to lead to Responding to enquiries ⎭ future appointments
Follow-up	– After-sales contact/relationship building Dealing with complaints
Administration	– Writing reports Coordinating with other departments, etc. Dealing with expenses, etc. Internal meetings/'kerbside conferences'
Other activities	– Training (either as learner or teacher) Exhibitions (either on stand or visiting) Competitor activity research Market trends research Chasing up late payments Preparing sales aids Involvement in special promotions

Figure 9.25
Typical salesperson
activities

In other words, the selling objectives are derived directly from the marketing objectives.

Sales staff undertake a range of activities. The salesperson is not selling all the time, in the sense of being in front of a customer. There are other activities, which combine to make up a typical week's work, and which are shown in Figure 9.25.

From the list in Figure 9.25, it can be seen that some activities are more productive than others. Clearly, it is in the company's interest to structure the sales job so that non-productive activities are kept to a minimum, thus freeing valuable time to be spent where it can make most impact.

Exactly how this is done, and how the sales force is kept motivated and operating at a high level of efficiency, is the task of sales management. Since this topic would merit a book in its own right, we propose to say little more on the subject, except that it is essential that quantitative objectives are set, whatever the sales activity. Whether these are for the number of visits made, sales achieved, letters written, complaints handled, or whatever, without a quantitative target against which to measure achievement, sales management is rendered impotent.

How many salespeople? By analysing the current activities of the sales force (using a categorization like the list in Figure 9.25), and finding out how much time is actually spent on each activity, the company is well on the way to answering this question. When this is undertaken for the first time, it often becomes apparent that the sales force needs to be redirected or that the sales job needs to be redefined.

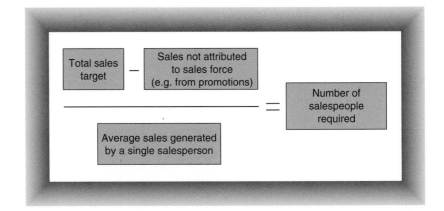

Figure 9.26
Formula for deriving
the size of the sales
force

> Nevertheless, it is possible to establish an ideal work pattern
> which holds a real prospect of generating a particular sales
> value.

The formula in Figure 9.26 can be used to calculate the size of the sales
force.

Of course, while the outcome of this calculation is obvious, the end
result has to be tempered with common sense. For example, if the coverage of some sales territories incurred a disproportionately high
amount of non-productive travel, then there could be a case for
employing additional sales staff in some regions. Alternatively, it
could act as a stimulus for finding new ways to tackle the problem,
perhaps by using telephone sales.

One life insurance company has developed a sophisticated computer
model based on the number of enquiries and a probabilistic estimate
of the gestation time of direct mail. The purpose of the model is to predict demand and then to recruit and train salespeople well ahead of
peak loads.

Preparing a sales plan   No two company sales plans will be the same,
because the role of the sales force might well be different.

> A properly developed sales plan will ensure the sales force
> does not just go out and sell whatever they can, to whomever
> they can.

Thus, the sales plan should indicate *how* the sales force is going to be
deployed in pursuit of the company's marketing objectives.

Task	The standard	How to set the standard	How to measure performance	What to look for
1 To achieve personal sales target	Sales target per period of time for individual groups and/or products	Analysis of • territory potential • individual customers' potential Discussion and agreement between salesperson and manager	Comparison of individual salesperson's product sales against targets	Significant shortfall between target and achievement over a meaningful period
2 To sell the required range and quantity to individual customers	Achievement of specified range and quantity of sales to a particular customer or group of customers within an agreed time period	Analysis of individual customer records of • potential • present sales Discussion and agreement between manager and salesperson	Scrutiny of • individual customer records • observation of selling in the field	Failure to achieve agreed objectives. Complacency with range of sales made to individual customers
3 To plan journeys and call frequencies to achieve minimum practicable selling cost	To achieve appropriate call frequency on individual customers. Number of live customer calls during a given time period	Analysis of individual customers' potential. Analysis of order/call ratios. Discussion and agreement between manager and salesperson	Scrutiny of individual customer records. Analysis of order/call ratio. Examination of call reports	High ratio of calls to an individual customer relative to that customer's yield. Shortfall on agreed total number of calls made over an agreed time period
4 To acquire new customers	Number of prospect calls during time period. Selling new products to existing customers	Identify total number of potential and actual customers who could produce results. Identify opportunity areas for prospecting	Examination of • call reports • records of new accounts opened • ratio of existing to potential customers	Shortfall in number of prospect calls from agreed standard. Low ratio of existing to potential customers
5 To make a sales approach of the required quality	To exercise the necessary skills and techniques required to achieve the identified objective of each element of the sales approach. Continuous use of sales material	Standard to be agreed in discussion between manager and salesperson related to company standards laid down	Regular observations of field selling using a systematic analysis of performance in each stage of the sales approach	Failure to • identify objective of each stage of sales approach • specify areas of skill, weakness • use support material

Figure 9.27   Example of salesperson's plan
Source: Based on work originally done by F. Norse whilst at Urwick Orr & Partners

The total sales target should be translated into regional objectives and then into individual goals. Bearing in mind the need for all activities to be quantifiable, and hence measurable, an individual salesperson's plan may look something like the example shown in Figure 9.27.

It is at this individual level that the sales plan stands or falls, and it is the role of sales management, supported by top management, to see that it is prepared thoroughly.

Summary

In this chapter, we have looked at the final phase of the marketing planning process concerned with budget setting, formulating one-year tactical marketing programmes for service products and communicating with customers, and monitoring, controlling and reviewing their progress. Budgets are a necessary first step to tying the marketing programmes to the economic realities of business life. Although working within a budget might limit the scope of a programme, it should impose no boundaries on its creative and imaginative content.

We saw that the tactical marketing programmes were essentially concerned with translating the marketing objectives and strategies into working one-year plans for service products and communications. We examined the service product plan and the promotions and communication plan and, in particular, discussed important developments in digital communications and social media. In the next chapter we continue our examination of the one-year detailed implementation programme by examining the marketing mix plans for price, place, people, processes and customer service.

10 Marketing planning Phase Four: resource allocation, monitoring and detailed planning (Part 2: price, place, people, processes and customer service)

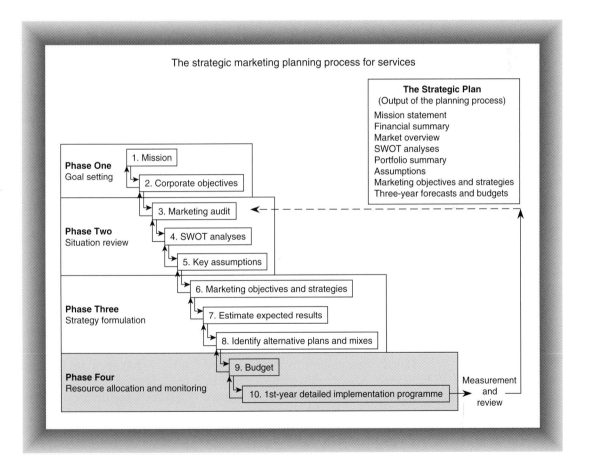

The strategic marketing planning process for services

The Strategic Plan
(Output of the planning process)

Mission statement
Financial summary
Market overview
SWOT analyses
Portfolio summary
Assumptions
Marketing objectives and strategies
Three-year forecasts and budgets

Phase One
Goal setting

1. Mission
2. Corporate objectives

Phase Two
Situation review

3. Marketing audit
4. SWOT analyses
5. Key assumptions

Phase Three
Strategy formulation

6. Marketing objectives and strategies
7. Estimate expected results
8. Identify alternative plans and mixes

Phase Four
Resource allocation and monitoring

9. Budget
10. 1st-year detailed implementation programme

Measurement and review

Chapter 9 addressed the budget and the first two components of the first year detailed implementation programme for marketing planning – the service product plan and the communications (promotion) plan. In this chapter we look at the remaining elements of this final phase of the marketing planning process for services. We start by addressing the pricing plan and then consider the remaining four elements in the detailed implementation programme for services marketing planning: the place plan – getting the service to customers; the people element; the process element; and the customer service element of the marketing mix.

Mix element 3: The pricing plan

Pricing is addressed as a separate element of the marketing mix because this provides a sensible way for the complex issues relating to pricing to be considered. In fact, the company may choose not to have a separate plan for pricing, and subsume pricing decisions into the individual service/segment plans. Whether or not the pricing element appears as a separate plan, careful thought will have to be given to the pricing structure.

The pricing decision is important for two main reasons:

> - It affects the margin through its impact on revenue.
> - It affects the quantity sold through its influence on demand.

It must, therefore, be seen as part of a consciously defined initiative, whose objectives have been clearly defined.

The terms used to describe the price charged to customers in service businesses vary considerably across different parts of the service sector. We pay fares for an airline or train ticket, fees for professional services, tariffs for mobile phone use, room rates for a hotel, premiums for an insurance policy and an honorarium for speaking at a conference. For convenience, we will use the terms 'price' and 'pricing' in this chapter.

Pricing decisions for services are particularly important, given the intangible nature of the service product. The price charged to customers signals information to them about the quality that they are likely to receive. Also, because they cannot be stored, services may attract premium prices when demand is high and discounts when demand is low.

Pricing is further complicated in that it is sometimes the subject of conflict between the accounting and marketing departments. On the one hand, the traditional accountant's viewpoint is concerned with covering costs and charging prices to get a fixed margin over and above these costs. Sometimes opposing them is the marketer, who recognizes that price is an important determinant of how much will be sold. The marketer may see the need for holding prices, or even reducing them, so as to maintain, or to increase, market share and thereby build the share needed for long-term success.

High-quality services have an intrinsic value for the customer and it is this value, rather than the cost of providing the service, that pricing decisions need to consider.

Prices need to reflect value

Pricing decisions need to reflect the strategic opportunities for the organization. A simple cost-plus approach to pricing disregards the advantages which can be gained by a well-researched and well-managed pricing policy.

Pricing objectives

The different pricing methods or approaches for services are broadly similar to those used for goods. The pricing method to be used should commence with a review of pricing objectives. These might include:

- *Survival* – In adverse market conditions the pricing objective may involve foregoing desired levels of profitability to ensure survival.

- *Profit maximization* – Pricing to ensure maximization of profitability over a given period. The period concerned will be related to the lifecycle of the service.

- *Sales maximization* – Pricing to build market share. This may involve selling at a loss initially in an effort to capture a high share of the market.

- *Prestige* – A service company may wish to use pricing to position itself as exclusive. High-priced restaurants and the first class 'suites' offered by Singapore Airlines in the A380 aircraft are examples.

- *ROI* – Pricing objectives may be based on achieving a desired return on investment.

These are some of the most common, but by no means all, pricing objectives. The decision a service organization makes on pricing will be dependent on a range of factors including:

- Prevailing economic conditions and service capacity
- Positioning of the service
- Corporate objectives
- Demand and demand elasticity

- Cost structures
- The nature of competition
- Lifecycle of the service(s).

Economic conditions and service capacity

Clearly factors such as the prevailing economic conditions and the capacity of the service firm will have an impact on pricing. In times of economic difficulty, service firms may need to adjust their prices downwards. For example, companies supplying electricity and other utilities in times of economic recession may have downward pressure on the pricing of their services as a result of either government intervention and consumer activism.

The capacity of a service firm will influence how a service company sets its prices. If it provides high-quality services and has limited capacity, a service business such as a restaurant or boutique hotel may be able to charge premium prices. If the firm has substantial capacity the organization's services is unlikely to be able to put their services into inventory. Thus, the firm may wish to discount its services, especially in times of low demand. Over recent years most international airlines have become particularly adept at what is termed 'yield management', which enables them to balance variations in demand at different times, their capacity and their pricing in order to optimize profitability.

Positioning of the service

The meaning of the term 'service product positioning' was explained in Chapter 7. For pricing, the concept of the positioning of the service product is a highly relevant concept. It is important to match the price to the positioning of the service. It is clearly inappropriate to position a service company's offer to customers as a high-quality exclusive service and then price the service at too low a level. We find many examples where there is a mismatch between the positioning of the service product and its price.

For example, some university business schools claim their courses for executives are among the best in the world, then they charge lower prices than their competitors. Research indicates that, for directors and very senior managers in industry, a low price charged for such executive courses is more likely to be counterproductive, because in this particular product field a high fee charged for such a course is considered by them to be an indicator of quality. Most services are largely intangible, so the price needs to accurately reflect the positioning of the service.

Corporate objectives

Unfortunately many arguments within firms about pricing take place in the sort of vacuum that is created when no-one has bothered to specify the objectives to which pricing is supposed to be contributing. We now know that it is important that the company should have a well-defined hierarchy of objectives to which all its activities and actions, including pricing, can be related, for example corporate objectives may well dictate achievement of short-term profits, long-term profit maximization, or some other requirement. Corporate objectives can also influence marketing objectives. This may result in the need to place emphasis on, say, market share rather than profitability and this will in turn likely impact the pricing strategy.

Where a company markets multiple services, decisions on pricing may be a function of its service's position compared to that of others within the portfolio. For example, it may well be that a financial services company chooses to heavily promote one service at the expense of another in order to gain market share. As a consequence relative margins and resulting prices may vary markedly across these two products.

Demand and demand elasticity

Service companies need to understand that there is a relationship between price and demand. Further, demand varies at different pricing levels. It may also vary by market segment. A useful framework to help understand this relationship is the 'elasticity of demand'. This concept helps service managers understand whether demand is elastic (a given percentage change in price produces a greater percentage change in demand) or inelastic (a significant change in price produces relatively little change in levels of demand). These different characteristics of demand are shown in Figure 10.1.

> It is important to know if demand is elastic or inelastic

Pricing levels are especially important if demand for the service is elastic. Examples where demand for services is elastic include airlines, railways, cinemas and package tours. Other services such as medical care and electricity supply exhibit more inelastic behaviour.

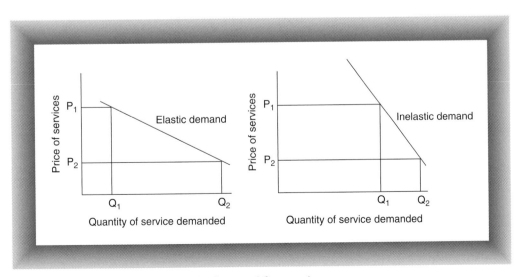

Figure 10.1 Elastic and inelastic demand for services

Cost structures

The costs of providing services and how these vary over time and with the level of demand also need to be understood. Two major types of costs, fixed costs and variable costs, need to be identified. In addition, some costs may be semi-variable. Fixed costs are those which do not vary with the level of output. They remain fixed over a given period and include buildings, furniture, staff costs, maintenance, etc. Variable costs vary according to the quantity of the service provided or sold. They include part-time employees' wages, expendable supplies, postage, etc. It should be noted that some costs have elements which are partly fixed and partly variable. These include telephone costs and salaried staff used for overtime work. If costs allocation appears to be assigned arbitrarily by accountants it will need to be re-examined. Activity-based costing can provide better insight into the cost structure as well as those factors that impact on costs.[1]

Many service businesses, such as airlines, have high levels of fixed costs because of the expense of the equipment and staff needed to operate them. For example, in financial services, fixed costs can represent more than 60% of total costs.

> Total costs represent the sum of the fixed, variable and semi-variable costs at a given level of output. Service managers need to understand how cost behaviour will vary at different levels of service output. This has important implications for decisions to expand capacity, as well as for pricing.

A useful tool to help managers understand cost behaviour in a service industry is the experience curve. The experience curve is an empirically derived relationship which suggests that as accumulated sales or output doubles, costs per unit (in real terms) typically fall by between 20 and 30%. Many financial service organizations have moved from paper-based processing, which offers no real economies of scale, to mechanization and use of electronic processing, which offer considerable potential for scale economies. Figure 10.2 shows an experience curve for electronic banking compared with paper processing of cheques.[2]

In retail banking, the use of automatic teller machines (ATMs) has had a profound effect on lowering costs. Although the cost of installing an ATM can be high, once installed the 'per transaction cost' is considerably less than using a human bank teller in the transaction. For many years volumes of ATM transactions have increased. While wage costs have risen with inflation, the cost of ATMs has fallen in real terms.

The experience curve can help service managers understand the potential to use scale to improve their firm's cost position. To date,

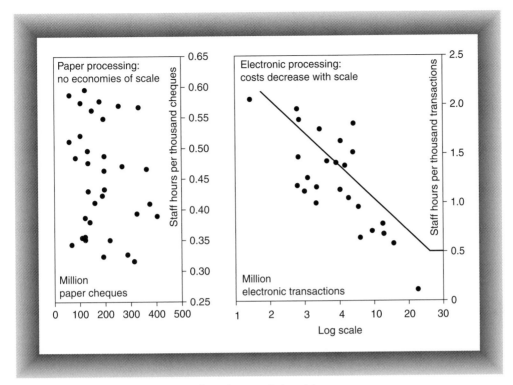

Figure 10.2   Experience curve for electronic banking

there has been relatively little published work dealing with the application of the experience curve to the service sector. One study that does explore experience curves in services was undertaken by Stuart Chambers and Robert Johnson.[3] These researchers examined a financial services organization and an airline and found strong experience curves existed in these firms. In particular, service firm 'back office' repetitive tasks and high-volume, high-customer contact operations such as call centres and supermarket checkouts are likely to benefit from the experience curve effect.

Competition

It is also essential to understand the costs and pricing behaviour of competitors. As well as seeking information about the prices of key competitors in each major segment, the cost position of major competitors needs to be considered.

An understanding of competitors' costs helps the service marketing manager to make a realistic assessment of competitors' ability to change their pricing structure.

For example, organizations such as Citibank in its US retail operations have sought to gain competitive advantage by achieving the lowest cost position in clearing transactions.

Benchmarking of competitors should be undertaken to determine their costs, prices and profitability. This can be done by a range of techniques including competitive shopping and market research and should include a price–quality comparison of each major competitor's offer. The competitors' positions in terms of profitability, cost position and market share, in each segment, can then be considered when making the pricing decision.

Some firms launch new services at high prices to recover their investment costs, only to find that they have provided a price umbrella to entice competitors into the market. Competitive firms that launch similar products at much lower prices can move down the experience curve more quickly, often taking the originating service company's market away from them in the process. A low launch price, with potentially a faster rate of diffusion and hence a greater rate of gaining experience (by achieving a more favourable position on the experience curve), may make it more difficult for a potential competitor to enter the market profitably.

Lifecycle of the service(s)

The importance of lifecycles has already been stressed in Chapter 7. For example, for a service estimated to be in the maturity stage of the lifecycle, with only a short time to run before it is replaced, it would usually be unwise to set market share growth as the marketing objective. Profit contribution would probably be a more appropriate goal, providing of course market share did not slip to a point below which it would jeopardize the service firm's ability to introduce a new or replacement service. It should be remembered that when the market reaches saturation level we may well have a very profitable cash cow on our hands for many years to come.

It is also important to stress that the role of pricing will change over a service's lifecycle. For example, during the high growth phase in the service's lifecycle, price may not to be the customer's primary consideration, since demand is growing at such a rapid rate and the service is still relatively new. Here there are plenty of opportunities, which have to be carefully balanced against market share considerations.

Pricing methods

When the basic pricing objectives have been considered and a review made of demand, costs, competitors' prices and costs, and other relevant factors, the services marketer needs to consider the method by which prices will be set.

Methods for setting prices vary considerably in the services sector and typically include:

- *Cost-plus pricing*, where a given percentage mark-up is sought.

- *Rate of return pricing*, where prices are set to achieve a given rate of return on investments or assets. This is sometimes called 'target return' pricing.

- *Competitive parity pricing*, where prices are set on the basis of following those set by the market leader.

- *Loss leading pricing*, usually done on a short time basis, to establish a position in the market or to provide an opportunity to cross-sell other services.

- *Value-based pricing*, where prices are based on the service's perceived value to a given customer segment. It represents a market-driven approach which reinforces the positioning of the service and the benefits the customer receives from the service.

- *Relationship pricing*, where prices are based on considerations of future potential profit streams over the lifetime of customers.

Most of these pricing methods are fairly straightforward. However, relationship pricing and value-based pricing merit some further discussion.

Relationship and value-based pricing

It is obvious that cost-plus-based pricing is often unacceptable, as customers are interested in their own costs, not those of their suppliers. Further, costs in many service businesses can be extremely hard to estimate, as companies offer a range of services and typically have a high level of resource sharing.

> Cost-plus pricing is rarely appropriate

Relationship pricing is the appropriate form of pricing where there is an ongoing contact between the service provider and the customer.

> Relationship pricing can be a major source of competitive advantage

> Relationship pricing follows closely the market-oriented approach of value-based pricing, but takes the lifetime value of the customer into account.

Relationship pricing is based on value considerations of all the services provided to the customer and makes an assessment of the potential profit stream over a given period of time – often the lifetime of the customer. While value-based pricing, which emphasizes benefits, drives this pricing philosophy, it allows the firm to use loss-leader,

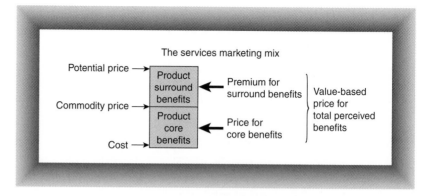

Figure 10.3
Value-based pricing

competitive or marginal costing at appropriate points in time, on relevant services, for both strategic and tactical purposes.

A value-based relationship approach to pricing aims at helping to position the service and reflects the fact that customers are prepared to pay extra for the perceived benefits provided by both the core product and the product surround. This concept is shown in Figure 10.3 and suggests that customers will pay a premium for perceived benefits and especially those supplied by the product surround in terms of brand image, brand values and service quality.

The size of the price premium is not meant to be to scale in Figure 10.3. In fact, the premium provided by the surround could be greater than the price for the core product or service benefit.

An approach increasingly being used by service firms to enhance their product surround and achieve premium prices is the unconditional service guarantee. 'Bugs' Burger Bug Killers (BBBK) are a US pest-extermination company who have charged up to 600% more than some of their competitors and have a high market share with clients who have severe pest problems. The company was so successful that it was purchased by S.C. Johnson Wax, which subsequently changed the name of the company to Prism. The significant price premium charged by BBBK for their services and the unconditional service guarantee do not imply staggeringly high costs. In the year it was purchased by S.C. Johnson, BBBK paid out only $120,000 in claims on their unconditional service guarantee, on sales of $33 million.[4] S.C. Johnson subsequently sold its Prism division. In 2003, the Burger family purchased the trade name back from S.C. Johnson Wax and 'Bugs' Burger Bug Killers is now operating again in the original family's ownership. The service guarantee offered to clients in the hotel and restaurant sectors in 2011 promises:

- You do not pay our initial charges until we totally eliminate every roach, rat or mouse nesting on your premises.

- If you are ever dissatisfied with the results and want to cancel our service, we will: (a) refund up to a one year's service charge, and (b) pay the cost of another extermina-tor of your choice for one year.

- Should a roach or rodent be seen by one of your guests, we will pay their bill, send them a letter of apology and invite them back as our guest.

- We will pay all fines that may be levied against your hotel or restaurant by the health authorities for the presence of roaches or rodents, and further . . .

- Should your hotel restaurant be closed by the health authorities for the presence of roaches or rodents, 'Bugs Burger' will pay profits lost while you were closed, plus $5,000.

Service guarantees such as this can impact greatly on the premium customers are willing to pay for product surround benefits. Service guarantees are used in a wide range of service industries including hotels, financial services and management consultancy.

As firms consider an appropriate pricing method, they need to take into account the potential pricing range at which they may finally set the prices. The pricing range a typical service company might consider is shown in Figure 10.4. As this figure shows, the usual discretionary pricing range for a company will be set by the lowest and the highest feasible price that could be charged. However, on occasion, the company may choose to price outside this pricing range. For example, the company may price close to its marginal cost when it has excess capacity, or it wishes to break into a new price-sensitive market. It may also do this for competitive reasons. The company may also offer a discount when the customer undertakes a trial of its services.

As the previous discussion has shown, there is a large range of pricing options. However, many of these can be simplified into what is referred to as either a skimming policy or a penetration policy. It is easiest to

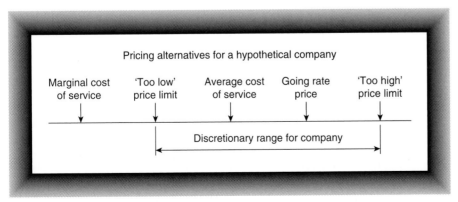

Figure 10.4   Pricing range for a service company

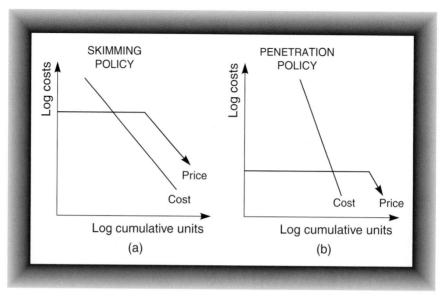

Figure 10.5 Skimming and penetration pricing policies

think about these policies in the context of the launch of the new service. Essentially a skimming pricing policy involves setting a high initial price and moving down the experience curve at a slower rate. A penetration pricing policy involves setting a lower initial price and seeking a much faster rate of service adoption, hence moving down the experience curve at a faster rate. These policies are illustrated in Figure 10.5.

The circumstances favouring a *skimming* pricing policy are as follows:

1. Demand is likely to be price inelastic.

2. There are likely to be different price–market segments, thereby appealing to those buyers in a segment that is keen to use the service first and who are less price sensitive.

3. Little is known about the costs of producing and marketing the service.

The circumstances favouring a *penetration* policy are as follows:

1. Demand is likely to be price elastic.

2. Competitors are likely to enter the market quickly.

3. There are no distinct and separate price–market segments

4. There is the possibility of large savings in operations and marketing costs if a large sales volume can be generated (experience curve effect).

In conclusion, it must be emphasized that pricing policy should only be determined after account has been taken of all factors which impinge on the pricing decision. The key factors that need to be taken into account in determining the pricing plan are shown in Figure 10.6.

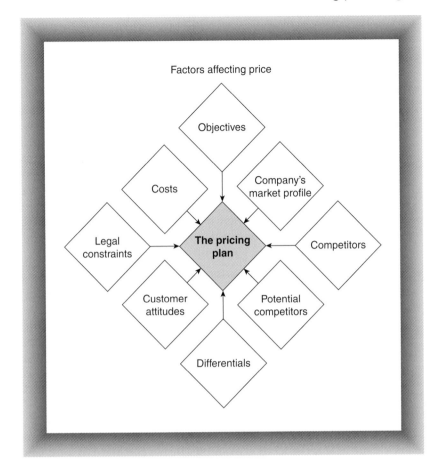

Figure 10.6
Factors to consider in the pricing plan

Mix element 4: The place plan – getting the service to the customers

Deciding on the location and channels for supplying services to target customers determines how the service will be delivered and where this should take place. Between them, these service delivery factors offer the prospect of establishing a competitive advantage, since they influence both the level of service to the customer and the cost of providing it.

Location decisions

The importance of location will, to a large extent, depend upon the nature of the service provided and the type of interaction it sets up between the suppliers and the customer. (These were discussed earlier in Figure 2.6 in Chapter 2.) There are three possibilities:

1. *The customer goes to the service provider* – In these circumstances, site location is very important. For some service businesses, like a restaurant or holiday centre, location may be the prime reason behind its success. Moreover, there is always a prospect of further growth from offering the service at more than one location, as long as each catchment area is well chosen. Indeed, some multisite operators

have developed sophisticated computer programs in order to optimize their location strategy.

2. *The service provider goes to the customer* – Here, site location is a far less critical issue, providing the service company remains sufficiently close to be able to maintain a quality service to its customers. In some cases, the supplier has no discretion in terms of going to the customer. This could be in businesses like plumbing, window cleaning, landscape gardening and so on. In other cases, the service company might have some discretion whether or not they provide the service at the customer's premises or their own. Such business could include personal fitness, hairdressing and TV repair. Some dry cleaning and laundry firms have even found that it is more effective to close down expensive high-street outlets and move their operations to a low-cost out-of-town location. They could maintain their business by providing a pick-up and delivery service.

3. *The service provider and customer transact business at arm's length* – Here, the location is largely irrelevant and so least cost might be the deciding factor. There will, of course, need to be a suitable communications infrastructure available, depending upon the nature of the service. Thus, an accountant offering low-cost Internet-based services will need an attractive website with good navigation and appropriate functionality; a mail-order company will need access to a reliable mail service; likewise an express parcels service will need good access to motorways and airports.

Many face-to-face services companies have successfully transferred to arm's-length transactions. For example, insurance and banking can now be done via the Internet, the telephone or mail.

Channel decisions

These decisions influence who participates in the service delivery, in terms of either organizations or people. A channel will consist of:

- The service provider
- Intermediaries (if appropriate), e.g. agents, brokers, franchisees
- Customers.

Whereas traditionally services were delivered by direct sales (e.g. professional services), increasingly intermediaries are now being used. For example, travel agencies act as middlemen for airlines, hotels and leisure services. Similarly, recruitment agencies provide a link between employers and potential employees.

The broad channel options are outlined in Figure 10.7. The ultimate choice of channel will depend upon a number of different factors, which can influence singly or in combination:

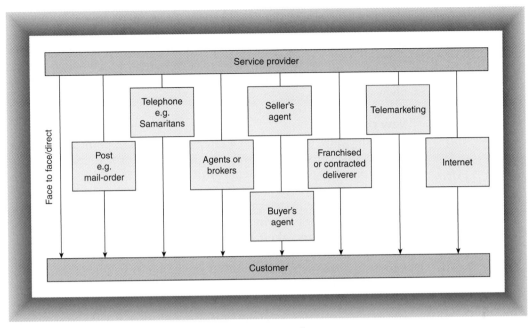

Figure 10.7   Channel options for service companies

- Ease and accessibility for customers
- The added value they provide
- The margins they seek
- The coverage they provide
- Their reputation and reliability
- Their compatibility with the supplier.

In strategic terms, the supplier should be concerned with:

- Understanding the distribution channels of its competitors
- Understanding the strengths and weaknesses of these channels
- Identifying how the company can avoid the problems experienced by competitors in existing channels, or creating alternative channel strategies by changing the type of intermediaries or what they traditionally do.

However, the choice of channel strategy can rarely be made in isolation from the issue of location. So, for example, a decision by a bank to switch to electronic systems, which require fewer face-to-face contacts, reduces the need for high-street premises. Instead, customer convenience is enhanced by having cash machines sited in, say, busy out-of-town superstores.

New channels

When deciding on a channel strategy, the starting point must be the customers themselves. If we do not offer them the channels they would prefer to use, a competitor will.

The starting point in determining customers' channel preferences is to identify customers' buying criteria, or the factors which determine which supplier gets their business. These may include cost, convenience (e.g. geographical proximity, ease of access, immediacy of response, home delivery, etc.), and reputation (e.g. service specialization, brand image or how well established the service provider is).

The ability of each current or future channel to deliver against each factor is then assessed judgementally on, say, a 1–10 basis (see Figure 10.8). In this hypothetical example, the various means by which a holiday can be purchased are compared. It can be seen that taking all the factors together, the Internet and physical stores have the best matches to this particular segment. In reality, different segments of the holiday market are clearly best matched to different channels.

The score of a channel against price-related factors, such as 'cost' in this example, will be affected by the channel economics, which will determine the price which any competitor using the channel chain will be able to offer. One factor in assessing the channel economics is the transaction costs involved. The TPN Network business-to-business exchange set up by General Electric, the first significant e-hub, saved

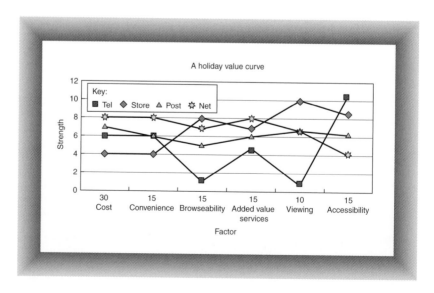

Figure 10.8
Choosing channels –
the value curve

GE 50–90% on processing costs for each order. But acquisition and retention costs should not be forgotten. The dotcom arm of one retail chain recently discovered that customer acquisition through a substantial investment in the Internet and banner advertising was costing approximately $900 per customer, when the average sale was only $75 – while the store-based arm of the retailer could acquire customers for its physical stores for around one quarter of this amount.

How channels work together

This example of a retailer using both physical stores and the Internet illustrates a complicating factor. In many markets, customers do not use a single channel. Rather, they use a number of channels in combination to meet their needs at different stages of their relationship with the supplier. To help define how this can best be done, we suggest the use of a tool we term channel chain analysis, which we illustrate in Figure 10.9.

Channel chain analysis involves describing which channels are used at which stages of the purchasing and value delivery process. The stages of the process are listed on the left of the diagram, and the channels used to accomplish the stage are listed against each stage. The

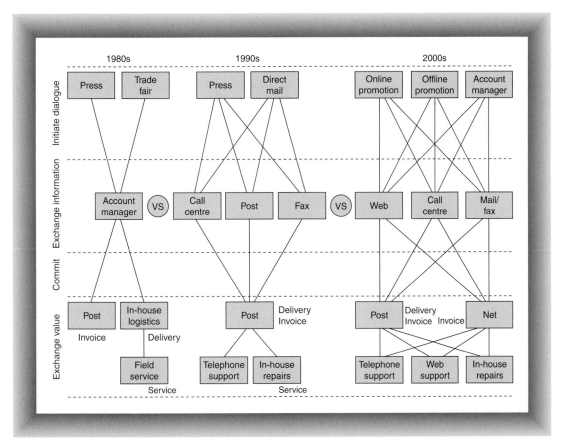

Figure 10.9 Channel chain analysis: the PC market

channel used for one stage will often affect which channel is likely to be used at the next stage, so the relevant boxes are joined with a line.

In this example from the business-to-business PC market, three of the common channel chains being offered by the various competitors are illustrated. The channel chain on the left shows the traditional account management approach, as used by most competitors at the start of the 1980s, when the sales process was largely handled face to face by account managers. Still a model used for larger computers or major contracts, it has tended, though, to be complemented by other channel chains which offer better channel economics for smaller deals.

One of these new channel chains, under way in the 1990s, was the direct model, illustrated in the middle of the figure. Here, press advertising formed the dominant marketing tool, with further information provided by product/service brochures and call centre staff. The actual order could be placed by a number of means – often a traditional fax or post order placed by the accounts department.

More recently, in the 2000s, many competitors have added the Internet to the channel mix, as illustrated on the right. But most of these are far from pureplay Internet providers. Account managers might serve major accounts, building relationships and negotiating discount levels. The account managers are freed from the details of product configuration and pricing by the website, while the order itself is as likely to be placed by fax or post as it is on the Web.

> Different channels, then, are needed at different points in the sales cycle, and different competitors may adopt different approaches. A fourth, pureplay Web channel chain which has a low-cost structure and is appropriate to certain price-sensitive segments has become increasingly common. Service companies in many sectors have now got competitors adopting this approach.

Having drawn the channel chains in current use, the next step is to consider possible future channel chains. This requires experimentation with channel chain diagrams to think through not just how the sale is to be made, but also how every other aspect of the customer's needs will be satisfied. Will a mobile phone purchaser buying over the Web be able to upgrade their service package at a nearby store?

The trick is to offer a channel chain that is appropriate to the differing needs of a company's target segments. In other words, the acid test as to whether a channel chain will flourish is whether it represents a better value proposition to some group of customers. To test this, we recommend drawing the value curve we described earlier, but comparing channel chains rather than individual channels.

There is a timing issue to be considered as well. Even if a channel chain offers a theoretically better proposition to customers, they may not yet be ready for it. A channel chain innovation, like a product or service innovation, is likely to proceed along the lines of Everett Rogers's bell-shaped diffusion of innovation curve.[5] If one hopes to convert customers to the Internet, for example, it is clearly necessary to consider what proportion of the customer base has Internet access and how mature their use of it is. We recall one department store which wasted millions on an aborted Web service in the mid-1990s because it was simply too far ahead of its market.

Our research suggests that service businesses can select from the following broad channel strategy options:

- A *single channel provider* provides at least the bulk of the customer interaction through one channel. Direct Line and First Direct both started as primarily telephone operations, while in the Internet world the approach is referred to as 'pureplay', represented by Amazon, eBay and so on.

- A *channel migrator* started with one single channel, but is attempting to migrate its customer base onto another channel on the grounds of increased value or reduced cost. easyJet initially sold tickets by telephone, but now provides financial incentives to its price-sensitive customers to buy online, most of whom now do so.

- An *activity-based strategy* uses different channels in combination to perform different tasks in the customer's lifecycle. Thomas Cook's corporate foreign exchange business uses the Internet to generate leads, a direct sales force to sign up new clients, and a call centre or the Internet to take orders.

- An *integrated multi-channel* approach involves offering different channels to the customer without attempting to influence which ones the customer uses. UK bank First Direct provides both telephone and Internet banking as an integrated service. While the Internet has much lower unit costs and also has proved better for cross-selling, First Direct chooses to position itself on customer service and accept the higher costs from those customers who primarily use the telephone without penalizing them or rewarding Internet users.

- A *needs-based segmentation strategy* offers different channels to different customer groups to meet their varying needs. The European insurance company Zurich Financial Services has strengths in different routes to market – the direct sales force, independent financial advisers and company pension schemes – in order to serve customer groups with differing needs and attitudes. Each of these routes to market may use the same brand name, or different names.

- A *graduated customer value strategy* uses channels selectively according to the financial value of the customers. Many IT firms use account managers for high-value customers, and steer smaller customers to lower-cost channels such as the Internet, call centres or value-added resellers. Many retail banks, though, are in danger of doing the precise opposite, offering the high-cost branch network to the lower-value customers who prefer not to bank by phone or Internet.

In brief, routes to market are being reconfigured in five main ways:

1. *Substitute/reconfigured products or services* (such as emails instead of physical post)

2. *Disintermediation* (e-commerce can make intermediaries redundant)

3. *Re-intermediation* (a previous intermediary is replaced by a new online intermediary)

4. *Partial channel substitution* (an intermediary's role may be reduced, but not eliminated – as in the case of a car retailer providing customer information, but pointing customers to particular outlets)

5. *Media switching/addition* (the links in the chain may remain the same, but communication between them may be partially or fully switched to the Internet from the previous mechanisms).

When the routes to market are being considered and potentially reconfigured it is important to review the channel intermediaries. We conclude our discussion on the 'place' plan with some evaluation criteria for channel intermediaries.

Evaluation criteria for channel intermediaries

Regardless of the type of intermediary to be used, there are a number of basic evaluation criteria, for example:

- Do they now, or will they, sell to our target market segment?

- Is their sales force large enough and trained well enough to achieve our regional sales forecasts?

- Is their regional location adequate in respect of the retail (and other) outlets serviced?

- If intermediaries rely on Internet channels, is their web platform attractive, easy to navigate and, if a significant increase in volume is likely in the channel, is it scalable?

- Are their promotional policies and budgets adequate?

- Do they satisfy customer after-sales requirements?

- Are their product policies consistent with our own?

- Do they sell competitive services?

- What are their policies regarding cover of the market?

- Are they creditworthy?

- Is distributor management receptive, aggressive and flexible?

All the above factors, and others, have to be considered when making specific decisions on choice of intermediaries, which in turn is part of the overall channel selection issue.

Mix element 5: The people element of the marketing mix

Another issue for the supplier is to ensure that the service received by the customer is of the same high quality, regardless of how it is delivered. This is particularly true where a franchised delivery system is used. Setting rigorous selection standards and providing training are two methods which can help to maintain quality in most situations. The difficult areas are where the service providers are of low education and tend not to remain in one job for very long, such as in the hotel and catering trades. Here, quality control is largely in the hands not of the operatives themselves, but of their supervisors and managers.

It is the people element, above all, that differentiates services marketing from product marketing

People in services

> It is clear that people loom large in the delivery of services. As indicated above, in the final analysis, it is largely a matter of how people are selected, trained, motivated and managed that influences the consistency of its quality. As more companies come to recognize this, so they are paying more attention to the different roles which people might play, both in customer contact and marketing in general.

One way of looking at roles is shown in Figure 10.10. This categorization, developed by Judd,[6] results in four groups:

> - *Contactors* have frequent or regular customer contact and are typically heavily involved with conventional marketing activities. They hold a range of positions in service firms, including selling and customer service roles. Whether they are involved in planning or execution of marketing strategy, they need to be well versed in the marketing strategies of the firm. They should be well trained, prepared and motivated to serve the customers on a day-to-day

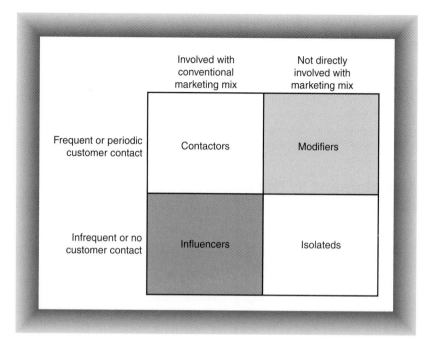

Figure 10.10
Employees and their
influence on customers

basis in a responsive manner. They should be recruited based on their potential to be responsive to customer needs and be evaluated and rewarded on this basis.

- *Modifiers* are people such as receptionists, credit department and switchboard personnel, and while they are not directly involved with conventional marketing activities to a great degree, they nevertheless have frequent customer contact. As such, they need to have a clear view of the organization's marketing strategy and the role that they can play in being responsive to customers' needs. They have a vital role to play especially, but not exclusively, in service businesses. Modifiers need to develop high levels of customer relationship skills. Training and monitoring of performance are especially important here.

- *Influencers*, while involved with the traditional elements of the marketing mix, have infrequent or no customer contact. However, they are very much part of the implementation of the organization's marketing strategy. They include roles such as product development and market research. In recruitment of influencers, people with the potential to develop a sense of customer responsiveness should be pursued. Influencers should be evaluated and rewarded according to customer-oriented performance standards, and opportunities to enhance the level of customer contact should be programmed into their activities.

> ● *Isolateds* are the various support functions which have nei-
> ther frequent customer contact nor a great deal to do with
> the conventional marketing activities. However, as support
> people, their activities critically affect performance of the
> organization's activities. Staff falling within this category
> include purchase department, personnel and data process-
> ing. Such staff need to be sensitive to the fact that internal
> customers as well as external customers have needs which
> must be satisfied. They need to understand the company's
> overall marketing strategy and how their functions contrib-
> ute to the quality of delivered value to the customer.

This type of analysis illustrates that not only do people play an
important part in the transactions between the supplier and the
customer, but also that they can be a source of differentiation for
the service.

> By adding value in the way they perform and by maximizing
> the impact of their activities, people have the capacity to give
> the company a competitive edge.

Internal marketing

It is now widely recognized that for service organizations to be successful in their external marketing, they also need to practise internal
marketing.

Internal marketing was discussed in Chapter 2 in the context of internal markets. There are at least two key elements to internal marketing:

● Every employee and every department within an organization have
roles both as internal customers and internal suppliers. To help
ensure high-quality external marketing, every individual and
department within a service organization must provide and receive
excellent service.

● People need to work together in a way that is aligned with the organization's stated mission, strategy and goals. This is obviously a
critical element within high-contact service firms where there
are high levels of interaction between the service provider and
customer.

Leading service companies such as Southwest Airlines, Virgin Atlantic, Disney and Nordstroms have recognized the importance of internal marketing and have developed organizational philosophies along

these lines. They subscribe to all members of staff providing the best possible contribution to the marketing activities, and engaging in all telephone, mail, electronic and personal encounters in a manner which adds value to the service. Such internal marketing initiatives are not passing gimmicks, but are backed up with rigorous and frequent training programmes, codes of behaviour, dress standards and awards for outstanding performers. This involvement of staff, in what for many organizations is a new and liberating policy, can set up an irreversible thrust, which only wanes when the organization's culture and climate change in a fundamental way.

Our research suggests that relatively few *formal* internal marketing programmes exist within service organizations. However, there are many service companies who have adopted elements of internal marketing. The research shows that, in companies practising internal marketing:

- Internal marketing is generally not a discrete activity, but is implicit in quality initiatives, customer service programmes and broader business strategies.

- Structured activities are accompanied by a range of less formal ad hoc initiatives.

- Communication is critical to successful internal marketing.

- Internal marketing performs a critical role in competitive differentiation.

- Internal marketing has an important role to play in reducing conflict between the functional areas of the organization.

- Internal marketing is an experiential process, leading employees to form their own conclusions.

- Internal marketing is evolutionary: it involves the slow erosion of barriers between departments and functions. It has an important role in helping with the balancing of marketing and operations – a problem that is discussed under the processes element of the marketing mix.

- Internal marketing is used to facilitate a spirit of innovation.

- Internal marketing is more successful when there is commitment at the highest level, when all employees cooperate, and an open management style prevails.

Internal marketing in all its forms should be recognized as an important activity in contributing to the people element of the marketing mix and in developing a customer-focused organization (see Chapter 11).

In practice, internal marketing is concerned with communications, with developing responsiveness, responsibility and unity of purpose. The fundamental aims of internal marketing are to develop internal and external customer awareness and remove functional barriers to organizational effectiveness.

The service–profit chain

Researchers at the Harvard Business School coined the term service–profit chain to describe a significant body of research carried out by them relating to service companies.[7] The generalized service–profit chain shown in Figure 10.11 clearly shows that there is a linkage between the people element of the marketing mix and the internal marketing activities associated with them and customer satisfaction and financial performance. These researchers found 'direct and strong' relationships between profit; growth; customer loyalty; customer satisfaction; the value of goods and services delivered to customers; employee capability, satisfaction, loyalty and productivity.

The important role of leaders in internal marketing has only recently been examined in any depth.[8] As suggested by Figure 10.11, when the leaders and managers of a company exhibit strong and positive management behaviour and provide high-quality support to employees as well as policies that enable employees to deliver results to customers, the people at all levels in organizations are more likely to be satisfied, loyal and productive employees. Loyal and empowered people in service organizations are motivated to fulfil their responsibilities and this has a direct positive impact on customer satisfaction. Highly satisfied customers are more likely to remain loyal to the company and will engage in repeat buying behaviour. Further, highly satisfied customers act as advocates of the company recommending it to friends, colleagues and acquaintances. This growing base of satisfied customers leads to improved financial performance in terms of profits, growth and reputation.

The service profit chain demonstrates how the people element of the marketing mix can make a profound impact on the success of the organization. Internal marketing is still at a relatively early stage of development. Readers wishing to explore internal marketing in greater detail should refer to the references for this part of the chapter.[9]

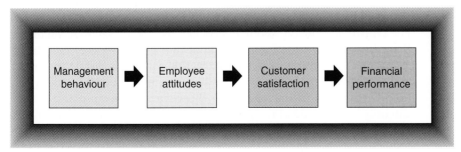

Figure 10.11 The service–profit chain

Mix element 6: The processes element of the marketing mix

> The processes by which services are created and delivered to the customer can be a major factor within the services marketing mix, for customers perceive the delivery system as part of the service itself. This means that operations management decisions can be of great importance regarding the competitive position of the service.

Process, in the sense it is used here, means work activity. Thus, any procedure, task, schedule, mechanism or routine which helps to deliver the service to the customer will fall under this heading. From this it follows that any policy decisions that are made about customer involvement or employee discretion have a direct impact on the processes element of the marketing mix.

Processes play a crucial role in service delivery

While people play a critical role in the mix, they will be severely handicapped if the process performance is inherently flawed. So, for example, if the processes supporting delivery cannot quickly respond and repair a service fault, or if the hotel kitchen takes too long to prepare a meal, all the initial positive impact of the contact staff is destroyed. This suggests that close cooperation is required between marketing and those who are involved in process management.

> Furthermore, any improvements in processes will inevitably lead to an improvement in service quality.

If the service runs efficiently, the service provider will have a clear advantage over less effective competitors.

Decision-making processes are also important in the context of this element of the marketing mix. Some service providers give their service deliverers the autonomy to make decisions up to a certain level. For example, an airline can give its staff powers to upgrade a passenger who is aggrieved about his or her treatment, thereby enabling them to defuse a situation on the spot in a satisfying way. Similarly, many service companies are now empowering junior staff to correct service errors, on the spot, up to a given limit. Not all services can lend themselves to this approach, however. For example, a waiter can only bill for food at the published price. Any discretionary powers are inevitably held by the restaurant manager, which means that customers have to demand to see the manager if their grievance is to be resolved.

It can be seen from these examples that, in general, the more special-ized the service, the more decision-making is entrusted to the service provider. This allows for greater customization and personalization of the service. Less specialized services, on the whole, have less scope for doing this.

The 'process plan', therefore, needs to address two main issues:

> ● How can processes be improved in order to help achieve an improved competitive positioning strategy?
>
> ● How can marketing and operations be managed in a way that is synergistic?

Analysing the processes

US academic Lynn Stostack[10] has developed a simple three-step approach for analysing a process:

> 1. Break down the process into logical steps and sequences.
>
> 2. Identify those steps which introduce the highest prospect of something going wrong because of judgement, choice or chance.
>
> 3. Set deviation or tolerance standards for these steps, thereby providing a performance band for functioning. (It will be unrealistic to expect process steps to be performed with complete precision every time.)

By adopting this approach, errant processes can be made to fulfil their purpose in a more consistent and service-enhancing way.

Processes can also be considered in terms of their *complexity*, i.e. the number or nature of the steps and sequences, and *divergence*, i.e. the latitude or variability involved. Thus, for example, a beach ice-cream salesperson has a delivery process which is neither complex nor divergent. In contrast, a bookkeeper's job might be quite high in complexity, but relatively modest in divergence. Another example, say a surgeon, would be high on both parameters.

Using this approach for looking at processes, four improvement strate-gies are possible:

> ● *Reduce divergence* – This option would tend to standardize the service and limit the extent to which it might be custom-ized. While this offers the prospects of reducing costs and

improving productivity, it could also alienate those customers for whom customization was a considerable benefit.

- *Increase divergence* – This would allow for greater customization and flexibility, for which it might be possible to charge premium prices. This may be a suitable strategy for niche positioning of the service, where high volume sales would not be anticipated.

- *Reduce complexity* – Here, steps and activities are omitted from the service process. This has the effect of making distribution and control easier, since some peripheral activities disappear.

- *Increase complexity* With this approach, more services are added to the core service product, usually with the intention of creating a competitive advantage and gaining market penetration. Financial services companies and supermarkets frequently use this approach.

All of these options carry with them advantages and disadvantages. In that sense, no single approach is any better than another. What is significant, however, is that the chosen process strategy will impact on customers' perceptions, in effect causing the service to be repositioned (Figure 10.12).

Assuming that the existing general management consultancy shown in Figure 10.12 could be positioned roughly in the centre of the map,

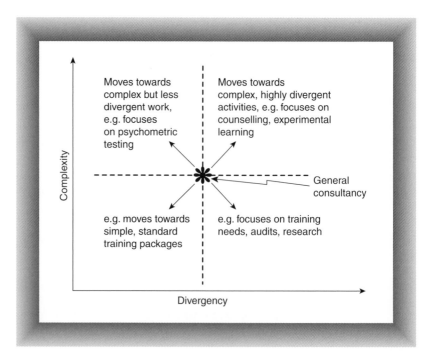

Figure 10.12
Example of service positioning through changing complexity and divergence (a management training consultancy)

repositioning could be achieved broadly in line with the suggestions in this figure. The alteration in complexity and divergence is analogous to changing elements of design of a product, thus their impact on the marketing mix is both obvious and influential.

Service blueprinting/process analysis

Service companies who wish to provide high levels of service quality and customer satisfaction need to understand all the factors which may impact on service processes. 'Blueprinting', or service process analysis, is a concept which breaks down the basic systems and structures of an organization to develop a greater understanding of the service process.

The approach requires identifying all of the points of contact between the customer and the service provider and documenting them in a service map or 'blueprint'. Possible breakdowns in the service experience can then be identified. These can then be acted upon and improved, thereby improving service quality.

Several approaches have been suggested to carry out a blueprinting exercise[11]:

1. *Blueprinting/cycle of service analysis* – The concept suggests that each contact with the customer is a 'moment of truth', each being an opportunity to either increase or decrease customer satisfaction. The perception of the customer is a continuous stream of experiences which together determine service quality. The company will very often not perceive the service in this way as their employees are constrained in their view by the particular part of the overall service with which they are involved. The blueprinting/cycle of service approach enables a service company to shift its employee's perception to better understand their customer's experience of their service.

2. *Value chain analysis* – This important analytical tool involves breaking down each of the activities of a firm into its various activities, and showing where value is added for its customers. Each activity can be analysed to determine its contribution to customer satisfaction and service quality.

3. *Storyboarding* – This concept was developed by the Walt Disney organization in designing its theme parks in order to engineer the customer experience and ensure the greatest customer satisfaction. When a film is made, each scene is outlined in advance, using a series of sketches arranged in a sequence known as a storyboard. Similarly, sketches of each contact a customer has with the service provider can be used to identify points for improvement in customer service. Scenes can be rearranged to improve the quality of the customer experience.

Blueprinting involves flow charting the service delivery system of each aspect, including both front office and back office, of the service process. It involves a number of steps[12]:

- The first step in blueprinting is to diagram all the components of a service so that the service can be clearly and objectively seen.

- The next important task in blueprinting is the identification of failure points – that is, the areas most likely to cause operational or consistency problems.

- Setting execution standards is the third critical part of the blueprint. These represent the main quality targets for the service. Execution standards not only define the costs of a service, they also define the performance criteria and tolerances for the completion of each service step.

- Finally, the manager must identify all of the evidence of the service that is available to the customer. Each item that is visible to the customer represents an encounter point, during which interaction with the service will occur.

Blueprinting involves identification and management of 'encounter points', 'pressure points', or 'moments of truth'. Moments of truth is a term used by Jan Carlzon of SAS to describe every interaction between the service provider and the customer. Karl Albrecht, a noted US commentator on service businesses, has outlined the typical moments of truth in the context of an airline:

1. Customer calls the airline for information

2. Customer books the flight with the airline representative

3. Customer arrives at airport counter

4. Customer waits in line

5. Ticket agent invites customer to the counter

6. Ticket agent processes payment and issues ticket

7. Customer goes looking for the departure gate

8. Gate agent welcomes customer to the flight, validates boarding pass

9. Customer waits in departure lounge for flight to depart

10. Boarding agent takes customer's ticket and invites customer on board

11. Customer boards aeroplane, is greeted by flight attendant

12. Customer looks for his/her assigned seat

13. Customer looks for a place to stow carry-on luggage

14. Customer takes his/her seat

15. Etc.

Each moment of truth represents a point where the service provider demonstrates elements of both functional and technical quality in different proportions. Every individual moment of truth adds to or detracts from the overall image of the service provider. Every moment of truth reinforces the quality of service or lack of it.

Virgin Atlantic has consciously adopted this approach in designing its service products. Its 'Upper Class' service is positioned between the business class and the first class service of other major airlines. Virgin Atlantic exemplifies seeing things from the customer's point of view and creating processes in line with customers' needs and desires. In many cities they have a limousine service that collects passengers from their home or office and drives them to the airport free of charge. At certain major airports around the world, including the airline's home capital city of London, they have a dedicated drive-in service where passengers may check their bags, have their passport inspected and received their boarding pass in the comfort of the limousine and then proceed immediately to Virgin Atlantic's business lounge without getting involved in long queues. The Virgin business lounge has high levels of customer intimacy and you feel like you are in a friendly restaurant with staff who are interested in helping you. This is unlike the more usual reception you get in a business class lounge where there is an offhand receptionist, stale sandwiches and disinterested catering staff.

The service blueprint is a valuable tool to help visualize the service process, understand what can go wrong and set performance standards for improvement in service quality. This helps not just with solving potential problems but also in designing ways to deal with service recovery. Many service companies are now using service blueprinting methods to improve their service quality.

Conflict between operations and marketing

While this might not be obvious in most service companies, there may be elements of conflict implicit in the way that operations and marketing people would view the same issue. Figure 10.13 illustrates some common areas of contention.[13]

Clearly, all of the issues listed in the figure affect both operations and marketing. However, where operations management is a more traditional part of the organizational fabric and marketing less deeply rooted, decision-making may be skewed in favour of operations. This is particularly likely to be the case if the organization tends to operate with a financial 'orientation', where everything is measured in terms of short-term profit or loss.

> The message for marketers is quite clear. They must take the initiative and make greater impact on operational decisions by providing cost–benefit trade-offs to back up their arguments.

Operational issues	Typical operations goals	Common marketing concerns
Productivity improvement	Reduce unit cost of production	Strategies may cause decline in service quality
Standardization versus customization	Keep costs low and quality consistent; simplify operations tasks; recruit low-cost employees	Consumers may seek variety, prefer customization to match segmented needs
Batch versus unit processing	Seek economies of scale, consistency, efficient use of capacity	Customers may be forced to wait, feel one of a crowd, be turned off by other customers
Facilities layout and design	Control costs; improve efficiency by ensuring proximity of operationally related tasks; enhance safety and security	Customers may be confused, shunted around unnecessarily, find facilities unattractive and inconvenient
Job design	Minimize error, waste and fraud; make efficient use of technology; simplify tasks for standardization	Operational-oriented employees with narrow roles may be unresponsive to customer needs
Management of capacity	Keep costs down by avoiding wasteful underutilization of resources	Service may be unavailable when needed; quality may be compromized during high-demand periods
Management of queues	Optimize use of available capacity by planning for average throughput; maintain customer order, discipline	Customers may be bored and frustrated during wait, see firm as unresponsive

Figure 10.13 Potential sources of conflict between operations and marketing on operational issues

Mix element 7: The customer service element of the marketing mix

As customers become more sophisticated and demand higher standards, so must companies improve customer service in order to remain competitive.

In most marketing literature, customer service has been subsumed under the broad heading of 'place' in the marketing mix. The reasoning for this is that since reliability and speed of delivery were thought to be the main elements of customer satisfaction, the way that services were delivered was seen to be a distribution and logistics problem. However, in the light of experience in recent years, service companies have developed a different perspective on customer service. For customer-centric organizations, customer service is a critical component of the marketing mix, and is not just about looking at customers or addressing complaints.

In their comprehensive text on services marketing, Lovelock, Patterson and Wirtz point out that customer service should be an integral part of the service firm's DNA. They define customer service as follows[14]:

> Customer service involves task-oriented activities [other than proactive selling] that involve interactions with customers in person or by technology for the purposes of service 'manufacture', delivery and service support. This function should be designed, performed and communicated with two goals in mind: customer satisfaction and operational efficiency.

Customer service is concerned with the building of bonds with customers and other markets or groups to establish long-term, mutually advantageous relationships which reinforce the other marketing mix elements.

In this context, and in the pursuance of time and place utilities for customers, customer service must take into account all activities which relate to customers before, during and after the transaction (Figure 10.14). The implication for the company operating in this comprehensive manner is that it must fully understand the reasons why customers buy, and recognize how additional value can be added to the offer.

Customer service takes into account all activities which relate to customers before, during and after the transaction

Many service companies have instinctively recognized this and have focused on their existing client base as never before. By increasing their

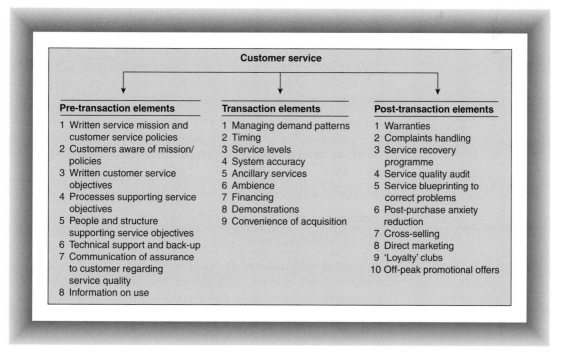

Figure 10.14 Illustration of key elements of customer service

understanding of client needs, they invariably find opportunities for additional cross-selling, thereby tying their customers even more closely to the company. However, because many services require close personal contact between the provider and the customer, improving customer service often hinges on the attitudes and behaviour of the contact staff. It is, therefore, essential that these key people are selected with great care and then given training which reflects the importance of their work.

Creating a customer service strategy

Recognizing the importance of customer service as a weapon, it is incumbent upon the marketer to be clear about how it will be created and used. There are four main steps in creating a customer service strategy[15]:

1. *Identify a service mission* – Just as there is a need for a corporate mission statement to clarify the organization's values and general sense of direction, so is there a need for a separate customer service mission. This will distil into a few words the company's philosophy and commitment to customer service.

2. *Setting customer service objectives* – This involves asking questions such as:

   - How important is customer service compared to other elements of the marketing mix?

   - Which are the most important customer service elements?

   - How do these vary by market segment?

   The answers to these questions will reflect such service quality variables as reliability, responsiveness and assurance. They will also take into account the nature of competitive offers.

   The customer service objectives which emerge from this type of analysis need to be considered in the context of pre-transaction, transaction, and post-transaction activities.

3. *Customer service strategy* – Not all customers will require the same level of service, therefore appropriate service packages have to be created for different market segments. In order to do this the company must:

   - Identify the most important services and segments

   - Prioritize service targets

   - Develop the service packages.

   The most appropriate service packages will be those which offer greater benefits to customers than those of competing services. Such benefits may be real or perceived.

4. *Implementation* – The selected service packages are then introduced into the marketing mix. Often, the benefits they provide can be used as part of the promotional campaign.

A key element of the customer service element of the marketing mix is the setting of service standards and key performance indicators (KPIs). This involves identifying the most important customer expectations and developing measures of these so the customer service performance can be measured on these key dimensions. We discuss this in the next section of the chapter.

It is important to remember that, just like the service product itself, customer service strategies can have a limited life. With this in mind, the forward-looking service company keeps customer satisfaction levels under constant review and stays in touch with the changing needs of its customers in terms of providing service.

The need for an overall marketing mix strategy

It is clear from the foregoing discussion about the seven elements of the marketing mix that they are closely related to each other. Such is the way they interact that to change one element is to impact on the others. It is essential, therefore, that an overall marketing mix is developed which ensures that all elements are mutually supportive and synergistic. This means that the interaction between the marketing mix elements should be[16]:

- *Integrated*, i.e. there is harmonious interaction
- *Consistent*, i.e. there is a logic behind how the major elements of the mix fit together
- *Leveraged*, i.e. each element is used to best advantage in support of the total marketing mix.

This process can be likened to the way that, in optics, a prism can split white light into its seven constituent colours of the rainbow. However, here it operates in reverse and the seven elements of the mix are focused into a distinctive output which determines the service quality and how the offer is positioned (Figure 10.15).

At this point, some comments should be made on service quality. (Positioning has already been discussed in Chapter 7.) Service quality is the ability of the service organization to meet or exceed customer expectations. The measure of performance is essentially a measure of *perceived* performance. Thus it is the customers' perceptions of performance which count, rather than the reality of performance. It has been argued that the quality of a service has two important components:

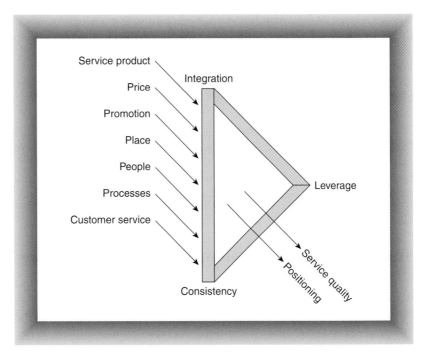

Figure 10.15
The marketing mix
'prism'

- *Technical quality* – the outcome dimension of the service operations process.

- *Functional quality* – the process dimension in terms of the interaction between the customer and the service provider.

These two dimensions of service quality highlight the subjective nature of quality assessments. Some authors refer to this as process quality and outcome quality. Generally, clients of professional service firms such as management consultants or insurance brokers have difficulty in distinguishing between good and outstanding technical quality of the service; thus judgements are often made on the subjective basis of how the client was treated. In the context of electronic commerce, Joel Collier and Carol Beinstock suggest that e-service quality in online service transactions involves process quality, outcome quality and recovery quality.[17]

Recently, research has been undertaken in an effort to try to understand the factors which influence service quality. Research by 'Parsu' Parasuraman, Len Berry and Valerie Zeithaml has focused on developing a conceptual model of service quality called 'SERVQUAL' in which service quality perceptions are influenced by a series of distinct gaps and empirical work, which identifies the importance of five key service areas.[18] These five key areas are:

- *Tangibles* – the physical facilities, equipment, appearance of personnel.

- *Reliability* – the ability to perform the desired service dependably, accurately and consistently.

- *Responsiveness* – willingness to provide prompt service and help customers.

- *Assurance* – employees' knowledge, courtesy, and ability to convey trust and confidence.

- *Empathy* – caring, individualized attention to customers.

While their empirical research in a number of service industries showed that all the above factors were important, two findings were especially important. First, tangibles have a relatively less important score than other dimensions. Second, reliability emerged as by far the most important dimension across all the services studied.

This work on SERVQUAL has recently been extended so that it can be utilized in the online context. This involved the development of an instrument with multiple scale items, called 'E-S-QUAL', for measuring service quality delivered on the Internet with a particular focus on shopping sites.[19]

The message for the service marketer seems clear. Above all, be reliable and deliver what is promised to the customer. Further, human performance plays a critical role in the customer's perception of service quality. Three of the five dimensions outlined above – assurance, empathy and response – result directly from human performance; and a fourth factor, reliability, is also largely dependent on human performance.

In developing the marketing mix that delivers service quality, it will be necessary to consider the impact of each marketing mix element on the target market segments. This implies that the marketer must ensure:

- A good fit between the marketing mix and each segment.

- A good fit between the marketing mix and the company's strategic capabilities, thus playing to its strengths and reducing the negative influences of its weaknesses.

- A recognition of competitors' capabilities, strategically avoiding their strengths and capitalizing on their weaknesses.

The optimum services marketing mix strategy, therefore, involves organizing marketing resources, deciding upon levels of marketing expenditure, and being clear about the expected results.

Monitoring, control and review

The marketing programmes which are formulated for each element of the marketing mix should:

> - Have an established timetable which indicates what activities have to be achieved at what time.
> - Indicate the priority tasks and activities.
> - Identify the resources and people needed to carry them out.
> - Provide for monitoring and control of performance.

This last point is vital if the marketing plan is to succeed, yet it is often overlooked. Without some means of monitoring, controlling and reviewing the programmes, it will be impossible to ensure that the short-term strategies of both small and large service organizations are working towards the planned long-term objectives.

> One of the reasons that monitoring and control is not covered very well in many companies is because they have been weak at setting quantifiable objectives in the first place. Without clearly measurable targets, monitoring progress becomes an extremely difficult, if not impossible, task.

Our work with smaller service companies, as well as academic research studies, suggests small firms often have poorer control procedures than larger ones. They also do a poorer job of setting objectives and monitoring them and often fail to analyse costs, evaluate advertising or examine sales force reports.

Tim Ambler, a leading researcher on performance metrics, identifies two key problems with larger companies. First, large companies frequently have too many measures, leading to confusion. Second, important control metrics such as customer satisfaction and customer retention often do not reach top management. In his research, he found customer satisfaction measures only reached the board of directors in 36% of companies and customer retention measures only reached the board of directors in 51% of companies.[20]

It is clear that accurate, timely and appropriate control data will not arrive by chance. Greater discipline is required by firms of all sizes to develop and monitor appropriate metrics to provide timely and better control for the leadership of the organization.

> A conscious effort must be made to set up information and reporting systems so that the right information for monitoring, control and review reaches the right people at the right time.

The level of detail, the format and the frequency of reporting will, to a large extent, be determined by the nature of the business, and the service markets in which it operates. In some companies, daily feedback will be required; in others, weekly, or even monthly, reporting periods might be perfectly adequate.

In a similar way, the performance criteria against which the market efforts are measured will need to be company specific, making sense only in the context of its marketing plan and particular business environment. Typical performance measures which might be monitored and controlled could include:

- Revenues
- Market share
- Marketing costs
- Overhead costs
- Profits
- Return on investments
- Consumer attitudes
- New customers
- Sales visits
- Conversion of visits to orders
- Complaints
- Customer retention
- Net promoter scores
- Bad debts
- Shifts in channel use
- Sales by service product
- Advertising effectiveness
- Service quality

The introduction of marketing planning can be a learning process for the whole organization. Its ultimate success comes from the willingness of everyone, from the boardroom down, to learn, to be prepared to experiment, and to adopt the planning system so that it delivers success to the company, regardless of its particular circumstances.

Summary

In this chapter we continued our examination of the first year detailed implementation programmes to address issues of: price; place; people; processes; and customer service, making sure that, in each of them, the ultimate choice of actions was designed to provide the service company with a competitive advantage. The challenge of responding to the opportunities and threats of new channels was given particular emphasis. Successful companies such as eBay, Amazon, Google and First Direct bank all compete by exploiting IT-enabled channels to add value, reduce costs or both. Channel selection and channel integration form key issues in marketing planning.

We also saw that the components of the marketing mix were interrelated in such a way that decisions made in one area could limit or enhance options in another. Therefore, it was important that all marketing programmes had an overall coherence which ensured that they were consistent and integrated with each other.

Finally, we saw that to wait until the end of the plan and only then discover that it had failed was no way to run a business. By monitoring progress as the plan unfolds, and taking corrective action whenever it proves necessary, the company not only brings the plan to fruition, but also learns from experience how to improve its planning and control processes.

In the last five chapters we have provided an overview of the marketing planning process and then looked at each of the four phases in detail. In the final three chapters we now examine some key organizational aspects relating to the introduction of marketing planning, consider how to measure the effectiveness of marketing plans and provide a step-by-step marketing planning system for service organizations which shows how the approach outlined in the previous chapters can be successfully implemented through the creation of structured three-year strategic and one-year tactical marketing plans.

11 Organizing for marketing planning

Introduction

From the foregoing chapters, it should be apparent that the decision to tackle marketing planning is not one that the service organization should take lightly. Taking up planning along the lines we have suggested will involve considerable time and effort being expended on a number of aspects of business activity which might earlier have been taken for granted and accepted uncritically. Although well-formulated marketing plans bring with them increased prospects for success, they are not achieved without cost. The forward-looking service organization recognizes this and is prepared to invest in the process, ensuring that the organization as a whole is geared up to supporting it. In these circumstances, marketing planning is identified as a critical planning activity and plays a key role in shaping organizational behaviour.

Undertaking marketing planning has profound organizational implications

Less far-seeing organizations perceive marketing planning as merely the imposition of a series of procedures which, if followed to the letter, deliver a plan at the end. It becomes a sort of 'bolt-on', optional extra. Such an unthinking, mechanical approach completely misses the point of having marketing planning.

Marketing planning is much more than a mechanical process

> For it is not the marketing procedures that achieve success, but the creative thinking processes that they stimulate.

Planning can never be a neat, remote approach that leaves the company largely untouched. It can be messy and uncomfortable, as attention is directed into organizational activities that have for too long been neglected. It can raise more questions than immediate answers.

Above all, it meets reality head on, as facts, rather than opinions, become the focus of organizational initiatives.

In Chapter 4 we looked at some of the organizational barriers which get in the way of marketing planning. We identified these as: short-termism; lack of support from top management; lack of a plan for planning; lack of line management support; confusion over planning terms; an over-reliance on numbers; too much detail, too far ahead; once-a-year ritual; confusion between operational and strategic planning; failure to integrate marketing planning into the corporate planning system; delegation of planning to a 'planner'; and uncertainty about what should appear in the plan. However, during our explanation of marketing planning, it should be obvious that many of these barriers stem from the lack of understanding of the marketing planning process and how it works.

Avoiding these potential hazards is clearly important, but there is still more that the company must do to organize for effective marketing planning. There are questions to be raised about marketing intelligence systems, the use of marketing research (and how much to spend on it) and database marketing, the impact of marketing planning on the organizational structure, and how to develop a market-focused organization. These are the issues which will be addressed in this chapter.

Marketing intelligence systems

> Since marketing intelligence is the fuel which powers marketing decision-making, the time and money spent on organizing information flows are inevitably a sound investment.

As the decision-making arena becomes more uncertain, so there is added pressure for more information. In fact, some managers are prepared to hide behind the lack of information as an excuse for putting off making decisions.

The advent and development of computer technology ought, in theory, to have simplified the gathering and presentation of marketing information. Sadly, this is not the case. Research has shown that it is one of the most badly organized areas of management. By and large, there seems to be a failure to identify both the decisions to be taken and the information essential to make them.

MIS must be based on the information needs of management

Thus, the construction of a successful marketing intelligence system (MIS) has to start with a clear definition of the management information needs. Unfortunately, this seemingly straightforward step is obscured by the fact that many executives fail to isolate the key determinants of success from the many other issues that attract their attention. For example, they misunderstand the meaning and significance of market share, or they over- or underestimate the strategic impact of service levels, and so on. By not providing a lead, they can be presented with a mass of unfocused data and information in such volume that it becomes virtually impossible for the recipients to isolate what is, or is not, important. Such is the regularity of the arrival of this material that some executives become, quite literally, overwhelmed.

The consequence of such systems is that their output is rarely used. Instead, management regresses to the old ways of relying on intuition and hunch when making marketing decisions.

In order to construct a productive MIS, there are four steps to be taken:

Too much data and information is counter-productive

> 1. Make a detailed list of all current data and information that are produced.
>
> 2. Separately, get each manager to list the important decisions he or she has to make, together with the essential information input required for making those decisions.
>
> 3. Compare these two lists and:
>
>   (a) remove all redundant information requirements, i.e. which are provided but not needed
>
>   (b) rationalize all the remaining manager/information combinations in a way that the managers' needs, in total, can be met with the fewest pieces of generated information.
>   This second category of action is not easy and is likely to involve a rigorous examination of the underlying purpose for all information requirements. While it might be nice for managers to know all sorts of information, much of this can turn out to be peripheral to decision-making.
>
> 4. Work towards the 'ideal' MIS.

It is tempting to think that it would be possible to build a new MIS starting from scratch. However, in the real world, this might not be possible for reasons of cost or IT resources. Experience suggests that the way forward is to use a building-block approach. This means that each block, which is a subsystem for meeting a particular group of information needs, is developed one at a time. Eventually an integrated and sophisticated MIS is put together to the benefit of its users.

Internal data sources and MIS[1]

In theory the internal audit should be relatively straightforward. Analysis and reporting of company results by region, product and segment should merely involve a bit of computer analysis of the sales ledger.

> In practice there are problems. Sales ledgers are owned by finance and designed to facilitate billings and collections. Their purpose does not include supporting marketing and they rarely do so.
>
> The information on sales ledgers is incomplete and miscoded from marketing's viewpoint. Ledgers contain accounts and stock-keeping units, which cannot easily be linked to customers, products, regions or segments.

Collecting, consolidating and using sales ledger information may also be difficult. Ledgers are designed to do accounting consolidations and analysis, not market consolidation and analysis.

Definition: ●————————
MIS facilitates information flows, ensuring appropriate inputs and that data gets to users in a sensible form

An **MIS** (marketing intelligence or marketing information system) is the solution. A system to facilitate information flows needs to be developed so that there are appropriate inputs and that data gets to the users in a sensible form. Building an MIS involves:

● Adding codes to the sales ledger to identify customers and products (in addition to accounts and stock-keeping units).

● Summarizing the customer transactions to a level of detail suited to marketing.

● Extracting the customer/product data.

● Storing it on a database.

● Adding extra codes to facilitate segmentation analysis.

● Obtaining software tools to analyse and report on the database.

This is easy to describe, but, as those who have tried will know, tremendously hard to implement. The main difficulty to overcome is to manage the expectations of computer staff, financial management (who own the sales ledger) and marketing users.

A problem facing anyone contemplating the development of an MIS is whether to hold data at the lowest level of detail or to hold summary statistics. The extra cost of storing and processing detailed data, at customer level, often deters planners. However, only storing summary data is a mistake in most circumstances, for two reasons:

● Flexibility to analyse and segment by different combinations of variables is only possible if the data is held at the lowest possible levels of detail.

● Customer data can subsequently be used for implementing the strategy (i.e. for direct mail, telemarketing and field sales call reporting).

Database marketing – reconciling the tactical with the strategic

Definition: ●————————
A database is a collection of data and information from outside and inside an organization which is stored in such a way that it can be accessed and analysed to provide intelligence for making decisions to achieve the company's objectives

Databases have traditionally been too large and expensive, and their performance too slow, for them to be cost-justifiable. Consequently, many of the MISs in use today are summary sales reporting systems. However, with the increased importance attached to direct marketing, telemarketing and sales performance management (using laptop computers), many companies are now more actively engaged in building customer databases.

Databases often represent a compromise between the strategic requirements of the planners and the tactical requirements of direct

Myth	Reality
The database collects what we need	We collect what is easily available
The database measures what matters	We measure what is least embarrassing
The database users understand what data they need	We know what we used last, what the textbooks say and what might be interesting on a rainy day
The database needs to hold more and more data	We feel safer with 'loadsadata', even when we haven't a clue how to use it
The database must integrate the data physically	We like neat solutions, whatever the cost
The database will save staff time	We need more and more staff to analyse data
The database will harmonize marketing, finance and sales	We all compete for scarce resources, and this involves fighting
The database is the one source of our market intelligence	We haven't thought through the business problems

Figure 11.1   Myths and realities about databases

marketers, telemarketers and sales managers. Another trouble for newcomers to the world of databases is that they fall prey to the many pitfalls, and believe many of the myths (Figure 11.1).

The consequence of these problems is that databases very often hold data that does not fit the purpose of the tacticians, far less the needs of strategic planners.

> The attempt to develop databases that serve both strategic and tactical purposes is often referred to as database marketing.

One of the most acute problems is that of reconciling the internal and external views of the markets. The usual problem is that data retrieved from the sales ledger rarely possesses the details needed to link customer records to market segments. Some of the problems are described in Figure 11.2.

Fusing together data from external sources and internal data is becoming increasingly common as a solution to the external–internal problem. This is often referred to as data fusion. Where large volumes of data are involved, computer programs, known as de-duplication routines, are used to automate the matching of the data. However, automation rarely achieves more than 80% accuracy in matching, and manual matching has to be applied to the remaining data.

External audit – variable	Problem with internal
What is bought	Internal systems have rich detail on accounts. However, information about types of products and services can often be missing. Information on the outlets or channels through which they are sold is very often lacking.
Who buys	Internal systems record who paid the invoice and who received delivery of the services. They rarely record who made the buying decision, or who influenced it. Even when the buyer details are on the system, it is rarely easy to determine their characteristics such as age, sex, etc. Information is typically based around quantity of services sold rather than on customers' total usage of various services.
Why	Reconciling external to internal involves: • matching accounts to customers • matching capacity to services required • matching external variables to internal records • collecting data from sources other than the sales ledger (e.g. from surveys of sales representatives) Internal sources of information on why people purchase is scarce. Enquiries can be qualified, using survey techniques, to provide some clues on why people respond, e.g. to an advertising campaign. Customer satisfaction surveys may also yield clues. Call reports from field sales and telesales can also provide valuable clues, especially if survey disciplines can be observed by the sales staff.

Figure 11.2 Problems of reconciling internal and external market audits

> The cost of matching external and internal market-coding schemes is driving a few companies to collect customer pro-files at source. This is either when they first enquire, or when their sales ledger records are first created.

However, the cost of the changes to the sales ledger, and the fact that it is owned by finance, are often barriers to success. In the future, marketing will need to work much more closely with finance and the IT department if it is to develop databases successfully. To address this problem, one major bank has moved its head of marketing into the role of head of the IT department.

What is the secret of using information successfully?

Information, in the minds of most marketing managers, lies in a strange no-man's land, part-way between the practical focus of marketing management and the abstractions of technologists, cyberneticists and boffins. Widely misunderstood, or equated to 'keyboard literacy', or 'technology awareness', the management of marketing information often ends up neglected or delegated to the most junior member of the marketing team.

Information is not the same as technology, nor is it information technology, nor is it necessarily derived from information technology. There are many problems associated with the use of computers to hold marketing data.

Information is not all hard, objective data; we will not necessarily become better informed by collecting more and more raw data, and storing it until we end up knowing 'everything'. Accounting systems are often seen as a source of hard facts, since most accounting transactions have to be audited and therefore must be reasonably accurate. Yet most accounting data has little direct relevance for marketing strategy.

What information is needed to support a marketing strategy? The answer to this question is something of a conundrum, since the information needed depends upon the marketing objectives that form the strategy. If you change the strategic marketing objectives, then you may need different kinds of information to support your strategy. Figure 11.3 illustrates how different objectives require different supporting information.

This observation goes some way towards explaining one of the great puzzles of marketing information:

> The information needs of marketing keep changing as a consequence of the evolution of the marketing strategy

Business objective	Segmentation method	Information source
Market extension		
– new locations	Geo-demographics	Electoral roll (consumer)
– new channels	Prospect profiles	Companies House (business)
– new segments	Survey analysis	Prospect lists and surveys
Market development	Customer profiling	Sales ledger and added profile data
	Behavioural scoring	Models from internal data source
Product development	Factor analysis	Surveys
	Qualitative methods	Panels/discussion groups

Figure 11.3   Examples of business objectives and segmentation methods

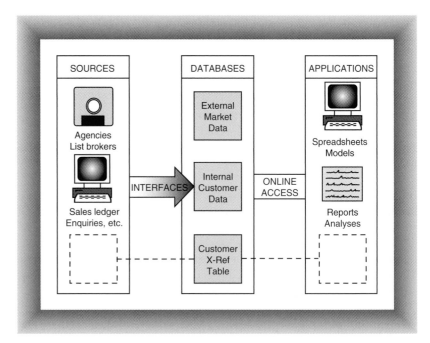

Figure 11.4
Information flows in a
marketing system

> Why is it so difficult to specify marketing's information needs?
> The answer is that, unlike accounting or service operations,
> which have fixed information needs, the information needs
> of marketing keep changing as a consequence of the evolu-
> tion of the marketing strategy in response to market changes.

At this point, the sales or marketing director might feel that, because
the situation changes so radically every year, there can be no hope for
developing an effective system or procedure for obtaining marketing
information. Many at this point delegate the need to an office junior,
with the result that they are very ill-informed when they come to
develop their marketing strategies.

For all the problems, there are a number of basic underlying marketing
issues with which all companies have to contend. Furthermore, the
solutions they have adopted can be seen as variations on relatively
few themes. The basic model of a marketing system can be visualized
as in Figure 11.4.

The main components of the system are as follows:

- *External market data*, which is purchased from external agencies.
  These include government agencies, market research firms, list
  brokers, etc.

- *Internal customer data*, which is collected from the sales ledger and
  other internal sources such as customer service, field sales, telesales,

etc. It is coded and segmented in such a way that market-share figures can be created by comparison with external data.

- *Customer reference table*, which is needed to make the system work effectively. It identifies customers (as defined by marketing) and provides a cross-reference to sales ledger accounts. Whenever a new sales ledger account is created, the cross-reference table is used to determine the customer associated with that account. This avoids the need for costly manual matching or de-duplication after the account is created. It is also used by marketing applications as a standard reference table for customers.

- *Database* refers to all three of the above data types. It needs to be structured using a technique known as *data modelling*, which organizes the data into the component types that marketing wants and not the structure that finance or anyone else provides. Usually, the data is held using *relational database* software, since this provides for maximum flexibility and choice of analysis tools.

- *Interfaces* refers to the computer programs that 'grab' the data from the source systems and restructure it into the components to go onto the marketing database. These programs have to be written by the in-house IT staff, since they obtain and restructure data from the in-house sales ledger and other in-house systems.

- *Applications* are the software programs that the planners use to analyse the data and develop their plans. They include data-grabbing tools that grab the items of data from their storage locations; reporting tools that summarize the data according to categories that marketing defines; spreadsheets that carry out calculations and what-if analyses on the reported summary data. Applications may also include specific marketing planning software such as EXMAR, Marketing Portfolio Planner, Market Segment Master and Key Account Planner.[2]

> The critical issue when building such a system is that it is not self-contained within marketing. It requires interface programs that will alter the systems used by finance, sales and other internal departments, as well as data feeds from external sources.

The secrets of success in developing systems for marketing are:

- Understanding what marketing needs and particularly how the internal and external views will be reconciled.

- Developing a strong cost–benefit case for information systems, including financial ones, to be altered to accommodate the needs of marketing.

- Working continuously with internal IT staff until the system is built. They are under pressure from other sources, especially finance, and unless marketing maintains momentum and direction, then other priorities will inevitably win.

Marketing planners need to become far less insular if they are to obtain the information they require to plan effectively. Cross-functional understanding and cooperation must be secured by marketing if they are to develop the systems they need. Building the interdepartmental cross-functional bridges to secure data, information and knowledge is one of the greatest challenges facing marketing today.

Who manages the MIS?

There is no hard and fast rule in answer to this question. It could be argued that, as the MIS is to facilitate decision-making company-wide, it should be managed within a central corporate information office. There are others who advocate that in a marketing-oriented company, it is feedback from the outside world which should drive decision-making. Therefore, it is claimed, the MIS should be managed by the marketing department.

> At the end of the day, where the system is located is of little consequence. Of far more significance is that the MIS is institutionalized and has procedures which facilitate information flows, both vertically and horizontally and both into and out of the information unit, to assist marketing planning.

It goes without saying that with an institutionalized system, all who are involved with it are trained to play their role, whether as providers of inputs or users of outputs.

Marketing research

While the MIS provides the data to make routine decisions and to keep the organization on track, from time to time new and specific pieces of information will be required by management.

Definition: ●
Marketing research is concerned with research into marketing processes

> Providing this is the role of **marketing research**, which is defined by the American Marketing Association as 'The systematic gathering, recording and analysis of data about problems relating to the marketing of goods and services'.

Marketing research is not the same as market research

Marketing research, therefore, is an approach which can look at the whole marketing process and is not to be confused with 'market research', which, as the name implies, is concerned specifically with research about markets. Marketing research can help to resolve problems, be they about distribution channels, competitive advantages of one's services, customer preferences, pricing, or, indeed, anything which is connected with matching the company's capabilities with customer needs. By collecting and analysing the appropriate data, the marketer can proceed to make decisions under conditions of known risk rather than uncertainty.

> Conversion of uncertainty into risk and the minimization of risk is perhaps marketing management's most important task, and in this process the role of marketing research is of paramount importance.

Information can be elicited in two broad ways:

- Through reactive methods
- Through non-reactive methods.

- *Reactive methods* – Here, the target audience reacts to test situations, or to questions posed to them by an interviewer, either face to face or over the telephone. Equally, they could respond to questionnaires or forms, which they might be handed or which are mailed to them. Figure 11.5 summarizes the main forms of reactive marketing research.
- *Non-reactive methods* – Here, methods are based on interpretation of observed phenomena, or extant data. They do not rely on data derived directly from respondents. Figure 11.6 summarizes the main forms of non-reactive marketing research.

All research methods have inherent advantages and disadvantages.[3] For example, structured interviews, controlled by the interviewer against a specific format, might be easy to analyse, but give little scope to explore what could be important departures from the chosen 'script'. In contrast, free-ranging interviews might provide a wealth of anecdotal and qualitative information, but prove to be very difficult to analyse overall.

> In many respects, the most important of all marketing research methods is the use of existing materials, particularly by means of *desk research*, which should always be the starting point of any marketing research programme.

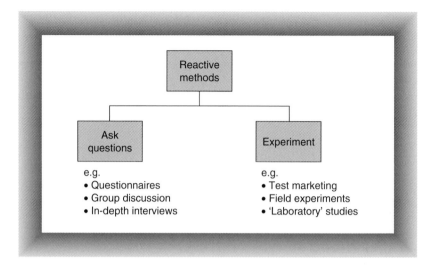

Figure 11.5
Focus of reactive
marketing research

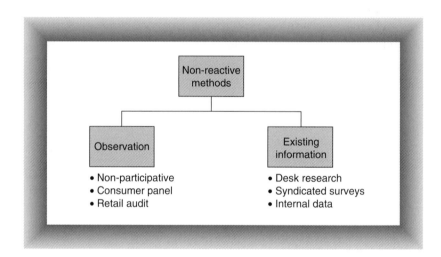

Figure 11.6
Focus of non-reactive
marketing research

There is often a wealth of information to be obtained from published information such as government statistics, OECD, EU, the United Nations, newspapers, technical journals, trade association publications, published market surveys, and so on. Two or three days spent on desk research nearly always provides pleasant surprises for the company that believes it lacks information about its markets. When combined with internal sales information, this can be the most powerful research method open to a company.

Cost-effectiveness is the ultimate determinant of the marketing research method to be used

Cost is also a consideration to take into account. For example, the logistics of sending interviewers door to door will clearly cost a lot more than a postal questionnaire. But, then again, whereas the former method achieves a very high 'hit rate' in terms of responses, the latter might yield very little. The advent of email and internet-based surveys now enables information to be collected faster and much more cheaply where such methods are relevant to the information being sought.

Cost, therefore, has to be seen as a determinant of the intrinsic quality of the information received. It has to be assessed, not in terms of the value of the research assignment input, but as the usefulness of the actual research output.

Increasing sophistication in the use of marketing research techniques has made it a highly specialized function within the field of marketing management. For this reason, many service companies turn to outside research agencies rather than attempting to develop their own internal resources.

Budgeting for marketing research

As we have seen, marketing information can be costly to obtain. Not surprisingly, how much to spend on marketing research is, therefore, a key question that marketers must address.

> Information can, in many ways, be seen as a product, for, like a product, it has to be 'made', stored and distributed. Similarly, it has a limited shelf-life, after which it can have a deleterious effect on company health if consumed.

As with a product, the more use that can be extracted from a piece of information, the greater is its value.

> The utility value of information is, of course, its ability to reduce the risk attached to making a wrong decision. The greater the risk, the higher the value of the marketing research.

Since any decision to buy any product or service would be subject to some form of cost–benefit appraisal, it should be possible to handle information likewise. Any investment in research would have to be justified by the return it provided. However, whereas the costs are relatively easy to identify, the benefits can be more elusive to pin down. They can only be expressed as the additional profits that might be achieved through identifying new marketing opportunities, and avoiding the costly failures which would otherwise have resulted without the information. Thus, while the cost–benefit approach looks to be eminently sensible, in practice it is beset with many 'ifs' and 'maybes'.

Another approach which is used with some success is based on the theory of probability and expected value. This operates in the following way. Suppose that the launch of a new service would incur costs of $500,000. The decision to go ahead is hampered by the fact that it is reckoned that there is a 10% chance that the service will fail. In these circumstances, the maximum loss expectation can be calculated as

Probability theory and expected value can be a useful method of calculating how much to spend on marketing research

$500,000 \cdot 0.10$, i.e. $50,000. This would suggest that it would be worth the company spending up to $50,000 to acquire information which would help to avoid such a loss.

However, the implication of this approach is that perfect information can be put at the company's disposal. Since the cost of gathering perfect information is likely to be prohibitive, the method shown above can only be seen to provide a rough guideline.

> In truth, budget setting is likely to be based upon a combination of cost–benefit analysis, probability and expected value, and empirical evidence that the service organization has accumulated over the years.

Marketing planning and company structure

Can marketing planning work in all organizations?

As should be clear by now, marketing planning is not something for the uncommitted manager. In order to get results, companies must undertake the task comprehensively.

> However, as we have described it, the planning process has a distinctive shape and pattern, whereas service organizations come in all shapes and sizes. It is reasonable to ask, therefore, if such a universal approach can actually be made to fit this wide range of potential customers.

Can it, for example, fit the large service company and the small one equally well? Will it be appropriate for the bank and the professional service firm? Or does it have to be tailored in order to become suitable? It is equally relevant to ask if the organization should modify its own activities in order to accommodate marketing planning. These questions are asked in order to throw light on often overlooked issues which have a bearing upon the ultimate success of the marketing planning initiative.

In order to address these issues, we need to switch our focus of attention away from the marketing planning process and, for a moment, take a look at service organizations themselves. First of all, let us look at how organizations develop and grow.

The organizational life-line

While in some ways organizations have an individuality all of their own, in much the same way as people, it can be shown that they also have many similarities when it comes to looking at their overall pattern of development.

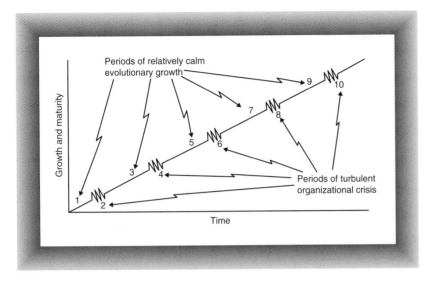

Figure 11.7
The organizational
life-line

Just as people go through life phases of infancy, youth, becoming an adolescent, and so on, do organizations experience a similar growth pattern?

Further, just as people experience problems in the transition from one phase of life to another, for example going through puberty or the menopause, do organizations have equivalent periods of discomfort and crisis?

There are several models upon which to draw to illustrate the organizational life-line, but that of Greiner[4] provides a comprehensive approach which is relevant to service (and most other) organizations. Figure 11.7 outlines the ten phases of evolution and crisis in this model.

> *Phase 1* – The first phase of organizational life is the *creative evolution* phase. Here, the organization is small, very informal and ill-organized, but powered by a sustainable business idea and the energy put in by the founder. This person is at the heart of everything – selling, creating, recruiting, rewarding, buying, and so on. The organization's plans are in the founder's head and the organization itself is used as an extension of the founder. They operate rather like a spider at the centre of a web. No activity in the organization, or indeed among customers, escapes their attention.
>
> Such a company can be very profitable, since the person running it knows the customers personally and can respond to their changing needs immediately. Coupled with this excellent service is an organization low on overhead costs.
>
> *Phase 2* – The company can grow successfully in a relatively controlled way until, one day, it starts to have problems. Its very

success overtaxes the central person, who finds it increasingly difficult to cope. The pressure might originate from extra customers, extra employees, extra machines, or whatever. The net result is that the source of decision-making becomes overcommitted. For example, he or she is with a customer when a problem crops up in the office, or they have to spend so much time negotiating a bank loan that they neglect bringing in new contracts. The organization has, in fact, reached its *leadership crisis* phase.

So serious is this phase that it overwhelms many organizations. This problem can be resolved in one of two ways:

- The entrepreneur/founder sells the business (and then, often, goes off somewhere to start something else).

- The company must manage a transition to its next phase of development.

Phase 3 – Here, the principles of textbook management start to be imposed on the organization. If the founder stays, he or she has to learn to devolve some jobs to others, start to employ specialists, define who does what, and introduce systems and procedures that 'run themselves'. From being a reactive type of organization, where planning was largely non-existent, the company starts to enter the world of scientific management, with a defined structure and sets of rules for coping with routines such as costing, payments, and the planning of work. Because it needs firm leadership to draw the company together and give it a new sense of purpose, there needs to be somebody strong at the helm, who knows more about management. With such a person in position, the company can look forward to another relatively calm period of evolutionary growth. This is the *directed evolution* phase.

Phase 4 – This period of growth eventually encounters problems, as the 'director's' expertise about markets, technology, or whatever is overtaken by subordinates whose day-to-day work ensures that they keep abreast of all the latest developments.

The leader may lose credibility to an extent that his or her judgement and ability to provide direction are no longer trusted by those in the organization. Subordinates who are on top of their jobs feel they could easily make better decisions faster than the out-of-touch boss. The company is now experiencing its *autonomy crisis* phase.

Phase 5 – This crisis is only solved by genuine power and authority being pushed down to lower levels in the organization. In this way, all the company's expertise is tapped and a new spirit of enterprise is released. Decisions are made by the people with the best and most current information, not by somebody remote from the situation, who cannot understand all the nuances of what is entailed. Again, if this transition is managed successfully, the company is equipped to benefit from another period of evolutionary growth, its *delegated evolution* phase.

Phase 6 – Once more, the seeds of the next crisis start as the company gets larger and more mature. Those at the top of the organization feel that they are losing control. Subordinates are making decisions which, in themselves, might be excellent, but which are essentially parochial and do not take into account the full ramifications for the organization as a whole. There is a *control crisis* as the issue of power and who is actually steering the business are addressed.

Phase 7 – As before, a solution is eventually found, whereby the organization is redefined on the basis of greater cooperation between different levels and functions. To facilitate this, roles are carefully defined and attention is paid to information flows. Rules, systems and procedures are developed to ensure that everyone knows their place and what is expected of them. When something slips through the organizational net, a new rule or procedure is established to ensure that it does not happen again. With the crisis of control resolved in this way, the company can enjoy another relatively trouble-free period of growth in its *coordinated evolution* phase.

Phase 8 – The next crisis phase occurs because, in its attempts to coordinate its decision-making and optimize the integration of all activities, too many bureaucratic procedures creep in. The company finds that rules, which once helped, now begin to slow down decision-making and blunt personal initiative. The organization becomes impersonal, and ensuring that procedures are completed seems to be the sole reason for its existence. Customers and markets may become distractions to the business of running the enterprise. The company is at its *red-tape crisis* phase and severely restricts itself unless action is taken.

Phase 9 – The answer seems to lie in returning to the days before the hand of bureaucracy took the energy out of the organization. A new approach to management needs to emerge. Once more, people have to be seen as more important than systems and procedures. Unnecessary routines are dismantled. Impersonal relationships are replaced with face-to-face transactions. Management is by exception, and over-control is replaced by trust. By adapting in this way, the company reaches its *collaborative evolution* phase. It becomes once more flexible and adaptive when it is beset by new challenges.

Phase 10 – As we have seen, every evolution phase is born out of a crisis and yet carried with it are the seeds of the next crisis. Since relatively few organizations have genuinely reached their collaborative evolution phase, the exact nature of the next crisis phase is somewhat speculative. There are suggestions that with the collaborative emphasis on teamwork and openness, managers lose the confidence to make decisions on their own. There is also a possibility that 'groupthink' takes over and too much time is spent looking at the functioning of internal teams, at the expense of keeping in touch with events in the outside world. However, as the *next crisis* phase materializes, no doubt human ingenuity will eventually find some way out of it.

There are two important points to make about the organizational life-line.

1. A company 'learns' by overcoming new problems and so its level of 'maturity' is not governed simply by its growth and size alone, but also by the complexity of its history. Thus, it is possible to have a very large company, in terms of turnover or number of employees, at an early stage in development terms, for example at its leadership crisis or directed evolution phase. Similarly, a relatively small company might just as easily be enmeshed in its red-tape crisis.

2. There is nothing to suggest that companies are more profitable at any one of the evolution phases than another. However, the organization can literally die at any of its crisis phases and so does not have a 'right' to experience all of the growth phases.

In his research, which examined marketing planning and corporate culture, Leppard[5] found that:

> • The process of marketing planning is sophisticated and carries with it hidden values regarding organizational openness and access to information. It therefore needs an equally sophisticated organization to be able to accept it in its totality. In this sense, the introduction of marketing planning is more than a matter of introducing some systems and procedures, for it can bring with it a challenge to the credibility, authority and style of the management regime.
>
> • It is difficult to introduce marketing planning at any of the crisis phases, because there are too many other unresolved contextual problems in the organization.
>
> • The marketing planning process has to be congruent with the corporate culture at each of the evolution phases. Broadly speaking, this suggests the emphasis shown in Figure 11.8.

> The conclusion to be reached is that the marketing planning process described in this book is of universal validity. Great care, however, is necessary to ensure that it does not strangle

personal initiative and creativity by an overly bureaucratic implementation of the associated systems and that it is implemented at the appropriate stage of the evolutionary development of the organization.

Stage of evolution	Marketing planning approach
Creative evolution	No formal marketing planning procedures exist. The owner/manager tends to operate more like a hunter than a farmer. At best, a sales plan might be acceptable, but in general, any kind of formal planning is alien in this culture.
Directed evolution	Here, the marketing planning process has to be imposed from the top, and so an essentially 'top-down' planning system provides the best organizational fit.
Delegated evolution	Here, an essentially 'bottom-up' marketing planning approach works best.
Coordinated evolution	Here, a 'top-down' and 'bottom-up' marketing planning approach can be combined to provide a good organizational fit.
Collaborative evolution	Since few organizations are at this stage of development, no firm conclusions can be drawn. The life-line concept suggests that a radical rethink might be made regarding marketing planning. This might mean the process becomes more non-functional and less mechanical.

Figure 11.8   Approaches to marketing planning for different stages of evolution

Centralized versus decentralized marketing

Regardless of where the service organization is on its life-line, it might at some time or other reach a stage, either from organic growth or by acquisition, where it operates with more than one unit. The question then arises regarding how best to locate the marketing function. The organizational structure might look like either of Figures 11.9 or 11.10.[6]

Centralized organizations are effective at controlling costs

In Figure 11.9, the centralized head office has taken over the strategic components of the business, including marketing, leaving the operational units A, B and C to produce services as directed. This approach clearly maintains control at the centre and ensures there is no duplication of effort in the operating units. However, unless communications are exceedingly good, it is conceivable that those with responsibility for marketing will lose touch with both the operating unit and its markets. This is particularly true if each unit has a wide range of services and customers. The sheer logistics of managing so many service product/customer combinations is too much to handle.

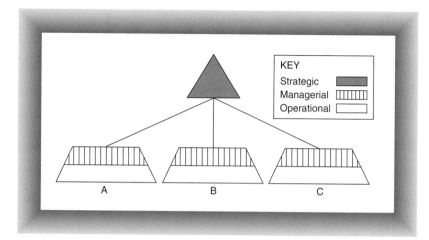

Figure 11.9
Centralized marketing, separate operating units

Decentralized organizations are effective at responding to market needs

The alternative possibility is shown in Figure 11.10. Here, the head office acts as a hub for largely self-autonomous units, which have their own marketing departments. Clearly, in these circumstances, the marketing activities will be highly relevant to the sub-units they are dedicated to serve. They will be well attuned to the specific needs of each business unit. However, unless all the marketing activities can be coordinated in some way, there could be a considerable duplication of work. For example, each unit might commission marketing research which is virtually identical, therefore spending much more than is necessary. If, however, some way can be found of gaining synergy from all this marketing energy, the rewards could be considerable.

As with so many aspects of marketing, there are no clear answers regarding which structure is the best. Both types have advantages and

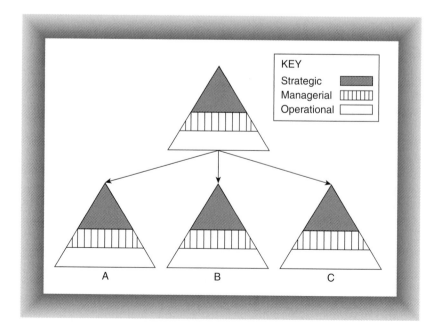

Figure 11.10
Decentralized marketing

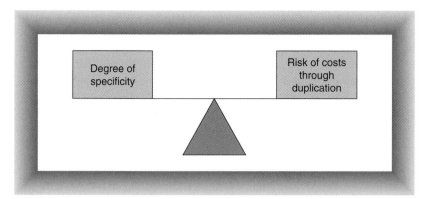

Figure 11.11
The specificity versus duplication balance in marketing planning

disadvantages. For this reason, each organization has to find a balance which allows for the right level of marketing specificity, yet imposes a mechanism for avoiding costly duplication (Figure 11.11).

There is no right or wrong answer for this organizational issue

It is the responsibility of the headquarters to draw up the boundaries regarding how the marketing activities shall be managed and coordinated. Until this is resolved, any attempts to introduce, or improve, marketing planning will be beset with problems.

The matrix organization

There is another way of considering organization design, which is based on one of the foundations of marketing thinking – that all companies must integrate the management of both their services and their markets. In the so-called 'matrix organization'[7] (Figure 11.12), it is common to find the posts of 'product manager' or 'service manager' and 'market manager', and sometimes all three.

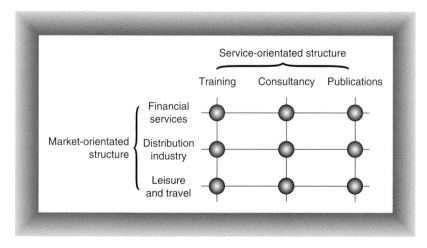

Figure 11.12
A matrix organization for a training and consulting firm

Having an overemphasis on services or markets can result in problems

In this example, we have a training/consultancy business which does business in three main markets: financial services; distribution; and leisure and travel. It could organize around 'service managers' so that, for example, one manager would be responsible for all training activities in all three markets. The advantage of doing this will be the strong service product orientation which results. While this is an undoubted plus, such a structure can easily lead to superficial market knowledge. Indeed, many companies have suffered from this approach by being slow to recognize changes in their markets.

In contrast to this approach, the 'market manager' orientation can maintain closeness to markets, but lead to unnecessary service duplication, service proliferation and the lack of a coherent policy for developing new services.

Because each approach has its strengths and weaknesses, there can be no simple answer regarding which might be the best. Common sense and experience of the market situation will, in the end, determine which approach is most appropriate.

> The third option in this range of possibilities is to have both service and market managers. This ought to provide the best of all possible worlds, since close attention is being paid to both services and markets.

However, for it to work well, there must be close liaison between the two types of manager. Also, it is suggested, in order to avoid deadlock, that one or the other is given the ultimate responsibility to make decisions. It therefore needs a high level of maturity from the staff involved, and a willingness to keep all communication channels open, if it is to work in practice. Too often it is found that vested interests get in the way of genuine service/market issues.

The purpose of this brief discussion into organizational structures was to underline some of the potential drawbacks and advantages which particular structures bring with them. Unfortunately, no single organizational form can be recommended unconditionally, because the final choice must always reflect the particular situation faced by the company.

> Even so, it is usually sensible to organize around customer groups or markets, rather than services, functions or geographical location.

By doing this, the whole organization can be mobilized to respond specifically to a unique set of market needs.

There are always a number of factors to take into consideration. We have touched upon these already. There are issues about authority and responsibility, ease of communication, coordination, flexibility, how the cross-functional interfaces are managed (e.g. between internal departments, or the company and its outside world), and, by no means least, human factors.

The way the company organizes for marketing will be one of the major determinants of the effectiveness of any marketing planning.

Plan for marketing planning

Just as important as getting the organization structure to complement the markets it serves, the company must also ensure that there is a plan for marketing planning. That is to say, everyone involved must not only be aware of the marketing planning process (as outlined in this book), but also be very clear about the role they are expected to play in it and the rate at which the planning process unfolds.

Often, when considering the reasons for marketing planning failures, we find that much of the blame can be attributed to chief executives.

The chief executive has to lead marketing planning

> It is their principal role to get the planning process accepted and, by way of their personal commitment and enthusiasm, maintain the energy and momentum of the initiative.

Too often, they have little familiarity with and interest in marketing planning.

In companies where chief executives have been successful in bringing about change, they have actively intervened in:

- Defining the organizational framework
- Ensuring that the strategic analysis covers critical factors
- Maintaining the balance between short- and long-term results
- Waging war on unnecessary bureaucracy
- Creating and maintaining the right level of motivation
- Encouraging marketing talent and skills to emerge.

Another area which sometimes causes concern is that of the role of the planning department. As we have seen, it cannot operate successfully if it is trapped inside an ivory-tower mentality. Instead of operating in isolation, it needs to be at the hub of the marketing planning information network. In playing this role it can:

- Advise on improved planning structures and systems

- Facilitate the transmission of relevant data

- Request inputs from managers, departments, or operating divisions

- Act as a catalyst to break down interdepartmental/inter-functional rivalry or barriers

- Evaluate marketing plans against the overall corporate strategy

- Monitor ongoing plans and keep top management informed

- Support and advise line managers and staff

- Initiate special research on industries, markets, etc.

Where top management is weak, it might try to avoid its responsibility and ask the planning department to provide not only the plan, but also the objectives and strategies. While this is technically feasible (assuming that the expertise is available), it is not a desirable outcome, for top management input about corporate direction is absolutely necessary.

The marketing planning cycle

The schedule should call for work on the plan for the next year to begin early enough in the current year to permit adequate time for market research and analysis of key data and market trends. In addition, the plan should provide for the early development of a strategic plan that can be approved or altered in principle.

A key factor in determining the planning cycle is bound to be the degree to which it is practicable to extrapolate from sales and market data, but, generally speaking, successful planning companies start the planning cycle formally somewhere between nine and six months from the beginning of the next fiscal year.

It is not necessary to be constrained to work within the company's fiscal year; it is quite possible to have a separate marketing planning schedule if that is appropriate, and simply organize the aggregation of results at the time required by the corporate financial controller.

Planning horizons

It is clear that, in the past, one- and five-year planning periods have been by far the most common, although three years has now become the most common period for the strategic plan, largely because of the dramatically increasing rate of environmental change. Lead time for the initiation of major new product innovations, the length of time necessary to recover capital investment costs, the continuing availability of customers and raw materials, and the size and usefulness of existing plant and buildings, are the most frequently mentioned reasons for having a five-year planning horizon. Increasingly, however, these plans are taking the form more of 'scenarios' than the detailed strategic plan outlined in this book. (We provide some references for scenario planning later in this chapter.)

Many companies, however, do not give sufficient thought to what represents a sensible planning horizon for their particular circumstances. A five-year time-span is clearly too long for some companies, particularly those with highly versatile machinery operating in volatile fashion-conscious markets. The effect of this is to rob strategic plans of reality. A five-year horizon is often chosen largely because of its universality. Also, some small subsidiaries in large conglomerates are often asked to forecast for seven, ten and, sometimes, 15 years ahead, with the result that they tend to become meaningless exercises. While it might make sense for, say, a glass manufacturer to produce 12-year plans or scenarios because of the very long lead time involved in laying down a new furnace, it does not make sense to impose the same planning timescale on small subsidiaries operating in totally different markets, even though they are in the same group. This places unnecessary burdens on operating management and tends to rob the whole strategic planning process of credibility.

The conclusion to be reached is that there is a natural point of focus into the future, beyond which it is pointless to look. This point of focus is a function of the relative size of a company.

> Small companies, because of their size and the way they are managed, tend to be comparatively flexible in the way in which they can react to environmental turbulence in the short term. Large companies, on the other hand, need a much longer lead time in which to make changes in direction. Consequently, they tend to need to look further into the future and use formalized systems for this purpose so that managers throughout the organization have a common means of communication.

How the marketing planning process works

There is one other major aspect to be considered. It concerns the requisite location of the marketing planning activity in a company. The answer is simple to give.

> Marketing planning should take place as near to the market place as possible in the first instance, but such plans should then be reviewed at high levels within an organization to see what issues have been overlooked.

It has been suggested that each manager in the organization should complete an audit and SWOT analysis on their own area of responsibility. The only way that this can work in practice is by means of a *hierarchy* of audits. The principle is simply demonstrated in Figure 11.13.

This illustrates the principle of auditing at different levels within an organization. The marketing audit format will be universally applicable. It is only the *detail* that varies from level to level and from company to company within the same group. For example, any one single company can specify without too much difficultly the precise headings under which information is now being sought.

At each operating level, this kind of information can be gathered in by means of the hierarchy of audits illustrated in Figure 11.13 with each

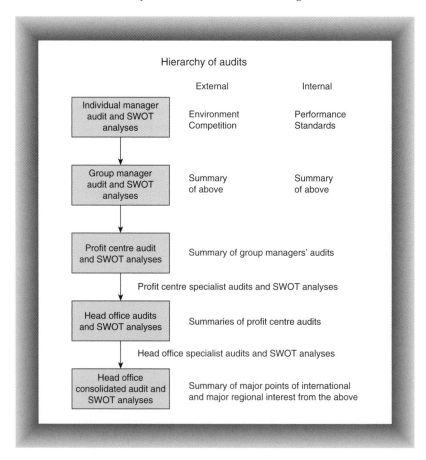

Figure 11.13
Hierarchy of audits

manager completing an audit for his or her area of accountability. While the overall format can be universal for a large and diversified group, uniformity is only necessary for units engaged in like activities. The advantages which accrue to the several headquarters' levels are substantial in terms of measuring worldwide potential for service products and market segments. Without such an information-collecting vehicle, it is difficult to formulate any overall strategic view.

> It has to be recognized that information and data are not always readily available in some parts of the world in the sort of format which is required but, given training, resources and understanding between headquarters and units, it is surprising how quickly information links can be forged which are of inestimable value to both sides. The same is also true of agents and distributors, who quickly respond to the give and take of such relationships in respect of audit-type information, which they inevitably find valuable for their own business.

Since, in anything but the smallest of undiversified companies, it is not possible for top management to set detailed objectives for operating units, it is suggested that at this stage in the planning process, strategic guidelines should be issued. One way of doing this is in the form of a *strategic planning letter*. Another is by means of a personal briefing by the chief executive at 'kick-off' meetings. As in the case of the audit, these guidelines would proceed from the broad to the specific, and would become more detailed as they progressed through the company towards operating units.

Under marketing, for example, at the highest level in a large group, top management may ask for particular attention to be paid to issues such as the impact of technology, leadership and innovation strategies, and vulnerability to attack from competitive services (e.g., a locally-based software developer or call centre company may be vulnerable to software developed in India or call centres being established in the Philippines). At operating company level, it is possible to be more explicit about target markets, service development, and the like.

It is important to remember that it is top management's responsibility to determine the strategic direction of the company, and to decide such issues as when businesses are to be milked, where to invest heavily in service development or market extension for longer-term gains, and so on. If this is left to operating managers to decide for themselves, they will tend to opt for actions concerned principally with *today's* service products and markets, because that is what they are judged on principally. There is also the problem of their inability to appreciate the larger, company-wide position.

> Nevertheless, the process just described demonstrates very clearly that there is total interdependence between top management and the lowest level of operating management in the objective and strategy setting process.

In a very large company without any procedures for managing this process, it is not difficult to see how control can be weakened and how vulnerability to rapid changes in the business environment around the world can be increased. This interdependence between the top-down/bottom-up process is illustrated in Figures 11.14 and 11.15, which show a similar hierarchy in respect of objective and strategy setting to that illustrated in respect of audits.

The same degree of formality is not required in all cases

Having explained carefully the point about *requisite* marketing planning, these figures also illustrate the principles by which the marketing planning process should be implemented in any company, irrespective of whether it is a small exporting company or a major multinational. In essence, these exhibits show a hierarchy of audits, SWOT analyses, objectives, strategies and programmes.

The time it takes to produce a strategic marketing plan can be determined by looking at the overall sequence of ten steps and working out what is a reasonable time for completing each one. Of course, for any particular company, the times required will relate to the size of the company (i.e. the number of people likely to get involved) and the complexity of the business (the multiplicity of services and markets). Both of these factors can influence the degree of formality of the final plan as shown in Figure 11.16.

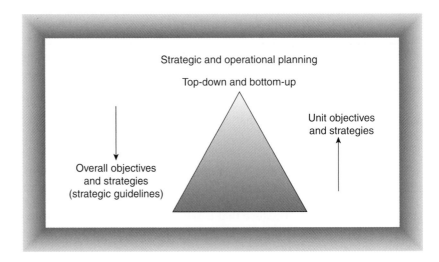

Figure 11.14
Strategic and operational planning hierarchy

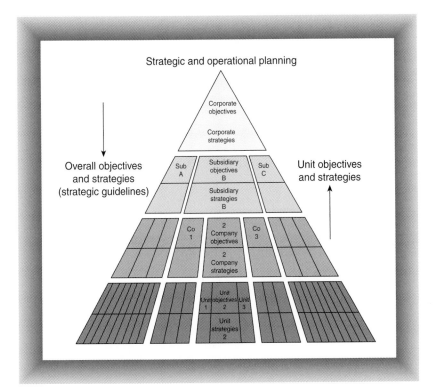

Strategic and operational planning

Corporate objectives

Corporate strategies

Overall objectives and strategies (strategic guidelines)

Unit objectives and strategies

Sub A

Subsidiary objectives B

Sub C

Subsidiary strategies B

Co 1

2 Company objectives

Co 3

2 Company strategies

Unit 1

Unit objectives 2

Unit 3

Unit strategies 2

Figure 11.15
Strategic and operational planning hierarchy in detail

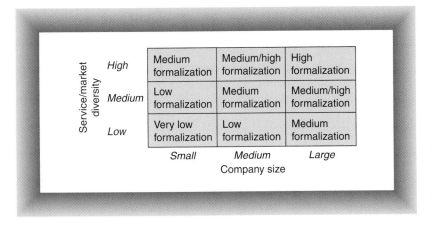

	Small	Medium	Large
High	Medium formalization	Medium/high formalization	High formalization
Medium	Low formalization	Medium formalization	Medium/high formalization
Low	Very low formalization	Low formalization	Medium formalization

Service/market diversity

Company size

Figure 11.16
Broad guidelines to the degree of marketing plan formality

> Not unexpectedly, this shows that small service organizations with, perhaps, only one or two products or services can get by with much less formal marketing plans than, say, a market leader operating on a global scale.

Having established the degree of formality that will be appropriate for the company marketing plan, it then becomes possible to 'plan' the planning cycle. It is often easier to consider the time when the

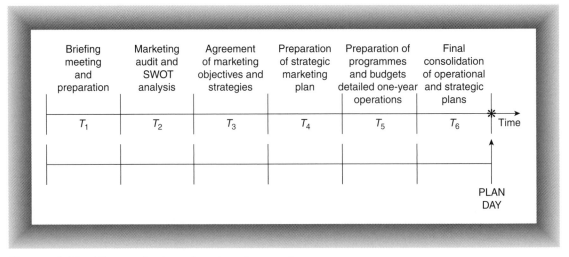

Figure 11.17 The marketing planning time cycle

plan should be available and then work backwards, as shown in Figure 11.17.

We can now see that the total planning time consists of $T_1 + T_2 + T_3 + T_4 + T_5 + T_6$, where:

T_1 represents the initial preparation time. This is an important, but often overlooked, part of the process. All those who have a part to play in the planning process should be briefed, so that they have a uniform approach to collecting and presenting data. Documentation should also be explained, so that there are no misunderstandings.

T_2 is the period for carrying out the marketing audit and distilling it into a SWOT analysis. Generally, this represents the largest span of time, because of the work involved. Nevertheless, there must be a deadline for this activity to be completed, otherwise the whole planning schedule will fall behind.

T_3 is the time it takes to formulate marketing objectives and strategies.

T_4 is the period in which the objectives and strategies are converted into a plan which covers the chosen marketing planning time horizon. Again, this will vary from company to company. In the past, the planning horizon was traditionally a five-year period. It is more common now, because of the accelerating rate of environmental change, to use a three-year horizon. To look too far ahead is meaningless, yet not to look sufficiently far ahead robs the company of the discipline to think long term. Because they can be more flexible and adaptable, small companies generally may not need to look ahead as far as their larger contemporaries.

Most companies will find that there is a natural point in the future beyond which it is meaningless to look. Those with a need to probe further into the future may do this through the use of 'scenario planning'. There are several approaches for doing this, but they all involve getting the most authoritative views about likely shifts such as advances in technology and changes in society and how they are likely to make impact on, and define, future markets. For those wishing to explore scenario planning in more detail, we provide some further reading in the references to this chapter.[8] Scenarios are a useful planning tool to enable organizations to consider longer-term opportunities and threats.

T_5 represents the time required to prepare detailed one-year operational programmes and budgets.

T_6 is the time required to consolidate the marketing plan, ensuring that the strategic and operational plans are consistent and represent the best options for the company.

All of these stages could be completed in a matter of weeks in smaller companies selling simple services. In larger, complex service organizations, it is likely to involve many months of work. Having estimated the likely time to complete a plan, it is now possible to look at the planning cycle in its entirety (Figure 11.18).

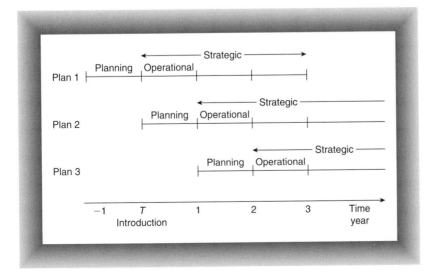

Figure 11.18
The marketing planning cycle – overview

We can now see that, in order to introduce our first strategic marketing plan on the date T, we must start our preparation in advance. This plan covers the year T to $T + 1$ in detail and that operational plan is derived from the strategic plan, which covers the period T to $T + 3$ (three years being taken as our planning horizon).

In order to produce an updated plan (Plan 2) a year later, preparation must start even before the first operational plan has run its course. The new operational plan will now cover the years $T + 1$ to $T + 2$, while the strategic plan covers $T + 1$ to $T + 4$.

This pattern is then repeated for each succeeding year. It is apparent from Figure 11.18 that the impact of the first strategic marketing plan cannot really be evaluated until it has run its course, i.e. at $T + 3$ years. For that reason, it could take up to three years before a fully refined planning process is developed.

> However, since each marketing audit will take into account how the plan is working out in practice, corrective action and improvements can be introduced into the planning process while the plan is still unfolding.

Finally, while Figures 11.17 and 11.18 have been set out as a linear process for the purpose of clarity, it would be more realistic to show it as a *circular* process, which more effectively links operational plans to corporate objectives and shows both the ongoing nature, the process and the interdependence between top-down and bottom-up inputs.

Figure 11.19 is another way of illustrating the total corporate strategic and planning process. It includes a time element and the relationship between strategic planning letters, and long-term corporate plans and short-term operational plans are clarified. It is important to note that there are two 'open loop' points. These are the key times in the planning process when a subordinate's views and findings should be subjected to the closest examination by a superior. It is by taking these opportunities that marketing planning can be transformed into the critical and creative process it is supposed to be, rather than the dull, repetitive ritual it so often turns out to be.

Developing a marketing orientation

Little of what we have outlined in this book will be achieved if the organization does not have a 'marketing orientation'. There are other orientations adopted by service organizations (see Figure 11.20). However, it is only the marketing orientation which specifically seeks to create an organization which proactively responds to customers and their needs.

Strategic and operational planning

Headquarters consolidation of operational and strategic plans

Start of budget year

Issue of strategic planning letters or chief executive's 'kick-off' meetings (open loop point 1)
Management audits
Marketing audits
SWOT analyses
Objectives, strategies
Budgets (proposed) long term (i.e. draft strategic marketing plans are prepared)

Preparation of short-term operational plans and budgets (1year)

Headquarters' review
Revise and agree long-term objectives, strategies, budgets (open loop 2)
(i.e. strategic marketing plans are finalized)

Figure 11.19
Strategic and operational planning cycle

Type of orientation	Typical associated attitudes
Marketing orientation	What we do is based on an in-depth understanding of the needs and aspirations of our customers and clients.
Product orientation	The technical quality of what we do means that our services sell themselves.
Response orientation	We will respond to any enquiry.
Financial orientation	If we can make money at anything, then we will do it.
Self-orientation	The company exists for the sole benefit of the owner/partners.
Sheep orientation	We will follow whatever is happening in the marketplace.
Erratic orientation	We run with new ideas only to drop them when a newer 'flavour-of-the-month' appears.

Figure 11.20
Some possible types of organizational orientation

Within the services sector, we have found that a marketing orientation cannot be taken for granted.

In Chapter 1, we described how we have surveyed over 1,500 senior managers from large and medium-sized service organizations and asked if the service companies they dealt with – both the suppliers of services to their companies and the services supplied to them as individual consumers – were 'market-led', 'customer-focused', or 'marketing-oriented'. The responses showed only 5–10% of the organizations they dealt with were considered to have a marketing orientation.

Most chief executives consider their companies to be marketing-oriented, but their customers do not consider them to be marketing-oriented

There is a considerable difference between how the CEOs of service organizations perceive their marketing orientation and how it appears to outsiders. This suggests to us that most service companies need to do much more in order to improve their market and customer focus.

In Chapter 1, we discussed the use of an audit tool which can be used to help a company audit its marketing effectiveness – a key component of marketing orientation. Executives wishing to use this audit tool in their organizations should refer to the appropriate section of Philip Kotler's book detailed in the references of this chapter.[9] This audit is generic to all organizations, but can to be adapted to suit a specific service sector or service organization.

We have used this audit with many different service organizations. The results have shown that most of these service businesses were operating at less than half their potential in terms of the scale of marketing effectiveness. As outlined in Chapter 1, the audit measures performance on five attributes: *customer philosophy*; *integrated marketing organization*; *adequate marketing information*; *strategic orientation*; and *operational efficiency*.

The attributes which generally tended to be especially low were in the areas of integrated marketing organization (the extent to which the firm is staffed to undertake market analysis, competitive analysis, planning, implementation and control) and 'operational efficiency' (does the firm have marketing plans which are implemented cost-effectively, and are the results monitored to ensure rapid action?), but in every service organization surveyed there was scope for improvement in all five areas of the audit.

Such an audit can provide useful data regarding how an organization can improve marketing orientation. It can also provide interesting comparisons between:

- Different operating divisions or subsidiaries
- Different departments or functional areas of the business
- Different companies in the same service industry.

Learning and planning for change

Change will not happen without considerable effort

Having identified a need for improvements to be made, it then becomes necessary to formulate a plan for achieving them. Such a plan will involve the steps outlined in Figure 11.21.

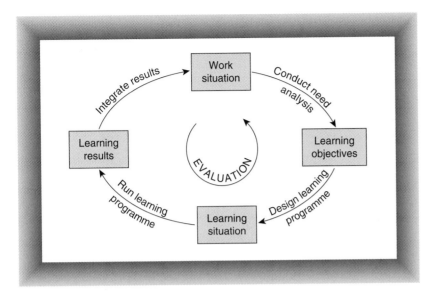

Figure 11.21
The learning/change process

The first stage will be to recognize that a problem exists in the work situation. A problem in this sense is a departure from the expected behaviour, or operational efficiency. Next, the situation has to be analysed so that the various factors that impinge on it can be put into perspective. From this analysis, it becomes possible to specify what learning objectives are required (i.e. who has to learn what and to what standard). Having established what needs to be learned/changed, it is then possible to design a 'learning' programme which, to a large extent, establishes the parameters of the learning situation. Is the learning best carried out on or off the job? Is it for an individual or a group? Does it require special facilities? The programme is run and achieves results, which are then integrated back into the work situation.

The particular advantage of following this learning 'model' is that it facilitates evaluation. For example, if the change does not bring about the required level of performance in the work situation, is this because the learning results were not properly integrated? The next evaluation question needs to address whether the right learning results were achieved. If they were not, was this to do with the way the programme was run? Was the learning situation the right one? Was the programme correctly designed? Were the learning objectives incorrect? Was the initial analysis at fault? In fact, the evaluation of the required change is achieved by following the model loop in Figure 11.21 in the *reverse* direction.

If the programme is not successful, finding exactly where the attempted improvement programme went wrong enables the organization to learn from its mistakes and do better next time.

The attitude of chief executives can be a determining factor in whether or not the change to marketing orientation succeeds or fails. Although they can lend weight and show considerable interest in the process, it

> The chief executive's role in this process is critical

is unlikely that they will have the time available to become deeply involved.

> For this reason, it is important that the chief executive nominates and gives full backing to a change agent, whose task is to facilitate the improvements and champion the marketing cause.

In some organizations this can be a full-time job, at least in the short term, until momentum gathers pace. It is not always easy to shift deep-rooted attitudes, thus the role of change agent requires a person with experience, imagination, tenacity and belief in what he or she is doing. The whole initiative has to be seen as more than a token management development exercise.

In-company workshops are often necessary to provide appropriate knowledge, skills and attitudes

The exact nature of what is to be done must, of course, relate to the individual company analysis. However, it is not unusual for the outcome to involve in-company workshops or programmes involving marketing staff and senior managers from all other functions. In general, the content will cover the skills, knowledge and attitudes necessary to develop and sustain a marketing-oriented service organization. The more that such development programmes can be focused on actual company marketing problems, the more relevant they become, as the development of skills to cope with real situations far outweighs the acquisition of knowledge.

In order to support the drive towards an improved marketing orientation, some additional support activities need to be considered. These are not necessarily relevant to all service companies.

- *Establish a marketing task force* – This should comprise a group of cross-functional senior managers. The group can work with the change agent, not only to provide ideas and suggestions about what might be done, but also to create change within their own parts of the organization.

- *Get rid of the 'wrong culture' carriers* – Senior managers convey by the way they react to situations, especially crises, what they really believe to be important. It is important to change the views or get rid of people who do not fit in with an organization dedicated to building a long-term relationship with its customers.

- *Acquire marketing talent* – A programme should be put in place to ensure that suitable marketing talent is hired.

This will involve external recruitment and internal development of staff.

- *Use external consultants* – Few companies possess the necessary in-house skills to be able to analyse, let alone organize and staff, all marketing activities such as advertising, marketing research, PR, information systems, and even training at senior levels. Therefore, there may be a case for using carefully chosen consultants to help solve problems and develop the company's own staff.

- *Promote market-oriented executives* – By making marketing orientation a significant criterion in the company's performance review, promotion and reward systems, the message can be clearly spelled out that it is important and career-enhancing for managers to be market-focused.

- *Maximize the impact of management development* – Ensuring that management development is endorsed by the chief executive, is well designed and produces results which can be measured and transferred to the business is often critical to success.

- *Keep the marketing structure under review* – As we have seen earlier, successful companies organize themselves around their markets and deliberately seek to maintain close contact with their customers. There should be a continual search for improving the way that marketing is organized.

- *Develop a marketing information system* – Again, as we saw earlier, information is critical to successful marketing decision-making. Developing an effective MIS can greatly assist the drive to an improved marketing orientation.

- *Recognize the long-term nature of the task* – The development of a marketing orientation where it has not previously existed will require a major change in attitudes and a fundamental shift in shared values. One major company set up a marketing orientation programme in which all senior managers were involved. Continuous activity lasting five years was necessary before a marketing orientation was achieved. It can take from three to six years before a real marketing orientation is developed.

- *Publicize successes* – Whenever something is achieved which demonstrates that the market orientation has paid off, ensure that it is publicized, either by word of mouth or by more formal channels. Success breeds further success.

From the above list, it is evident that the drive for marketing orientation must have a high profile. It must also operate across a broad front and leave no part of the organization untouched. It has become clear from the studies of excellent companies that their success was no accident. It was won by the total commitment of top management and staff alike to do whatever was necessary to overcome all obstacles in the way of serving customers.

Summary

In this chapter, we looked at some of the issues which, although not directly part of the marketing planning process itself, nonetheless have a direct and profound impact on its ultimate effectiveness.

The first of these was the underlying need for there to be a well-thought-out marketing intelligence system. Without provision of accurate data, marketing planning will not be effective. Attention was paid not only to how a system should be designed, but also to how it might be managed.

Marketing research was also considered in terms of how special information requirements might be identified. In addition to a brief look at research techniques, we addressed the issue of how much to spend on marketing research.

We then looked at marketing planning in terms of how the process might need to be adapted in order to be congruent with the organization's stage of development. We saw that, at some stages of a company's life, it was inappropriate to consider the introduction of marketing planning until more immediate organizational issues had been resolved. There are also other problems facing the marketer, in terms of where to position marketing planning in centralized or decentralized marketing organizations and issues around matrix management in terms of the relative importance placed on product/service management versus market management.

The service organization company still also needs a plan for the introduction of planning. It needs to establish a schedule and a planning cycle in which everyone involved knows when to make their particular contribution.

Finally, we looked at perhaps the most critical issue of all, how the service organization might develop or improve their marketing orientation. We saw that the gap between the degree of marketing orientation that the top management of a service organization believes it has and what actually exists could, in many companies, be vast. Part of the reason for this is a lack of understanding, but often it is because other orientations are too deeply engrained in the organization to allow a marketing orientation to develop. We saw that it was possible to measure marketing effectiveness, an important component of marketing orientation, by analysing the company's approach to customer philosophy, integrating its marketing organization, gathering marketing information, strategy formulation and operational efficiency.

Knowing the extent of a company's marketing orientation is one thing – setting out to improve it is another and far more difficult task. As we saw, it needs a high level of commitment in the company to change and to give marketing initiatives a chance of succeeding. Any change programme has to be underpinned by a number of supporting activities designed to make an impact on the corporate culture. Above all, seeking to raise the level of market orientation is a different task and it requires a carefully formulated approach to achieve success. Such initiatives, while difficult and time-consuming, are critical to the success of marketing planning activity.

We have now covered most of the key phases of marketing planning and the related organizational issues in detail. In the next chapter we examine the measurement of marketing plan effectiveness including a number of marketing investment appraisal techniques which form an important part of marketing strategy and marketing planning. In the final chapter we provide an overview and summary of the book and a detailed step-by-step approach for developing a services marketing planning system.

12 Measuring the effectiveness of marketing plans for service businesses

A three-level marketing accountability framework

The ultimate test of marketing investment, and indeed any investment, is whether it creates value for shareholders. But few marketing investments are evaluated from this perspective, and many would argue that it is almost impossible to link financial results to any specific marketing activity.

But increasingly, boards of directors and city analysts the world over are dissatisfied with this lack of accountability for what are, very often, huge budgets. Cranfield School of Management has been addressing this problem through its Marketing Value Added Research Club and Marketing Accountability Research Club, formed with a number of blue-chip companies. The club set out to create and test a new framework which shows how marketing systematically contributes to shareholder value, and how its contribution can be measured in an objective and comparable way.

> There is an urgent need for such a framework. Not only does marketing need it, to answer the widespread accusations of poor performance,[1] but corporate and financial strategists need it too, to understand how to link marketing activities to the wider corporate agenda. All too often marketing objectives and strategies are not aligned with the organization's overall plans to increase shareholder value.

The purpose of this chapter is to set out the logic of this framework, which is underpinned by two Cranfield University PhD theses by Wilson[2] and Smith.[3]

The chapter starts with a brief justification of the need for a wholly new approach to measuring the effectiveness of marketing.

It then proceeds to set out another accountability framework also developed in the Cranfield Research Clubs.

What counts as marketing expenditure?

Historically, marketing expenditure has tended to escape rigorous performance appraisal for a number of reasons. First, there has been real confusion as to the true scope and nature of marketing investments. Too often, marketing expenditure has been assumed to be only the budgets put together by the marketing function, and as such a (major) cost to be controlled rather than a potential driver of value. Second, the causal relationship between expenditure and results has been regarded as too difficult to pin down to any useful level of precision.

Now, because of the demands of increasingly discerning customers and greater competition, marketing investments and marketing processes are under scrutiny as never before. From the process point of view, as a result of insights from management concepts such as the quality movement and re-engineering, marketing is now much more commonly seen as a cross-functional responsibility of the entire organization rather than just the marketing department's problem.

> Howard Morganis, past chairman of Procter and Gamble, said, 'There is no such thing as a marketing skill by itself. For a company to be good at marketing, it must be good at everything else from R&D to manufacturing, from quality controls to financial controls.' Hugh Davidson in *Offensive Marketing*[4] comments, 'Marketing is an approach to business rather than a specialist discipline. It is no more the exclusive responsibility of the marketing department than profitability is the sole charge of the finance department.'

But there is also a growing awareness that, because of this wider interpretation of marketing, nearly all budgets within the company could be regarded as marketing investments in one way or another. This is especially the case with IT budgets. The exponential increase in computing power has made it possible to track customer perceptions and behaviours on a far greater scale, and with far greater precision than previously. When used correctly, these databases and analytical tools can shed a much greater light on what really happens inside the 'black box'. However, the sums involved in acquiring such technologies are forcing even the most slapdash of companies to apply more rigorous appraisal techniques to their investments in this area.

This wider understanding of what 'marketing' is really all about has had a number of consequences. First, the classic textbook treatment of strategic issues in marketing has finally caught up with reality. Topics such as market and customer segmentation, product and brand development, databases and customer service and support are now regularly discussed at board level, instead of being left to operational managers or obscure research specialists.

CEOs and MDs are increasingly accepting that they must take on the role of chief marketing officer if they want to create truly customer-led organizations. Sir Clive Thompson commented, 'I am convinced that corporate and marketing strategy are more or less the same things. The chief executive has to be the chief marketer. If you delegate that responsibility, you are not doing your job.'

Second, because of their 'new' mission-critical status, marketing investments are attracting the serious attention of finance professionals. As part of a wider revolution in thinking about what kind of corporate assets are important in today's business environment, intangibles such as knowledge about customers and markets, or the power of brands, have assumed a new importance. The race is on to find robust methods of quantifying and evaluating such assets for the benefit of corporate managements and the wider investment community.

> Unfortunately, this new focus on the importance of marketing has not improved the profile of marketing professionals. Instead, the spotlight has merely highlighted their weaknesses and shortcomings. After one 1997 survey on the perceived status of the profession, John Stubbs, CEO of the UK Marketing Council, was forced to comment, 'I was taken aback by just how little reputation marketing actually has among other functions . . . marketing and marketers are not respected by the people in their organisations for their contributions to business strategy, results or internal communication. We often do not know what or who is good or bad at marketing; our measurements are not seen as credible; our highest qualifications are not seen to have compatible status with other professions.'

> A survey at Cranfield during a two-year period has revealed that marketers are seen as 'slippery, expensive, unreliable and unaccountable'.[5]

What does 'value added' really mean?

The term 'value added' is fast becoming the new mantra for the early 21st century business literature, and is often used quite loosely to indicate a business concept that is intended to exceed either customer or investor expectations, or both. However, from the point of view of this chapter, it is important to realize that the term has its origin in a number of different management ideas, and is used in very specific ways by different sets of authors. Most of the ideas come from the US, and have originated in business school and consultancy research in the mid-1980s.

Value chain analysis

First, there is Michael Porter's well-known concept of value-chain analysis.[6] Porter's concept of value added is an incremental one; he focuses on how successive activities change the value of goods and services as they pass through various stages of a value chain. The analysis disaggregates a firm into its major activities in order to understand the behaviour of costs and the existing and potential sources of differentiation. It determines how the firm's own value chain interacts with the value chains of suppliers, customers and competitors. Companies gain competitive advantage by performing some or all of these activities at lower cost or with greater differentiation than competitors.

Shareholder value added (SVA)

Value chain analysis is used to identify potential sources of economic advantage

Second, there is Alfred Rappaport's equally well-known research on shareholder value added.[7] Rappaport's concept of value added focuses less on processes than Porter's, and acts more as a final gateway in decision-making, although it can be used at multiple levels within a firm. The analysis measures a company's ability to earn more than its total cost of capital . . . Within business units, SVA measures the value the unit has created by analysing cash flows over time.

SVA is described as 'The process of analysing how decisions affect the net present value of cash to shareholders'

> At the corporate level, SVA provides a framework for evaluating options for improving shareholder value by determining the tradeoffs between reinvesting in existing businesses, investing in new businesses and returning cash to stockholders.

There are a number of different ways of measuring shareholder value added, one of which, *market value added* (MVA), needs further explanation. *Market* value added is a measure first proposed by consultants Sterne Stewart in 1991, which compares the total shareholder capital of a company (including retained earnings) with the current market value of the company (capitalization and debt). When one is deducted from the other, a positive result means value has been added, and a negative result means investors have lost out. Within the literature, there is much discussion of the merits of this measure, versus another approach proposed by Sterne Stewart – EVA (economic value added).

However, from the point of view of *marketing* value added, Walters and Halliday[8] usefully sum up the discussion thus: 'As aggregate measures and as relative performance indicators they have much to offer . . . [but] how can the manager responsible for developing and/ or implementing growth objectives [use them] to identify and select from alternative [strategic] options?'

Market value added is one of a number of tools that analysts and the capital markets use to assess the value of a company. *Marketing value added* as a research topic focuses more directly on the processes of creating that value through effective marketing investments.

Customer value

A third way of looking at value added is the customer's perception of value. Unfortunately, despite exhaustive research by academics and practitioners around the world, this elusive concept has proved almost impossible to pin down: 'What constitutes [customer] value – even in a single product category – appears to be highly personal and idiosyncratic', concludes Zeithaml, for instance.[9] Nevertheless, the individual customer's perception of the extra value represented by different products and services cannot be easily dismissed: in the guise of measures such as customer satisfaction and customer loyalty, it is known to be the essence of brand success, and what became known during the late 1990s as relationship marketing.

Accounting value

Effectively, this is a snapshot picture from the annual accounts of how the revenue from a sales period has been distributed, and how much is left over for reinvestment after meeting all costs, including shareholder dividends. Although this figure will say something about the past viability of a business, in itself it does not provide a guide to future prospects.

Finally, there is the accountant's definition of value added: 'value added = sales revenue – purchases and services'.

One reason that the term 'value added' has come to be used rather carelessly is that all these concepts of value, although different, are not mutually exclusive. Porter's value chain analysis is one of several extremely useful techniques for identifying potential new competitive market strategies. Rappaport's SVA approach can be seen as a powerful tool which enables managers to cost out the long-term financial implications of pursuing one or other of the competitive strategies which have been identified. Customer perceptions are clearly a major driver (or destroyer) of annual audited accounting value in all companies, whatever strategy is pursued.

> However, most companies today accept that value added, as defined by their annual accounts, is really only a record of what they achieved in the past, and that financial targets in themselves are insufficient as business objectives. Many companies are now convinced that focusing on more intangible measures of value added such as brand equity, customer loyalty, or customer satisfaction are the new route to achieving financial results.

Unfortunately, research has found that there is no neat, causal link between offering additional customer value and achieving value added on a balance sheet. That is, good ratings from customers about perceived value do not necessarily lead to financial success. Nor do financially successful companies necessarily offer products and services which customers perceive as offering better value than competitors.

In order to explain the link that does exist between customer-oriented strategies and financial results, a far more rigorous approach to forecasting costs and revenues is required than is usual in marketing planning, coupled with a longer-term perspective on the payback period than is possible on an annual balance sheet. This cash-driven perspective is the basis of the SVA approach, and can be used in conjunction with any marketing-strategy formulation process.

> However, despite its apparent compatibility with existing planning systems, it is important to stress that adherents of the SVA approach believe that, after all the calculations have been made about the impact of different strategic choices, the final decision about which strategy to pursue should be the one which generates the most value (cash) for shareholders.

This point of view adds a further dimension to the strategic debate, and is by no means universally accepted: there is a vigorous and ongoing debate in the literature as to whether increasing shareholder value should be the ultimate objective of a corporation.

Despite these arguments, there is no denying that during the last 15 years, SVA (or variants on the technique) has become the single most dominating corporate valuation perspective in developed western economies. Its popularity tends to be limited to the boardroom and the stock exchanges, however. Several surveys (e.g. CSF Consulting in 2000, KPMG in 1999) have found that less than 30% of companies were pushing SVA-based management techniques down to an operational level, because of difficulties in translating cash targets into practical, day-to-day management objectives.

This is a pity because, apart from its widespread use at corporate level, the SVA approach particularly merits extensive attention of researchers interested in putting a value on marketing, as it allows marketing investments (or indeed any investments) to be valued over a much longer period of time than the usual one-year budget cycle.

Although common sense might argue that developing strong product or service offerings, and building up a loyal, satisfied customer base, will usually require a series of 1–2 year investment plans in any business, such is the universal distrust of marketing strategies and forecasts that it is common practice in most companies to write off marketing as a cost within each year's budget. It is rare for such expenditure to be treated as an investment which will deliver results over a number of years, but research shows that companies who are able to do this create a lasting competitive edge.

Meanwhile, over the past 15 years, research into marketing accountability continues apace at Cranfield, particularly into the application of the SVA concept. This was followed by research into the effectiveness of marketing strategies. As a result, a three-level model has been developed and tested and it is to this model that we now turn.

Three distinct levels for measuring marketing effectiveness

When one of the authors was marketing director of a fast moving consumer goods company 30 years ago, there were many well tried-and-tested models for measuring the effectiveness of marketing promotional expenditure. Indeed, some of these were quite sophisticated and included mathematical models for promotional campaigns, for advertising threshold and wear-out levels and the like.

Indeed, it would be surprising if marketing as a discipline did not have its own quantitative models for the massive expenditure of FMCG companies. Over time, these models have been transferred to business-to-business and service companies, with the result that, today, any organization spending substantial sums of shareholders' money on promotion should be ashamed of themselves if those responsible could not account for the effectiveness of such expenditure.

> Nonetheless, with the advent of different promotional methods and channels, combined with an empowered and more sophisticated consumer, the problems of measuring promotional effectiveness have increased considerably.

Consequently, this remains one of the major challenges facing the marketing community today and, as mentioned above, the research and practice of specialists at Cranfield School of Management continue apace.

But, at this level, accountability can only be measured in terms of the kinds of effects that promotional expenditure can achieve, such as awareness, or attitude change, both of which can be measured quantitatively.

But to assert that such expenditure can be measured directly in terms of sales or profits is intellectually indefensible, when there are so many other variables that affect sales, such as product efficacy, packaging, price, the sales force, competitors and countless other variables that, like advertising, have an intermediate impact on sales and profits. Again, however, there clearly is a cause and effect link, otherwise such expenditure would be pointless. This issue is addressed later in this chapter.

> So, the problem with marketing accountability has never been how to measure the effectiveness of promotional expenditure, for this we have had for many years. No, the problem occurs because marketing isn't just a promotional activity. As explained in detail in Chapter 1, in world class organizations where the customer is at the centre of the business model, marketing as a discipline is responsible for defining and understanding markets, for segmenting these markets, for developing value propositions to meet the researched needs of the customers in the segments, for getting buy-in from all those in the organization responsible for delivering this value, for playing their own part in delivering this value and for monitoring whether the promised value is being delivered.

Indeed, this definition of marketing as a function for strategy development as well as for tactical sales delivery, when represented as a map (see Figure 12.1), can be used to clarify the whole problem of how to measure marketing effectiveness. This is expanded on in Table 12.1.

Level 1: Shareholder value added (SVA)

SVA is profit after tax, minus net capital employed multiplied by the cost of capital. There are only three things you can do to affect SVA:

- increase revenue
- decrease costs
- decrease the amount of capital tied up in the business.

All of these are highly influenced by the strategic marketing plan. A very simple example of how SVA can be calculated follows: A has £15,000 invested in the company. The cost of capital is 10%. The company makes a net profit of £2,000. Therefore, the company has created £500 SVA ($£15,000 \times 10\% - £2000 = +£500$).

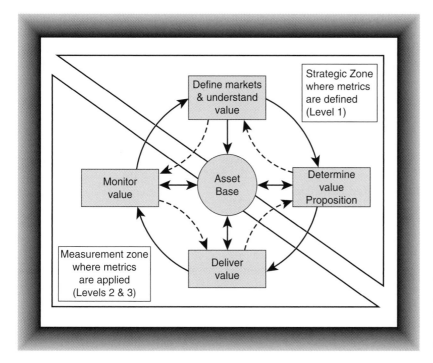

Figure 12.1
Map of the marketing domain and the three-level accountability framework

Level of marketing effectiveness	Areas considered	Outputs
Level 1 Marketing Due Diligence	The marketing strategy, i.e. the choice of target customers and value proposition	An objective assessment of whether or not the marketing strategy will create or destroy shareholder value, together with the identification of how the strategy may be improved
Level 2 Marketing Effectiveness	The marketing tactics (i.e. the full range of products, pricing, promotional and channels), employed for each segment identified and targeted by the marketing strategy	The likelihood of the marketing tactics creating the necessary competitive advantage in each segment
Level 3 Promotional Effectiveness	The marketing communications strategy (i.e. advertising, sales team, etc.), employed to communicate with each segment	The effectiveness of the communications activity in contributing to marketing objectives

Table 12.1
Three levels of marketing measurements

Level 1 is the most vital of all three, because this is what determines whether or not the marketing strategies for the longer term (usually three to five years) destroy or create shareholder value added. It is justified to use the strategic marketing plan for assessing whether shareholder value is being created or destroyed because, as Sean Kelly[10] agrees:

> The customer is simply the fulcrum of the business and everything from production to supply chain, to finance, risk management, personnel management and product development, all adapt to and converge on the business value proposition that is projected to the customer.

Thus, corporate assets and their associated competences are only relevant if customer markets value them sufficiently highly that they lead to sustainable competitive advantage, or shareholder value added. This is our justification for evaluating the strategic plan for what is to be sold, to whom and with what projected effect on profits as a route to establishing whether shareholder value will be created or destroyed.

A company's share price, the shareholder value created and the cost of capital are all heavily influenced by one factor: risk. Investors constantly seek to estimate the likelihood of a business plan delivering its promises, while the boards try to demonstrate the strength of their strategy.

How much is a company really worth? In most companies there is a huge discrepancy between the tangible assets and the share price; there are innumerable tools that try to estimate the true value of intangibles and goodwill. However, these mostly come from a cost-accounting perspective. They try to estimate the cost of re-creating the brand, intellectual property or whatever is the basis of intangible assets. Our research into companies that succeed and fail suggests that approach is flawed, because what matters is not the assets owned, but how they are used. We need to get back to the basics of what determines company value.

We should never be too simplistic about business, but some things are fundamentally simple. We believe that a company's job is to create shareholder value, and the share price reflects how well the investment community thinks that is being done. Whether or not shareholder value is created depends on creating profits greater than investors might get elsewhere at the same level of risk. The business plan makes promises about profits, which investors then discount against their estimate of the chance a company will deliver it. So it all comes down to that. A company says it will achieve $1bn; investors and analysts think it is more likely to be $0.8bn. The capital markets revolve around perceptions of risk. What boards and investors both need therefore is a strategic management process that gives a rigorous assessment of risk and uses that to assess and improve shareholder value creation. Just such a process has emerged from many years of research at Cranfield, a process we have called, appropriately, Marketing due diligence.

There is a whole book dedicated to explaining this process,[11] so we will provide only a brief summary here.

Where does risk come from?

Marketing due diligence begins by looking for the risk associated with a company's strategy. Evaluation of thousands of marketing plans and business plans suggests that the many different ways that companies fail to keep their promises can be grouped into three categories:

- The market wasn't as big as they thought

- They didn't get the market share they hoped for

- They didn't get the profit they hoped for.

Of course, a business can fail by any of these routes or a combination of them. The risk inherent in a plan is the aggregate of these three categories, which we have called, respectively, market risk, strategy risk and implementation risk. The challenge is to accurately assess these risks and their implications for shareholder value creation.

Our research found that most estimates of business risk were unreliable because they grouped lots of different sources of risk under one heading. Since each source of risk is influenced by many different factors, this high-level approach to assessing business risk is too simplistic and inherently inaccurate. A better approach is to subdivide business risk into as many sources as practically possible, estimate those separately and then recombine them. This has two advantages. First, each risk factor is 'cleaner', in that its causes can be assessed more accurately. Second, minor errors in each of the estimations cancel each other out. The result is a much better estimate of overall risk.

How risky is a business?

Marketing due diligence makes an initial improvement over high-level risk estimates by assessing market, strategy and implementation risk separately. However, even those three categories are not sufficiently detailed. We need to understand the components of each, which have to be teased out by careful comparison of successful and unsuccessful strategies. Our research indicated that each of the three risk sources could be subdivided further into five risk factors, making 15 in all. These are summarized in Table 12.2.

Armed with this understanding of the components and subcomponents of business risk, we are now half-way to a genuine assessment

Table 12.2
Factors contributing
to risk

Overall risk associated with the business plan		
Market risk	*Strategy risk*	*Implementation risk*
Product category risk, which is lower if the product category is well established and higher for a new product category.	Target market risk, which is lower if the target market is defined in terms of homogeneous segments and higher if it is not.	Profit pool risk, which is lower if the targeted profit pool is high and growing and higher if it is static or shrinking.
Segment existence risk, which is lower if the target segment is well established and higher if it is a new segment.	Proposition risk, which is lower if the proposition delivered to each segment is segment specific and higher if all segments are offered the same thing.	Competitor impact risk, which is lower if the profit impact on competitors is small and distributed and higher if it threatens a competitor's survival.
Sales volumes risk, which is lower if the sales volumes are well supported by evidence and higher if they are guessed.	SWOT risk, which is lower if the strengths and weaknesses of the organization are correctly assessed and leveraged by the strategy and higher if the strategy ignores the firm's strengths and weaknesses.	Internal gross margin risk, which is lower if the internal gross margin assumptions are conservative relative to current products and higher if they are optimistic.
Forecast risk, which is lower if the forecast growth is in line with historical trends and higher if it exceeds them significantly.	Uniqueness risk, which is lower if the target segments and propositions are different from that of the major competitors and higher if the strategy goes 'head on'.	Profit sources risk, which is lower if the source profit is growth in the existing profit pool and higher if the profit is planned to come from the market leader.
Pricing risk, which is lower if the pricing assumptions are conservative relative to current pricing levels and higher if they are optimistic.	Future risk, which is lower if the strategy allows for any trends in the market and higher if it fails to address them.	Other costs risk, which is lower if assumptions regarding other costs, including marketing support, are higher than existing costs and higher if they are lower than current costs.

of our value creation potential. The next step is to accurately assess our own business against each of the 15 criteria and use them to evaluate the probability that our plan will deliver its promises.

This gradation of risk level is not straightforward. It is too simplistic to reduce risk assessment to a tick-box exercise. However, a comparison of a strategy against a large sample of other company's strategies does provide a relative scale.

> By comparing, for instance, the evidence of market size, or the homogeneity of target markets, or the intended sources of profit against this scale, a valid, objective, assessment of the risk associated with business plan can be made.

What use is this knowledge?

Marketing due diligence involves the careful assessment of a business plan and the supporting information behind it. In doing so, it discounts subjective opinions and side-steps the spin of investor relations. At the end of the process the output is a number, a tangible measure of the risk associated with a chosen strategy. This number is then applied in the tried and trusted calculations that are used to work out shareholder value. Now, in place of a subjective guess, we have a research based and objective answer to the all-important question: Does this plan create shareholder value?

Too often, the answer is no. When risk is allowed for, many business plans create less value than putting the same money in a bank account or index-linked investment. Such plans, of course, actually destroy shareholder value because their return is less than the opportunity cost of the investment. An accurate assessment of value creation would make a huge difference to the valuation of the company. The result of carrying out marketing due diligence is, therefore, of great interest and value to both sides of the capital market.

For the investment community, marketing due diligence allows a much more informed and substantiated investment decision. Portfolio management is made more rational and more transparent. Marketing due diligence provides a standard by which to judge potential investments and a means to see through the vagaries of business plans.

For those seeking to satisfy investors, the value of marketing due diligence lies in two areas. First, it allows a rigorous assessment of the business plan in terms of its potential to create shareholder value. A positive assessment then becomes a substantive piece of evidence in negotiations with investors and other sources of finance. If, on the other hand, a strategy is shown to have weaknesses, the process not only pinpoints them but also indicates what corrective action is needed.

For both sides, the growth potential of a company is made more explicit, easier to measure and harder to disguise.

> For anyone involved in running a company or investing in one, marketing due diligence has three messages. First, business needs a process that assesses shareholder value creation, and hence the value of a company, in terms of risk rather than the cost of replacing intangible assets. Second, business risk can be dissected, measured and aggregated in a way that is much more accurate than a high-level judgement. Finally, marketing due diligence is a necessary process for both investors and companies.

Eventually, we anticipate that a process of marketing due diligence will become as de rigueur for assessing intangible value as financial due diligence is for its tangible counterpart. Until then, early adopters will be able to use it as a source of competitive advantage in the capital market.

The following is a summary of how SVA should be calculated using the marketing due diligence process (see Figures 12.2 and 12.3).

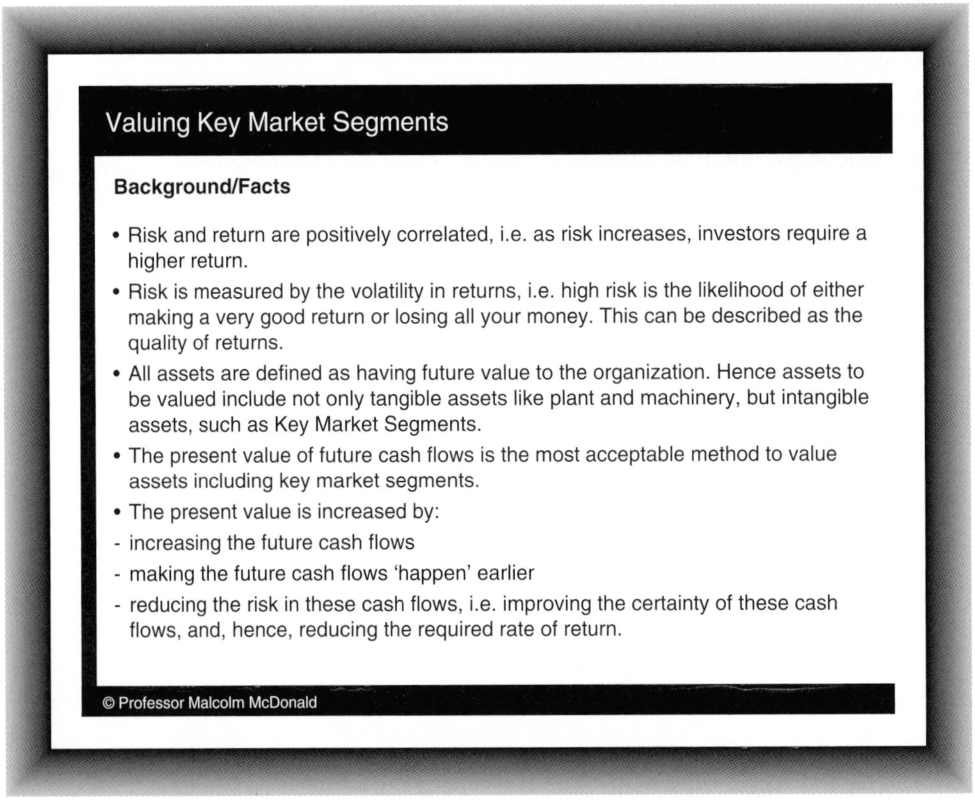

Valuing Key Market Segments

Background/Facts

- Risk and return are positively correlated, i.e. as risk increases, investors require a higher return.
- Risk is measured by the volatility in returns, i.e. high risk is the likelihood of either making a very good return or losing all your money. This can be described as the quality of returns.
- All assets are defined as having future value to the organization. Hence assets to be valued include not only tangible assets like plant and machinery, but intangible assets, such as Key Market Segments.
- The present value of future cash flows is the most acceptable method to value assets including key market segments.
- The present value is increased by:
- increasing the future cash flows
- making the future cash flows 'happen' earlier
- reducing the risk in these cash flows, i.e. improving the certainty of these cash flows, and, hence, reducing the required rate of return.

© Professor Malcolm McDonald

Figure 12.2   Valuing key market segments (sheet 1 of 2)

Suggested Approach

- Identify your key market segments. It is helpful if they can be classified on a vertical axis (a kind of thermometer) according to their attractiveness to your company. 'Attractiveness' usually means the potential of each for growth in your profits over a period of between 3 and 5 years. (See Figure 12.4)
- Based on your current experience and planning horizon that you are confident with, make a projection of future net free cash in-flows from your segments. It is normal to select a period such as 3 or 5 years.
- These calculations will consist of three parts:
  - revenue forecasts for each year;
  - cost forecasts for each year;
  - net free cash flow for each segment for each year.
- Identify the key factors that are likely to either increase or decrease these future cash flows.
- These factors are likely to be assessed according to the following factors:
  - the riskiness of the product/market segment relative to its position on the ANSOFF matrix;
  - the riskiness of the marketing strategies to achieve the revenue and market share;
  - the riskiness of the forecast profitability (e.g. the cost forecast accuracy).
- Now recalculate the revenues, costs and net free cash flows for each year, having adjusted the figures using the risks (probabilities) from the above.
- Ask your accountant to provide you with the overall SBU cost of capital and capital used in the SBU. This will not consist only of tangible assets. Thus, £1,000,000 capital at a required shareholder rate of return of 10% would give £100,000 as the minimum return necessary.
- Deduct the proportional cost of capital from the free cash flow for each segment for each year.
- An aggregate positive net present value indicates that you are creating shareholder value – i.e. achieving overall returns greater than the weighted average cost of capital, having taken into account the risk associated with future cash flows.

Figure 12.3 Suggested approach (sheet 2 of 2)

This high-level process for marketing accountability, however, still does not answer the dilemma of finding an approach which is better than the plethora of metrics with which today's marketing directors are bombarded, so Cranfield's Research Club took this issue on board in an attempt to answer the following questions:

- What needs to be measured

- Why it needs to be measured

- How frequently it needs to be measured

- To whom it should be reported

- And the relative importance of each.

This leads to a discussion of Level 2.

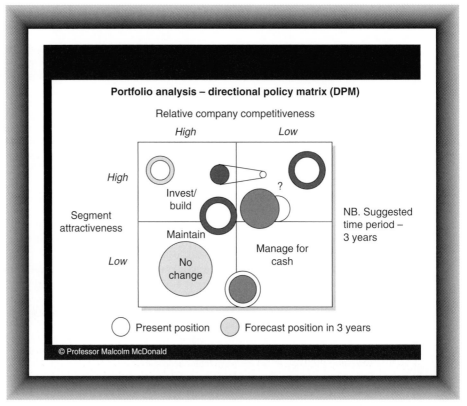

Figure 12.4 Portfolio analysis – directional policy matrix (DPM)

Level 2: Measuring marketing effectiveness

The approach we took to answering these questions was to drive metrics from a company's strategy and the following model, shown as Figure 12.5, was developed. This clearly shows the link between Lead Indicators and Lag Indicators. There are other factors, of course, that influence what is sold and to whom. The 'Hygiene Factors' (HF), 'Productivity Factors' (PF) and 'Critical Success Factors' (CSF) shown under the strategy element of the lead indicators are explained shortly.

This process model is explained in much greater detail in *Marketing Accountability*,[12] so here we will provide a brief summary only.

To date, few academics or practitioners have addressed this second level, which links marketing actions to outcomes in a more holistic way. We shall describe it briefly here, although it must be stressed that it is central to the issue of marketing metrics and marketing effectiveness.

First, however, let us destroy once and for all one of the great myths of measurement – marketing return on investment. This implies 'return' divided by 'investment' and, for marketing expenditure such as promotional spend, it is an intellectually puerile notion. It's a bit like demanding a financial justification for the wings of an aircraft! Also, as McGovern *et al*. say,

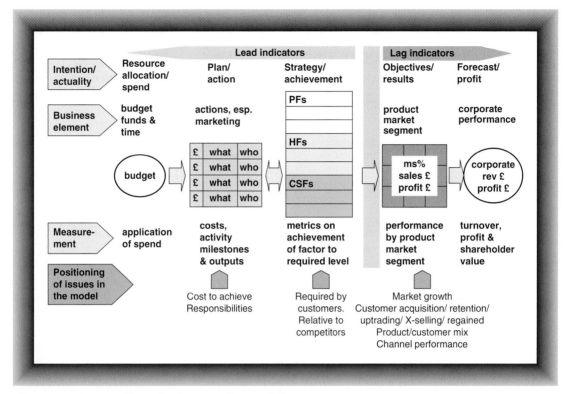

Figure 12.5   Overall marketing metrics model

Measuring marketing performance isn't like measuring factory output – a fact that many non-marketing executives don't grasp. In the controlled environment of a manufacturing plant, it's simple to account for what goes in one end and what comes out the other and then determine productivity.

But the output of marketing can be measured only long after it has left the plant.[13]

Neither is the budget and all the energy employed in measuring it a proxy for measuring marketing effectiveness.

In Figure 12.5, reading from right to left, it can be seen that the corporate financial objectives can only be met by selling something to someone – represented in the figure as the Ansoff matrix (shaded box).

So how do we set about linking our marketing activities to our overall objectives? We will start with the Ansoff matrix shown in Figure 12.6.

Each of the cells in each box (cells will consist of products/services for segments) is a planning unit, in the sense that objectives will be set for each for volume, value and profit for the first year of the strategic plan.

For each of the products for segment cells, having set objectives, the task is then to determine strategies for achieving them. The starting

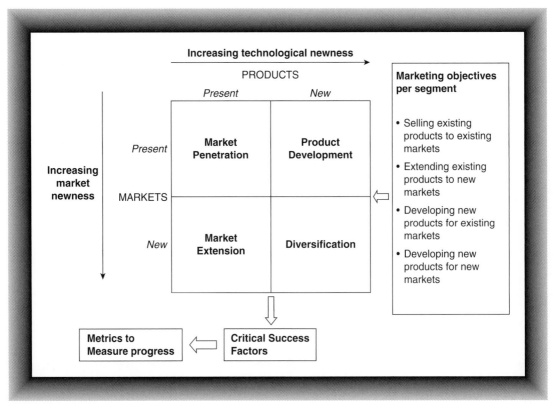

Figure 12.6 Ansoff matrix

point for these strategies is Critical Success Factors (CSFs), the factors critical to success in each product/service for segment, which will be weighted according to their relative importance to the customers in the segment. See Figure 12.7.

In these terms, a strategy will involve improving one or more CSF scores in one or more product-for-segment cells. It is unlikely though that the marketing function will be directly responsible for what needs to be done to improve a CSF. For example, issues like product/service efficacy, after sales service, channel management and sometimes even price and the sales force are often controlled by other functions, so marketing needs to get buy-in from these functions to the need to improve the CSF scores.

It is very rare for this information to be perfectly available to the marketer. While models such as price sensitivity, advertising response or even marketing mix or econometric approaches may help to populate the CSF form, there are generally several other factors where information is less easy to gather. Nevertheless, a CSF analysis indicates where metrics are most needed which can steer the organization towards measuring the right things.

Critical Success Factors	Weighting factor	Your organization	Competitor A	Competitor B	Competitor C
CSF 1					
CSF 2					
CSF 3					
CSF 4					
Total weighted score (score x weight)	100				

(Within the table, overlaid on CSF 1 and CSF 2 rows:)
- Strategies to improve competitive position/achieve objectives over time (4Ps)
- Metrics (each CSF) to measure performance over time in achieving goals

Figure 12.7   Critical success factors: in each segment, defined by the segment

Figure 12.8 shows the actions that have to be taken, by whom and at what cost in order to improve the CSFs.

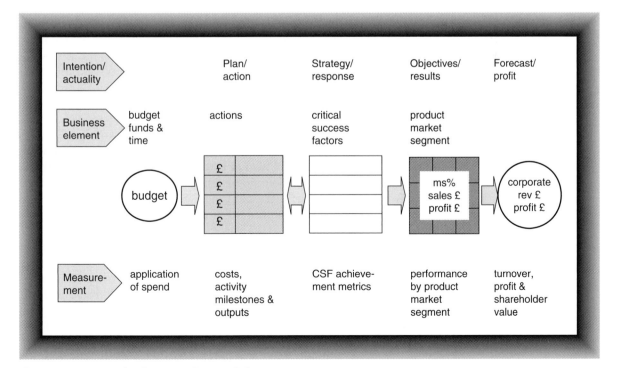

Figure 12.8   Marketing metrics model

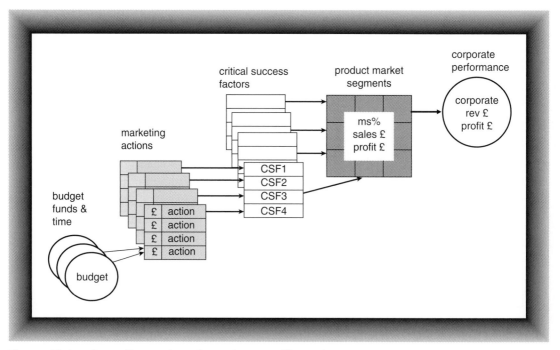

Figure 12.9   Cascading actions from the Ansoff matrix

Figure 12.9 shows how these actions multiply for each box of the Ansoff matrix.

There are other factors, of course, that influence what is sold and to whom. These may be referred to as 'Hygiene Factors' (HF) – i.e. those standards that must be achieved by any competitor in the market. Other factors may be referred to as 'Productivity Factors' (PF) – i.e. those issues which may impact on an organization's performance unless the required productivity is achieved in its relevant activities.

Thus, it can be seen how the expenditure on marketing and other functional actions to improve CSFs can be linked to marketing objectives and, ultimately, to profitability, and it becomes clear exactly what must be measured and why. It also obviates the absurd assumption that a particular marketing action can be linked directly to profitability. It can only be linked to other weighted CSFs which, if improved, should lead to the achievement of volumes, value and, ultimately, profits.

Figure 12.3 is reintroduced here in Figure 12.10, as it summarizes all of this in one flow chart, which clearly spells out the difference between 'Lag Indicators' and 'Lead Indicators'. Lead indicators are the actions taken and the associated expenditure that is incurred. These include, of course, promotional expenditure, which will be addressed later in this chapter. Lag indicators are the *outcomes* of these actions and expenditures and need to be carefully monitored and measured. Thus, retention by segment, loss by segment, new customers, new product sales, channel performance and the like are *outcomes*, but these need to

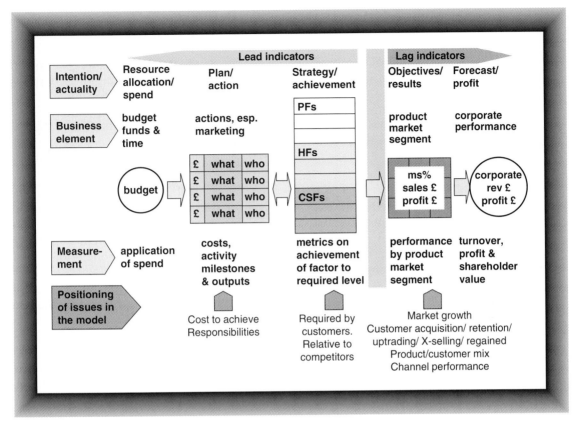

Figure 12.10   Overall marketing metrics model

be linked back to the appropriate *inputs*, an issue which is addressed later in this chapter.

There is one other crucial implication to be drawn from this model. Most operating boards on scrutinizing profit and loss accounts typically see only one line for revenue, while costs are covered in considerable detail, and it is around costs that most of the discussion takes place. In the view of the authors, there should be at least two sets of figures – one to detail where the sales revenue has come from, another to detail costs. A key task of marketers, rarely carried out, is to link the two documents together. Figure 12.10 goes some way towards this.

We stress, however, that the corporate revenue and profits shown in the right of Figure 12.10 are not the same as shareholder value added, which takes account of the risks involved in the strategies, the time value of money and the cost of capital. This brings us to Level 3.

Level 3: Promotional Effectiveness

Level 3 is the fundamental and crucial level of promotional measurement.

It would be surprising if marketing as a discipline did not have its own quantitative models for the massive expenditure of FMCG companies. Over time, these models have been transferred to business-to-business and service companies, with the result that, today, any organization spending substantial sums of shareholders' money on promotion should be ashamed of themselves if those responsible could not account for the effectiveness of such expenditure.

Nonetheless, with the advent of different promotional methods and channels, combined with an empowered and more sophisticated consumer, the problems of measuring promotional effectiveness have increased considerably. Consequently, this remains one of the major challenges facing the marketing community today.

For example, in fast moving consumer goods, supermarket buyers expect and demand a threshold level of promotional expenditure in order to be considered for listing. Indeed, in most commercial situations, there is a threshold level of expenditure that has to be made in order just to maintain the status quo – i.e. keep up the product or service in consumer consciousness to encourage them to continue buying. The author refers to this as 'maintenance' expenditure.

In most situations, however, not to maintain existing levels of promotion over time results in volume, price and margin pressure, market share losses and a subsequent declining share price.

There is some evidence from the IPA's analysis of almost 900 promotional campaigns, presented in a report.[14] The graph in Figure 12.11 shows that, in one experimental scenario, the promotional budget was cut to zero for a year, then returned to normal, while in another, the budget was cut by 50%. Sales recovery to pre-cut levels took five years and three years, respectively, with cumulative negative impacts on net profits of £1.7 million and £0.8 million.

It is important to make one final point about measuring the effectiveness of promotional expenditure in taking account of 'maintenance' expenditure. This point relates to the tried and tested method of measuring the financial impact of promotional expenditure – net present value.

As can be seen from the following, by not taking account of the expenditure to maintain current sales and by including total promotional expenditure in the NPV calculations, a totally false result ensues. However, by taking account of maintenance expenditure, a much better result emerges.

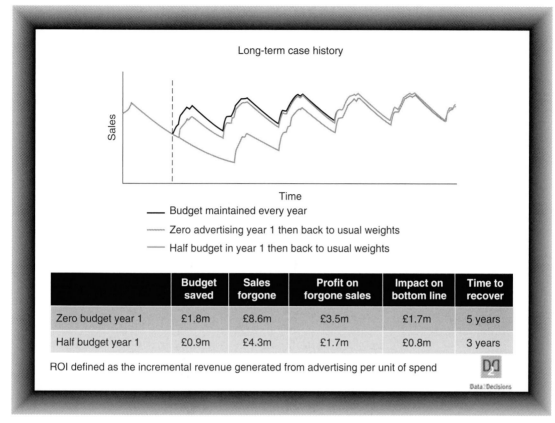

Figure 12.11 ROI. Long-term case history

Present values

Discounting a future stream of revenue into a 'Present Value' assumes that a rational investor would be indifferent to having a dollar today, or to receiving in some future year a dollar plus the interest that could have been earned by investing that dollar for those years.

Thus it makes sense to assess investments by dividing the money to be received in future years by $(1 + r)$, where r is the discount rate (the annual return from investing that money) and n is the number of years during which the investment could be earning that return.

PV or NPV or DCF is denoted as:

$$PV = \frac{\sum C_t}{(1 + r)^n}$$

Σ is the sum of the cash flows in years t (1, 2, 3, 4, etc.).

This summation of the cash flows is then divided by $(1 + r)^n$ where r is the discount rate and n is the number of years the investment could be earning that return.

Hence, for a net free cash flow of $2 million a year over 4 years and a cost of capital of 10%, the net present value is:

$$\frac{2}{(1.1)} + \frac{2}{(1.1)^2} + \frac{2}{(1.1)^3} + \frac{2}{(1.1)^4} = \$6.4 \; million$$

Minus an initial investment of, say, $5 million, the NPV of this investment is $1.4 million.

However:

A promotional investment of, say, $7 million, using the above figure, would produce a loss of $0.6 million.

If, however, a company needs to spend say $6 million just to maintain current sales, the investment is only $1 million and the NPV would then be:

$$-\$1 \; million + \frac{2}{(1.1)} + \frac{2}{(1.1)^2} + \frac{2}{(1.1)^3} + \frac{2}{(1.1)^4} = \$5.4 \; million$$

The research issue facing our community is how to estimate what might be classified as 'maintenance' promotion and what as 'investment' promotion. This is complicated by the different forms of promotion and the many different channels available today, but it is not impossible.

Conclusion

Having provided some insights into marketing accountability, it should make it slightly easier to answer the following questions:

● What needs measuring?

● Why?

● When?

● How?

● How frequently?

● By whom?

● Reported to whom?

● At what cost?

● Etc.

It is suggested that the following questions also need to be explored:

1. What counts as marketing expenditure?

2. What does 'added value' really mean?

- value chain analysis
- shareholder value added (SVA)
- customer value
- brand value
- accounting value
- value-based marketing

3. What are the major 'Schools of Thought'? What are the strengths and weaknesses of each?

4. Preliminary conclusions from the above with our own recommendations/hypotheses.

5. Some small-scale field work to test findings on world class companies.

The metrics below show a summary of some of the more common metrics in use in companies today:

- Brand awareness
- Channel efficiency
- Cost per lead
- Customer satisfaction
- Growth in customers
- Lead conversion rate
- Orders: number average, total value
- Repurchase rate
- Share of customer
- Total marketing cost per order.

Whatever models emerge from the above, it is highly unlikely that any organization will be using them all. There will be examples of excellence along a number of dimensions which will help us to refine and develop the models.

Summary

The chapter outlined a number of marketing investment appraisal techniques which form an important part of marketing strategy and marketing planning, starting with a discussion of what counts as marketing expenditure. It continued by describing three levels of marketing measurement:

Level 1: Marketing Due Diligence (MDD). MDD assesses the risks associated with the three main components of strategic marketing plans: the market; the marketing strategy; and the profit pool. The forecast net free cash flows for the planning period are reduced if appropriate by the probability that they can be archived. The accountant will then take account of the cost of capital to assess whether these risk-adjusted net free cash flows will create or destroy shareholder value.

Level 2: Marketing Spend Evaluation. The model provided a framework for linking principal products for market (the Ansoff matrix) to critical success factors, productivity factors and to hygiene factors. These are then translated into actions, with costs and responsibilities associated with each action.

Level 3: Promotional Spend Evaluation. Here, the difference between maintenance and investment expenditure was explained and examples provided which illustrated the very different net present value outcomes based on maintenance and investment expenditure.

We have now covered each of the major phases of marketing planning, examined related organizational issues in detail and, in this chapter, reviewed measurement of the effectiveness of marketing plans. In the final chapter, which follows, we provide an overview and summary of the key issues we have covered and a detailed step-by-step approach for developing a services marketing planning system. This chapter will provide a detailed structure, with accompanying pro-formas, for creating:

- A three-year strategic marketing plan

- A one-year detailed tactical marketing plan

- A headquarters consolidated plan of several strategic business unit (SBU) strategic marketing plans.

The authors are indebted to Professor Robert Shaw of Cass Business School, who worked with them in running Cranfield University School of Management's Value Added Research Club. They are also indebted to Peter Mouncy, who worked with the authors in Cranfield's Marketing Accountability Research Club.

13 A step-by-step marketing planning system for service businesses

Introduction

This chapter is in two parts, as follows:

Part 1:

- A summary of the strategic marketing planning process for services

Part 2:

- A step-by-step approach to preparing a strategic marketing plan
- A step-by-step approach to preparing a tactical marketing plan
- A format for those who have to consolidate many strategic marketing plans
- Forms and templates are provided to turn the theory into practice

It is, of course, possible to complete the pro-formas provided without reading this book, but we stress that this is very dangerous and may well lead to a plan without any real substance. Consequently, we advise readers to consult the relevant sections of the main text.

Part 1 Marketing planning summary

The purpose of marketing planning

The overall purpose of marketing and its principal focus is the identification and creation of competitive advantage.

What is marketing planning?

Marketing planning is simply a logical sequence and a series of activities leading to the setting of marketing objectives and the formulation of plans for achieving them.

Why is marketing planning necessary?
Marketing planning is necessary because of:

- Increasing turbulence, complexity and competitiveness

- The speed of technological change

- Services are often less tangible, variable and perishable

- The need for *you*

  - to help identify sources of competitive advantage

  - to force an organized approach to develop specificity

  - to ensure consistent relationships

- The need for *superiors*

  - to inform

- The need for non-marketing functions

  - to get support

- The need for *subordinates*

  - to get resources

  - to gain commitment

  - to set objectives and strategies.

What should appear in the strategic marketing plan for a service organization?

A summary of what appears in a strategic marketing plan and a list of the principal marketing tools/techniques/structures/frameworks which apply to each step is given in Figure 13.1.

It must be understood, however, that marketing planning never has been just the simple step-by-step approach described so enthusiastically in most prescriptive texts and courses. The moment an organization embarks on the marketing planning path, it can expect to encounter a number of complex organizational, attitudinal, process and cognitive problems, which are likely to block progress (see Chapter 11). By being forewarned about these barriers, there is a good chance of successfully using the step-by-step marketing planning system which follows in Part 2 of this chapter and of doing excellent marketing planning that will bring all the claimed benefits, including a significant impact on the bottom line, through the creation of competitive advantage. If they are ignored, however, marketing planning will remain the Cinderella of business management.

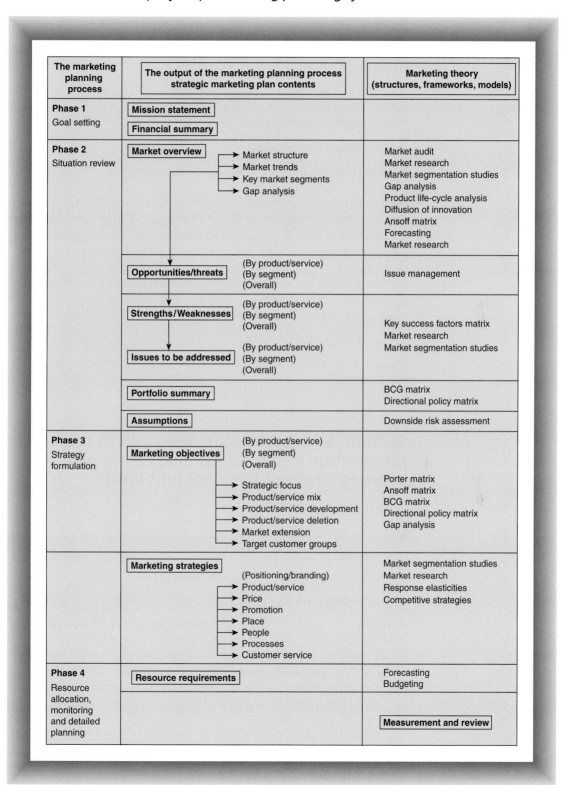

The marketing planning process	The output of the marketing planning process strategic marketing plan contents	Marketing theory (structures, frameworks, models)
Phase 1 Goal setting	Mission statement Financial summary	
Phase 2 Situation review	Market overview → Market structure → Market trends → Key market segments → Gap analysis	Market audit Market research Market segmentation studies Gap analysis Product life-cycle analysis Diffusion of innovation Ansoff matrix Forecasting Market research
	Opportunities/threats (By product/service) (By segment) (Overall)	Issue management
	Strengths/Weaknesses (By product/service) (By segment) (Overall)	Key success factors matrix Market research Market segmentation studies
	Issues to be addressed (By product/service) (By segment) (Overall)	
	Portfolio summary	BCG matrix Directional policy matrix
	Assumptions	Downside risk assessment
Phase 3 Strategy formulation	Marketing objectives (By product/service) (By segment) (Overall) → Strategic focus → Product/service mix → Product/service development → Product/service deletion → Market extension → Target customer groups	Porter matrix Ansoff matrix BCG matrix Directional policy matrix Gap analysis
	Marketing strategies (Positioning/branding) → Product/service → Price → Promotion → Place → People → Processes → Customer service	Market segmentation studies Market research Response elasticities Competitive strategies
Phase 4 Resource allocation, monitoring and detailed planning	Resource requirements	Forecasting Budgeting
		Measurement and review

Figure 13.1 Principal marketing tools which can be utilized at different phases of the marketing planning process

Part 2 A Marketing Planning System

Introduction

This chapter contains a step-by-step system for completing:

- a strategic marketing plan
- a tactical marketing plan
- a consolidated multi-SBU strategic marketing plan.

Section A takes you through a step-by-step approach to the preparation of a strategic marketing plan. What actually appears in the strategic marketing plan is given under the heading 'Strategic marketing plan documentation', which appears later in this chapter.

Section B takes you through the preparation of a one-year marketing plan. What actually appears in a one-year marketing plan is given under the heading 'The one-year marketing plan documentation'.

Finally, Section C refers to the need for a headquarters consolidated plan of several SBU strategic marketing plans and provides a suggested format.

Section A   Step-by-step approach to the preparation of a strategic marketing plan for a services strategic business unit (SBU)

A strategic business unit:

- will have common segments and competitors for most of its products
- will be a competitor in an external market
- will be a discrete and identifiable unit
- will have a manager who has control over most of the areas critical to success.

SBUs are not necessarily the same as operating units and the definition can, and should if necessary, be applied all the way down to a particular product or customer or group of products and customers.

The marketing planning process is formally expressed in two marketing plans, the strategic marketing plan and the tactical marketing plan, which should be written in accordance with the format provided in this system. It is designed for strategic business units (SBUs) to be able to take a logical and constructive approach to planning for success.

Two very important introductory points should be made about the marketing plan:

1. The *importance of different sections* – in the final analysis, the strategic marketing plan is a plan for action, and this should be reflected in the finished document. The implementation part of the strategic plan is represented by the subsequent one-year marketing plan.

2. The *length of the analytical section* – to be able to produce an action-focused strategic marketing plan, a considerable amount of background information and statistics needs to be collected, collated and analysed. An analytical framework has been provided in the forms, included in the database section of the 'Strategic marketing plan documentation', which each SBU should complete. However, the commentary given in the strategic marketing plan should provide the main findings of the analysis rather than a mass of raw data. It should compel concentration upon only that which is essential. The analysis section should, therefore, provide only a short background.

Basis of the system

Each business unit in the organization will have different levels of opportunity depending on the prevailing business climate. Each business unit, therefore, needs to be managed in a way that is appropriate to its own unique circumstances. At the same time, the chief executive officer of the SBU must have every opportunity to see that the ways in which these business units are managed are consistent with the overall strategic aims of the organization.

This system sets out the procedures which, if adhered to, will assist in achieving these aims.

Sections A, B and C set out the three basic marketing planning formats and explain how each of the planning steps should be carried out. They explain simply and clearly what should be presented, and when, in the three-year marketing plan, in the more detailed one-year operational plan and in the headquarters consolidated marketing plan.

The overall marketing planning format is described in Figure 13.2. (Note that, for the sake of simplicity, it has been assumed that the organization's year runs from January to December.) The following sections explain how each of the steps in the planning process should be completed.

The marketing audit

(For completion between February and May each year.)

Note: the marketing audit is not for inclusion in the plan or its presentation.

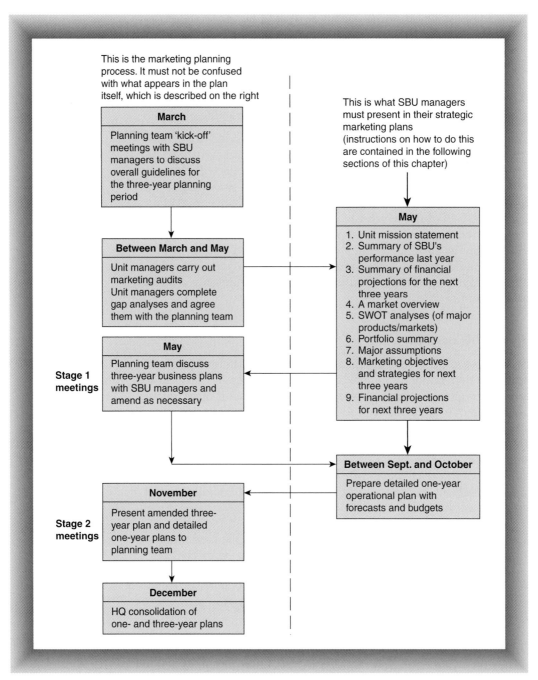

Figure 13.2 Marketing planning timetable

For the purpose of a marketing planning system, it is usual to provide users with an agreed list of what should be audited so that all SBUs using the system use similar nomenclature for products and markets.

All managers carrying out their audit should use internal sales data and the SBU marketing information system to complete their audit. It is helpful at this stage if the various SBU managers can issue to any subordinates involved in the audit a market overview covering major industry and market trends. The audit will inevitably require considerably more data preparation than is required to be reproduced in the marketing plan itself. Therefore, all managers should start a *running reference file* for their area of responsibility during the year, which can also be used as a continual reference source and for verbal presentation of proposals.

It is essential to stress that the audit, which will be based on the running reference file, is not a marketing plan and under no circumstances should voluminous documents relating to the audit appear in any marketing or business plans.

The contents of a strategic marketing plan

The following sections describe what should be presented in strategic marketing plans. These should be completed by the end of May each year.

The actual documentation for the strategic marketing plan is also provided in this section.

Strategic marketing plan documentation

Form 1   Unit Mission Statement

Unit mission statement

This is the first item to appear in the marketing plan.

The purpose of the mission statement is to ensure that the *raison d'être* of the unit is clearly stated. Brief statements should be made which cover the following points:

1 *Role or contribution of the unit*
   e.g. profit generator
         service department
         opportunity seeker

2 *Definition of the business*
   i.e. the needs you satisfy or the benefits you provide. Don't be too specific (e.g. 'we sell insurance') or too general (e.g. 'we're in the communication business').

3 *Distinctive competence*
   This should be a brief statement that applies only to your specific unit. A statement that could equally apply to any competitor is unsatisfactory.

4 *Indications for future direction*
   A brief statement of the principal things you would give serious consideration to (e.g. move into a new segment).

Form 2 Summary of SBU's performance

Summary of SBU's performance

This opening section is designed to give a bird's eye view of the SBU's total marketing activities.

In addition to a quantitative summary of performance, as follows, SBU managers should give a summary of reasons for good or bad performance.

Use constant revenue in order that comparisons are meaningful. Make sure you use the same base year values for any projections provided in later sections of this system.

	3 years ago	2 years ago	Last year
Volume/turnover			
Gross profit (%)			
Gross margin (000 euro)			

Summary of reasons for good or bad performance

Form 3   Summary of financial projections

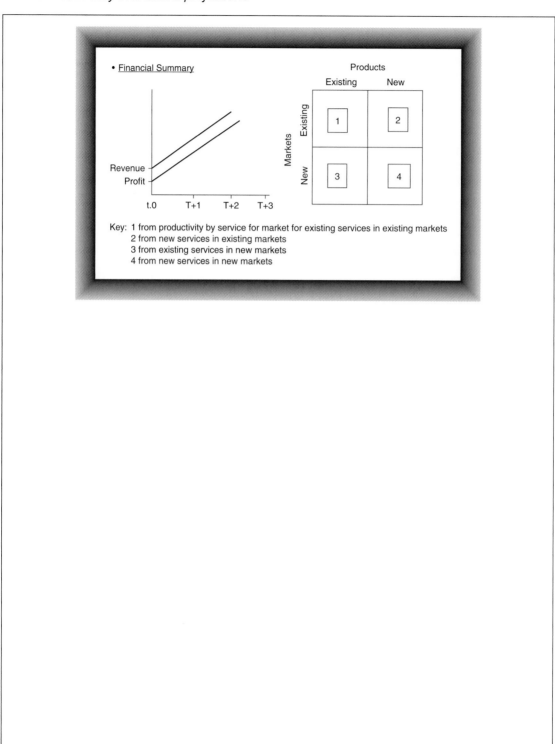

Form 4   Market overview

Market overview (with 'market map', if appropriate, together with implications for the organization)

It is also helpful if the principal segments can be described here.

- Market definition
- Market map showing vol/rev flows from supplier through to end user, with major decision points highlighted
- Where appropriate, provide a future market map
- Include commentary/conclusions/implications for the company
- At major decision points, include key segments.

Form 5   Strategic planning exercise (SWOT Analysis)

(Note: This form should be completed for each service for market and segment under consideration.)

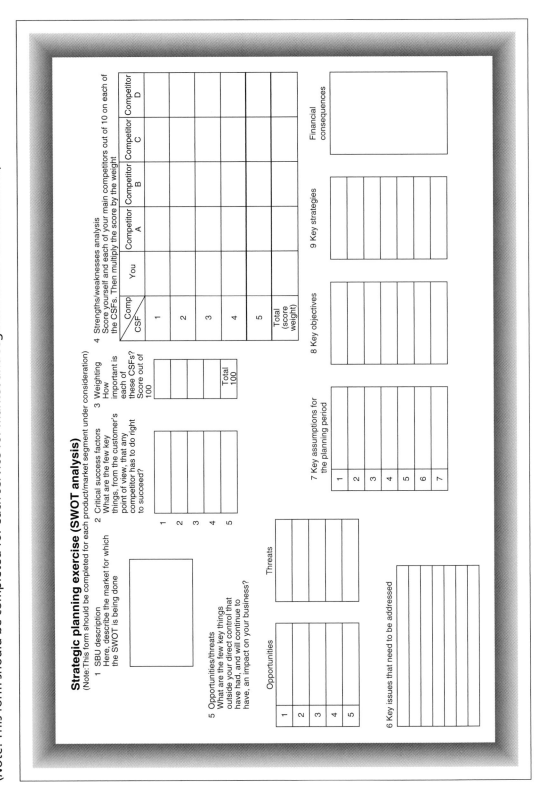

Strategic planning exercise (SWOT analysis)
(Note: This form should be completed for each product/market segment under consideration)

1 SBU description
Here, describe the market for which the SWOT is being done

2 Critical success factors
What are the few key things, from the customer's point of view, that any competitor has to do right to succeed?

1
2
3
4
5

3 Weighting
How important is each of these CSFs? Score out of 100

Total 100

4 Strengths/weaknesses analysis
Score yourself and each of your main competitors out of 10 on each of the CSFs. Then multiply the score by the weight

Comp CSF	You	Competitor A	Competitor B	Competitor C	Competitor D
1					
2					
3					
4					
5					
Total (score weight)					

5 Opportunities/threats
What are the few key things outside your direct control that have had, and will continue to have, an impact on your business?

Opportunities

1
2
3
4
5

Threats

6 Key issues that need to be addressed

7 Key assumptions for the planning period

1
2
3
4
5
6
7

8 Key objectives

9 Key strategies

Financial consequences

Form 6   Competitor analysis

(Note: This form should be completed for each service market segment under consideration.)

Note: This form should be completed for each service market segment under consideration

Main competitor	Serviced products/ markets	Business direction and current objectives and strategies	Strengths	Weaknesses	Competitive position

Form 7   Portfolio summary of the SWOTs

Portfolio summary

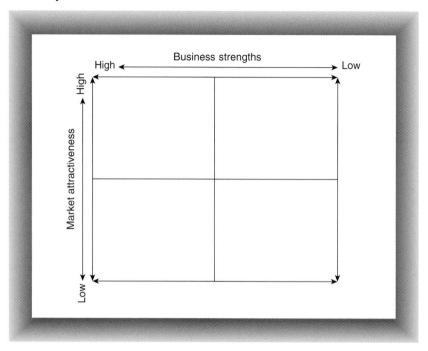

Show pictorially:

● the attractiveness of the segments over the next 3–5 years

● the current competitive position of your organization in each segment

● the planned competitive position of each segment over the next 3–5 years

Form 8   Assumptions

Assumptions

Overall, assumptions should be few in number. If the plan can happen irrespective of the assumption, it should not be included.

Form 9   Marketing objectives and strategies for the next 3–5 years

Database and summary of marketing objectives
Market segment sales values

Sales values	Last year (t – 1)	Current year (t0)	Next year (t + 1)	(t + 2)	(t + 3)
Key market segments (list)	Total company market segment sales share	Total company market segment sales share	Total company market segment sales share	Total company market segment sales share	Total company market segment sales share
Total					

Form 10   Database and summary of marketing objectives – profits

Database and summary of marketing objectives
Market segment sales values gross profits

Sales values	Last year (t – 1)	Current year (t0)	Next year (t + 1)	(t + 2)	(t + 3)
Key market segments (list)	Total company market segment sales share	Total company market segment sales share	Total company market segment sales share	Total company market segment sales share	Total company market segment sales share
Total					

Form 11   Consolidated budget for the next 3–5 years

Service group analysis

Service Groups	Last year (t – 1)		Current year (t0)			Next year (t + 1)			(t + 2)			(t + 3)		
	Sales value	Gross profit	Gross margin (%)	Sales value	Gross profit	Gross margin (%)	Sales value	Gross profit	Gross margin (%)	Sales value	Gross profit	Gross margin (%)	Sales value	Gross profit	Gross margin (%)
Total															

Form 12   Summary of marketing objectives and strategies

Summary (in words) of main marketing objectives and strategies

Section B   The one-year marketing plan

(This should be kept separate from the three-year strategic marketing plan and should not be completed until the planning team has approved the strategic plan in May each year.)

Specific sub-objectives for services and segments, supported by more detailed strategy and action statements, should now be developed. Here, include *budgets* and *forecasts* and a *consolidated budget*. These must reflect the marketing objectives and strategies, and in turn the objectives, strategies and programmes *must* reflect the agreed budgets and sales forecasts. Their main purpose is to delineate the major steps required in implementation, to assign accountability, to focus on the major decision points, and to specify the required allocation of resources and their timing.

If the procedures in this system are followed, a hierarchy of *objectives* will be built up in such a way that every item of budgeted expenditure can be related directly back to the initial financial objectives (this is known as task-related budgeting).

Thus when, say, advertising has been identified as a means of achieving an objective in a particular market (i.e. advertising is a strategy to be used), all advertising expenditure against items appearing in the budget can be related back specifically to a major objective. The essential feature of this is that budgets are set against both the overall marketing objectives and the sub-objectives for each element of the marketing mix.

The principal advantage is that this method allows operating units to build up and demonstrate an increasingly clear picture of their markets. This method of budgeting also allows every item of expenditure to be fully accounted for as part of an objective approach. It also ensures that when changes have to be made during the period to which the plan relates, such changes can be made in a way that causes the least damage to the SBU's long-term objectives.

Contingency plan

It is important to include a *contingency plan* in the one-year marketing plan. Notes on this are included below.

Guidelines for completion of a one-year marketing plan

Because of the varying nature of strategic business units, it is impossible to provide a standard format for all SBUs. There is, however, a minimum amount of information which should be provided to accompany the financial documentation between September and October. There is no need to supply market background information, as this should have been completed in the three-year strategic marketing plan.

Suggested format for a one-year marketing plan

1. (a) Overall objectives (see Forms 1 and 2 in the one-year marketing plan documentation) – these should cover the following:

Volume or value	Value last year	Current year estimate	Budget next year
Gross margin	Last year	Current year estimate	Budget next year

Against each there should be a few words of commentary/explanation.

   (b) *Overall strategies* – e.g. new customers, new services, advertising, sales promotion, selling, customer service, pricing.

2. (a) *Sub-objectives (see Form 3 in one-year marketing plan documentation)* – more detailed objectives should be provided for services, or markets, or segments, or major customers, as appropriate.
   (b) *Strategies* – the means by which sub-objectives will be achieved should be stated.
   (c) *Action/tactics* – the details, timing, responsibility and cost should also be stated.

3. Summary of marketing activities and costs (see Form 4 in the one-year marketing plan documentation).

4. Contingency plan (see Form 5 in the one-year marketing plan documentation) – it is important to include a contingency plan, which should address the following questions:
   (a) What are the critical assumptions on which the one-year plan is based?
   (b) What would the financial consequences be (i.e. the effect on the operating income) if these assumptions did not come true? For example, if a forecast of revenue is based on the assumption that a decision will be made to buy a new plant by a major customer, what would the effect be if that customer did not go ahead?
   (c) How will these assumptions be measured?
   (d) What action will you take to ensure that the adverse financial effects of an unfulfilled assumption are mitigated, so that you end up with the same forecast profit at the end of the year?
   To measure the risk, assess the negative or downside, asking what can go wrong with each assumption that would change the outcome. For example, if a market growth rate of 5% is a key assumption, what lower growth rate would have to occur before a substantially different management decision would be taken? For a capital project, this would be the point at which the project would cease to be economical.

5. Operating result and financial ratios (see Form 6 in the one-year marketing plan documentation. *Note*: This form is provided only

as an example, for, clearly, all organizations will have their own formats) – this should include:

- Net revenue
- Gross margin
- Adjustments
- Marketing costs
- Administration costs
- Interest
- Operating result
- ROS
- ROI.

6. *Key activity planner (see Form 7 in the one-year marketing plan documentation)* – finally, you should summarize the key activities and indicate the start and finish. This should help you considerably with monitoring the progress of your annual plan.

7. *Other* – there may be other information you wish to provide, such as sales call plans.

One-year marketing plan documentation

Form 1

Overall objectives

Service/market/ segment/application/ customer	Volume			Value			Gross margin			Commentary
	t − 1	t0	t + 1	t − 1	t0	t + 1	t − 1	t0	t + 1	

Form 2

Overall strategies

	Strategies	Cost
1		
2		
3		
4		
5		
6		
7		
8		
9		
10		

Comments

Form 3

Sub-objectives, strategies, actions, responsibilities, timing, cost

Service/market/ segment/application/ customer	Objective	Strategies	Action	Responsibility	Timing	Cost
Total						

Form 4

Summary of marketing activities and costs				
	t − 1	*t0*	*t + 1*	*Comments*
Depreciation				
Salaries				
Postage/telephone/stationery				
Legal and professional				
Training				
Data processing				
Advertising				
Sales promotion				
Travelling and entertainment				
Exhibitions				
Printing				
Meetings/conferences				
Market research				
Internal costs				
Other (specify)				
Total				

Form 5

Suggested downside risk assessment format

Key assumption	Basis of assumption	What event would have to happen to make this strategy unattractive?	Risk of such an event occurring (%)			Impact if event occurs	Trigger point for action	Actual contingency action proposed
			High P(7–10)	Medium P(4–6)	Low P(0–3)			

Form 6

Operating result and financial ratios			
	$t-1$	$t0$	$t+1$
Net revenue			
Gross margin			
Adjustments			
Marketing costs			
Administration costs			
Interest			
Operating result			
Other interest and financial costs			
Result after financial costs			
Net result			

Section C   Headquarters' consolidation of several SBU strategic marketing plans

The authors are frequently asked how several SBU strategic marketing plans should be consolidated by senior headquarters' marketing personnel. A suggested format for this task is provided below.

Directional statement

1. *Role/contribution* – this should be a brief statement about the company's role or contribution. Usually, it will specify a minimum growth rate in turnover and profit, but it could also encapsulate roles such as opportunity seeking service and so on.

2. *Definition of the business* – this statement should describe the needs that the company is fulfilling, or the benefits that it is providing for its markets, for example 'the provision of information to business to facilitate credit decision-making'. Usually, at the corporate level, there will be a number of definitions for its strategic business units. It is important that these statements are not too broad so as to be meaningless (e.g. 'communications' – which could mean satellites or pens) or too narrow (e.g. credit cards – which could become obsolete if a better method of fulfilling the need for credit is found).

Form 7

Key activity planner

Date/activity	Jan				Feb				March				April				May				June				July				Aug				Sept				Oct				Nov				Dec			
	1	2	3	4	1	2	3	4	1	2	3	4	1	2	3	4	1	2	3	4	1	2	3	4	1	2	3	4	1	2	3	4	1	2	3	4	1	2	3	4	1	2	3	4	1	2	3	4

3. *Distinctive competence* – all companies should have a distinctive competence. It does not have to be unique, but it must be substantial and sustainable. Distinctive competence can reside in integrity, specialist skills, technology, distribution strength, international coverage, reputation, and so on.

4. *Indications for future direction* – this section should indicate guidelines for future growth. For example, does the company wish to expand internationally, or to acquire new skills and resources? The purpose of this section is to indicate the boundaries of future business activities.

Summary of the main features of the plan

1. Here draw a portfolio matrix indicating the current and proposed relative position of each of the strategic business units. Alternatively, this can appear later in the plan.

2. Include a few words summarizing growth in turnover, profit, margins, etc.

3. Draw a graph indicating simply the total long-term plan. At least two lines are necessary – turnover and profit.

Financial history (past five years)

Include a bar chart showing the relevant financial history but, at the very least, include turnover and profit for the past five years.

Major changes and events since the previous plan

Here, describe briefly major changes and events (such as divesting a subsidiary) which occurred during the previous year.

Major issues by strategic business unit

Market characteristics
Here, it might be considered useful to provide a table listing strategic business units, alongside relevant market characteristics. For example:

	SBU1	SBU2	SBU3	SBU4
Market size				
Market growth				
Competitive intensity				
Relative market share				
etc.				

Competitive characteristics

Here, it might be considered useful to list the critical success factors by strategic business unit and rate each unit against major competitors. For example:

Critical success factors/competitors	Our company	Competitor 1	Competitor 2
CSF 1			
CSF 2			
CSF 3			
CSF 4			
CSF 5			

Key strategic issues

This is an extremely important section, as its purpose is to list (possibly by strategic business unit) what the key issues are that face the company. In essence, this really consists of stating the major strengths, weaknesses, opportunities and threats and indicating how they will be either built on or dealt with.

Key strategic issues might consist of technology, regulation, competitive moves, institutional changes, and so on.

Strategic objectives by strategic business unit and key statistics

This is a summary of the objectives of each strategic business unit. It should obviously be tailored to the specific circumstances of each company. However, an example of what might be appropriate follows:

Objectives / Strategic business unit	Market Share		Relative market share		Real growth		Key statistics				
							Sales per employee		Contribution per employee		etc.
	Now	+5 years	Now	+5 years	+5 years	p.a.	Now	+5 years	Now	+5 years	
SBU1											
SBU2											
SBU3											
SBU4											
SBU5											

Alternatively, or additionally, put a portfolio matrix indicating the current and proposed relative position of each of the strategic business units.

Financial goals (next five years)

Here, draw a bar chart (or a number of bar charts) showing the relevant financial goals. At the very least, show turnover and profit by strategic business unit for the next five years.

Appendices

Include whatever detailed appendices are appropriate. Try not to rob the total plan of focus by including too much detail.

Timetable

The major steps and timing for the annual round of strategic and operational planning are described in the following pages. The planning process is in two separate stages, which are interrelated to provide a review point prior to the detailed quantification of plans. 'Stage One' involves the statement of key and critical objectives for the full three-year planning period, to be reviewed prior to the more detailed quantification of the tactical one-year plan in 'Stage Two' by 30 November, for subsequent consolidation into the company plans.

Planning team's 'kick-off' meetings (to be completed by 31 March)

At this meeting, the planning team will outline their expectations for the following planning cycle. The purpose of the meeting is to give the planning team the opportunity to explain corporate policy, report progress during the previous planning cycle, and to give a broad indication of what is expected from each SBU during the forthcoming cycle. The planning team's review will include an overall appraisal of performance against plan, as well as a variance analysis. The briefing will give guidance under some of the following headings (as appropriate):

1. *Financial*

   - Gross margins

   - Operating profits

   - Debtors

   - Creditors

   - Cash flow.

2. *Manpower and organization*

   - Organization

   - Succession

- Training
- Remuneration.

3. *Export strategy*

4. *Marketing*

- Service development
- Target markets
- Market segments
- Volumes
- Market shares
- Pricing
- Promotion
- Marketing research
- Quality control
- Customer service.

This is an essential meeting prior to the mainstream planning activity which SBUs will subsequently engage in. It is the principal means by which it can be ensured that plans do not become stale and repetitive due to over-bureaucratization. Marketing creativity will be the key-note of this meeting.

Top-down and bottom-up planning
A cornerstone of the marketing planning philosophy is that there should be widespread understanding at all levels in the organization of the key objectives that have to be achieved, and of the key means of achieving them. This way, the actions and decisions that are taken by managers will be disciplined by clear objectives that hang logically together as part of a rational, overall purpose. The only way this will happen is if the planning system is firmly based on market-centred analysis which emanates from the SBUs themselves. Therefore, after the planning team's 'kick-off' meetings, audits should be carried out by all managers in the SBUs down to a level which will be determined by SBU managers. Each manager will also do SWOT analyses and set tentative three-year objectives and strategies, together with proposed budgets for initial consideration by their superior manager. In this way, each superior will be responsible for synthesizing the work of those managers reporting to them.

The major steps in the annual planning cycle are listed below and depicted schematically in Figure 13.3 (shown earlier as Figure 11.19).

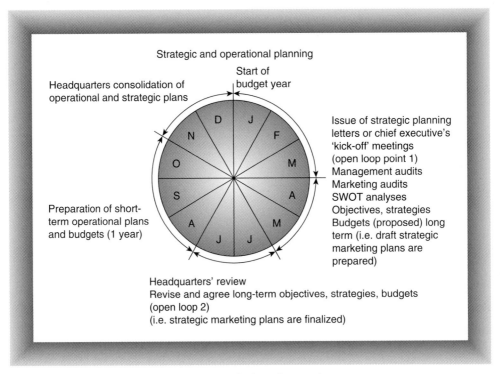

Figure 13.3 Strategic and operational planning cycle

Activity	*Deadline*
● Planning team's 'kick-off' meetings with SBU managers to discuss overall guidelines for the three-year planning period	31 March
● Prepare marketing audits, SWOT analyses, proposed marketing objectives, strategies and budgets (cover the full three-year planning horizon)	31 May
● *'Stage One'* meetings: presentation to the planning team for review	31 May
● Prepare short-term (one-year) operational plans and budgets, and final three-year SBU managers' consolidated marketing plans	31 October
● *'Stage Two'* meetings: presentation to the planning team	30 November
● Final consolidation of the marketing plans	31 December

And finally, a test to check the quality of your strategic marketing plan

This test has been developed by Brian Smith, one of the author's PhD students at Cranfield. It is the result of much in-depth research into the output of the process of strategic marketing planning. It consists of 12 tests. Please answer them honestly, otherwise there is no point in doing them.

If you get a high score, congratulations. If you get a low score, you have much work to do, but nothing that cannot be accomplished by implementing what has been written in this book.

Test 1
- Our marketing strategy makes it clear what markets or parts of the market we will concentrate our efforts on

  - If your strategy attacks all of your market sector (e.g. retail groceries, super-conducting magnets) equally $= 0$

  - If your strategy is focused by descriptor group (e.g. ABC1s, large firms, SMEs, etc.) $= 1$

  - If your strategy attacks needs-based segments (e.g. efficacy focused customers with high ego needs) $= 2$

  - If you don't know $= -1$

Test 2
- Our marketing strategy makes clear what actions fit with the marketing strategy and what do not

  - If your strategy allows complete freedom of action $= 0$

  - If your strategy allows a high degree of freedom of action $= 1$

  - If your strategy makes most of your action plan decisions for you $= 2$

  - If you don't know $= -1$

Test 3
- Our marketing strategy clearly defines our intended competitive advantage in the target market segments

  - If there is no strong and supported reason why the customer should choose you $= 0$

  - If there is a reason the customer should buy from you but no strong proof $= 1$

  - If you can state clearly the reason the customer should buy from you and not the competitor and substantiate that reason $= 2$

  - If you don't know $= -1$

Test 4
- Our marketing strategy allows synergy between the activities of the different parts of the organization

  - If the strategy is a compromise of what each department is capable of $= 0$

- If the strategy uses the strengths of only one or two departments $= 1$

- If the strategy uses the best strengths of all departments $= 2$

- If you don't know $= -1$

Test 5
● Our marketing strategy is significantly different from that of our competitors in our key market segments

- If we attack the same customers with the same value proposition $= 0$

- If we attack the same customers OR use the same value proposition $= 1$

- If we attack different customers with a different value proposition $= 2$

- If you don't know $= -1$

Test 6
● Our marketing strategy recognizes and makes full allowance for the needs and wants of our target customers

- If you only meet the basic functional needs (safety, regulation, efficacy) $= 0$

- If you also meet the higher functional needs (efficiency, service, price) $= 1$

- If you also meet the emotional and ego needs (brand, confidence) $= 2$

- If you don't know $= -1$

Test 7
● Our marketing strategy recognizes and makes full allowance for the strategies of our competitors

- If you are ignoring the competitors' strategy $= 0$

- If you are allowing for some of the competitors' strategy $= 1$

- If you are allowing for all of the competitors' strategy $= 2$

- If you don't know $= -1$

Test 8
● Our marketing strategy recognizes and makes full allowance for changes in the business environment that are beyond our control, such as technological, legislation or social change

- If your strategy is designed for today's conditions $= 1$

- If your strategy allows for one or two changes (e.g. technology or demographics) $= 1$

- If your strategy considers the combined effects of all the external factors = 2

- If you don't know = –1

Test 9
- Our marketing strategy either avoids or compensates for those areas where we are relatively weak compared to the competition

  - If you have taken little or no account of your relative weaknesses = 0

  - If you are trying to fix your relative weaknesses = 1

  - If your strategy means that your relative weaknesses don't matter = 2

  - If you don't know = –1

Test 10
- Our marketing strategy makes full use of those areas where we are relatively strong compared to the competition

  - If you have taken little or no account of your relative strengths = 0

  - If you are trying to use your relative strengths = 1

  - If your strategy means that your relative strengths become more important = 2

  - If you don't know = –1

Test 11
- Our marketing strategy, if successfully implemented, will meet all the objectives of the organization

  - If your strategy, fully and successfully implemented, does not deliver your financial or non-financial objectives = 0

  - If your strategy, fully and successfully implemented, delivers only your financial objectives = 1

  - If your strategy, fully and successfully implemented, delivers your financial and non-financial objectives = 2

  - If you don't know = –1

Test 12
- The resources available to the organization are sufficient to implement the marketing strategy successfully

  - If you have neither the tangible nor the intangible resources to implement the strategy = 0

  - If you have only the tangible or the intangible resources, but not both = 1

- If you have both the tangible and the intangible resources needed to implement the strategy = 2
- If you don't know = –1

How did you Score?

- 18–24 – Well done! (are you sure?) – Can I buy some shares?
- 12–17 – You will succeed – If your competition is weak!
- 6–11 – You will survive – If your competition is weak!
- Less than 6 – Oh dear, it was nice knowing you.

Examples of marketing plans

Introduction

The marketing plans produced here are intended solely to provide readers with a variety of ideas about the process and content of a strategic marketing plan. They are not intended to be perfect examples. Rather, they are real plans produced by real organizations struggling to produce their first serious effort to move from turgid long-range forecasts and budgets to something more sophisticated. The names and data, of course, have been changed to protect confidentiality.

We recommend that you read through all of them, as each one has its own merits (and faults). All, however, exemplify many of the processes and ideas contained in this book.

Contents

1. Alison, Hazlewood and Partners – Solicitors
2. Steadfast Design Corporation – Design and purchasing
3. Wilcox and Simmonds – Project management
4. Moritaki Computers (UK) Ltd – Computer consultancy.

Alison, Hazlewood and Partners[*]

Introduction

Alison, Hazlewood and Partners are solicitors based in the Home Counties to the west of London. The firm was started by the original Mr Alison, who later took on Hazlewood as a partner. It was run as a family business until several decades ago, when the sons of the original partners retired. Thus, despite the name, there is no longer an Alison or a Hazlewood featured among the partners.

The firm is situated in an imposing listed building, just off the high street of a thriving town, and has experienced steady, if unspectacular, growth over the years. At present there are six partners and 14 fee earners, together with the necessary back-up secretarial staff.

Like many of its contemporaries, the firm has tended to be reactive in its approach to business. Local reputation and word of mouth seemed to ensure that enough clients crossed the threshold and generated fees.

However, the turbulent times in which we live have caused the partners to reappraise whether or not the firm would remain viable by retaining such a traditional stance. The outcome of their deliberations was that the firm should have a marketing plan, something entirely new for them.

Lacking the expertise to do this themselves, they approached a consultant. What follows are, in essence, the key components that went into their strategic marketing plan.

Three-year strategic marketing plan

1. Mission statement

(a) *Definition of the business* The firm's aim is to ensure that clients are treated in an attentive and personal manner, and that their legal problems are handled speedily and accurately.

Internally, the firm aims to provide satisfying and fulfilling work for all who work here, directed to a profitable business.

(b) *Distinctive competence* We believe our ability to produce good quality work for our clients, at a reasonable price, in a friendly manner is something that sets us apart from our competitors. As firms become larger and more impersonal, our approach will become even more important.

---

[*]Alison, Hazlewood and Partners will not be found in any directory, because the name is fictitious. The real company preferred to remain anonymous, and even then in order to safeguard its identity, some of the business information has been changed from the original.

For similar purposes, fee incomes for various parts of the business are expressed as percentages rather than actual figures.

Having said this, the marketing plan which follows is an accurate representation of the diagnostic process which was used.

(c) *Indications for the future* A more business-like approach must be taken to finding new clients and winning new business. However, growth will always go hand in hand with our developing capabilities, not pursued as an end in itself.

We will invest in the development of our staff and attempt to recruit people of high calibre and potential. In doing this we will develop new competencies and thereby broaden the range of services we can offer, and boost productivity and profitability.

2. Summary of performance

(a) *Fee income* In the last year this was generated as follows:

Trusts, wills and probate	30%
Family	40%
Conveyancing	22%
Commercial	8%

More significantly, in terms of growth or decline, three years ago these business areas looked like this:

Trusts, wills and probate	36%
Family	30%
Conveyancing	30%
Commercial	4%

This shows that Trusts, wills and probate work is slightly reducing. Family is exhibiting quite substantial growth, as is Commercial. In contrast to this, Conveyancing is reflecting the downturn of the housing market.

(b) *Profitability* It is not possible to calculate the profitability of the different types of work, because systems do not exist to allocate costs with any degree of accuracy. This is something which will be addressed in the next financial year.

3. Financial projections

Average growth in recent years has been in the order of 10%. However, this was achieved by passive, evolutionary growth and is, therefore, far less than might be expected with a more focused, business-like approach.

Accordingly, financial projections over the next three years aim for a 15% growth in fee income each year.

This marketing plan will indicate how this level of growth will be achieved.

4. Market overview

(a) Segmentation of customers and markets

Clients for the products offered by the firm could be described thus:

Trusts, wills and probate	Private clients, mainly socioeconomic classes A and B.
Family	Private clients, mainly A, B, C1 and C2 classes, mainly divorce related.
Conveyancing	Private clients, mainly domestic, but some retail. Some local property developers.
Commercial	Local firms and some private clients.

From this information, clients of the firm as a whole could be summarized as follows:

1. Private clients (generally wealthy)

2. Private clients (with domestic problems)

3. Property developers

4. Local companies.

The potential for growth in fee income between these four categories varies quite significantly, and goes some way towards explaining the relative growth and decline of some parts of the business.

1. *Private clients* On the whole this group is reluctant to meet large legal bills unless their particular circumstances merit it. However, a large number of people, by dint of owning property, have a sufficiently sized estate to make it worth their while making a will. This market is unknown in size locally, but must be considerable, especially in high-value neighbourhoods.

   At another level, divorce and other family matters show no signs of being on the decrease. Indeed, more legislation, such as the Children's Bill, can provide new areas of work.

2. *Property developers* At present this group is not very productive, but if the housing market is experiencing a cyclical downturn, they could feature prominently again.

3. *Local companies* These fall into two categories:

   (i) *Successful ones* Here the work is concerned with contracts, intellectual property, and the like.

   (ii) *Unsuccessful ones* Here the work is involved in failure to meet contracts, insolvency, etc.

   While short-term growth can be expected from the latter category, the firm's long-term interests are best met by cultivating relationships with successful local companies.

5. Changes in the market

A General

(a) *The Courts and Legal Services Bill* will have an impact on the market in four ways:

   (i) Banks and building societies will be able to do conveyancing work.

(ii) Trust corporations will be allowed to do probate work.

(iii) Barristers will be able to operate from firms of solicitors.

(iv) Lawyers can defer their fees in certain cases and take an increase at the end of the case, if they are successful. (A form of payment by results.)

Of these, only item (i) is likely to impact on us. Even so, banks and building societies have yet to establish credibility in this area.

(b) *European developments* This can affect us in two main areas:

(i) Giving general advice on European law.

(ii) Legal work arising from cross-border commercial business.

This will require us to develop new expertise.

(c) *The legal industry* There is a growing tendency for large city firms to expand by acquisition or planned growth, and set up offices in strategically situated localities. Such firms can offer a wide range of services to their clients, by having specialists in all fields.

B Local

(a) It is rumoured that a small local firm is going to close on the imminent retirement of the senior partner. The only other partner is in ill-health.

We can expect to pick up a proportion of the business which at present goes to this practice.

6. SWOT Analysis on key business areas

Trusts, wills and probate

(a) Critical success factors

These are as follows:

Personal service and aftercare	(40%)
Quality of advice	(40%)
Promptness of service	(15%)
Standard of presentation of documents	(5%)

The relative importance of these factors is shown in parentheses. Comparing us with our three main competitors in our catchment area, we come out as shown. (Raw scores are given out of 10 and multiplied by the above weighting.)

	AH & P	COMP A	COMP B	COMP C
Personal service	3.6	3.6	2.0	3.2
Quality	2.8	3.6	3.2	2.8
Promptness	1.2	0.75	1.2	1.2
Presentation	0.4	0.4	0.4	0.4
	8.0	**8.35**	**6.8**	**7.6**

Using this comparison, in absolute terms we come second best to Competitor A. However, closer analysis shows that it is only on quality of advice where we fall down, something which can be remedied.

(b) *Opportunities and threats*

Apart from the obvious threat posed by needing to match Competitor A on quality of advice, other authorized practitioners will be allowed to work in this area. Opportunities centre on making other clients aware of our service and reputation. This can be achieved by cross-referral.

There is an untapped potential among those in high property value households and the elderly without wills.

(c) *Key issues to be addressed*

(i) What action is required to improve quality of advice? For example, shall we 'buy in' expertise or develop it ourselves?

(ii) What is the realistic level at which to target this sector of business so that it doesn't compete for resources from other parts of the firm?

Family

(a) Critical success factors

Most of this work centres on divorce. There are two critical factors:

(i) The client must have absolute confidence in the firm's representative (60%).

(ii) The firm must have experience and a good reputation (40%).

Again, the relative weighting of these factors is shown in brackets. In comparison with our main competitors, we emerge as shown.

	AH & P	COMP A	COMP B	COMP C
Confidence	4.8	4.2	4.8	4.2
Experience and reputation	3.2	2.8	2.8	3.2
	8.0	7.0	7.6	7.4

In overall terms we rate the best and are not surpassed on these two factors by any competitor, although some are equally as good as us on one or the other.

(b) *Opportunities and threats*

Opportunities stem from new legislation, mainly associated with the Children's Bill. Issues concerned with international marriages could also be a growth area.

The main threat is the unwillingness of private clients to meet the ever-increasing fee levels this sort of work generates.

(c) *Key issues to be addressed*

We need to take measures to increase the amount of work referred from other departments.

We need to look for means of reducing costs.

Conveyancing
(a) Critical success factors

By far the most important factor is speed, for time equals money. However, there are other factors, as shown here. Again, weightings are in parentheses.

Speed   (80%)
Quality of service   (15%)
Personalized service   (5%)

	AH & P	COMP A	COMP B	COMP C
Speed	7.2	7.2	5.6	5.6
Quality	0.9	1.2	1.35	1.2
Personalization	0.4	0.3	0.35	0.35
	8.5	**8.7**	**7.30**	**7.15**

In overall terms, we come second to Competitor A, against whom we fall down on quality. In fact, our quality score is the lowest of all the competing firms.

In contrast to this, our personalization score is the highest, and nobody actually beats us on speed.

We must improve quality.

(b) *Opportunities and threats*

The downturn of the property market is the most obvious threat, although there are some signals that an upturn might be expected.

Banks, building societies and 'other authorized practitioners' can now do conveyancing work. We will have to monitor to what extent their entry affects the market, especially in terms of the prices they charge for the service.

Opportunities exist for providing more 'insolvency advice' for hard-pressed mortgage payers. Also, cross-referencing from family clients could provide new prospects, e.g. when one partner of a divorce seeks to move to a new property.

(c) *Key issues to be addressed*

We must monitor the effect of new 'players' in this sector.

We must cross-reference prospective clients.

We must get a more accurate assessment of how many conveyances can be expected in the local market, thereby gaining insights about our market share.

Commercial

(a) Critical success factors

The overriding priority in this sector is high-quality service and having equally high-quality staff. However, other factors also come into play, as shown below, and they are weighted accordingly:

High-quality service	(30%)
Highly competent staff	(30%)
Speed of service	(15%)
Price/value for money	(15%)
Location (accessibility)	(5%)
Flexibility/capacity	(5%)

	AH & P	*COMP A*	*COMP B*	*COMP C*
Quality	2.1	2.7	2.1	2.4
Staff	2.1	2.7	2.1	2.4
Speed	1.2	1.2	1.2	1.2
Price	0.9	1.2	0.9	1.2
Location	0.5	0.4	0.5	0.4
Flexibility	0.3	0.5	0.3	0.4
	7.1	**8.7**	**7.1**	**8.0**

We do not compare favourably with our main competitors. We are not sufficiently professional in terms of the quality of work and staff, nor do we have the flexibility/capacity to respond to sudden and unusual requests.

However, we are favourably located and easy to reach, and the speed of our work is not bettered.

(b) *Opportunities and threats*

The main threat stems from potential clients going to larger, more commercially oriented firms. However, to offset this, there are advantages in having local, readily accessible advice – if the quality is right.

Another opportunity is the wider recognition of clients of the potential pitfalls associated with the opening of European markets, and the all-pervading EU law.

(c) *Issues to be addressed*

This work has just evolved in the past and no serious attempt has been made to develop the expertise and capacity, or to make our capabilities known to local industry and commerce. We should be clearer about what we offer, and to whom.

Even within individual client companies, there are different legal requirements according their different functional departments.

For example:

Functional area	Legal requirements
Finance	Capital and project finance deals
	Corporate tax
Marketing	Property leasing
	Covenants
	Franchise agreements
Product development	Intellectual property (patents and copyright)
Purchasing	Contractual arrangements
Production	Employment issues
	Safety legislation
	Environmental issues
	Compliance
Distribution	Contracts
	Consumer protection

In addition to these, there are legal requirements associated with diversification, mergers and acquisitions, and international trading.

This wide diversity of potential legal requirements poses additional problems, in terms of:

(i) Should we focus on just one or two legal areas and attempt to develop a reputation as local 'specialists'?
  or

(ii) Should we exploit all of our commercial contracts and try to broaden our areas of contact in each one, i.e. become something of a 'one-stop legal shop'?

Either decision can have far-reaching consequences for the way this part of the firm develops.

7. Product portfolio and directional strategy

Considering the firm's main business areas in terms of how they match up with its relative strengths and market attractiveness, it is possible to construct a directional policy matrix as shown below.

The factors which were taken into account in calculating the positions on the matrix are as follows:

● Relative business strengths

 – Reputation/successful track record

 – Quality of staff

 – Capacity

 – Personalization of service

- Market attractiveness

  - Prospects for continued growth

  - Not unduly price sensitive

  - Geographically close

  - Lacking own legal expertise.

The reasons for the projected trends come out of the SWOT analysis:

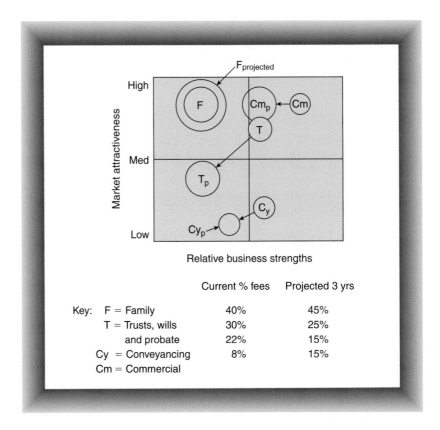

Key:		Current % fees	Projected 3 yrs
F = Family		40%	45%
T = Trusts, wills		30%	25%
and probate		22%	15%
Cy = Conveyancing		8%	15%
Cm = Commercial			

Family	Still a growth area, especially with more proactive stance.
Trusts, wills and probates	Competition from 'authorized practitioners' makes it less attractive.
Conveyancing	Depressed housing market and competition from banks and building societies make the market less attractive.
Commercial	Proactive stance plus improved capability should improve our business strengths.

In terms of generating funds, the directional policy matrix indicates that Conveyancing and Trusts, Wills and Probate will need to be 'milked' to finance expansion of Commercial business.

Family will also need some investment, but will be largely self-financing.

8. Marketing stance and objectives

Broadly speaking, our marketing objectives are concerned with what products/services go to which clients. Therefore, the options open to us can be represented by the following diagram:

Using this framework:

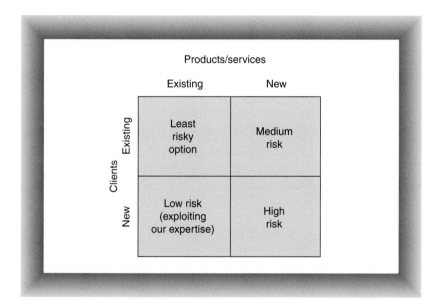

Trusts, wills and probate   Existing services to existing and new clients
Family   Existing services to existing and new clients
Conveyancing   Existing services to mainly new clients
Commercial (mixture of)   Existing services to new clients and new
                            services to existing clients.

Thus, overall, our marketing objectives do not entail high levels of risk, except for part of the commercial business. However, since this is a relatively new area for the firm, some experimentation, hence risk, is only to be expected. Our safeguard here is the analysis we have applied to this sector, which ensures that our stance is as realistic as possible.

Overall, the objective is to increase fee income by 15% p.a. for the next three years.

Taking the business sector by sector, here is a more detailed record of what we aim to achieve.

(a) Trusts, wills and probate

Objectives — To manage the sector so that it is contributing 25% of fee income in three years' time. This represents an 8% increase from the current level in real terms.

Assumptions — There will be no significant changes in either legislation or competition, other than that already mentioned earlier.

Strategy — To gain clients from those who are already using other services of the firm. This will require a selective analysis of clients in order to identify the 'right' ones.

To redesign the brochure for this service, emphasizing client benefits. Have copies prominently displayed in reception.

To contribute articles, advice columns, etc. to local newspapers as a means of advertising.

To distribute brochures to local accountants and financial advisers so that they can recommend us.

To develop/reinforce staff in order to improve the quality of our advice, and hence our competitive position.

(b) Family

Objectives — To manage this sector so that it is contributing 45% of fee income in three years' time. In real terms, this means a 28% increase on today's income.

Assumptions — No significant players enter the local market over the strategic time-frame.

Strategy — Keep fees at the lower end of the competitive range for divorce matters by reducing costs. This means increasing the number of clients as the main means of increasing income.

This will be achieved by:

(i) Encouraging satisfied clients to recommend us
(ii) Local advertising
(iii) Increasing and publicizing our ability to handle new children's legislation
(iv) Maintaining our differential advantage over competing firms. High fees can be charged for this new children's legislation.

(c) Conveyancing

Objectives — To manage this sector so that it contributes 15% of total fee income in three years' time. With the targeted growth of 15% p.a. overall, this means that, in real terms, fee income has to be maintained at its current level.

Assumptions	That the recession in the housing market has bottomed out and will not get worse. Also, that some business will be taken by banks and building societies.
Strategy	To cross-reference suitable clients who are using other services.
	To develop/maintain good relationships with local builders and estate agents.
	To charge fees at the top end of the competitive range.

To advertise in local newspapers at a modest level.

(d) Commercial

Objectives	To manage this sector so that it contributes 15% of total fee income in three years' time. In real terms, that means that this sector has to increase 23% on the current level.
Assumptions	None of our immediate competitors will develop faster than ourselves. Large commercial law firms will concentrate on high potential earning jobs (which would be too big for us).
Strategy	To target our marketing effort on all small to medium-sized commercial organizations that are successful, within easy reach, and have no 'in-house' legal expertise.
	To gain introductions by running half-day seminars about pertinent legal issues.
	To develop a brochure and good quality supporting promotional material.
	To use cross-referrals from clients using our other services.
	To price very competitively to win initial assignments, and then to exploit contacts and other departments in client companies to acquire additional work.

Footnotes

1. Information systems

   In order to enable cross-referencing and analysis of existing clients to take place, our internal systems need to be modified.

   Equally, in order to control costs, it is important to know exactly how staff allocate their time. This means setting up an effective management control system.

   Both of these initiatives should begin as soon as possible.

2. Review

As this is our first attempt at producing a marketing plan, it is essential that progress after the first year is reviewed critically, and any deviations from the expected are analysed and understood.

By building in such a rigorous review procedure, our future planning will become increasingly accurate.

Steadfast Design Corporation

Background information

SDC is a long-established and successful company providing design and purchasing services, mainly to the building industry. It operates in five main building markets: Industrial, Offices, Retail, Private residential and Leisure (sports centres and hotels).

The company originated in the Midlands and has a head office in Birmingham. However, it operates throughout the mainland UK and has regional offices in Birmingham (Midlands and Wales), Stockport (North and Scotland) and Basingstoke (South).

Due to the nature of the business, SDC deals with a wide range of customers, including large public limited companies, banks, building societies, pension funds, local authorities and housing associations.

The company has long been interested in marketing and many of the senior managers have attended courses at Cranfield. Although, traditionally, the building and associated trades and service providers have not been noted for innovation in management thinking, SDC is striving to be an exception to this rule.

What follows is the company marketing plan for the next three years.

Executive summary

1. Financial targets

Year	Income (£m)	Expenditure (£m)	Profit (£m)	Income growth over previous year (%)	Profit growth over previous year (%)
Current	84.00	71.40	12.60	46.1	85.3
11	112.90	95.70	17.20	34.4	36.5
12	132.20	109.40	22.60	16.9	31.4
13	162.60	132.30	30.30	23.2	34.1

2. Analysis of customer base

Customer survey	Highly compatible + good business potential (%)	Highly compatible + low business potential (%)	Not very compatible + high business potential (%)	Low compatibility + low business potential (%)	No repeat business (%)
Last year	27	27	5	18	23
Current year	36	28.5	7.5	16	12

This illustrates the beginning of a favourable trend towards having more customers who are compatible and who have good business potential.

However, there must be an effort made to reappraise those customers who are not compatible or who have low business potential in terms of whether they are still worth cultivating or whether they should be allowed to drop from our portfolio.

The reduction in 'no repeat business' is in line with what we hoped to achieve.

3. Regional trends

	Southern (%)	Midland (%)	North and Scotland (%)
National last year	49.5	30.7	19.8
National current year	52.5	29.5	18.0
Relative change	13.0	21.2	21.8
SDC last year	38.0	35.0	27.0
SDC current year	42.5	30.0	27.5
Relative change	14.5	25.0	10.5

This table shows that in the Southern Region we are increasing our share of the business at a faster rate than the national trend. This is true also for the Northern Region. However, in our traditional stronghold, the Midlands, we seem to be doing less well.

4. Analysis

Full details are included in the report but probably the most noteworthy elements are as follows:

Strengths

(a) The size and status of the company

(b) The quality of our staff

(c) Our willingness to innovate (both technically and managerially).

Weaknesses

(a) We have yet to match the company to many of the potential high business potential customers

(b) Continued growth is bringing with it communication problems and a danger that our high standards might be compromised.

Opportunities

(a) Buy out some small quality builders who are strategically placed to improve our national coverage

(b) Government preparedness to increase public spending

(c) EU deregulation.

Threats

(a) Ability to keep key personnel and/or get adequately skilled recruits

(b) Increased marketing sophistication by competitors

(c) EU deregulation

(d) The national economy goes into deep recession.

5. *Major objectives over next three years*

(a) Increase turnover

(b) Improve profitability

(c) Continue to broaden customer base so that no single customer in any market accounts for more than 20% of the turnover

(d) Maintain high standards of ethics in all our business transactions

(e) Maintain a level of social responsibility in all the building projects we undertake.

6. *General progress*

The company is moving along the right lines and is stronger than it was a year ago. Broadly speaking, our last year's marketing plan was achieved and brought with it the benefits we anticipated.

However, there is no room for complacency. We really need to have more information about our competitors and their activities. We need to explore the potential of new markets. The EU deregulation can be a two-edged sword; it can bring both opportunities and threats. Above all, if the economy should be depressed for too long, the challenge for all of us at SDC to meet our targets will be considerable.

Introduction

This Corporate Marketing Plan incorporates all three operational regions' activities and has been compiled with their assistance.

The layout of this plan is as follows:

Section 1   Situation review

Section 2   SWOT analysis

Section 3   Assumptions

Section 4   Marketing objectives and strategies

Section 5   Alternative plans and mixes

Section 6   Targets and programmes

Section 1 Situation review

We deal with five different 'business sectors'

- Industrial building
- Office building
- Retail
- Private residential
- Leisure

1. Relative market share

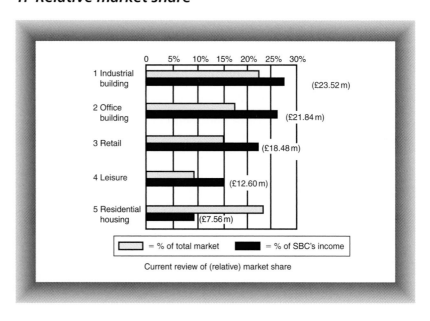

Current review of (relative) market share

Conclusion

Our relative market share (in terms of income) is greater than that for each sector of the building industry as a whole, except for Residential housing.

This can be explained because much of the residential building has been on small sites which are uneconomical for us.

The actual revenue figures are shown in parentheses. Total income was £84 m.

2. *Characteristics of these business sectors*

- Industrial building

    There is considerable growth in medium to small industrial parks in the south-east and in areas where heavy industry has declined. Also many old industrial buildings are unsuitable for high technology industries. Prospects look good in this sector.

- Office building

    In most urban renewal schemes there is considerable scope for office building. Also, property developers can tap cash-rich pension funds and investment houses. Good prospect area.

- Retail

    This has been a considerable growth area, with the popularity of shopping precincts either in or out of towns. Possibility of growth slowing down as major retail chains rethink their strategies for a period of high interest rates.

- Leisure

    There is still reckoned to be a shortfall in hotel rooms for business and tourism needs. Similarly, more health and recreation centres are required to meet fitness lifestyle needs, either provided by private funding or local authorities.

- Residential housing

    Demand for first-time housing is high, but greenfield development opportunities are reducing in those areas with growth potential. We need large projects to separate ourselves from small local suppliers who could not tackle anything on such a scale. This business sector is beginning to look less attractive unless we position ourselves more creatively by redefining our market.

3. Income

Business sector	Last year (£)	Current year (£)	% change
Industrial	12.40 m	23.52 m	190
Office	12.20 m	21.84 m	179
Retail	15.00 m	18.48 m	123
Leisure	9.60 m	12.60 m	131
Residential	8.30 m	7.56 m	29
Total	**57.50 m**	**84.00 m**	146

Conclusion

Our income per sector, comparing last year with the current year, confirms our subjective analysis of the characteristics of each of our markets.

4. Distribution of Income

Analysis of our current year shows that our customer base of 260 contributed to our income as follows:

% customers	10	20	30	40	50	60	70	80	90	100
Cumulative income	58.3	74.5	83.6	89.6	93.7	96.3	98.0	99.1	99.8	100
Income per % of customers	58.3	16.2	9.1	6.0	4.1	2.6	1.7	1.1	0.7	0.2
Grade		A	B	C		D			E	

This approximates to the conventional Pareto distribution, with our 20% largest customers accounting for 74.5% of our income.

The customer grading bounds are somewhat arbitrary but make it possible to extract more useful data in the customer matrix analysis which follows.

5. Customer matrix

The customer matrix was designed around two dimensions, compatibility with our business and business potential. Each customer was allocated scores using these criteria.

- Compatibility

Quality of our relationship with customer	0–3 points (for very good)
Needs complete range of services	0–3 points
Low sensitivity to price	0–2 points
Needs high quality	0–2 points
	–
	10 points max.

- Business potential

Customer's business is showing average to high growth	0–3 points
Potential for further business	0–3 points
Potential for high profit projects	0–4 points
	–
	10 points max.

Looking at the Total Business

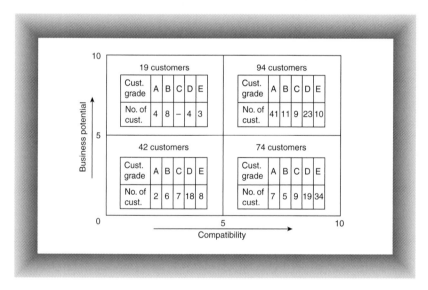

Note: Of the customer base of 260, 31 no-repeat business clients were eliminated from the matrix. The breakdown of these companies by customer grading is:

Customer grade	A	B	C	D	E
No. of customers	–	1	1	12	17

Conclusion

This high compatibility/high business potential quadrant of the matrix contains 76% of Grade A customers, 35% of Grade B and 35% of Grade C.

In contrast, the no-repeat business group was predominantly Grades D and E.

Both of these results are consistent with our previous marketing objectives.

6. *Regional breakdown of customer matrix*

(i) Southern

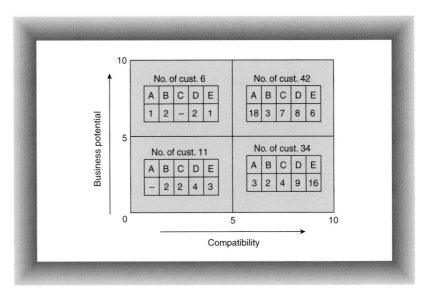

(ii) Midlands

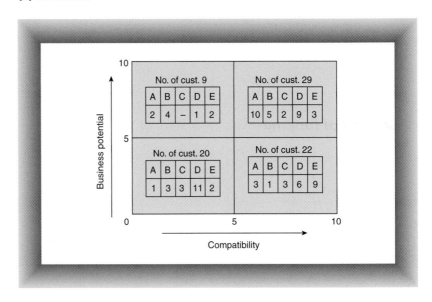

(iii) Northern

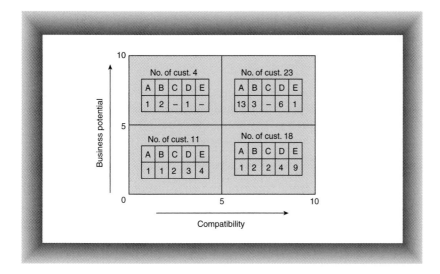

Conclusion

Each region will need to take steps to reduce the number of customers in the low/low quadrant and to increase those in the high/high quadrant. Also in this quadrant: work on B, C, D and Es to win larger contracts where possible.

For high business potential/low compatibility, eliminate the Es and consider how we might adapt our offer to other grades and achieve better matching.

For low business potential/high compatibility, reduce the number of D and E grades and offer consultancy to improve business potential of A and B customers.

7. Sources of funding

Source	As % of total income	
	Last year	Current year
Owner-occupied, industrial	33	20
Owner-occupied, non-industrial	7	18
Public sector	3.5	21
Pension and investment funds	42.5	34
Developers	14	7
	100	100

Conclusion

The biggest increases are in public sector spending and owner-occupied non-industrial projects, with an apparent slowdown in other areas.

8. Environmental review

- The economy

- The current balance of payments deficit and the high interest strategy to remedy the situation are sending ripples throughout the economy. Nevertheless, assuming the situation does not deteriorate further, there are some positive signs:

  - Public spending is on the increase again.

  - Work on the infrastructure and urban renewal is being given high priority.

  - There is still a high demand for leisure facilities and from tourism.

  - Foreign companies are coming to the UK and wanting custom-built premises.

  - There is pressure on government to invest more in industry and adopt a regional policy.

  - Forecasts for industrial and commercial premises still show an upward trend, as do those for retail premises in the Southern Region.

- Technology

  There is a continued growth in Design and Build and a requirement for fast-build techniques.

  Computerized inventory control and procurement systems should make our operations even more efficient.

  New materials and techniques will have to be continually monitored.

- Competition

  Our two nearest competitors are going through a transitionary period and are reorganizing themselves. While this currently acts in our favour, they are likely to re-emerge in a more competitive shape.

  There is a danger if there is a substantial downturn in the economy that a 'price war' will start as everyone scrambles for the little business that would be available. We need contingency plans for such an eventuality, or a refocusing of our corporate objectives.

  Overall we do not know very much about our competitors and their marketing strategies. We have been too busy getting our own house in order. This situation will need to be redressed.

  EU deregulation might present us with new competitors.

Section SWOT analysis

Strengths

- Size and status of the company
- Our experience and track record
- National coverage
- Quality we provide
- Quality of our staff
- Willingness to innovate
- Relationships with customers
- Improved marketing skills
- Computerized services

Weaknesses

- Coordination between regional offices
- We deal with too many 'mismatched' customers
- Shortage of some key skill
- Inconsistent quality standards
- Inexperience of new recruits

Opportunities

- Increase in public spending
- Buy out other builders
- Use some of our services, e.g. quantity surveying, as a separate profit centre
- Extend regional coverage in south with new office
- Investigate new markets, e.g. private hospitals
- Make better use of our computer systems
- EU deregulation
- Look for a partner on mainland Europe

Threats

- Downturn of the economy
- Loss of key personnel
- Problems in recruiting right calibre people
- EU deregulation
- Material shortages
- Revitalized and more sophisticated competitors
- Continued growth will stretch us too far and lead to inefficiencies
- Changes in key market segments
- Environmental lobby makes it more difficult to get land and/or planning permission

Section 3 Assumptions

Three main assumptions have been made as a backdrop to the thinking behind this plan.

1. The economy will not go into deep recession.

2. We maintain a similar organizational structure over most of the next three years.

3. Any new EU competitor will not make a significant impact in the period under consideration.

Section 4 Marketing objectives and strategies

Objectives	Strategies
1. Increase turnover by the amounts shown in Section 6	Increase market penetration and customer base Target new customers more accurately Work to develop more business from existing high potential customers Actively market our specific competences Acquire three small existing businesses

Note: As a safeguard, no one customer in any segment is to account for more than 20% of turnover.

2. Improve profitability by the amounts shown in Section 6	Eliminate 'mismatched' unprofitable customers from the portfolio and concentrate efforts on those with high business potential Improve inventory control and logistics

Other objectives and strategies

3. Maintain a high level of social responsibility	Respond to contacts from schools regarding careers talks, etc. Support local charities, etc. Maintain safe working practices Each region to have someone to keep abreast of local environmental issues
4. Maintain a high standard of ethics in all our transactions	An internal 'code of practice' to be developed A video to be made to explain to staff why the directors see this as such an important issue

| 5. Keep one step ahead | Explore potential of new markets, e.g. hospitals
Examine prospects of EU deregulation and/or partnership with Euro-company
Explore more attractive employment 'packages' to attract new and keep existing staff |

Section 5 plans and mixes

1. The time is coming for each region to become an individual profit centre and be responsible for its own marketing plan, rather than being controlled and compiled centrally. However, it is probable that there is not enough marketing expertise throughout the organization to allow that to happen yet.

   Nevertheless, this should be considered as a longer-term organizational goal to guide our short-term thinking.

2. Another possibility was to exploit the profit potential of some of our internal services, e.g. quantity surveying, computer applications to the construction industry, project management, etc.

   However, this development was shelved temporarily, for two main reasons:

   (a) With our relatively rapid growth rate, it is probably helpful if we consolidate as opposed to diversifying and perhaps putting additional pressures on our hard-pressed organization.

   (b) Such a move might compromise the eventual move of making the regions more autonomous.

3. If the economy goes into a deep recession then much of this marketing plan will have to be reviewed, particularly our growth targets.

Section 6 targets and programmes

1. Financial targets

Southern

Year	Income (£m)	Expenditure (£m)	Profit (£m)
Current	35.50	30.10	5.40
11	48.55	41.25	7.30
12	56.80	47.08	9.72
13	69.90	56.90	13.00

Midlands

Year	Income (£m)	Expenditure (£m)	Profit (£m)
Current	22.40	19.10	3.30
11	29.35	24.85	4.50
12	34.40	28.52	5.88
13	42.30	34.40	7.90

Northern

Year	Income (£m)	Expenditure (£m)	Profit (£m)
Current	26.10	22.20	3.90
11	35.10	29.80	5.30
12	41.00	34.00	7.00
13	50.40	41.00	9.40

2. Customer base

Targets to be achieved over three-year period:

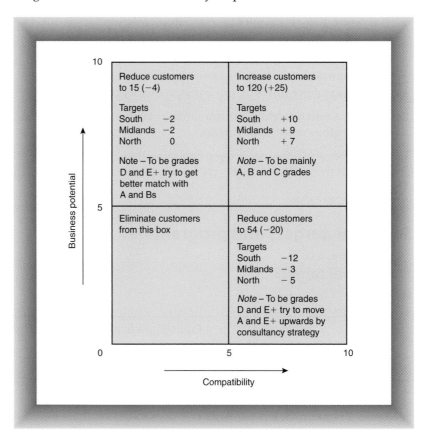

Note: New customers should be selected using the criteria upon which the customer matrix was based (Section 1.5). While these criteria are not meant to override local knowledge, regions will have to present a good case for accepting customers who do not meet them.

3. Advertising and promotion

This will be at the discretion of each regional manager, consistent with the targets and budgets he or she is allowed.

4. Pricing

Our policy of providing high-quality services and pleasing and functional design, plus our reputation of completing projects on time, vindicates our strategy to price at the top end of the market.

Wilcox and Simmonds Project Management Ltd

Introduction

Wilcox and Simmonds have a long and, on the whole, distinguished record of supplying the UK construction industry with a range of specialist goods and services.

The Project Management Division was recently set up to run as an autonomous unit to provide project management services to the construction industry, something which is a relatively new idea in this business sector.

Project management originally developed in the heavy, civil and process engineering industries. It involves taking the responsibility for the overall planning, control and coordination of a project from inception to completion, with the objective of meeting the client's requirements of achieving completion on time, within the target cost and to the required quality standards.

During a construction project a whole range of functional specialists might get involved. Typically these would be architects, structural engineers, service engineers, quantity surveyors and building contractors. Very large projects might also include town planners and civil engineers.

The project manager's task can be to recommend those who can fulfil these roles, or to work with those of the client's choice. Essentially the project manager becomes the 'hub' of a network of interrelated activities, the output of which is dictated by his or her budgetary planning skills and ability to influence and cajole everyone to deliver their particular contribution at the required time.

The key benefit for the client is that all progress can be monitored through one person. Equally, if things are going wrong, there is again only one person to deal with. Although a client company might have a department capable in theory to tackle such work, in practice there is often not the required wide range of expertise and experience to sustain the project management role.

Thus the UK construction industry, with its tradition of separating design from construction, and its propensity for developing managers as functional specialists, appeared to be a suitable candidate for an overall, project management approach. It was this opportunity which spurred the company to set up its new division.

So new is project management in the building industry that its role is not yet fully accepted, nor is there an established pricing structure.

It is against this background that the chief executive and his team prepare for the next three years, following an eventful and quite successful first year in business. What follows is the business plan produced by the Project Management Division.

In order to protect identity, all names, locations and values have been changed. However, the integrity of the company's planning process still remains to provide an interesting example of business planning from which we can all learn.

1. Review of first full year's trading

Although financial targets were met, a substantial amount of time was devoted to setting up and staffing our three offices. In addition it was difficult to recruit staff experienced in both project management and the construction industry, therefore a considerable amount of training had to be provided.

However, we now have an administrative base, the personnel and technical procedures. This means that project managers can start to focus on building up the business in a planned and sustained way, rather than chasing work as and when opportunities present themselves.

Financial

	£000	
	Budget	*Actual*
Income	2,352	2,573
Expenditure	1,970	2,052
Profit	*382*	*521*

Personnel

	Actual	Deviation from plan
Professional staff		
Croydon	13	23
Coventry	14	0
Manchester	5	0
Administrative		
Croydon	7	11
Coventry	5	21
Manchester	1	0
Total	**45**	

Analysis of profit

	Turnover (£)	Profit (£)
Project management	1,750,000	250,000
Construction management	860,000	271,000
Total	521,000	

2. Mission statement

Our review of our first year has not caused us to be swayed from our original statement of intent:

To become the leading company supplying project management within the construction industry.

We will achieve this by:

● Establishing a reputation for quality and successful completions

● Having the largest market share

● Being the first choice of clients seeking project management

● Being the first choice of the best candidates in the job market.

Above all, we must be clear about what we are striving to achieve at a time when there are many potential opportunities in the market place.

We believe a key to success is to break our organization into strategic business units.

3. Financial projections

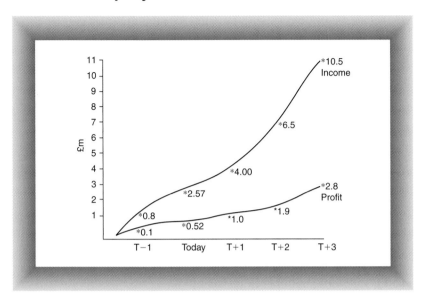

4. Market overview

Competition

There are probably at most only about 40 companies set up to offer a similar service to ours. Of these companies we are one of the largest, in terms of project managers employed.

However, there are a number of other types of competitors who partially compete with us by offering a reduced range of services. These companies fall into the following broad categories:

Organization category	Services
1. Management consultants These are often parts of major accounting firms	Specialist advice, feasibility studies
2. Management contractors Usually parts of large building contractors	Management of site work, little involvement in design
3. Civil engineering contractors (with project management depts)	Tend to stay in civil engineering. Also undertake feasibility studies

| 4. Quantity surveyors with PM depts | Tend to limit their role to providing ongoing information at meetings, etc. Some duplicate the work of building contractors |
| 5. PM depts of client companies | Do not have the all-round expertise to compete with us on quality. |

Market trends

The construction industry is a very large, if fragmented, overall market. Over the last ten years it has grown steadily at an average rate of approximately 5.5%.

The project management market we estimate to have a potential value of £120 m. Our current market share of this is 2.1%.

However, we believe there will be a rapid increase in sales of project management for a number of reasons:

- More clients will perceive the need for it as it becomes increasingly accepted in the industry.
- Clients seek new solutions to improve their performance.
- The rate of change in building technology makes project management ever more complex and difficult for those not trained in it (the majority of construction managers).
- Architects are failing to fulfil clients' needs in terms of providing value-for-money solutions.
- There is increasing pressure to shorten the inception-to-completion time-span.

Market structure

There are two driving forces for the construction industry:

1. Property developers and investors who create facilities for sale or lease

   Included in this category are insurance companies, banks, pension funds, investment companies.

2. Property occupiers who create facilities for their own use

   In this category are firms from the private sector, such as manufacturing, retailing, distribution and leisure. There is also a sizeable public sector which includes government ministries, local authorities, public utilities, public transport and health authorities.

Strategic business units

It would make sense to manage our business through five specific business units:

1. Regional project management

   Managing medium-to-large projects (ideally over £250,000 construction turnover per month) in all principal markets.

2. Construction management

   Managing fast-track, complex projects (ideally over £1 m construction turnover per month) which require a site-based construction team. This SBU would focus on commercial owner-occupier/developers in the south-east.

3. Special projects

   A design and management service to small building projects, operating mainly in the developer, pension fund, owner-occupier markets.

4. Manufacturing process projects

   Managing manufacturing plants, machinery installations and associated commercial buildings. The principal markets will be industrial and warehousing.

5. Major Projects

   Projects which require a dedicated team and are likely to be in the order of £2 m construction turnover per month. The initial market to be targeted will be investor/developer, although this unit will operate in all principal markets.

   Note: SBUs 4 and 5 will not come on-stream for another year.

Ansoff matrix

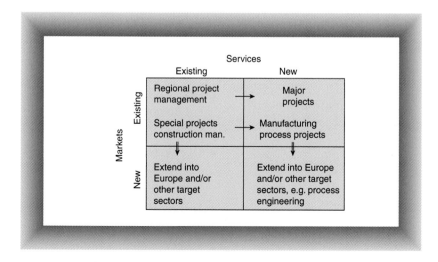

Gap analysis

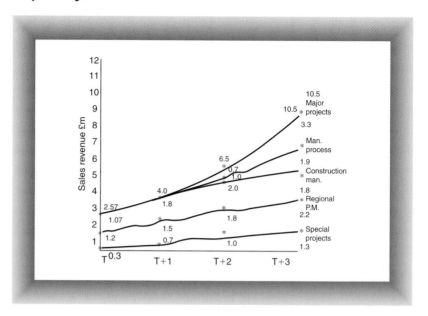

5. SWOT analysis

The following analysis holds true for all the SBUs:

Strengths

- Reputation of W & S in the construction industry in general

- Regional representation in growth areas of UK economy

- High expertise in PM of staff

- One of the largest companies

- Now have a business plan

- Wealth of contacts in the industry via W & S

- Starting with a 'clean sheet' and can get it right from the start.

Weaknesses

- Training of new staff needs to be improved, both in quality and duration (too long)

- Lack of detailed market information

- Need more/better promotional material

- We have made mistakes in recruiting PMs. Some do not fit our 'culture'. More attention to selection and better employment package required

- PMs are excellent individuals but do not yet function well in teams

- To date we have been chasing any work just to meet targets and have not been focused

- Technical procedures still need to be improved

- Need to establish unique selling points/selling skills.

Opportunities
- PM is in its infancy in the construction industry
- Large potential market
- Expand by acquisition if necessary
- Joint ventures, in UK and Europe
- Traditional structure of construction industry lends itself to PM
- Few serious competitors at present.

Threats
- Interest rates increase even higher, and trigger off a recession
- Entry of new competitors
- Large contractors develop their own PM depts
- Inability to recruit sufficiently high calibre staff to sustain growth
- PM does not really 'catch on' in the the construction industry.

6. Critical success factors

Regional project management

CSF	Weighting	Score vs competition	Total
1. Staff are perceived by clients as highly professional	3	5	15
2. We provide value for money	2	6	12
3. Our corporate reputation and track record	2	8	16
4. Staff are motivated to win business	3	5	15
	(10)	(out of 10)	**58/100**

Issues to be Addressed
1. Improve professionalism and motivation of staff, by training and better field management.
2. Improve service surround to provide better value for money.

Construction management

CSF	Weighting	Score vs competition	Total
1. Early identification of opportunity	3	7	21
2. Demonstrate knowledge of client's business	2	8	16
3. High level of PM consultant teamwork	2	4	8
4. Value for money	2	6	12
5. Track record	1	7	7
	(10)	(out of 10)	**64/100**

Issues to be Addressed

1. Improve consultant teamwork.

2. Look for ways to offer more value for money.

Special projects

CSF	Weighting	Score vs competition	Total
1. Close contact with clients	1	6	6
2. Demonstration of early success	3	6	18
3. Flexibility to adapt to changing client needs	3	8	24
4. Value for money	2	8	16
5. Track record	1	6	6
	(10)	(out of 10)	**70/100**

Issues to be Addressed

1. Improve contact with clients – establish schedules.

2. Improve and publicize track record.

3. Reappraise staffing levels at front end of projects in order to develop more momentum and hence quicker results.

Manufacturing process projects

CSF	Weighting	Score vs competition	Total
1. Early identification of opportunity	3	5	15
2. Can 'talk clients' language'	4	5	20
3. Value for money	2	8	16
4. Track record	1	7	7
	(10)	(out of 10)	**58/100**

Issues to be Addressed

1. Improve intelligence sources.

2. Develop more expertise about client business through recruiting people with different appropriate career backgrounds *or* buy out a suitable company to gain right expertise.

Major projects

CSF	Weighting	Score vs competition	Total
1. Dedicated team of high quality	3	6	18
2. Value for money	2	7	14
3. Swift evidence of impact of services	2	7	14
4. Early identification of opportunity	3	5	15
	(10)	(out of 10)	**61/100**

Issues to be Addressed

1. Improve market intelligence.

2. Develop teamwork.

3. Look for ways of demonstrating quick paybacks to client.

7. Assumptions

Underlying all of the foregoing analysis were the following assumptions:

1. The growth rate of the construction industry will continue at its average rate of the last few years (1%).

2. Interest rates will not go any higher.

3. Investor confidence stays reasonably buoyant in the short and medium term.

4. There is a continuing growth in the demand for project management.

5. A change of government (should it happen) will not lead to a significant change in the economic prospects of the construction industry.

8. Portfolio analysis

Within Regional project management it was possible to break down the current and potential business in terms of our competence in dealing with key market segments and their attractiveness. The results are shown here. It is intended to develop this type of analysis for each SBU as data becomes available.

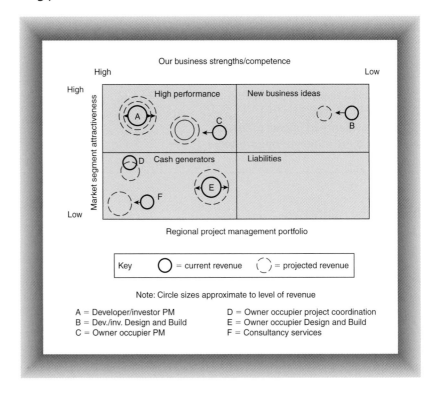

Overall comment

The portfolio is reasonably well balanced at present. There are no services in the liabilities quadrant. We will need to start thinking about another new business idea fairly soon in order to keep a 'flow' going. We need more revenue from existing cash generators so that we can invest in the high performers and new business ideas. The implications are that we review our pricing and look at ways of saving on costs.

9. Marketing objectives and strategies

To increase from £2.57 m to £10.5 m over the next three years, while at the same time growing net profits from £0.52 m to £2.8 m. This will come from the following:

Existing business

1. Regional project management

   To increase income from £1.2 m to £2.2 m over the next three years.

   To increase average project size by 25% over that period.

Each project manager to start two new projects per year.

Opening of new regional offices or acquisition of existing company will be reviewed throughout the planning period.

2. Construction management

   To increase income from £1.07 m to £1.8 m over the next three years.

   Focusing on commercial owner-occupiers and developers in the south-east.

   One additional project required each year over the total managed in previous year. Average project value to increase by 10% per annum minimum.

3. Special projects

   To increase income from £0.3 m to £1.3 m over the next three years.

   Treble the number of contacts made with potential clients each year and improve conversion rate by 25%.

   Average contract value to increase by 10% per annum minimum.

New business

4. Manufacturing process projects

   To initiate the business by $t - 1$ and to earn revenue of £1.9 m over the next two years.

   Focus on small to medium-sized projects in order to gain quick results and demonstrate a track record.

5. Major projects

   Starting in $t - 1$, to earn revenue of £3.3 m over the next two years.

   Focus on developers and investors.

   Look for opportunities in public sector.

Long-term strategies beyond the three-year plan

Build on the expertise we will have developed in terms of planning procedures, systems, quality procedures and staff to lead into new growth market segments. These are likely to be:

- Large design and build projects (UK and Europe)
- Direct development of property (UK and Europe)
- Major manufacturing process projects (worldwide).

Marketing strategies (i.e. the marketing mix)

	Regional project management	*Construction management*	*Special projects*	*Manufacturing process projects*	*Major projects*
Market share	Increase	Increase	Increase	Establish	Establish
Promotion	Rely on face-to-face selling skills and developing good personal relationships with clients. Indirect promotion will focus on press releases about success stories, articles in journals and presentations at conferences, etc. Any promotional material will have to be high quality, and consistent with our image				
Price	High end of range	High end of range	High end of range	Competitive for entry	Competitive for entry
Product	Increase product surround and provide added value for money			Experiment with 'most acceptable' product	
Place	Regional representation will be provided whenever possible to establish closeness to clients. This might entail opening new offices in the UK and Europe				
Developments	Develop USPs re value management. Establish better data re costs and prices	Consider use of joint venture approach with suitable partners	Develop USPs re value management	Maximize profile with suitable launch. Sales campaigns into target industries	Maximize profile with suitable launch. Consider acquisition strategy from early days

Note: Ideas for developing value management are attached (Appendix A) and criteria for acquisition are provided (Appendix B).

Appendix A Developing value management

The project manager's task is twofold: to manage the physical construction chain and to manage the value-added chain.

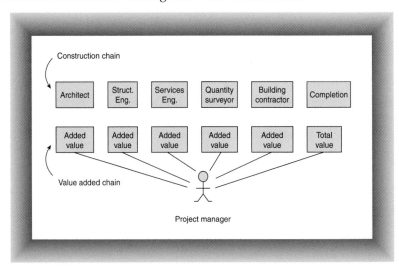

It is not from the completion of the project that we earn anything. It is the *total added value* from which we earn our profits and reputation.

Added value will accrue from the project manager's ability to reduce costs (in real terms) and to save time. For example, a day saved at an early stage of the chain might lead to many being saved at the later stages of the project, which in turn could dramatically alter the whole cost structure of the construction, both for the client and ourselves.

There must be regular reappraisals of our current working procedures by all project managers and teams in order that we can improve upon the value-added chain.

Appendix B Criteria for acquisition

Should the growth of the project management market outstrip our capabilities to meet demand we will need to consider acquiring existing businesses. However, in order to be a genuine asset, such a purchase should meet these criteria.

The company will:

- Have a good reputation in the industry
- Add to our collective experience due to its track record and/or its contacts
- Provide us with advantageous geographical coverage
- Provide expertise in terms of its operating systems and procedures, and/or staff
- Have the financial resources to share in the investment costs of technical development, sales and marketing, and staff training.

For us to be certain we will be making a good investment we will need to:

- Research and monitor our competition, both in the UK and abroad
- Prioritize the above criteria
- Select from the competition those which best meet our requirements
- Identify the mutuality of our objectives and assess the synergistic potential from acquisition
- Have a short-list of potential candidates
- Plan a suitable campaign which will maximize goodwill and a trouble-free integration.

Note: Acquisition might also be considered as a solution to overcoming skill shortages in the short term. In this instance care should be taken that too much extraneous 'baggage' is not taken on board at the same time.

Moritaki computers (UK) Ltd

Background and information

The company was set up four years ago by the parent organization, which is in Tokyo. In total the group employ just over a hundred people, with approximately half of them based in London.

Between them the two companies provide an international computer consultancy specializing in the installation, enhancement and support of corporate accounting systems. Both units operate virtually autonomously in terms of seeking new business. Territorially, the London office deals with the northern hemisphere and Tokyo the southern.

Primarily the target customers are large, international companies who continually invest in their management information systems. The Tokyo office already has a client base which includes five of the largest Japanese companies.

Although the London office is expected to focus its activities primarily on Europe, it does have a small sales office in New York.

The company specializes in the Cassandra (Comprehensive Accounting Spread Sheet and Revenue Analysis) financial accounting system, which is supplied by the author Genesis Inc. from California, USA. In addition there is a systems development group, and multi-user hardware is also supplied.

The total group turnover is expected to be in the order of £3 m this year, with London accounting for about 60% of the total.

However, the Managing Director in London was both pleased about the trading success of the young company and yet worried. He knew that his sales team were good at spotting new opportunities as they arose, but could see that there was a danger of a proliferation of products and markets. Indeed, there seemed to be a general lack of focus for the company. It was tending to be reactive to the market rather than proactive.

This line of thinking prompted the MD to recruit a marketing director who was given this initial brief:

1. Define a strategy for the company as it moves through a period of rapid expansion and change.

2. Establish some marketing objectives for the company.

3. Lay down some compatible strategies for all of our products and services within each of the major market segments in which we compete.

4. Design a framework against which the directors can evaluate and sensibly judge a wide range of marketing opportunities which are uncovered by the sales force.

What follows is the three-year marketing plan developed by the new marketing director for Moritaki Computers (UK) Ltd.

1. Corporate mission

1. To provide a complete service in the design, enhancement, support and development of corporate accounting systems across the major industrial centres of the world.

2. To seek sustained growth through operating with high margins and reinvesting a substantial part of our profits. Our profit goal should never be less than 12.5% (after tax and interest charges).

3. To provide a professional service which generates quality solutions to client problems and maintains a high level of customer service.

4. To encourage our staff to use their initiative by giving them responsibility and control over their own spheres of work, and rewarding them according to their contribution to the business.

5. To avoid any business activity which is peripheral and not consistent with our core business. In doing this we expect to double our turnover over the next three years.

6. To keep the company privately owned.

2. Situation review

Market review

It is possible to describe several key identifying characteristics which typify Moritaki customers:

- They have high expectations of their systems and demand systems capable of providing comprehensive management information about their business activities.

- They are above average in sophistication in their approach to computerization.

- They are perhaps installing a computerized accounting system for the second or third time.

- They are large companies with specialist financial and accounting functions.

- They are faced with multi-currency or other difficult reporting requirements.

- They consider their investment in information systems in terms of their strategic value to the company as well as cost benefits.

- They demand high quality and superior support services.

The following three market segments would appear to offer us the best opportunities for providing complete business systems, consistent with the above customer profile.

1. European multinational companies

   These offer the prospect of multiple installations on an international scale.

2. Large UK firms with complex currency/information requirements

   Our expertise and ability to enhance the product give considerable scope in this segment.

3. Japanese multinational companies who are clients of Moritaki in Japan, but with a presence in the northern hemisphere

   Introductions are easy and logistically it is better to service test clients from London rather than Japan.

Competition and company image

A survey was conducted by telephoning a number of existing and potential client companies.

1. *How well is Moritaki known?* (Sample 20 typical client companies selected at random)

	Percentage
Competitor A	75
Competitor B	95
Competitor C	60
Competitor D	50
Competitor E	65
Competitor F	80
Competitor G	100
Moritaki (UK)	55

Conclusion Compared with our major competitors we are one of the least well-known suppliers (together with Competitor D). In contrast, everyone has heard of Competitor G.

2. *Quality of the product* (Sample 18 users, scoring 1–10 points, 10 = highest quality)

	Average score
System W	6.3
System X	5.8
System Y	7.9
System Z	6.7
Cassandra	9.2

Conclusion The Cassandra system is perceived to be superior in quality to competing systems by users who are in a position to make a comparison.

3. *Marketing ability* (Sample 20 companies where we are known, scoring between 1 (low) and 10 (high)) *Average score*

Competitor A	5.4
Competitor B	6.2
Competitor C	7.8
Competitor D	4.8
Competitor E	5.0
Competitor F	5.5
Competitor G	9.4
Moritaki (UK)	4.5

Conclusion Competitor G is seen to have the highest level of marketing ability, whereas we have the lowest average score.

Overall conclusions

Little information is known about competitors, but on the basis of some admittedly rather crude surveys, it appears that:

- We are little known outside our existing bank of clients.

- Our product is the best on the market.

- We are not perceived as having much marketing ability.

This helps to explain why 65% of our business is either from repeat sales or referrals from existing customers. Useful though this is, we will need to be capable of breaking out of our existing customer network if we are to achieve the corporate objectives of doubling our turnover over the next three years.

Market positioning

It is possible to define our existing position and determine our repositioning strategy by using the 'map' shown here.

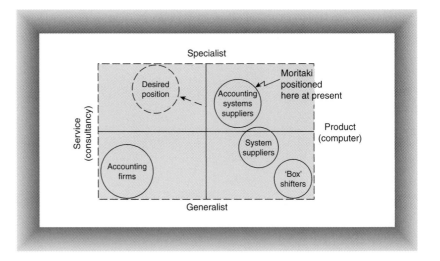

The new position is more consistent with the corporate objective of being a professional, specialist, consultancy company, providing a high level of customer service.

Marketing environment

The foreseeable threats and their potential to damage us are best described in the following table.

Threat analysis

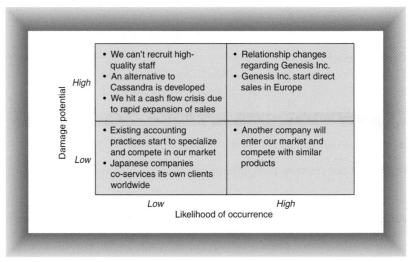

Equally there are a number of opportunities, as described below.

Opportunity analysis

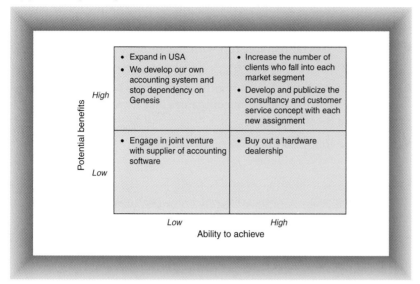

3. Product plans and analyses

The organization could be said to have this configuration:

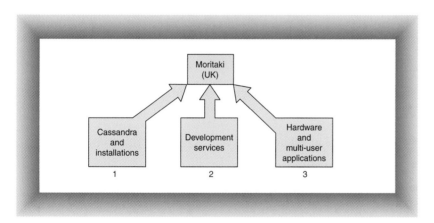

What follows are individual analyses of the three component parts that comprise Moritaki (UK) Ltd.

Cassandra system

● Best available product on the market.

● We have a very high level of experience with this system and a track record of successful installations and satisfied clients.

- Our development staff understand the open architecture of the product and can identify cross-selling opportunities for enhancement services.

- We have a special relationship with the authors, Genesis, who provide us with customer leads.

- It has a lifecycle of at least another two years, because of the conservative nature of the client companies and its relative lack of penetration in the market.

- Sales have followed this pattern up to now:

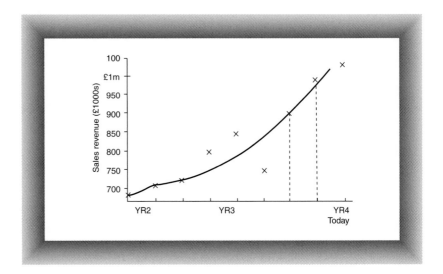

We need to:

- Monitor sales to get better at establishing lifecycle trends
- Monitor competitor activity
- Start thinking about the system to succeed Cassandra.

Critical installation factors which generate success
Ranked in order of importance they are:

1. Ability to provide a complete system including installation.
2. Ability to understand the client's needs and talk in their language.
3. Demonstrable technical competence, e.g. track record.
4. Value for money, e.g. value added or cost savings.
5. Ability to customize product to meet special requirements.
6. High level of service and customer support.

SWOT analysis
Strengths

Our technical knowledge and expertise

Accounting background

Track record

Relationship with Genesis.

Weaknesses

High perceived level of charges

Not well known in market

Dependency on Genesis

Lack of customer service skills/consulting skills.

Opportunities

Expand level of consultancy with each installation

Add other services to enhance system.

Threats

Not getting right quality staff as we expand

Genesis might use own sales team in Europe

Maintaining standards with rapid expansion.

Key issues
- We must focus on our 'customer services' not our 'product'.
- Our perceived high level of fees is because we are associated with 'computer companies', not professional service companies.
- We need to develop selling and customer service skills in installation staff, thereby generating more leads and business.
- We must maintain the high quality of installations.
- We need to keep Genesis out of Europe by persuasion.

Objectives

	Now	*13 years*
Turnover (£m)	£1.1	£1.98
Contribution (£k)	£105	£175
Growth	31	31.8

Key assumptions

- No system superior to Cassandra comes on the market in the next three years.

- The relationship with Genesis stays cordial.

- There is no worldwide trade recession.

Strategies

- Present our range of products and services as a complete corporate accounting system.

- Add as much value as possible to each installation.

- More meetings with clients prior to installation in order to:

  - explore all accounting and systems issues

  - create in the customer's mind the distinction between the software and the final completed system.

Pricing

Our current charges are 20–30% higher than our main competitors and have probably inhibited our level of business in the past.

Our proposed market positioning can sustain this price differential, but as an interim measure we will need to carry out some research to find out:

- Customer perceptions about our fee levels

- What the market will bear

- How we can adopt a pricing strategy which will be consistent with our changing image.

Promotional strategy

Get the company better known in general by:

- Getting articles, etc. into clients' trade journals

- Running seminars about specific problems which will interest potential clients

- Re-evaluating our existing promotional materials and upgrading where necessary

- Exhibiting at one or two prestigious venues

- Investing in a limited advertising campaign.

Because of our relative lack of experience in the visual impact of designing promotional materials, exhibitions and advertising, outside consultants will have to be used.

Sales strategy

- Recognize that every contact with a client is a sales opportunity
- Train all installation staff in selling and customer service skills
- Ensure that installation staff are aware of all other products and services and can sell 'through the range'
- Develop a client contact plan as a means of improving our relationships with clients before and after a sale.

Product strategy

- Develop installation checklists to ensure consistent standards
- Standardize pre- and post-installation evaluation checks.

Development services

- Can provide bespoke systems to extend the facilities of Cassandra
- Use COBOL – the same as Cassandra, hence no additional learning required by clients
- Provide database requirements for clients
- Several similar bespoke systems have been amalgamated into specific 'products' which include:
  - 'loans and overdraft' system
  - 'futures investment' system.

Critical Success Factors for Development Work

Ranked in order of importance they are:

1. Our services outmatch the client's internal services in terms of charges and completion times.
2. We can talk the client's language.
3. Being able to demonstrate a track record.
4. Availability, when client has a problem.

SWOT analysis

Strengths

- Very high technical skills
- Intimate knowledge of Cassandra system
- Staff have financial background
- Have accumulated a 'portfolio' of bespoke solutions to many client problems.

Weaknesses

- Tend to be more interested in the technical problems than the client's lack of customer awareness
- Lack of coordination regarding similar projects
- Lack of control/project management on large projects
- No promotional material for this service.

Opportunities

- To exploit some of the 'bespoke' systems.

Threats

- Recruiting and keeping quality staff are problems
- Quality will suffer if department is overloaded.

Key issues

- How to get better control and coordination of projects at all stages
- Getting better customer service skills
- Recruitment, training and rewards package for development staff to be improved.

Objectives

	Now	*13 years*
Turnover (£m)	£400	£800
Contribution (£k)	£38	£79
Growth	31	32

Key assumptions
- There are no crashes in the financial markets.

Pricing strategy
In order that we maximize our profits there are two considerations:

- Our prices are competitive
- We do not run over the time allowed for each project.

The better the record of delivering on time, the more we can justify above-average prices.

The whole situation regarding prices for development needs reviewing. Current market prices have been distorted by the inclusion of the fees of 'one-man bands' who could not tackle most of the projects we undertake.

Promotional strategy

The main promotional thrust for Cassandra and installations will also publicize our development services.

In addition, staff will be trained in selling and customer service skills.

Product strategy

- Develop a 'house style' in terms of design, coding and testing so that consistent quality and appearance are perceived by clients.

- We must continually take full advantage of the latest developments in both software and hardware.

Hardware and multi-user applications

- Two-thirds of our installations are integrated with some form of PC network

- New and existing machines can be linked via a network

- Increasing interest in market re multi-user systems

- We supply maintenance and support contracts.

Critical success factors

Ranked in order of importance they are:

1. Confidence client places in technical skills and abilities of the consultant.

2. Ability to provide general advice as well as the mainstream topic.

3. Speed of response and back-up services.

4. Prices of products and services.

5. Selling and customer contact skills.

SWOT analysis

Strengths

- Technically astute

- Customer-oriented.

Weaknesses

- We are small compared with specialist firms in this part of the market

- Limited on dealerships with major equipment manufacturers

- Outdated promotional material.

Opportunities

- Growing demand for networks
- Our preferred multi-user system is becoming very popular and could be promoted
- Become agent for overseas equipment manufacturer.

Threats
- Larger companies enjoy economies of scale
- Dependent on sales of Cassandra to generate business
- Competition is getting fiercer in this market.

Key issues
- Targets to be set for non-Cassandra work
- More promotion effort to get known in market
- Capitalize on growing demand for networks and multi-user applications.

Objectives

	Now	*13 years*
Turnover (£m)	£250	£720
Contribution (£k)	£24	£66
Growth	31	32.9

Key assumptions
- Current growth trends for networks and multi-user systems will continue
- Sales for Cassandra reach their projected levels.

Pricing strategy
We need to focus on 'added value' not 'cheapness'. We provide very good products, excellent and impartial technical advice, above average installation and maintenance services, a fast response to client problems and a flexible approach.

The product is only part of this 'package', therefore we will avoid discounting as practised by the 'box shifters'.

In the short term (up to one year) prices will stay the same. Thereafter we will push to charge the highest the market will bear, in line with our publicity and company image campaigns.

Promotional strategy

- Develop promotional materials

- Set realistic sales targets for non-Cassandra linked work

- Ensure staff can sell 'through the range'.

Product strategy

- Keep abreast of all new developments

- Standardize as much as possible on configurations, installation checks, pre- and post-installation tests

- Develop closer ties with major hardware suppliers.

Glossary of marketing planning terms

Assumptions   The *major* assumptions on which the marketing plan is based.

Benefit   A perceived or stated relationship between a product feature and the need the feature is designed to satisfy. *See also* Differential advantage *and* Feature.

Brand   A name or symbol which identifies a product or service. A successful brand identifies a product or service as having sustainable, competitive advantage.

Budget   The revenue and costs associated with forecasts used in planning.

Business plan   A plan commonly intermediate between a company's strategic plan and its annual marketing plan. The purpose of the business plan is to establish the broad business objectives and strategies to be pursued by the business unit or centre over a time period of as many as five years. In this respect, business plans are similar to strategic plans which concern themselves with equally long time-frames. Business plans are like strategic plans in one other respect: usually they deal with such strategic considerations as new product development, product acquisition, and new market development to achieve desired financial goals. Business plans also require extensive marketing input for their formulation and, in this respect, they share characteristics in common with marketing plans. However, business plans generally do not include action programmes – a feature typical of marketing plans – but simply spell out intentions and directions. For example, if new product development was among the strategies to be pursued, this would be stated along with appropriate supporting rationale. However, the statement of this strategy would not be accompanied by a new product development plan.

Charter   A statement of the chief function or responsibility of an operating unit within an organization made up of several operating units. *See also* Mission.

Closed loop system   A bureaucratic planning system that consists mainly of pro-formas for completion by managers according to pre-determined headings and formats. Such systems frequently degenerate into stale form-filling exercises and there is little opportunity for adding creative insights.

Consumer   The final consumer of goods or services. Customers are people or organizations who buy directly from us.

Core strategy   A term used in marketing to denote the predominant elements of the marketing mix, selected by marketing management to achieve the optimum match between the benefits customers seek and those the product offers. This process of selection is sometimes referred to as 'making the differential advantage operational'.

Critical success factors (CSFs)   The factors (strengths and weaknesses) that most affect an organization's success. These are measured relative to those of its competitors. For example, product performance, breadth of services, low costs, etc.

Customer service   A system organized to provide a continuing link between the first contact with the customer, through to the time the order is received and the goods/services delivered and used, with the objective of satisfying customer needs continuously. It is also sometimes defined as the percentage of occasions the product or service is available to the customer *when* and *where* he or she wants it.

Data   Words, pictures, sounds, etc. Data by themselves are of little use until they are combined with direction and hence become information.

Database   A collection of data and information from outside and inside an organization which is stored in such a way that it can be accessed and analysed to provide intelligence for making decisions to achieve the organization's objectives.

Data warehouse   Similar to an Executive Information System or EIS, it stores all external and internal information (both historical and current data) in a format that can be easily accessed.

Data mining   Software that allows users to access the data warehouse to search for statistics and for correlations between data that can be used in decision-making.

Demographics   Commonly used descriptions of customers and consumers according to public and measured criteria.

Differential advantage   A benefit or cluster of benefits offered to a sizeable group of customers which they value (and are willing to pay for) and which they cannot obtain elsewhere. *See also* Feature *and* Benefit.

Distribution   A term used in marketing to refer to the means by which a product or service is made physically available to customers. Distribution encompasses such activities as warehousing, transportation, inventory control, order processing, etc. Because distribution is the means of increasing a service or product's availability, it is also a tool which can be used by marketing management to improve the match between benefits sought by customers and those offered by the organization.

Experience effect   It is a proven fact that most value-added cost components of a product or service decline steadily with experience and can be reduced significantly as the scale of operation increases. In turn this cost (and therefore price advantage) is a significant factor in increasing the company's market share.

Feature   A characteristic or property of a product or service such as reliability, price, convenience, safety and quality. These features may or may not satisfy customer needs. To the extent that they do, they can be translated into benefits. *See also* Benefit *and* Differential advantage.

Forecast In planning terms a forecast is usually associated with predicting the volume and value of products and services at some future point in time.

Gap In marketing terms, the difference between a service or product's present or projected performance and the level sought. Typically, the gaps in marketing management are those relating to return on investment, cash generation or use, return on sales and market share.

Gap analysis The process of determining gaps between a service or product's present or projected performance and the level of performance sought. *See also* Gap.

Growth/share matrix A term synonymous with 'product portfolio' which in essence is a means of displaying graphically the amount of 'experience' or market share a product or service has and comparing this share with the rate of growth of the relevant market segment. With the matrix, a manager can decide, for example, whether he or she should invest in getting more 'experience' – that is, fight for bigger market share – or perhaps get out of the market altogether. These choices are among a number of strategic alternatives available to the manager – strategic in the sense that they not only affect marketing strategy but determine use of capital within the organization. *See also* Experience effect.

Intelligence Information which is consumable and usable by management in converting uncertainty into risk.

Market A customer need described in a way which covers the aggregation of all the alternative products or services which customers regard as being capable of satisfying the same or similar needs.

Market map A map which defines the distribution and value chain between service provider and final user, which takes into account the various buying mechanisms found in a market, including the part played by 'influencers'.

Market research Research specifically about markets.

Market segment A group of actual or potential customers who can be expected to respond in approximately the same way to a given offer (who share the same or similar needs); a finer, more detailed breakdown of a market.

Market segmentation The process of splitting customers, or potential customers, in a market into different groups, or segments. A critical aspect of marketing planning and one designed to convert product/service differences into a cost differential that can be maintained over the product's lifecycle. *See also* Product lifecycle/service lifecycle.

Market share The percentage of the market represented by a firm's sales in relation to total sales. Some marketing theorists argue that the term is misleading since it suggests that the dimensions of the market are known and assumes that the size of the market is represented by the amount of goods sold in it. All that is known, these theorists point out, and correctly, is the volume sold; in actuality, the market may be considerably larger.

Marketing audit   A situational analysis of the company's current marketing capability. *See also* Situational analysis.

Marketing concept   The marketing concept, as opposed to the marketing function, implies that all the activities of an organization are driven by a desire to satisfy customer needs.

Marketing intelligence/information system (MIS)   A system to facilitate information flows so that there are appropriate inputs and the correct data gets to the users in a sensible form.

Marketing mix   The 'tools' or means available to an organization to improve the match between benefits sought by customers and those offered by the organization so as to obtain a differential advantage. Among these tools are product, price, promotion and distribution service. *See also* Differential advantage.

Marketing objectives   A statement of the targets or goals to be pursued and achieved within the period covered in the marketing plan. Depending on the scope and orientation of the plan – whether, for example, the plan is designed primarily to spell out short-term marketing intentions or to identify broad business directions and needs – the objectives stated may encompass such important measures of business performance as profit, growth and market share.

   Marketing objectives with respect to profit, market share, sales volume, market development or penetration and other broader considerations are sometimes referred to as 'primary' marketing objectives. More commonly, they are referred to as 'strategic' or 'business' objectives since they pertain to the operation of the business as a whole. In turn, objectives set for specific marketing sub-functions or activities are referred to as 'programme' objectives to distinguish them from the broader business or strategic objectives they are meant to serve.

Marketing plan   Contains a mission statement, SWOT analysis, assumptions, marketing objectives, marketing strategies and programmes. Note that the objectives, strategies and policies are established for each level of the business.

Marketing planning   A logical sequence of events leading to the setting of marketing objectives and the formulation of plans for achieving them.

Marketing research   Research into marketing processes.

Mission   A definite task with which one is charged; the chief function of an institution or organization. In essence it is a vision of what the company is or is striving to become. The basic issue is: 'What is our business and what should it be?' In marketing planning, the mission statement is the starting point in the planning process, since it sets the broad parameters within which marketing objectives are established, strategies developed and programmes implemented. Some companies, usually those with several operating units or divisions, make a distinction between 'mission' and 'charter'. In these instances, the term 'mission' is used to denote the broader purpose of the organization as reflected in corporate policies or assigned by the senior management of the company; the term 'charter', in comparison, is used to denote the purpose or reason for being of individual units with prime responsibility for a specific functional or product-marketing area. *See also* Charter.

Objective A statement or description of a desired future result that cannot be predicted in advance but which is believed, by those setting the objective, to be achievable through their efforts within a given time period; a quantitative target or goal to be achieved in the future through one's efforts, which can also be used to measure performance. To be of value, objectives should be specific in time and scope and attainable given the financial, technical and human resources available. According to this definition, general statements of hopes or desire are not true 'objectives'. *See also* Marketing objectives.

Planning The process of predetermining a course or courses of action based on assumptions about future conditions or trends which can be imagined but not predicted with any certainty.

Policies Guidelines adopted in implementing the strategies selected. In essence, a policy is a summary statement of objectives and strategies.

Positioning The process of selecting, delineating and matching the segment of the market with which a product or service will be most compatible.

Product A term used in marketing to denote not only the product itself – its inherent properties and characteristics – but also service, availability, price, and other factors which may be as important in differentiating the product from those of competitors as the inherent characteristics of the product itself. *See also* Marketing mix.

Product lifecycle/service lifecycle A term used in marketing to refer to the pattern of growth and decline in sales revenue of a product over time. This pattern is typically divided into stages: introduction, growth, maturity, saturation and decline. With time, competition among firms tends to reduce all products in the market to commodities – products which can only be marginally differentiated from each other – with the result that pioneering companies – those first to enter the market – face the choice of becoming limited volume, high-priced, high-cost speciality producers or high-volume, low-cost producers of standard products. (Similar definition applies to 'service lifecycle'.)

Product portfolio A theory about the alternative uses of capital by business organizations formulated originally by Bruce Henderson of the Boston Consulting Group, a leading firm in the area of corporate strategy consulting. This theory or approach to marketing strategy formulation has gained wide acceptance among managers of diversified companies, who were first attracted by the intuitively appealing notion that long-run corporate performance is more than the sum of the contributions of individual profit centres or product strategies. Other factors which account for the theory's appeal are: (1) its usefulness in developing specific marketing strategies designed to achieve a balanced mix of products that will produce maximum return from scarce cash and managerial resources; and (2) the fact that the theory employs a simple matrix representation useful in portraying and communicating a product's position in the market place. *See also* Growth/share matrix.

Programme   A term used in marketing planning to denote the steps or tasks to be undertaken by marketing, field sales and other functions within an organization to implement the chosen strategies and to accomplish the objectives set forth in the marketing plan. Typically, descriptions of programmes include a statement of objectives as well as a definition of the persons or units responsible and a schedule for completion of the steps or tasks for which the person or unit is responsible. *See also* Strategy statement *and* Marketing objectives.

Psychographic segmentation   Dividing a market into different groups based on social class, lifestyle, behaviour, attitudes and personality characteristics.

Relative market share   A firm's share of the market relative to its largest competitor. *See also* Market share.

Resources   Broadly speaking, anyone or anything through which something is produced or accomplished; in marketing planning, a term used to denote the unique capabilities or skills that an organization brings to a market or business problem or opportunity.

Revenue   The monetary value received by a company for its goods or services. It is the net price received, i.e. the price less any discounts.

Service   A service (or product) is the total experience of the customer or consumer when dealing with an organization. A service product cannot be made in advance and stored for selling 'off the shelf' at some later stage.

Service business   A business specifically focused on providing a service or services to customers. The service product may involve goods.

Situational analysis   The second step in the marketing planning process (the first being the definition of mission), which reviews the business environment at large (with particular attention to economic, market and competitive aspects) as well as the company's own internal operation. The purpose of the situational analysis is to identify marketing problems and opportunities, both those stemming from the organization's internal strengths and limitations, and those external to the organization and caused by changes in economic conditions and trends, competition, customer expectations, industry relations, government regulations and, increasingly, social perceptions and trends. The output of the full analysis is summarized in key-point form under the heading SWOT (strengths, weaknesses, opportunities and threats) analysis; this summary then becomes part of the marketing plan. The outcome of the situational analysis includes a set of assumptions about future conditions as well as an estimate or forecast of potential market demand during the period covered by the marketing plan. Based on these estimates and assumptions, marketing objectives are established and strategies and programmes formulated.

Strategic plan A plan that covers a period beyond the next fiscal year. Usually this is for three to five years.

Strategy statement A description of the broad course of action to be taken to achieve a specific marketing objective such as an increase in sales volume or a reduction in unit costs. The strategy statement is frequently referred to as the connecting link between marketing objectives and programmes – the actual concrete steps to be taken to achieve those objectives. *See also* Programme.

Tactical plan A plan that covers in detail the actions to be taken and by whom, during a short-term planning period. This is usually for one year or less.

Target Something aimed at; a person or group of persons to be made the object of an action or actions intended, usually to bring about an effect or change in the person or group of persons.

References

Chapter 1

1 Central Intelligence Agency (2011) *The World Factbook*, Central Intelligence Agency. Available at https://www.cia.gov/library/publications/the-world-factbook/fields/2012.html Accessed 25 January 2011.
2 Spohrer, J. (2005) 'Services Sciences, Management, Engineering (SSME): A next frontier in education, innovation, and economic growth and the role of knowledge representation techniques in services innovation', Presentation by IBM SSME Education, Innovation, and Economic Growth, 25 October 2005.
3 Kotler, P. (2003) *Marketing Management*, 11th edn, Upper Saddle River, New Jersey: Prentice Hall, pp. 695–797. (The marketing effectiveness audit is reproduced in full in this book.)
4 This section owes much to McDonald, M. and Wilson, H. (2003) *The New Marketing*, Oxford: Butterworth-Heinemann. Thanks to the authors for giving permission for its use here.
5 McDonald, M. and Wilson, H. (2011) *Marketing Plans: How to prepare them, how to use them*, 7th edn, Chichester: John Wiley & Sons Ltd.
6 Lanning, M. (2003) *'An Introduction to the Market-focused Philosophy, Framework and Methodology called Delivering Profitable Value'*. Available at http://www.exubrio.com/white-papers/DPVIntro-eXubrio.pdf Accessed 27 February 2008.
7 Frow, P. and Payne, A. (2008) 'The Value Proposition Concept: Evolution, Development and Application in Marketing', Academy of Marketing Conference, Aberdeen, UK, July.

Chapter 2

1 Moeller, S. (2010) 'Characteristics of Services – A New Approach Uncovers their Value', *Journal of Services Marketing*, **24** (5), 359–368.
2 Lovelock, C. and Gummesson, E. (2004) 'Whither Services Marketing?: In Search of a New Paradigm and Fresh Perspectives', *Journal of Service Research*, **7** (1), 20–41.
3 Vargo, S. and Lusch, R.F. (2004) 'The Four Service Marketing Myths: Remnants of a Goods-based, Manufacturing Model', *Journal of Service Research*, **6** (May), 324–335.
4 Kotler, P. (1997) *Marketing Management: Analysis, Planning and Control*, 9th ed., Englewood Cliffs, NJ: Prentice Hall.
5 Lovelock, C., Patterson, P.G. and Wirz, J. (2011) *Services Marketing: An Asia-Pacific and Australasian Perspective*, Frenchs Forest, NSW: Pearson Australia.
6 Ando, R. (2011) *'IBM Blows Past Forecasts, Services Contracts Rise'*, Jan 20, 2011. http://www.itnews.com.au/News/245425,ibm-blows-past-forecasts-services-contracts-rise.aspx (accessed 15 February 2011).
7 Levitt, T. (1974) *Marketing for Business Growth*, New York: McGraw Hill, p. 5.

8 Gummesson, E. (2010) 'The New Service Marketing', in Baker, M.J. and Saren, M., eds, *Marketing Theory: A Student Text*, 2nd edn, London: Sage, pp. 399–421.

9 Vargo, S.L. and Lusch, R.F. (2004) 'Evolving to a New Dominant Logic for Marketing', *Journal of Marketing*, **68** (January), 1–17. Also see: Vargo, S.L. and Lusch, R.F. (2008) 'Service-dominant Logic: Continuing the Evolution', *Journal of the Academy of Marketing Science*, **36** (1), 1–10.

10 Maglio, P.P. and Spohrer, J. (2008) 'Fundamentals of Service Science', *Journal of the Academy of Marketing Science*, **36** (1), 18–20.

11 Payne, A., Storbacka, K. and Frow, P. (2008) 'Managing the Co-Creation of Value', *Journal of the Academy of Marketing Science*, **36** (1), 83–96.

12 Gummesson, E. (2010), *op. cit.*

13 Lovelock, C.H. (1983) 'Classifying Services to Gain Strategic Marketing Insights', *Journal of Marketing*, **47** (Summer), 9–20. (The matrices shown in this chapter are based on those developed by Lovelock.)

14 Ng, S., Russell-Bennett, R. and Dagger, T. (2007) 'A Typology of Mass Services: The Role of Service Delivery and Consumption Purpose in Classifying Service Experiences', *Journal of Services Marketing*, **21** (7), 471–480.

15 Vandermerwe, S. and Rada, J. (1988) 'Servitization of Business: Adding Value by Adding Service', *European Management Journal*, **6** (4), 314–423. Also see:. Baines, T.S., Lightfoot, H.W., Benedettini, O. and Kay, J.M. (2009) 'The Servitization of Manufacturing: A Review of Literature and Reflection on Future Challenges', *Journal of Manufacturing Technology Management*, **20** (5), 547–567.

16 For example, see Booms, B.H. and Bitner, M.J. (1981) 'Marketing Strategies and Organizational Structures for Service Firms', in Donnelly, J.H. and George, W.R. (eds), *Marketing of Services*, Chicago: American Marketing Association Proceedings Series, p. 48.

17 For a more detailed discussion of the services marketing mix, see: Kasper, H., van Helsdingen, P. and Gabbott, M. (2006) *Services Marketing Management*, 2nd edn, Chichester: John Wiley & Sons Ltd.

18 Fisk, R.P. and Grove, S.J. (2010) 'The Evolution and Future of Service: Building and Broadening a Multidisciplinary Field', in Maglio, P.P., Kieliszewski, C.A. and Spohrer, J.C. (eds), *Handbook of Service Science: Research and Innovations in the Service Economy*, New York: Springer.

19 See Reichheld, F.F. and Sasser, W.E. (Jr.) (1990) 'Zero Defections: Quality Comes to Services', *Harvard Business Review*, September–October, 105–111; Reichheld, F.F. (2001) *Loyalty Rules*, Boston: Harvard Business School; and Reichheld, F. (1994) 'Loyalty and the Renaissance of Marketing', *Marketing Management*, **12** (4), 17.

20 Payne, A., Ballantyne, D. and Christopher, M. (2005) 'Relationship Marketing: A Stakeholder Approach', *European Journal of Marketing*, **39** (7/8), 855–871. Also see: Christopher, M., Payne, A. and Ballantyne, D. (2002) *Relationship Marketing: Creating Shareholder Value*, Oxford: Butterworth-Heinemann.

Chapter 3

1 Buzzell, R.D. (2004) 'The PIMS Program of Strategy Research: A Retrospective Appraisal', *Journal of Business Research*, **57**, 478–483. (This article provides a review of the overall research programme.) The results of the earlier work appear in: Buzzell, R.D. and Gale, B.T. (1987) *The PIMS Principles: Linking Strategy to Performance*, New York: The Free Press.

2 McDonald, M. (1992) 'Strategic Marketing Planning: A State-of-the-Art Review', *Marketing Intelligence and Planning*, **10** (4), 4–22.

3 For an up-to-date summary, see: McDonald, M. and Wilson, H. (2011) *Marketing Plans: How to prepare them; How to use them*, 7th edn, Chichester: John Wiley & Sons Ltd. The start of the ongoing research project on marketing planning commenced with: McDonald, M. (1982) 'The Theory and Practice of Marketing Planning for Industrial Goods in International Markets', PhD thesis, Cranfield Institute of Technology.

4 For a later treatment of Ansoff's work, see: Ansoff, H.I. and Antoniou, P.H. (2006) *The Secrets of Strategic Management: The Ansoffian Approach*, Book-Surge Publishing. His original model was published in: Ansoff, H.I. (1957) 'Strategies for Diversification', *Harvard Business Review*, **35** (September–October), 113–121.

Chapter 4

1 Chisnall, P. (1975) 'Marketing Planning in a Service Economy', *Long Range Planning*, December, 43–52.

2 Hooley, G.J., West, C.J. and Lynch, J.E. (1984) *Marketing in the UK: A Study of Current Practice and Performance*, London: Institute of Marketing.

3 Greenley, G. (1983) 'An Overview of Marketing Planning in UK Service Companies', *Marketing Intelligence and Planning*, **1** (3), 55–68.

4 Cousins, L. (1991) 'Marketing Plans or Marketing Planning?' *Business Strategy Review*, Summer, 35–54.

5 Greenley, G. and Bayus, B. (1994) 'Marketing Planning Processes in UK and US Companies', *Journal of Strategic Marketing*, **2**, 140–154.

6 Sutton, H. (1990) *The Marketing Plan in the 1990s*, New York: The Conference Board.

7 Dibb, S., Farhangmehr, M. and Simkin, L. (2001) 'The Marketing Planning Experience: A UK and Portuguese Comparison', *Marketing Intelligence and Planning*, **1** (6), 409–417.

8 Smith, B. (2003) 'The Effectiveness of Marketing Strategy Making Process', PhD thesis, Cranfield School of Management.

9 Greenley, G., Hooley, G. and Saunders, J. (2004) 'Management Processes in Marketing Planning', *European Journal of Marketing*, **38** (8), 933–955.

10 Brooksbank, R., Garland, R. and Taylor, D. (2010) 'Strategic Marketing in New Zealand Companies', *Journal of Global Marketing*, **23** (1), 33–44.

11 Taghian, M. (2010) 'Marketing Planning: Operationalising the Market Orientation Strategy', *Journal of Marketing Management*, **26** (9), 825–841.

12 Keegan, W.J. (2004) 'Strategic Marketing Planning: A Twenty-First Century Perspective', *International Marketing Review*, **21** (1), 13–16.

13 Taghian, M. (2010) *op. cit.*

Chapter 5

1 David, F.R. (1989) 'How Companies Define their Mission', *Long Range Planning*, **22** (1), 90–97.

2 Byars, L.L. and Neil, T.C. (1987) 'Organisational Philosophy and Mission Statements', *Planning Review*, July/August, 32–35.

3 Bart, C., Bounties, N. and Tagger, S. (2001) 'A Model of the Impact of Mission Statements on Firm Performance', *Management Decision*, **39** (1), 19–36.

4 Barks, B., Glassman, M. and McAfee, R. (2004) 'A Comparison of the Quality of European, Japanese and US Mission Statements: A Content Analysis', *European Management Journal*, **22** (4), 393–402.

5 Desmids, S. and Prize, A.A. (2009) 'The Effectiveness of Mission State-ments: An Explorative Analysis from a Communication Perspective', *Academy of Management Annual Meeting Proceedings*, August.

6 Jones, I.S., Lovett, M.G. and Blankenship, D. (2006) 'Mission Statements on Fortune 500 Web Sites: A Descriptive Analysis', *Journal of Business and Behavioral Sciences*, Fall, 74–84.

7 King, D.L., Case, C.J. and Primo, K.M. (2010) 'Current Mission Statement Emphasis: Be Ethical and Go Global', *Academy of Strategic Management Journal*, **9** (2), 71–87.

8 Bain & Company (2009) *Management Tools and Trends*, Boston.

9 Levitt, T. (1960) 'Marketing Myopia', *Harvard Business Review*, July–August, 45–56.

10 Bain & Company (2011) http://www.joinbain.com/this-is-bain/what-we-do/our-mission.asp (accessed 18 January 2011).

11 IBM (2011) http://www.ibm.com/ibm/jam/ (accessed 21 January 2011).

12 DHL (2011) www.dhl-graduates.com/the-producers/our-vision.html (accessed 21 January 2011).

13 Davidson, H. (2002) *The Committed Enterprise*, Oxford: Butterworth-Heinemann.

14 Campbell, A., Devine, M. and Young, D. (1990) *Sense of Mission*, Economist Books/Hutchinson, London; Campbell, A. and Young, S. (1990) *Do You Need a Mission Statement?*, London: Economist Publications Management Guides, Abrahams, J. (2007) *101 Mission Statements from Top Companies*, Ten Speed Press; King, D.L. and Case, C.J. (2010) 'The Evolving Mission State-ment: An Essential Communication Tool', *American Society of Business and Behavioral Sciences Journal*, **6** (1), 71–78.

15 Richards, M.D. (1986) *Setting Strategic Goals and Objectives*, St Paul, Minn: West Publishing.

16 Chattered, S. (2005) 'Core Objectives: Clarity in Designing Strategy', *California Management Review*, **47** (2), 33–47.

17 Ambler, T (2000) *Marketing and the Bottom Line*, London: Financial Times Prentice Hall.

Chapter 6

1 McDonald, M. and Dunbar, I. (2010) *Market Segmentation: How to Do It; How to Profit from It*, Oxford: Goodfellow Publishing.

2 Buzzell, R.D. and Gale, B.T. (1987) *The PIMS Principles: Linking Strategy to Performance*, New York: The Free Press.

3 Jenkins, M. and McDonald, M. (1997) 'Market Segmentation: Organisa-tional Archetypes and a Research Agenda', *European Journal of Marketing*, **31** (1), 17–30.

4 Smith, W. (1956) 'Product Differentiation and Market Segmentation as Alternative Marketing Strategies', *Journal of Marketing*, **21**, July, 3–8.

5 Wind, Y. (1978) 'Issues and Advances in Segmentation Research', *Journal of Marketing Research*, **15**, 317–337.

6 Bailey, C., Baines, P., Wilson, H. and Clark, M. (2009) 'Segmentation and Customer Insight in Contemporary Services Marketing Practice: Why Grouping Customers is no Longer Enough', *Journal of Marketing Manage-ment*, **25** (3–4), 228–251.

7 Coviello, N.E., Brodie, R.J., Danaher, P.J. and Johnston, W.J. (2002) 'How Firms Relate to their Markets: An Empirical Examination of Contemporary Marketing Practice', *Journal of Marketing*, **66** (3), 33–46.

8 Wilson, H., Daniel, E. and McDonald, M. (2002) 'Factors for Success in Rela-tionship Marketing', *Journal of Marketing Management*, **18** (1/2), 199–218.

9 Rigby, D.K., Reicheld, F.F., Schefter, P. (2002) 'Avoid the Four Perils of CRM', *Harvard Business Review*, **80** (2), 101–109.

10 Christensen C., Cook, S. and Hall, T. (2005) 'Marketing Malpractice: The Cause and the Cure', *Harvard Business Review*, **83** (12) December, 74–83.

11 Yankelovitch, D. (2006) 'Rediscovering Market Segmentation', *Harvard Business Review*, **84** (6) February, 122–131.

12 Smith, B. (2003) 'The Effectiveness of Marketing Strategy Making Processes in Medical Markets', April, Cranfield Doctoral Thesis.

Chapter 7

1 Fleisher, C. and Bensoussan, B. (2002) *Strategic Competitive Analysis: Methods and Techniques for Analyzing Business Competition*, Englewood Cliffs, NJ: Prentice Hall; Pollard, A. (1999) *Competitor Intelligence – Strategy, Tools and Techniques for Competitive Advantage*, Pitman; Fuld, L. (1994) *The New Competitor Intelligence: The Complete Resource for Finding, Analyzing, and Using Information about Your Competitors*, New York: John Wiley & Sons Inc.

2 Porter, M. (1980) *Competitive Strategy*, New York: The Free Press.

3 Hamel, G. and Prahalad, C.K. (1994) *Competing for the Future*, Boston: Harvard Business School.

4 Based on Kotler, P. (1991) *Marketing Management*, 7th edn, Englewood Cliffs, NJ: Prentice Hall, p. 301.

5 For a review of positioning research, see: Holey, G. and Saunders, J. (2003) *Competitive Positioning*, Prentice Hall, Ch. 10. For a more general discussion of positioning, see: Ries, A. and Trout, J. (2000) *Positioning: The Battle for Your Mind*, 20th Anniversary Edition, New York: McGraw Hill.

6 Based on Kosnik, T. (1989) *Corporate Positioning: How to Assess and Build a Company's Reputation*, Boston: Harvard Business School, Note 9–589–087.

7 Sasser, W.E., Olsen, R.P. and Wyckoff, D.D. (1978) *Management of Service Operations: Text, Cases and Readings*, London: Alleyn & Bacon, pp. 534–566.

8 Wilson, A. (2002) *The Marketing Audit Handbook*, London: Kogan Page.

9 McDonald, M. and Leppard, J. (1991) *The Marketing Audit*, Oxford: Butterworth-Heinemann; Parmerlee, D. (2000) *Auditing Markets, Products and Marketing Plans*, New York: McGraw Hill.

Chapter 8

1 Cooper, R., Edgett, S. and Kleinschmidt, E. (2001) 'Portfolio Management for New Product Development: Results of an Industry Practices Study', *R&D Management*, **31** (4), 361–380.

2 Porter, M.E. (1980) *Competitive Strategy*, New York: The Free Press.

3 See Myers, K. (1999) *Manager's Guide to Contingency Planning for Disasters*, New York: John Wiley & Sons Inc.

Chapter 9

1 Abratt, R., Beffon, M. and Ford, J. (1994) 'Relationship Between Marketing Planning and Annual Budget', *Marketing Intelligence and Planning*, **12** (1), 22–28.

2 Vancil, R. and Ferrantino, J.A. (2010) *Marketing Investment Planner 2011: Benchmarks, Key Performance Indicators, and CMO Priorities*, IDC #225478, 1 November 2010.

3 Constantinides, E. (2006) 'The Marketing Mix Revisited: Towards the 21st Century Marketing', *Journal of Marketing Management*, **22**, 407–438.

4 Adapted from McDonald, M. and de Chernatony, L. (2001) 'Corporate Marketing and Service Brands: Moving Beyond the Fast-moving Consumer Goods Model', *European Journal of Marketing*, **35** (3/4), 335–352.

5 Thorbjørnsen, H. and Supphellen, M. (2011) 'Determinants of Core Value Behavior in Service Brands', *Journal of Services Marketing*, **25** (1), 68–76.

6 Berry, L.L. and Parasuraman, A. (1991) Marketing Services: Competing Through Quality, New York: The Free Press, p. 131.

7 For an excellent discussion on physical evidence, see: Zeithaml, V.A., Bitner, M.J. and Gremler, D.D. (2009) *Services Marketing: Integrating Customer Focus across the Firm*, 5th edn, New York: McGraw Hill, Chapter 11.

8 Lovelock, C., Patterson, P.G. and Wirtz, J. (2011) *Services Marketing: An Asia-Pacific and Australian Perspective*, 5th edn, Frenchs Forest, NSW: Prentice Hall, p. 265.

9 Grönroos, C. (2007) *Service Management and Marketing*, 3rd edn, Chichester: John Wiley & Sons Ltd.

10 Shultz, D. and Shultz, H. (2003) *IMC – The Next Generation: Five Steps for Delivering Value and Measuring Financial Returns*, New York: McGraw Hill.

11 For a detailed discussion of CRM, see: Payne, A. (2006) *The Handbook of CRM: Achieving Excellence in Customer Management*, Oxford: Elsevier Butterworth Heinemann. Also see: Frow, P. and Payne, A. (2009) 'Customer Relationship Management: A Strategic Perspective', *Journal of Business Market Management*, **3** (1), 7–28.

12 Spenner, P. (2010) 'Why you Need a New-Media "Ringmaster"', *Harvard Business Review*, December, 78–79.

13 Rogers, E.M. (1995) *Diffusion of Innovations*, 4th edn, New York: Free Press.

14 Based on Johnson, E.M., Scheuing, E.E. and Gaida, K.A. (1986) *Profitable Services Marketing*, Homewood, Ill: Dow Jones-Irwin, p. 212.

Chapter 10

1 See, for example: Bahnub, B.J. (2010) *Activity-Based Management for Financial Institutions: Driving Bottom-Line Results*, New York: John Wiley & Sons Inc.

2 Based on material from Boston Consulting Group.

3 Chambers, S. and Johnston, R. (2000) 'Experience Curves in Services: Macro and Micro Level Approaches', *International Journal of Operations & Production Management*, **20** (7), 842–859.

4 See: Burger, A. (2005) 'The Son also Rises', *Pest Control*, **72** (4), 116; and Heskett, J.L., Sasser, W.E. and Hart, C.W.L. (1990) *Service Breakthroughs*, New York: The Free Press, p. 89.

5 Rogers, E.M. (1995) *Diffusion of Innovations*, 4th edn, New York: Free Press.

6 See also: Judd, V. (2003) 'Achieving a Customer Orientation Using "People Power", the "5th P"', *European Journal of Marketing*, **37** (10), October, 1–13; and Judd, V.C. (1987) 'Differentiate with the 5th P: People', *Industrial Marketing Management*, **16**, 241–247. (The descriptions of the four categories are based closely on his work.)

7 See: Heskett, J.L. and Sasser, W.E. (2010) 'The Service Profit Chain: From Satisfaction to Ownership', in Maglio, P.P., Kieliszewski, C.A. and Spohrer, J.C. (eds), *Handbook of Service Science: Research and Innovations in the Service Economy*, New York: Springer, pp. 19–30; Heskett, J.L., Sasser, W.E. and Schlesinger, L.A. (1997) *The Service Profit Chain*, New York: The Free Press; and Hallowell, R., Schlesinger, L.A. and Zornitsky, J. (1996) 'Internal Service Quality, Customer and Job Satisfaction: Linkages and Implications', *Human Resource Planning Journal*, **19** (2), 20–31.

8 Wieseke, J., Ahearne, M., Lam, S.K. and van Dick, R. (2009) 'The Role of Leaders in Internal Marketing', *Journal of Marketing*, **73**, March, 123–145.

9 See: Varey, R. and Lewis, B. (2000) *Internal Marketing: Directions for Management*, London: Routledge; and Pervaiz K.A. and Rafiq, M. (2002) *Internal Marketing: Tools and Concepts for Customer-Focused Management*, Oxford: Elsevier.

10 This section is based on Stostack, G.L. (2001) 'Service Positioning through Structural Change', in Lovelock, C., Patterson, P.G. and Walker, R.H. *Services Marketing: An Asia-Pacific Perspective*, 2nd edn, Frenchs Forest, NSW: Prentice Hall, pp. 577–587.

11 See: Bitner, M.J., Ostrom, A.L. and Morgan, F.N. (2008) 'Service Blueprinting: A Practical Technique for Service Innovation', *California Management Review*, **50** (3), 66–94; and Band, W. (1989) 'Blueprint your Organisation to Create Satisfied Customers', *Sales & Marketing in Canada*, April, 6–8. The latter author refers specifically to these approaches.

12 Shostack, G.L. (1985) 'Planning the Service Encounter', in Czepiel, J.A. (ed.), *The Service Encounter*, Lexington, Mass: Lexington Books.

13 See: Lovelock, C. (2000) 'Functional Integration in Services: Understanding the Links between Marketing, Operations, and Human Resources', in Schwartz, T.A. and Iacobucci, D. (eds), *Handbook of Services Marketing and Management*, Thousand Oaks, CA: Sage, pp. 421–438; and Lovelock, C. (1992) 'Seeking Synergy in Service Operations: Seven Things Marketers Need to Know About Service Operations', *European Management Journal*, **10** (1), 22–29.

14 Lovelock, C., Patterson, P.G. and Wirtz, J. (2011) *Services Marketing: An Asia-Pacific and Australian Perspective*, 5th edn, Frenchs Forest, NSW: Prentice Hall, p. 265.

15 We are grateful to Professor Christopher of Cranfield University for his commentary on these steps.

16 Shapiro, B. (1985) 'Rejuvenating the Marketing Mix', *Harvard Business Review*, September–October, 28–33. Also see: Akroush, M. (2006) 'The Services Marketing Mix Paradigm: Is it Still Appropriate for Today's Service business?' *AL-Balqa Journal for Research and Studies*, **11** (2), 49–74.

17 Collier, J.E. and Bienstock, C.C. (2006) 'Measuring Service Quality in e-re-retailing', *Journal of Service Research*, **8** (February), 260–275.

18 See Parasuraman, A., Zeithaml, V.A. and Berry, L.L. (1985) 'A Conceptual Model of Services Quality and Its Implications for Future Research', *Journal of Marketing*, **49**, Autumn, 41–50. For an overview of the work of Berry, See: Keaveney, S. (2004) 'Reviews of Books', *Journal of the Academy of Marketing Science*, **32** (2), 203–211.

19 Parasuraman, A., Zeithaml, V.A. and Malhotra, A. (2005) 'E-S-QUAL: A Multiple-Item Scale for Assessing Electronic Service Quality', *Journal of Service Research*, **7** (3), 213–233.

20 Ambler, T. (2003) *Marketing and the Bottom Line*, 2nd edn, London: Financial Times Prentice Hall.

Chapter 11

1 This section on MIS and database marketing is based on McDonald, M. and Wilson, H. (2011) *Marketing Plans: How to Prepare Them; How to Use Them*, 7th edn, Chichester: John Wiley & Sons Ltd.

2 EXMAR is a major decision-support tool for strategic marketing planning. These software application systems are available from marcus.clark@themarketingprocessco.com.

3 Those wishing to examine the topic of marketing research in detail should see standard texts such as: Malhotra, N. (2010) *Marketing Research: An Applied Orientation*, Harlow, UK: Pearson; and Aaker, D.A., Kumar, V., Day, G.S and Leone, R.P. (2010) *Marketing Research*, John Wiley & Sons, Ltd.

4 Greiner, L.E. (1998) 'Revolution is Still Inevitable', *Harvard Business Review*, **3**, 62–63; and Greiner, L.E. (1967) 'Patterns of Organisation Change', *Harvard Business Review*, **45**, 119–128.

5 Leppard, J. (1989) 'Marketing Planning and Organisational Culture', M. Phil. thesis, Cranfield University.

6 This section is based on original work by Visiting Professor Simon Majaro of Cranfield School of Management and is used with his kind permission.

7 Gottlieb, M.R. (2007) *The Matrix Organization Reloaded: Adventures in Team and Project Management*, Westport, CT: Praeger. (This book provides a managerial perspective on matrix management.)

8 Varum, C.A. (2010) 'Directions in Scenario Planning Literature: A Review of the Past Decades', *Futures*, **42** (4), 355–369; Hughes, N. (2009) *A Historical Overview of Strategic Scenario Planning*, UK Energy Research; Worthington, W.J., Collins, J.D. and Hitt, M.A. (2009) 'Beyond Risk Mitigation: Enhancing Corporate Innovation with Scenario Planning', *Business Horizons*, **52** (5), September–October, 441–450. (These references provide provide more detailed background to scenario planning.)

9 Kotler, P. (2003) *Marketing Management*, 11th edn, Upper Saddle River, New Jersey: Prentice Hall, pp. 695–797. (The marketing effectiveness audit is reproduced in full at these pages in his book.)

Chapter 12

1 Deloitte (2007) *'Marketing in 3D'*, Deloitte and Touche, www.deloitte.co .uk/marketing

2 Wilson H. (1997) 'An Investigation into the Impact of Decision Support Systems on Strategic Marketing Planning Practice', PhD thesis, Cranfield University School of Management.

3 Smith, B.D. (2003) 'The Effectiveness of Marketing Planning in Medical Markets', PhD thesis, Cranfield University School of Management.

4 Davidson, H. (1997) *Even More Offensive Marketing*, London: Penguin Books.

5 Baker, S. (2000) 'Defining a Marketing Paradigm', Unpublished Research Report, Cranfield University School of Management.

6 Porter, M.E. (1980) *Competitive Strategies*, New York: Free Press.

7 Rappaport, A. (1986) *Creating Shareholder Value*, New York: Free Press, Revised Edition 1998.

8 Walters, D. and Halliday, M. (1997) *Marketing and Finance: Working the Interface*, Allen and Unwin.

9 Zeithaml, V.A. (1998) 'Consumer Perceptions of Price, Quality and Value', *Journal of Marketing*, **52**, 2–22.

10 Kelly, S. (2005) *Customer Intelligence: From Data to Dialogue*, Chichester: John Wiley & Sons Ltd.

11 McDonald, M., Smith, B. and Ward, K. (2006) *Marketing Due Diligence: Reconnecting Strategy with Share Price*, Oxford: Butterworth-Heinemann.

12 McDonald, M. and Mouncey, P. (2009) *Marketing Accountability: How to Measure Marketing Effectiveness*, London: Kogan Page.

13 McGovern, G., Court, D. and Quelch, J. (2004) 'Bringing Customers into the Boardroom', *Harvard Business Review*, November, 70–80.

14 Binet, L. and Field, P. (2007) 'Marketing in an Age of Accountability', IPA Datamine.

Index

Index compiled by Indexing Specialists (UK) Ltd